Cruel and Unu...  P9-CJG-600

Cruel and Unusual

Punishment and US Culture

Brian Jarvis

Pluto Press

LONDON • STERLING, VIRGINIA

First published 2004 by
Pluto Press
345 Archway Road, London N6 5AA
and 22883 Quicksilver Drive, Sterling, VA 20166–2012, USA

www.plutobooks.com

British Library Cataloguing in Publication Data
A catalogue record for this book is available from the British Library

ISBN   0 7453 1543 7 hardback
ISBN   0 7453 1538 0 paperback

Library of Congress Cataloging in Publication Data
Jarvis, Brian.
    Cruel and unusual : punishment and US culture / Brian Jarvis.
        p. cm.
Includes bibliographical references.
    ISBN 0–7453–1543–7 — ISBN 0–7453–1538–0 (pbk.)
    1. Punishment—United States—History. 2. Punishment in
literature. I. Title.

    HV9466.J37 2004
    364.6'0973—dc22

                                                    2003023260

10   9   8   7   6   5   4   3   2   1

Designed and produced for Pluto Press by
Chase Publishing Services, Fortescue, Sidmouth, EX10 9QG, England
Typeset from disk by Stanford DTP Services, Northampton, England
Printed and bound in the European Union by
Antony Rowe Ltd, Chippenham and Eastbourne, England

Excessive bail shall not be required, nor excessive fines imposed, nor cruel and unusual punishments inflicted.

Amendment IX, Bill of Rights, US Constitution

Contents

1
The Birth of a Prison Nation

[T]here was some deep meaning in it, most worthy of interpretation, and which, as it were, streamed forth from the mystic
symbol... On the breast of [Hester Prynne's] gown, in fine red
cloth, surrounded with an elaborate embroidery and fantastic
flourishes of gold thread, appeared the letter A.

The Scarlet Letter, Nathaniel Hawthorne[1]

Throughout *The Scarlet Letter*, Hawthorne underlines the hermeneutic
allure of this immoderate sign. Since its first appearance this first
letter has been read perhaps more closely than any other symbol in
American literary history and yet the 'deep meaning' of this article
has proved most indefinite. The 'A' has been explicated as 'Artist'
and 'Angel', as 'America' and 'Anarchy', as 'Abject' and 'Alienation'
and even as an allegory of 'Allegory'. There is a danger in these
readings, however, not exactly of interpolation, but of focusing so
intently on what the sign does not say that one loses sight of its
explicit social signification as a form of punishment. The Puritan
letter penalty for adultery, like Poe's 'Purloined Letter', lies hidden in
plain view. In *Discipline and Punish*, his gothic genealogy of the
prison, Michel Foucault claimed that modern modes of discipline
aim to render punishment increasingly invisible. The aim of this
study is to resist that process. *Cruel and Unusual* will highlight the
extent to which punishment has been a conspicuous feature of
American history and culture from the Puritan colonies to the present
day. Although it is sometimes hidden, although it may not be
recognised even when in plain view, punishment has been as
intricately woven into the fabric of American society as Hester
Prynne's crewelwork.

Hawthorne's preoccupation with needlepoint performs an
historical correction. By expunging the practice of branding and
tattooing the criminal body the son exculpates his Puritan
forefathers. The guilty flesh was often used as folio for an indelible
sermon on sin. Given a strict sartorial code that insisted on covering
as much skin as possible, Puritan disciplinary mnemonics were

typically inscribed on the face and hands. 'A' or 'AD' indicated adultery, 'B' was for blasphemy, 'D' for drunkenness, 'F' for fighting or fornication, 'I' for incest, 'M' for manslaughter, 'P' for prostitution, 'R' for roguery, 'S' for swearing, 'T' for thievery and 'V' for 'venal' or lewd behaviour. One legacy of Puritan stigma was the nineteenth-century practice of tattooing inmates with the name of their prison. A more recent patrimony is suggested by Martin Scorcese's 1991 remake of *Cape Fear*. As the semi-naked Max Cady exercises in his cell, the camera catechises a body covered in scripture. The centrepiece, on the subject's spine, is a set of scales weighing Justice (a knife) and Truth (the Bible). A detective remarks on this display during a line-up: 'I don't know whether to look at him or read him.' Cady's body might be read as a parodic emblem of the New Puritanism in US corrections and of the vogue amongst prisoners for scarification. It has been estimated that around 60 per cent of white and 85 per cent of Hispanic-American prisoners have ignored the injunction in Leviticus, 19.28: 'You are not to gash your bodies when somebody dies, and you are not to tattoo yourselves.' The significance of the tattoo in contemporary prison subculture is underscored by *Oz*. The opening credit sequence of this cult prison drama is sutured with shots of a figure, rumoured to be the series creator, Tom Fontana, having 'Oz' tattooed on his biceps. From branding to brand names, from letter penalties designed to enforce ostracism to gang markings that are a badge of belonging, from sadistic wounding to self-inflicted torture that signifies an elision between desire and hurt: a genealogy of punitive signs illustrates that their meanings are far less ingrained than a criminal's tattoo.

Like the scarlet letter, 'punishment' is a protean sign. Hester's judges intended that the 'A' would denote the sinful act which Hawthorne, with a prudery only partly feigned, never mentions by name. According to the letter of Puritan law adultery was punishable by death. By the mid nineteenth century, at the time *The Scarlet Letter* was published, numerous novels of adultery still registered the perceived dangers of this transgression by dramatising its unravelling of economics and desire. Adultery, of course, is no longer codified in most Western societies as an offence under criminal law, although pecuniary penalties may be incurred in civil proceedings. In ancient Greece, however, the punishment for adultery was decided by the 'victim'. Cuckolded husbands enjoyed considerable latitude, but often plumped for the insertion of root vegetables in the anus of their rivals. Revenge by *rhapanidosis* was a favourite as radishes, although small, produced a particularly unpleasant burning sensation. Conversely, anal sex between consenting males was not considered a punishable act in ancient Greece or Rome, but was illegal throughout the US until the 1960s and is currently defined as criminal according to sodomy laws in 14 states and the US military.

Even a cursory glance at the history of punishment proves that penal practices vary dramatically between societies and across time. Although the specific forms are constantly changing, the brute fact of punishment itself is immutable. *The Scarlet Letter* opens with 'The Prison Door' and Hawthorne's insistence that all societies begin by preparing to punish those who pose a threat:

> The founders of a new colony, whatever Utopia of human virtue and happiness they might originally project, have invariably recognised it among their earliest practical necessities to allot a portion of the virgin soil as a cemetery, and another portion as the site of a prison. (p.47)

Boston established its inaugural 'House of Correction' in 1632, just two years after the founding of the Massachusetts Bay Colony. This key penal institution has since been the subject of a lexical proliferation that foregrounds how difficult it is to contain the meanings of 'prison'. The American prison has acquired a range of formal titles that reflect differences in organisation and philosophy (county jail and state penitentiary, federal correctional and detention facility, reformatory, boot camp and brig) and colloquialisms that capture the regional and ethnic diversity of the inmates (bird and the Big House, the can, the clink and the cooler, the calaboose and the chokey, the glasshouse, the hoosegow and the joint, the pen and the pokey, the slammer and the skookum house). Historical links between America and the Big House predate even the first Puritan prisons. Ogden Nash joked that 'Columbus discovered America and they put him in jail for it'.[2] On his release from Las Cuevas monastery in Seville, Columbus organised a final expedition to a continent which had since been christened after a rival explorer. Emerson bemoaned the decision of Waldseemuller, the German mapmaker, to name the New World after a figure suspected by many of fraud: 'Strange that broad America must wear the name of a thief! Amerigo Vespucci ... in an expedition that never sailed, managed in this lying world to supplant Columbus, and baptise half the earth with his own dishonest name!'[3] Doing a six-year stretch for burglary between 1946 and 1952, an inmate at Charlestown State Prison renounced his own 'dishonest name' in favour of a symbol, 'X', that signified a 300-year history of theft and imprisonment. Malcolm X, alongside a generation of African-Americans politicised by incarceration, insisted that for his people 'America' had always meant 'prison'.

Enslaved Africans were amongst the first arrivals in the New World for whom the American experience was of imprisonment rather than new-found liberty, but they were not alone. Throughout the colonial period, America received significant numbers of transported convicts, indentured servants, impressed sailors and military conscripts, united by their carceral condition. In Virginia, by 1618, only 600 of the original 1,800 colonists had survived. The early colonial period witnessed acute labour shortages and these were resolved, in part, by the deportation of convicts. Seventeenth-century English law saw a steady increase in the number of crimes punishable by death (including stealing a lady's petticoat or a silver spoon), but a decline in the number of executions. Deportation to the colonies was often the only alternative to death, and this established a long-lasting precedent in American history for the integration of capital and punishment. Despite the profits made by colonial merchants, the prisoner trade was not met with unequivocal enthusiasm. The General Court of Virginia expressed concern about the 'danger to the colony caused by the great number of felons and other desperate villains sent over from the prisons of England'.[4] When Sir John Popham tried to establish a community in Maine, some critics complained that it was made up from 'all the gaols of England'.[5] For much of the seventeenth century in Britain, prior to the revolutionary war, deportation was the most common sentence imposed on felons. During this period, over 50,000 convicts were transported to America, accounting for almost 25 per cent of all British emigrants. When news of colonial resentment at this practice made its way back to England, Samuel Johnson retorted: 'Why they [Americans] are a race of convicts, and ought to be thankful for anything we allow them short of hanging.'[6]

The attempt to cultivate a New Eden in the Wilderness was itself a response to original deportation from the Garden. As well as acknowledging affinities between early America and the penal colony, it is essential to recognise the punitive caste of the religion which the Pilgrim Fathers took to the New World. For the Puritan sensibility the central sign in Christian culture, the cross, retained much of its significance as an instrument of torture and execution. The Puritan

God was a profoundly disciplinary deity. Seventeenth-century sermons embarrass the apocalyptic imagination on display in the Hollywood disaster film: floods and rivers running red with blood; famine, disease and fire; plagues of insects, vermin and reptiles; brimstone and fire raining down on cities; the sacrifice of sons, and mothers ordered to eat their own babies. Alexis de Tocqueville judged that '[t]here is no country in the world where the Christian religion retains a greater influence over the souls of men than in America'.[7] Whilst the power of the church has waned in most other western societies, religion has remained a potent force in the US and has always been entangled in notions of divine vengeance and earthly retribution. The Heavenly Father, in God's own country, has often been cast as a strict disciplinarian, and according to Thomas Paine, 'belief in a cruel God makes a cruel man'.[8]

Paine's writings helped inspire the push for independence and the Revolution furthered the fledgling Republic's sensitivity to the subject of punishment. In the War of Independence more Americans died as prisoners than were killed in combat. The British held rebels in overcrowded and unhygienic conditions in camps and a flotilla of prison ships. In the wake of the war, the debate concerning the shape and direction of American government returned frequently to the importance of criminal and civil justice. A determination to fulfil the ideals established in the Declaration, and to distance themselves from the tyrannical treatment of prisoners by their former masters, encouraged a reconsideration of penal practice. Alongside programmes to improve transport infrastructure, education and houses of refuge for the poor, the fledgling Republic sought to forge a national identity that was distinct from Old World despotism through humane treatment of the criminal population. One of the signatories on the Declaration, Benjamin Rush, called for the abolition of capital punishment and the establishment of a new penal philosophy founded on the ideal of social and spiritual rehabilita-tion. Rush believed that 'a prison sometimes supplies the place of a church and out-preaches the preacher in conveying useful instruction to the heart'.[9] Punishment ought, therefore, to be tailored 'according to the temper of criminals and the progress of their reformation'.[10] Pennsylvania, with its sizeable Quaker population, was a focal point for the reforms that Rush requested. It was the first state to abolish capital punishment for all but the most serious felonies, and replace it with hard labour. The Quakers were also instrumental in the evolution of a new form of prison, modelled on the monastery and

geared towards the spiritual instruction of inmates. In the 'penitentiaries' that appeared in the late eighteenth and early nineteenth
centuries, regimes based on solitary confinement, silence and hard
work were introduced for the first time. Incarceration was no longer
simply a punishment, but an opportunity to redeem lost souls.

These innovations in penal style generated considerable interest in
Europe. In 1831 the French government sent two magistrates to
investigate and report on the penitentiary system. Alexis de
Tocqueville, travelling with Gustave de Beaumont, toured various
facilities, including Eastern State and Sing Sing, before submitting
*On the Penitentiary System in the United States and Its Application in
France*. This report was guarded in its optimism. The authors
suggested that the penitentiary had developed into a monomania
which reformers saw as 'a remedy for all the evils of society'.[11] They
went on to conclude that 'while society in the United States gives
the example of the most extended liberty, the prisons of the same
country offer the spectacle of the most complete despotism'.[12]
Democracy in America, regarded as a seminal statement on the
'extended liberty' enjoyed by US citizens, grew out of de Tocqueville's
study of the nation's prison system. Although he was troubled by
the failure to realise the ideals of the penitentiary, de Tocqueville
remained convinced that the Land of the Free lay just beyond the
prison walls. However, when the situation of those deprived of
fundamental liberties is considered – the slaves held on plantations
in the South, the native Americans coerced onto reservations, the
industrial working class corralled in factories, and the women increasingly confined to the domestic sphere – the distinctions between
inside and outside are not as clear-cut as de Tocqueville assumed.
The legends of 'extended liberty' evolved partly in response to
increasing historical pressures placed on romantic ideals at the heart
of the Republic's formation. The focus on frontier freedom, for
example, cloaked the increasingly carceral experiences of many to
the east of this mythical line. As David Rothman notes, the pinnacle
of enthusiasm for prison reform coincided with the era of Jacksonian
democracy:

> At the very moment that Americans began to pride themselves on
> the openness of their society, when the boundless frontier became
> the symbol of opportunity and equality ... notions of total
> isolation, unquestioned obedience, and severe discipline became
> the hallmarks of the captive society.[13]

A century and a half later, the same disparity is starkly evident. Political and business rhetoric insists routinely on the democratic virtues of small government and the free market, at the same time as an unprecedented lockdown of US citizens is taking place. Since the end of the Vietnam war, the prison population has increased tenfold, from approximately 200,000 to over 2,000,000 inmates. If public works embody the spirit of the age, then the *zeitgeist* of millennial America is profoundly carceral. When Clinton declared, in 1996, that the 'era of big government is over', he could not have been referring to the Department of Corrections. Between 1990 and 1995, a massive building programme produced 168 state and 45 federal prisons, bringing the total to 1,500, alongside 3,300 local jails and over 5,000 additional correctional facilities. Historically, plans for prison building have been met with vociferous opposition from local communities. In the current climate, however, the same groups lobby feverishly to secure the boost to regional economies promised by a new prison. A maximum-security facility can cost anywhere between $30 million and $75 million. The average cost of a single cell, at around $80,000, now rivals suburban property values. Construction expenditure is quickly dwarfed by operating costs. It takes more tax dollars to send someone to prison than to study law at Harvard, and the education they receive at both institutions helps keep the wheels rolling on the Justice Juggernaut.

The 'celling' of America increasingly involves lucrative partnerships between private capital and state and federal authorities.[14] Between 1985 and 1995 there was a 500 per cent increase in the number of private prisons. The privatisation of the prison landscape has been accompanied by increasing use of convict labour. Alongside the traditional manufacture of licence plates, prisoners now make uniforms for McDonald's employees, pack Microsoft products and golf balls, make motherboards and furniture, as well as being involved in telemarketing and drug testing for pharmaceutical companies. This convergence of business and political interests has made the concept of decarceration 'unthinkable'. The rise and rise of a multi-billion dollar corrections industry is largely unopposed, and prison hegemony is systematically reinforced within mainstream media culture. Dostoyevsky famously declared that 'the degree of civilisation in a society can be judged by entering its prisons'.[15] Even before we examine the interior, however, degrees are suggested by the sheer number of prison doors to open in contemporary US society. The prison that Hester Prynne emerges from is described by

Hawthorne as 'weather-beaten' and the 'rust on the ponderous iron-work of its oaken door looked more antique than anything else in the New World' (p.48). The prisons produced by the New Puritanism in US corrections belong increasingly to the realm of science fiction: automated locking systems, unbreakable polycarbonate screens, infrared surveillance cameras, digital voice-recognition software, impulse radar systems for perimeter security and guards armed with stun guns and tasers. The SuperMax is the new City on the Hill and a flagship monument for the Big House nation.

Officially, from the birth of the penitentiary system to the early 1970s, there were no prisons or prisoners in America. According to ruling definitions, the Department of Corrections provided its 'inmates' with vocational training, educational opportunities, counselling and psychiatric treatment. The contemporary expansion of the penal system, however, has witnessed a wholesale rejection of rehabilitative ideals and a return to a profoundly Puritanical insistence on punishment as retribution. This regression poses problems for the influential historical model offered by Foucault in *Discipline and Punish*. Foucault argues for a fundamental break in the practice of punishment between the preindustrial and industrial eras. The *ancien régime* is exemplified by an account of the execution, in 1757, of a regicide. The body of the condemned man, Damiens, was subjected to prolonged public torture, before being pulled apart by horses and burnt to ashes. The function of this spectacle was to make visible the absolute power of the sovereign, and thus intimidate his subjects into obedience. The opening pages of *Discipline and Punish* juxtapose this execution with a timetable that establishes a strict daily routine in a house of young prisoners in 1838 in Paris. Foucault asserts that the characteristics of this new technology of power are discipline, surveillance and self-control. The transition between these two penal styles displays an increasing interiority. The privatisation of punishment replaces public spectacles of torture. The gallows, the stocks and pillories disappear, and discipline is administered behind locked doors. In the new system, the focal point of punitive violence is no longer the body but the criminal 'soul'. The infliction of pain is secondary to psychological correction. Within this regime it is not enough to punish the criminal; the criminal must learn to punish himself. Whilst liberal histories have traditionally seen the birth of the prison as part of the march of civilisation, Foucault sees instead the appearance of new modes of social control that are if anything more pervasive and insidious. These new tactics were pioneered in prison and then applied throughout society, in asylums, hospitals, schools, workplaces and the home. For Foucault, the birth of the prison means the birth of a prison society.

The paradigmatic form for these developments is the panopticon. Jeremy Bentham's model prison was a tiered, circular structure with a watchtower at the centre. The advantage of this design was that the prisoners, held in barred cells around the circumference walls, could be ceaselessly monitored. In fact, Bentham contended, over time the prisoners would learn automatically to feel and fear a disciplinary gaze, and at this point a human presence in the watchtower would be redundant. Panopticon principles may be evident in other institutions, but currently, in US corrections, the *ancien régime* is enjoying a renaissance. Rather than being internalised and hidden, punishment is arguably more conspicuous in American public life than it has ever been. At current rates of construction, Bentham's dream of having a panopticon at the heart of every town and city may even be realised. There is, however, little room in the modern Big House for the rehabilitative ideals that initially informed experimental prison design. Contemporary American justice is unashamedly founded on the ethos of *lex talionis* (an eye for an eye). A number of states have reintroduced the chain gang and judges have rediscovered a Puritan zeal for sentencing offenders to public penance for misdemeanours. Crucially, the ultimate expression of the power of the state over its subjects remains in the US despite its abolition in most other nation-states in the west. The death penalty, first codified as law by King Hammurabi of Babylon in the eighteenth century BC, still plays a vital role in American punishment practice. Following *Furman v. Georgia* in 1972, a moratorium was ruled in accordance with the Ninth Amendment, but this lasted only until 1976, when in *Gregg v. Georgia*, *Proffitt v. Florida* and *Jurek v. Texas* it was ruled that the death penalty per se did not constitute cruel and unusual punishment. Between 1977 and 2000 there were almost 700 executions in the US, with 98 in 1999 alone. This has been accompanied by clamouring for televised executions. Various interest groups, especially in relation to high-profile cases, such as that of Timothy McVeigh, have lobbied on behalf of the public's constitutional right to witness the administration of justice.

When the Foucault model follows in the footsteps of de Tocqueville to visit the US penal system it encounters problems caused by the resilience of the *ancien régime*. Additional problems stem from one of the most telling lacunae in *Discipline and Punish*.

Somewhat surprisingly for the devotee of de Sade and author of *The History of Sexuality*, Foucault seems largely uninterested in the erotics of punishment. Sadism and masochism, the desire to punish and be punished, play a vital role in discipline and are a key feature in the history of cruelty in the US. According to psychoanalytical theory, relationships with the law are shaped by oedipal dynamics. This terrain was originally mapped by Freud in *Three Essays on the Theory of Sexuality*, 'A Child is Being Beaten' and 'The Economic Problem of Masochism'. Although S&M subsequently passed into the collective imagination as synonymous with sexual deviancy, Freud's work sometimes narrowed the gap between perversion and normality. In classical psychoanalysis, the roots of sadism lie less in aberrance than in a perfection of the oedipal complex. The sadist is the subject who over-identifies with the Father and his Law. In the sadistic personality, the superego becomes so powerful that it requires subjects to punish as surrogates for internal weaknesses associated with the maternal imago.

Although the Marquis de Sade's infamy is more widespread than Leopold von Sacher-Masoch's, sadism has enjoyed less critical coverage than masochism. This preference is evident in Freud's work where, building on Krafft-Ebing's *Psychopathia Sexualis*, masochism is subdivided into three categories: erotogenic, moral and feminine. Erotogenic masochism involves deriving sensual gratification from physical pain. Moral masochism concerns the subject whose ego is tortured incessantly by a distended superego and whose desire for punishment becomes so irresistible that he is constantly tempted to commit those deviant acts that will result in self-castigation. Freud devised the term 'feminine masochism' to categorise male patients who desired to assume the 'feminine position' and female patients who ventured beyond the bounds of socially-sanctioned submissiveness. The history of this perversion is traced to infantile fantasies of being bound, beaten and 'treated like ... a naughty child'.[16] Whether it is physical correction or self-chastisement, the 'true masochist ... always turns his cheek whenever he has a chance of receiving a blow'.[17] But who is delivering this punishment, and why is it desired? Freud read the beating scene as a passage from the oedipal script in which cruelty was the cipher of love: 'the wish, which so frequently appears in phantasies, to be beaten by the father stands very close to the other wish, to have a passive (feminine) relation to him and is only a regressive distortion of it'.[18]

Classical psychoanalysis has established the parameters within which the meanings of masochism have been contested, and it is important to recognise that Freud's own models were themselves somewhat conflicted. In *Male Subjectivity at the Margins*, Kaja Silverman offers a persuasive deconstruction of the Freudian paradigm that begins with the recognition that 'feminine masochism doesn't have much to do with women, [and] moral masochism doesn't have much to do with virtue'.[19] Silverman illustrates how classical Freudianism itself jeopardises the hegemonic sexual coding of 'healthy' and 'sick'. The prominence of male subjects in case studies of female masochism, for example, suggests that there are socially-acceptable levels of self-torture for women: 'It is an accepted – indeed a requisite – element of "normal" female subjectivity, providing a crucial mechanism for eroticising lack and submission ... what is acceptable for the female subject is patholog-ical for the male.'[20] For both sexes, masochism differs from the psychic economy of the 'normal' subject only in 'degree and erotic intent'.[21] The margins between the upstanding citizen and the pervert are less certain than Freud may have wanted to concede. Those mainstays of Victorian ideology – the Protestant Work Ethic, 'suffer and be still', spiritual self-surveillance – lie on a continuum with masochistic desire.

Silverman quite rightly challenges the moral imperatives of classical psychoanalysis, but confirms Freud's judgement that masochism is a 'dangerous' condition, one with the 'revolutionary' potential to spill out of the boudoir and onto the barricades, 'con-taminating the proprieties of gender, class, and race'.[22] According to this reading, the masochist 'radiates a negativity inimical to the social order'; he is involved in the transgression of boundaries (pain/pleasure, male/female, animal/human, victim/aggressor, life/death) and forms of 'phallic divestiture' that might result in the 'ruination of masculinity'.[23] This hard-core and brazenly utopian definition of masochism is partly indebted to Deleuze. In *Masochism: Coldness and Cruelty*, Deleuze turns Freudian orthodoxy on its head to propose that sadism and masochism, rather than being reciprocal complexes, are in fact profoundly antithetical and politically charged. The sadistic desire to dominate the other is oedipal in origin, whilst masochism is motivated by a desire to recover a pre-oedipal bond with the mother. For Freud, the classical S&M scenario is a drag, with the dominatrix as Daddy in disguise. Conversely, Deleuze insists that the female 'master' is not masquerading as the oedipal father, but instead embodies a forceful return of repressed maternal power: 'a pact between mother and son to write the father out of his dominant position within both masochism and culture, and to install the mother in his place'.[24] Male masochism is not, as Freud believed, a symptom of repressed homosexual attraction to the patriarch, but a desire to overturn the father's law as it is embodied in the willing slave: 'what is beaten, humiliated and ridiculed in him is the image and likeness of the father'.[25] Neither Deleuze nor Silverman are especially precise about the means by which private acts are translated into public transgressions, and it is perhaps a recognition of this that leads the latter to conclude with a cautionary note: 'Perversion always contains the trace of Oedipus within it – it is always organised to some degree by what it subverts.'[26] Pursuing the logic of this position to its extreme, as is his wont, Foucault argues in *The History of Sexuality* that perversions, rather than subverting the grammar of the oedipal narrative, simply extend it into the margins. Masochism is not a modern manifestation of Dionysian energies, but a masquerade that mimics cruelty within the family. Those desires and practices labelled 'masochistic' are produced and managed by the dominant fictions of sexuality, helping to reinforce the norm by simply inverting the hegemonic dualities of heterosexuality.

Cruel and Unusual will examine cultural representations of punishment in relation to these rival definitions of sadism and masochism. The aim of this study is to foreground not only the bonds between discipline and desire, but also to explore the entanglement of erotics and economics. Punishment can be read as a lynchpin between relations of domination and submission in political and libidinal economies. If psychoanalysis can contribute to our understanding of the latter, Marxist critical theory is essential to grasping the operations of the former, since as Rusche and Kirchheimer argue: 'Every system of production tends to discover punishments which correspond to its productive relationships.'[27] According to the Marxist reading, the concept of the 'political prisoner' is tautological, since the history of punishment is always a 'history of the relations [between] the rich and the poor'.[28] Or, as Norman Mailer suggests more romantically:

> There is a paradox at the core of penology, and from it derives the thousand ills and afflictions of the prison system. It is that not only the worst of the young are sent to prison but the best – that

is the proudest, the bravest, the most daring, the most enterprising, and the most undefeated of the poor. There starts the horror.[29]

Whether it occurs in public or private, punishment is always enacted in a network of social relations. As Scott Christianson insists, any history of punishment must expand to include

> the slave traders and spirits and crimps and transporters and outfitters and masters and drivers and overseers and locksmiths and jailers and wardens and judges and bail bondsmen and guards and chaplains and prison reformers and inspectors and jurors and executioners and sheriffs and marshals and cops and probation officers and parole officers and correction officers and their families.[30]

At the same time, any history of punishment cannot consider the punitive act in temporal isolation, but must address the before and after. Every narrative of punishment is also a crime story. Every disciplinary act leaves its mark. Foucault contends that punishment is always a mode of representation. At times, *Discipline and Punish* seems preoccupied with the perspective of those who practise the punitive arts rather than the subjects who are their raw materials. To consider punishment from the perspective of the victims of torture, the prisoners and the condemned is to recognise the extent to which punishment is the end of representation. The effects of punishment – bodily pain, trauma and death – produce crises in signification that destroy both word and world. A history of punishment must therefore move simultaneously out into the material contexts of social relations and inwards towards the body, its desires and the silent centres of unspeakable hurt.

To this end, *Cruel and Unusual* will offer readings of a range of cultural representations in relation to key phases and cohorts within the history of punishment in the US. We will begin with the early colonial period and the role played by Puritan religion in regulating social, sexual and punitive relations. Hawthorne's *The Scarlet Letter* will be closely scrutinised both for what it has to say about punishment in Puritan New England and the antebellum North. The fiction of Hawthorne's friend and contemporary, Herman Melville, will be inspected with regard to developments in discipline in the nineteenth century. The ghosts of Puritanism will be hunted in the Cold War era through a consideration of the execution of the Rosenbergs and its fictional recreation in E. L. Doctorow's *The Book of Daniel* and Robert Coover's *The Public Burning*. The African-American experience and representation of punishment will be surveyed from slave narratives to recent prison writings. In conclusion, the prison film will be examined in relation to discipline and punishment on the contemporary American scene. Although the materials examined in each part of this survey are disparate, the intention remains the same: to explore the conflict between hegemonic fables of American national identity and the secret and silenced sexual and economic histories of punishment. In 1921 the LAPD arrested Upton Sinclair for reading aloud the Declaration of Independence in a public space. This might be read as a paradigmatic moment in the long history of punishment in North America. The mythology of the Land of the Free can be seen as an ideological smokescreen designed to obscure the systematic deprivation of liberty and infliction of punishments, both cruel and unusual.

2
The Scarlet Letter and the Long Forever of Puritan Punishment

He turned towards the scaffold, and stretched forth his arms.

The Scarlet Letter, Nathaniel Hawthorne[1]

To begin a history of punishment in America with the Puritans is problematic. Although the Pilgrim Fathers believed otherwise, they did not invent discipline in the 'wilderness'. Spanish soldiers constructed a substantial prison in 1570 at St Augustine in Florida. The first recorded execution in North America took place in 1608 when George Kendall was hanged for allegedly betraying Virginia Colony to the Spanish.[2] In 1611, almost a decade before the *Mayflower* moored near Plymouth Rock, Jamestown had already instituted a code of 'Laws Divine, Moral and Martial'. 'Dale's Laws', named in honour of the governor, could be as unforgiving as the marshland on which the colony was founded. One of the earliest recorded punishments at Jamestown documents a seamstress being whipped for sewing her lady's skirts too short. For uttering 'base and detracting words' against Dale, Richard Barnes was sentenced to the following:

> [he shall be] disarmed and have his arms broken and his tongue bored through with an awl and [he] shall pass through a guard of 40 men and shall be butted by every one of them and at the head of the troop kicked down and footed out of the fort; and he shall be banished out of James City and the Island, and he shall not be capable of any privilege of freedom in the country.[3]

In recognition of the punitive severity of early Jamestown, Karen Kupperman has compared the first permanent European settlement in North America to a prison camp.[4] The history of punishment in America thus pre-dates the Puritans, and not just by the odd decade. For centuries prior to the establishment of Camp Jamestown, what came to be known as America had already been the site of punishments as diverse (tribal, martial, religious, domestic, erotic) as the indigenous population who practised them.[5]

The problems confronting a history of punishment that begins with the Puritans do not end here. Historians of the colonial period have warned against collapsing early America into Puritanism and Puritanism into caricature. The colonial period stretches over 150 years (1620–1776) and sees a population increase from a few thousand to over 3 million. The majority of this demographic were not Puritans. There were significant numbers of Quakers, Antinomians, Anabaptists, Jesuits, Diggers, Seekers, Familists and Ranters. In addition, there were many colonists who did not belong to a church or were excluded from one (including many servants and slaves). Diversity in the colonial period can be obscured by a preoccupation with the Pilgrim faithful. Equally, differentiation within this community can be erased by casual assumptions about a monolithic Puritan order. There were critical differences between and sometimes within Puritan communities and these extend to the punishment practices that were continually evolving throughout the pre-revolutionary era.

To commence a history of punishment in America with the Puritans is thus problematic, but also necessary. Although they did not invent discipline, the Puritans' code either supplanted or helped to shape most other penal styles. In part the potency of this code is a function of the importance placed on punishment by the Puritan colonies from their inception. In his historical study, *Of Plymouth Plantation*, William Bradford described the Pilgrim Fathers' exodus as itself a flight from punitive persecution: 'what wars and oppositions ever since [the Reformation], Satan hath raised, maintained and continued against the Saints ... Sometimes by bloody death and cruel torments; other whiles imprisonments, banishments and other hard usages.'[6] The irony of fleeing persecution in the Old World only to repeat it in the New has often been noted. Popular conceptions of the colonial period gravitate towards the 'cruel torments' of witches, Quakers, backsliders and others unfortunate enough to incur the wrath of stern Puritan judges. The tactics and technologies of discipline are amongst the most significant patrimonies bequeathed by the Puritans to the Republic. This chapter will explore the nature of punishment in Puritan society and its continuing legacy in relation to *The Scarlet Letter*. Hawthorne's canonical text has been instrumental in shaping popular conceptions and misconceptions about Puritan society. This novel will be examined both in relation to punishment in the early colonial period (the novel's historical setting) and then alongside disciplinary developments in antebellum America (the novel's historical context).

THE 'BODY OF LIBERTIES'

> With dismal chains, and strongest reins,
> like Prisoners of Hell,
> They're held in place before Christ's face,
> til He their Doom shall tell.
> These void of tears, but fill'd with fears,
> And dreadful expectation
> Of endless pains and scalding flames,
> stand waiting for Damnation.
>
> ....
>
> It's now high time that ev'ry Crime
> be brought to punishment.

The Day of Doom, Michael Wigglesworth[7]

The Scarlet Letter is entitled by the letter of the law. Hester Prynne is sentenced to wear an 'A' on her person, at all times, to signify her guilt as an adulteress. When Hester is introduced as a subject of shame on the scaffold, she clutches her bastard child, Pearl, to her breast and is addressed by her secret lover, the Reverend Dimmesdale. Subsequently, the scaffold is the site of a clandestine meeting between these three in the middle of the narrative (in private, at midnight) and of the climactic revelation of Pearl's paternity at the close (in public, at noon). Hawthorne's narrative patterns are as carefully woven as his heroine's symbol, and the prominence of the scaffold on which the three figures converge three times underlines the centrality of punishment to this tale. *The Scarlet Letter* is sometimes mistakenly cited as a novel of adultery. The 'crime' itself, however, is banished from the narrative in much the same manner that one of its perpetrators is expelled from the community. This most unromantic of romances is preoccupied with the punishment that pursues 'lawless passion'. Alongside Miller's *The Crucible*, the other canonical text set in this milieu, *The Scarlet Letter* has encouraged a conception of Puritan New England as virtual penal colony. But just how important was punishment to the Puritans?

John Winthrop records a meeting between leading members of the Puritan elite that took place in 1636 in Boston. The meeting was convened by Henry Vane to discuss the subject of discipline, and specifically whether, 'in the infancy of a plantation, justice should be administered with more lenity than in a settled state'.[8] Winthrop found himself in the minority, forwarding a case for the political expediency of a clement criminal justice system. Church leaders, however, insisted on rigid adherence to the Levitical code, and the meeting resolved that 'strict discipline, both in criminal and martial affairs, were more needful in plantations than in a settled state, as tending to the honour and safety of the gospel'.[9] In the light of this decision Nathaniel Ward, a retired minister, drafted the 'Body of Liberties', which was duly ratified in 1641 by the General Court. This document was the first attempt at a fully codified penal system in the English-speaking world. The meeting documented by Winthrop can thus be seen as a watershed, since it helped establish the legal framework and general character of the Puritan judiciary for subsequent generations. Although colonial justice in some respects mirrored the forms of English common law, its animating spirit was Mosaic. At the same time Liberty, that key word in national myth, was conjoined in its earliest official usage with the practice of punishment.

The 'Body of Liberties' included an injunction against punishments 'that are inhumane, barbarous or cruel'.[10] This did not, however, dissuade Puritan judges from sentencing offenders to violent, shaming rituals in the stocks and pillories, whipping, mutilations of face and body, banishment and execution. It is important to recognise the cruelty of Puritan punishment, but it should not be overstated. At this time such practices were commonplace throughout the Old World. The notorious Salem witch trials resulted in 19 executions, a figure dwarfed by the number of hangings and public burnings for witchcraft in early modern Europe, estimates of which vary from 60,000 to a holocaust of 9 million. Criminal justice in colonial New England was not significantly more barbaric than that in Europe. What was more distinctive, however, was its extent and the fervour with which it was administered. During Hester's ordeal on the scaffold, Hawthorne describes the Puritans as 'a people amongst whom religion and law were almost identical, and in whose character both were so thoroughly interfused, that the mildest and the severest acts of public discipline were alike made venerable and awful' (p.55). Lawrence Friedman confirms Hawthorne's assessment of Puritan theocracy, insisting that it would be hard to overemphasise the influence of religion … in shaping the criminal codes, in framing modes of enforcement, and, generally, in creating a distinctive legal culture. The criminal justice system was in many ways another arm of religious orthodoxy.[11]

Puritan punishment was invested with religious vehemence, and its religion inspirited with a punitive zeal. The Puritan deity in Jonathan Edwards' *Sinners in the Hands of an Angry God* was a merciless judge:

'I will tread them in mine anger, and will trample them in my fury, and their blood shall be sprinkled upon my garments, and I will stain all my raiment' (Isaiah, 63.3) … There will be no end to this exquisite horrible misery. When you look forward, you shall see a long forever, a boundless duration before you … So that your punishment will indeed be infinite.[12]

Edwards' jeremiad was delivered in 1741, the centennial anniversary of the 'Body of Liberties', and sustained the tradition in Puritan culture of representing the Father as cruel disciplinarian. Michael Wigglesworth's *The Day of Doom*, the best-selling poem in seventeenth-century America, suggests that Puritan eschatology was at least as concerned with His vengeance as with the prospect of salvation:

already under a sentence of condemnation to hell … justice calls aloud for an infinite punishment of their sins … the pit is prepared, the fire is made ready, the furnace is now hot, ready to receive them; the flames do now rage and glow. The glittering sword is whet, and held over them, and the pit hath opened its mouth under them.[13]

According to the doctrine of predestination, the Preterite had no possibility of pardon from this 'infinite punishment'. This did not imply, however, that the Elect were automatically exempt from chastisement. The Saints, as God's Chosen People, were in fact more, not less likely to feel His Wrath. As Winthrop explained in *A Model of Christian Charity*: 'the more Jealous of our love and obedience so he tells the people of Israel, you only have I known of all the families of the Earth therefore will I punish you for your Transgressions'.[14] Since it was a coded expression of His Love, the Puritans were keen to encounter signs of divine punishment all around them: in famines and floods, in battles and deaths, even in the humdrum details of everyday life. An entry in Wigglesworth's diary interprets the nightly banging of a neighbour's door as punishment for his own lascivious thoughts. Since, as Minister Samuel Danforth declared, 'the holiest man hath as vile and filthy a nature as the Sodomites', the New Canaan was not a sanctuary, but a site permanently on the brink of experiencing Divine Justice as apocalyptic as that administered at Sodom and Gomorrah.[15] Inspired by heavenly precedent the Puritans devised their own severe retributions, but rather than eliminating wrong-doing, their unforgiving regime seemed to increase its likelihood. In his history of Plymouth Colony William Bradford detected a fiendish circuitry between the righteous justice adminis- tered by Puritan law and the preternatural tortures visited upon them:

> Marvellous it may be to see and consider how some kind of wickedness did grow and break forth here, in a land where the same was so much witnessed against and so narrowly looked unto, and severely punished when it was known, as in no place more, that I have known of or heard of ... the devil may carry a greater spite against the churches of Christ and the gospel here, by how much the more they endeavour to preserve holiness and purity amongst themselves and strictly punisheth the contrary when it ariseth.[16]

Despite, or perhaps because of this double bind, the Puritan judiciary continued to administer punishment with devotion. The 'Body of Liberties' annotated an exhaustive list of crimes with biblical citation. There were crimes against the church, against figures of authority (from parents to government officials), crimes of a sexual nature, crimes that disturbed the peace, crimes against property and person; but ultimately all were seen as offences against God. This perspective had various consequences. Firstly, it collapsed distinc- tions between 'crime' and 'sin'. Puritan theocracy drew no lines between man-made laws and God's Law. Any transgression was thus an affront to the covenant between God and His Chosen People. Secondly, as a consequence of this, Puritan penality found it difficult to distinguish between 'major' and 'minor' offences. The concept of the misdemeanour was anathema. As Wigglesworth warned in the *Day of Doom*: 'Eternal smart is the desert,/ ev'n of the least offence.'[17] Encouraged by the Calvinist doctrine of innate depravity, the Puritans perceived a continuum between all classes of offence, so that the most petty could be treated as a harbinger of the most heinous. Thirdly, this perspective provided ideological sanction for draconian measures and for the colonisation of everyday life by discipline. Court records are crowded with accounts of offenders severely castigated for apparently trivial acts: idleness, cursing an animal, the wearing of a silk hood.

> In a given day ... the court might take notice of persons who drank too much, who were 'without the use of their reason', who lived a scandalous life, who dressed in inappropriate clothes or let their hair grow too long, who swore, bragged, or talked too much, who disobeyed their parents or engaged in frivolous games. The saints did not appreciate the distinction invented by later generations between persons who infringe the customs of the group and persons who flatly violate the law, for the Word of God governed everything and had to be protected with all the machinery at the state's disposal.[18]

The Puritans did not allow for peccadilloes, and similarly, as Hawthorne recognised, there were no inconsequential corrections: 'a penalty which, in our days, would infer a degree of mocking infamy and ridicule, might then be invested with almost as stern a dignity as the punishment of death itself' (p.55). The import of any transgression and its retribution was magnified by the Puritan communal ethic: 'If one member suffers, all suffer with it; if one be in honour, all rejoice with it.'[19] Puritan sermons interminably underlined the possibility that a crime by an individual could jeopardise His Judgement on the Holy City. In a classic Durkheimian analysis of deviance in Puritan society, Kai Erikson argues that crime waves in the colonial period (including the outbreak of witchcraft at Salem) do not suggest breakdown in social structure so much as an essential means of solidifying it. Punishment – divine, demoniac and social – seems to have been a cement that encouraged social cohesion in early colonial America.

THE PRISON DOOR, THE ROSE-BUSH AND THE WILDERNESS WITHIN

[Hawthorne] wrote about a wild woman. This woman challenged the society by fucking a guy who wasn't her husband and having his kid. The society punished her by sending her to gaol, making her wear a red 'A' for adultery right on her tits ... *Wild* in the Puritan New England society Hawthorne writes about means *evil anti-society criminal*. Wild. Wild. Wild.

Blood and Guts in High School, Part Two, Kathy Acker[20]

This cursory glance at criminal and cultural history seems to confirm Hawthorne's positioning of punishment near the heart of Puritan society. Recognising its prominence, however, does not guarantee the accuracy of Hawthorne's depiction. *The Scarlet Letter* opens with 'The Prison Door' and the insistence that new communities must begin by preparing to punish those who threaten social stability:

The founders of a new colony, whatever Utopia of human virtue and happiness they might originally project, have invariably recognised it among their earliest practical necessities to allot a portion of the virgin soil as a cemetery, and another portion as the site of a prison. (p.51)

Following the building of Boston's first 'House of Correction' in 1632, prisons became increasingly conspicuous in seventeenth-century New England, far outnumbering other public buildings such as hospitals or schools. Fines were introduced to encourage every county to prioritise prison construction. By the 1650s, a few years after the historical setting of *The Scarlet Letter*, almost every small town and village in the colonies could boast a purpose-built detention facility. It is worth remembering that imprisonment as a punishment was still extremely rare, costly and contrary to the Puritan emphasis on public retribution. Nevertheless, the establishment of a network of jails served vital social, economic and symbolic imperatives. The imposing presence of a prison near the heart of each Puritan community underscored the insistence on discipline. Prisons were also integral to relations of production and were used to detain and discipline convict labour exported from England in the prisoner trade, as well as servants, slaves and those who refused to work.

Hawthorne's description of the Boston prison aims to transcend these historical contingencies:

Certain it is that, some fifteen or twenty years after the settlement of the town, the wooden jail was already marked with weather-stains and other indications of age, which gave a yet darker aspect to its beetle-browed and gloomy front. The rust on the ponderous iron-work of its oaken door looked more antique than anything else in the New World. Before this ugly edifice, and between it and the wheel-track of the street, was a grass-plot, much overgrown with burdock, pig-weed, apple-pern, and such unsightly vegetation, which evidently found something congenial in the soil that had so early borne the black flower of civilised society, a prison. But, on one side of the portal, and rooted almost at the threshold, was a wild rose-bush, covered, in this month of June, with its delicate gems. (pp.52–3)

The naturalising metaphor here is carefully cultivated, uprooting the prison from history and planting it in a timeless, organic tradition. The opposition of the wild rose-bush and the prison door ushers in a Puritan cartography whose antipodes are desire and the law. Throughout *The Scarlet Letter* this polarity is mapped onto the dark forest (where lovers meet alone) and the marketplace (whose cynosure is the scaffold, where lovers and others are disciplined). At times, however, this opposition seems less secure than the Boston prison. The juxtaposition of the 'black flower' and the 'rose-bush' hints at cross-fertilisation between desire and the law and this fecundity produces anxiety. The rose-bush offers 'delicate gems', but is also 'wild'. Closer inspection might reveal those thorns that signify, like the dark forest beyond, the dangers attendant on desire. The prison door is similarly decorated 'with iron spikes' and is 'antique' and 'gloomy.' It lacks the enchantments of the rose, but denotes stability and permanence. The romance reader knows which side of that door Hester ought to be on but Hawthorne is perhaps less certain: he may regret the suffering produced by punishment in the prison and the marketplace, but he seems even more concerned about the pleasures of the forest.

The black flower of punishment promises redemption, but nature in *The Scarlet Letter* is still blighted by Puritan phobias. The 'primeval forest' has the 'wild, free atmosphere of an unredeemed, un-christianised, lawless region' (p.159). The Puritan geographical imagination located itself on a middle ground between the hyper-trophied corruption of Old World civilisation and the heathen wilderness of the New World. Their 'errand in the wilderness' was to cultivate the pleasant gardens of Christ. Thomas Hooker warned that 'there is wild love and joy enough in the world, as there is wild thyme and other herbs, but we would have garden love and garden joy'.[21] Puritan horticultural tropes are part of a cultural pathology that often borders on the agoraphobic. The wilderness was shunned as the home of savages, diseases, environmental dangers and assorted shapes of the devil. Even more worryingly, these badlands did not end at the edge of the Puritan's well-tended gardens:

> the Puritan community had helped mark its location in space by keeping close watch on the wilderness surrounding it on all sides; and now that the visible traces of that wilderness had receded out of sight, the settlers invented a new one by finding the shapes of the forest in the middle of the community itself.[22]

Mistress Hibbins, Hawthorne's witch, invites Hester to come into the woods at night and meet her master, 'the Black Man'. Hester declines, but throughout *The Scarlet Letter* 'shapes in the forest' make the return journey. 'Wild' is the keyword that marks their presence and the frequency with which it appears suggests the rampant colonisation of the Puritan garden by the lawless wilderness. Hester is vitalised by a 'wild energy' that is merely contained by punishment, never extinguished: '[a] passion, once so wild, and even yet neither dead nor asleep, but only imprisoned within the same tomb-like heart' (p.144). This wildness is also her daughter's defining feature. Pearl has 'bright, wild eyes', makes 'wild, inarticulate, and sometimes piercing music' and is prone to 'wild outbreak[s] ... fit[s] of passion, gesticulating violently, and throwing her small figure into the most extravagant contortions' (pp.164, 177). As the 'effluence of her mother's lawless passion', '[Pearl] could not be made amenable to rules', '[t]here is no law, nor reverence for authority ... mixed up with [her] composition' and she has no 'principle of being ... save the freedom of the broken law' (pp.82, 112). The lawlessness of the daughter is linked to the mother's stigmatic sign. Pearl is 'the scarlet letter in another form; the scarlet letter endowed with life' (p.90). The ease with which the letter of the law, through its conjunction with Pearl, comes to signify 'Anarchy', accents Hawthorne's anxieties about both social and semantic instability.

Although Hester declines Mistress Hibbins' invitation she is still associated by Hawthorne with witchcraft. The indeterminacy of the law's letter is foregrounded through references to the 'spell' cast by the scarlet sign, a hex that encloses the lawless body of the female criminal and her 'witch-baby' in a 'magic circle.' Witchcraft was arguably the most feared form of *wildness* in Puritan New England. It was established as a capital crime in the 'Body of Liberties' and early victims of this law included Margaret Jones in 1648, Mistress Hibbins in 1656, and four alleged witches executed in 1662 in Hartford, Connecticut. Events at Salem in 1692 were less a freak occurrence than the climax to a punitive persecution spanning 50 years. In addition to the 19 recorded executions, the witchcraft hysteria resulted in one death by interrogation (Giles Corey was crushed to death under rocks), two further necromancers died in prison and hundreds of suspects endured lengthy incarceration.

Various explanations have been offered for the Puritan punishment of witches. Carol Karlsen, for example, has examined patterns of property ownership and inheritance to reveal how many of the women who were convicted and executed enjoyed levels of economic self-sufficiency that perturbed Puritan patriarchs.[23] Although economics may have been an underlying determinant, erotics played a defining role in the demonology. Riding her phallic broom and screaming into the night, the witch was accused of wild sexual crimes. She allowed both body and soul to be entered by Satan, had intercourse with her familiar and assumed the form of a succubus to assault victims in their beds. Interrogation of witches involved intrusive physical examination for proof of these deviant practices. The discovery of a 'witch's teat', at which the familiar was suckled in grotesque perversion of maternity, invariably resulted in execution. Bridget Bishop was hanged after discovery of the 'Devil's Mark', a 'preternatural Excrescence of flesh between the pudendum and Anus much like to Teats & not usual in women'.[24] As the dark, wild Pearl is suckled on the scaffold and is subsequently seen forever at her mother's side, Hawthorne hints at the folklore that condemned Hester's historical sisters and sustains the Puritan equation between the devil and female desire.

THE 'STRANGE JOY' OF PURITAN PUNISHMENT

The 'Devil's Mark' was a sign of fearful libidinal excesses that were not exclusive to witches. All Puritans were forced to struggle with what Wigglesworth termed the 'Sodom within'. When New Haven introduced ordinances classifying masturbation as a capital crime, it reflected the suspicion that Puritan society was being subjected to an erotic endo-colonisation: 'many, many are guilty ... so many that if stoning were the punishment a mountain could not afford stones enough'.[25] Prohibitions did not finish at sexual pleasure, leading H. L. Mencken to deride Puritanism as 'the haunting fear that someone, somewhere, may be happy'.[26] It is important not to rely on platitudes concerning Puritan prudery. The considerable degree of repression in Puritan society implies, of course, that there was a lot to repress. At the same time, the ferocity with which 'deviant' pleasures were pursued and the sheer number of injunctions against them cannot be ignored. The statutes prohibiting games (such as cards and shuffle board), forms of fashion (pertaining to colours and materials) and indulgence (especially drinking) were legion, and were reinforced by interminable sermons and tracts (Increase Mather's *Arrow against Profane and Promiscuous Mixt Dancing* is not untypical of Puritan literature in this respect).

Alongside these interdicts colonial justice possessed an alarmingly expansive definition of crimes that were sexual in nature. Captain Kemble was confined to the stocks for two hours when, after returning from three years at sea, he was seen kissing his wife, in public, on the Sabbath. Section 94 of the 'Body of Liberties', 'The Capital Laws of New-England', ranks 15 offences in order of seriousness. Five of the top ten were sex crimes (bestiality, sodomy, adultery, sex with a child under the age of ten, rape) and one of the remaining five, witchcraft, was automatically associated with sexual deviance. The crime that Hester is convicted of was one of the most common in colonial New England. Mosaic Law was unambiguous on the penalty for adultery: 'And the man that committeth adultery with another man's wife ... the adulterer and the adulteress shall surely be put to death' (Leviticus 20.10). Although, in accordance with the Pentateuch, adultery was classified as a capital crime, the full penalty was very rarely enforced. A few years prior to the historical setting of *The Scarlet Letter*, Mary Latham and James Britton were executed for adultery, but following this case juries grew reluctant to find offenders guilty and magistrates settled for lesser charges of 'lewd misconduct'.

As the capital punishment of adulterers became a dead letter, alternative strategies were devised that often involved the use of letters. Puritan logocentricism is apparent in its propensity for letter penalties, with its translation of the criminal body into script. Offenders were typically taken through the streets in a cart, or required to stand for a specified period in prominent public spaces whilst wearing a letter that signified their crime. The Plymouth Colony records document the use of letter penalties for adulterers as early as 1639, and this practice was codified in 1658 by the Boston General Court. In *The Scarlet Letter*, Hester is made a 'type of sin' and the narrator underlines the potency of this punishment:

> Tomorrow would bring its own trial with it; so would the next day, and so would the next ... she would become the general symbol at which the preacher and the moralist might point, and in which they might vivify and embody their images of woman's frailty and passion ... the figure, the body, the reality of sin. (p.74)

The Puritans were notoriously hostile towards theatre, and yet their punishments were staged with a keen eye for dramatic effect. Puritan justice, with its emphasis on public performance, conforms in this respect to Foucault's model of classical punishment. The guilty were carted through the streets, confined to the stocks or the whipping post, displayed on the pillory, gallows, or church steps, often at midday to guarantee exposure to the largest possible audience. Lengthy sermons were routinely delivered prior to an execution, with the intention of extracting a spectacular last-minute confession and repentance from the condemned.

In a 'scene of public witnessing', Hester is placed centre-stage in a carefully chosen costume to be heckled by the crowd and lectured by her critics (p.193). In this opening set-piece Hawthorne captures the theatricality of Puritan punishment, but much of its cruelty is kept backstage. The element which Hawthorne masks is that which Nietzsche sought to unveil in *The Genealogy of Morals*:

> all religions are at their deepest foundations systems of cruelty ... there is, perhaps, nothing more frightening and more sinister in the whole prehistory of man than his *technique for remembering things*. Something is branded in, so that it stays in the memory: only that which *hurts* incessantly is remembered.[27]

The punishments devised for those who transgressed the 'Body of Liberties' invariably focused on the body. Culprits charged with adultery, or any crime of a sexual nature, were automatically whipped. Failure to comply with a letter penalty, or the repetition of an offence, would often result in the sign being branded into flesh. Branding was not the only form of mutilation practised by the magistracy. The head was a focal point for disfigurement, with ears removed, nostrils slit and holes bored through tongues.

The Scarlet Letter wills amnesia concerning the Puritan 'technique for remembering things'. Hawthorne's narrator insists on the 'cunning cruelty of [Hester's] sentence', but the physicality of Puritan discipline is erased by exclusive concentration on psychological trauma (p.120). This omission is further obscured by the corporeal tropes deployed to depict Hester's suffering. The criminal's first steps from the prison, the gaze of the crowd, the touch of her daughter, husband and lover and the glow of the scarlet letter itself are all described as 'torture', but these torments remain strictly figurative. Hester is not whipped (as all adulterers were) and she is permitted to keep her child (as all adulterers were not). Her prison experiences are similarly sanitised. Early colonial jails tended to be crowded, unhygienic and disease-ridden. For the female offender enduring same-sex incarceration, sexual assaults by other inmates and jailers were commonplace. Hester's confinement, however, appears to have been solitary, aside from her daughter and a jailer benevolently watching over his charge.

Hawthorne's sanitisation of Puritan punishment represses the slippage between desire and law that characterised corrections in the colonial era. Puritanism frowned on sexual deviancy, but offered surrogates in the form of socially-sanctioned sadism and masochism. The Puritan God was a cruel master always prepared to correct his servants. The Puritan faithful were willing victims, cringing in submission. In *Meat Out of the Eater*, Wigglesworth reminds his reader that 'God doth chastise his own in Love'; his children must learn, therefore, to find pleasure in pain and 'the Rod in Meekness kiss'.[28] Wigglesworth's *Day of Doom* typifies the Puritan jeremiad with its catalogue of lacerations, bristling with erotic undercurrents, that await the fallen. Fantasies of heavenly hurt could be acted out in punishment practice whilst simultaneously disavowing the libidinal energies that fuelled them.

The response to the erotic economy of Puritan punishment in *The Scarlet Letter* is somewhat conflicted. Hawthorne appears to valorise the masochistic personality, whilst the sadistic excesses routinely practised in public are cathected towards the private sphere. Following Hester's 'exquisitely painful' humiliation before the crowd, she learns how to sublimate her wild desires into the 'positive and vivacious suffering' of self-punishment: 'Hester Prynne had no selfish ends, nor lived in any measure for her own profit and enjoyment' (p.200). This self-disciplining threatens to realise the capital punishment required for adultery by Puritan law:

> imitation of the Virgin Mary and Christian martyrs ... self-sacrifice and self-denial ... serve as proof of physical and spiritual purity, [and] can be seen as embodying fantasies of a masochistic turning inward of the death drive that results in self-negation and self-obliteration.[29]

Rather than opposing this self-imposed death sentence, Hawthorne endorses the curative benefits of masochism: the 'lees of bitterness' is a 'cordial of intensest potency', offering 'to cure by wholesome pain' (pp.176, 153). Hester's daughter illustrates the importance of taking your medicine: 'She wanted – what some people want throughout life – a grief that should deeply touch her, and thus humanise and make her capable of sympathy' (p.147). Pearl punishes her parents, laughing in 'extravagant ecstasy' at their pain; she is the scourge of Puritan children and the community faithful, and in the dark forest her cruelty is given free rein to drown snails, lay jelly-fish out to melt in the sun and stone small birds in 'perverse merriment' (p.112). Critically, it is pain on the scaffold that is the catalyst to her transformation from unrepentant sadist. The imp of polymorphous perversity is exorcised as her father dies in the shadow of the gallows: 'Pearl kissed his lips. A spell was broken. The great scene of grief, in which the wild infant bore a part, had developed all her sympathies' (p.196). The only kiss Hawthorne permits in this romance is public, involving family members, and it produces a therapeutic flood of grief rather than desire. The premise behind Puritan penology, that pain is the essential prerequisite for moral growth, is thus dramatically confirmed.

Dimmesdale's acceptance of paternity and punishment on the scaffold facilitates his daughter's entry into the symbolic. The law accepted by the father dispels the wild witchcraft of women. The gender opposition that informs Hawthorne's drama of punishment, however, is both confused and confirmed by the insistent feminisation of Dimmesdale. Although he is introduced alongside Puritan patriarchs and participates in their interrogation of Hester, the gap between the male judges on the balcony and the female offender on the scaffold is bridged by a preoccupation with Dimmesdale's appearance:

a white, lofty, and impending brow, large, brown, melancholy eyes, and a mouth which, unless when he forcibly compressed it, was apt to be tremulous, expressing both nervous sensibility and a vast power of self-restraint ... coming forth, when occasion was, with a freshness, and fragrance, and dewy purity of thought, which, as many people said affected them like the speech of an angel ... the young pastor's voice was tremulously sweet, rich, deep. (pp.66–7)

When Dimmesdale recognises that Hester will not fold under interrogation and reveal the name of the father, his own name, he clutches his hand to his heart and sighs 'with a long respiration' (p.68). Unlike her loquacious and practically pre-Raphaelite partner in crime, Hester is courageous, reticent, determined on a course of noble self-sacrifice, and thus plays the part in this punitive drama of the hardened con: '[her] temperament was not of the order that escapes from too intense suffering by a swoon ... With the same hard demeanour, she was led back to prison' (ibid.).

The 'A' branded on Dimmesdale's breast may then signify an androgyny that was anathema to Puritan patriarchy. At the witch trials, George Jacobs was hanged after physical examination uncovered '3. Teats, which according to the best of our Judgement we think is not natural'.[30] Puritan gender codes encouraged a robust manliness that problematises the reverence that Dimmesdale, a veritable Angel in the House of God, receives from his parishioners. Wrestling, weight-lifting, hunting and vigorous outdoor pursuits were popular pastimes within the clergy. Roger Thompson's report of a 'church member [who] scorned a limp minister as "fitter to be a lady's chamberman"', suggests that his flock would have limited tolerance for the perpetually ailing Dimmesdale.[31] Predictably, Puritan masculine ideals were accompanied by a vigorous homophobia. 'Sodomitical uncleaness' was classified as a capital crime in the 'Body of Liberties', and generally regarded as 'far more abominable than adultery ... the most abominable unnatural sin'.[32]

Although *The Scarlet Letter* is nominally concerned with adultery (without ever mentioning this crime by name), the 'lawless passion' of homosexuality plays a pivotal role. The heterosexual romance between Hester and Dimmesdale is in part a catalyst to a homoerotic plot centred on Chillingworth and Dimmesdale. The public punishment of the female offender is in fact eclipsed by a private drama, suffused with sadomasochistic overtones, between her husband and lover. The relationship between these two confirms Girard's influential assertion, that in 'any erotic rivalry, the bond that links the two rivals is as intense and potent as the bond that links either of the rivals to the beloved'.[33] Hester recognises this bond and appears threatened by it: 'no man is as near to him as you. You tread behind his every footstep. You are beside him, sleeping and waking ... Your clutch is on his life' (p.137).

In the private drama of punishment between illicit lover and cuckold, Dimmesdale is the masochistic partner. The persistent references to his 'secret' are double-edged and intimate heteroclite desires beyond the purely adulterous. Dimmesdale punishes himself for avoiding his punishment, only to relish the erotic compensations of self-torture. Hawthorne describes a midnight visit to the scaffold by Dimmesdale as a 'vain show of expiation', but penitence hardly seems to be the reverend's motivation: 'a thrill of the heart, – but he knew not whether of exquisite pain, or pleasure as acute ... [he] was already trembling at the conjunction in which – with a strange joy, nevertheless – he now found himself' (p.125). In a repetition of his heterosexual partner's appearance on the scaffold, there is something 'exquisitely painful' about Dimmesdale's anguish. The proximity of this 'strange joy' and Puritanism's taboo desires is accented by supernatural allusions: his tortured cry is mistaken, at the witching hour, for necromancy. Dimmesdale feverishly performs acts of penitence guaranteed to intensify his guilty displeasure. He attempts to transform the pulpit into a pillory, publicly castigating himself for his sinful nature, but the more he punishes himself the more he is revered: 'his heart vibrated in unison with theirs, and received their pain unto itself, and sent its own throb of pain through a thousand hearts ... It is inconceivable, the agony with which this public veneration tortured him!' (pp.118–19) Following Cotton Mather and other Puritan dignitaries, Dimmesdale resorts to flagellation:

> In Mr Dimmesdale's secret closet, under lock and key, there was a bloody scourge. Oftentimes, this Protestant and puritan divine had plied it on his own shoulders; laughing bitterly at himself the while, and smiting so much the more pitilessly, because of that bitter laugh. (p.120)

Whilst Hester grows ever-stronger as a result of accepting her punishment, Dimmesdale undergoes physical and spiritual collapse for trying to avoid public correction. When Hester persuades the minister to run away, his self-destructive masochism, freed from guilt, threatens to flower into anarchic sadism. On the road back from the dark forest he undergoes 'a revolution in the sphere of thought and feeling' that confirms Puritan moral mappings of the 'Sodom within':

> ... nothing short of a total change of dynasty and moral code ... At every step he was incited to do some strange, wild, wicked thing or other, with a sense that it would be at once involuntary and intentional; in spite of himself, yet growing out of a profounder self than that which opposed the impulse. (pp.169–70)

Dimmesdale's decision not to run, but to reveal his sinful self on the scaffold, may betoken a triumph over his 'profounder self', or the id's most spectacular success. As he tears off his tunic to reveal the scarlet letter 'imprinted in the flesh', Dimmesdale stands with 'a flush of triumph in his face, as one who, in the crisis of acutest pain, had won a victory' (p.196). The 'death' that follows might be stained by metaphoric connotations commonplace in the Elizabethan theatre the Puritans loved to loathe.

Dimmesdale's partner in this S&M play, Chillingworth, pursues a path of 'cruel purpose' against his willing victim in which punishment is similarly bonded with aberrant desires: 'He could play upon him as he chose. Would he arouse him with a throb of agony? The victim was for ever on the rack; it needed only to know the spring that controlled the engine; – and the physician knew it well!' (p.116). Whilst Dimmesdale's masochism is associated with insidious feminisation, Chillingworth's sadism is tied to an equally problematic hyper-masculinisation. In contrast to his victim, whose spirit is so 'shattered and subdued it could hardly hold itself erect', Chillingworth appears as a phallic agent of punitive vengeance: '[he] thrust himself through the crowd, or, perhaps ... he rose up out of some nether region' (pp.156, 193). The climax to Chillingworth's torture takes place whilst his victim is sleeping:

> The physician advanced directly in front of his patient, laid his hand upon his bosom, and thrust aside the vestment, that, hitherto, had always covered it even from the professional eye. Then, indeed, Mr Dimmesdale shuddered, and slightly stirred ... the physician turned away. But with what a wild look of wonder, joy, and horror! With what a ghastly rapture ... bursting forth ... and making itself riotously manifest by the extravagant gestures

with which he threw his arms towards the ceiling, and stamped his foot upon the floor! (pp.115–16)

Chillingworth's 'moment of ecstasy' in Dimmesdale's chambers recalls Pearl's relish at the suffering of others. The physician and the elf-child are kindred sadistic spirits, plaguing their willing victims, the adulterous couple. These mirrorings confirm the Puritan demonisation of desire. Deviant eroticism (adultery, homosexuality, S&M) is not opposed to a healthy heterosexuality; desire itself is defined as a threat to social stability and gender identity. Because she has been subjected to the proper public discipline, Hester proves best able to control the 'lawless passion' unleashed elsewhere. The 'perverse merriment' of children, the 'ghastly rapture' of physicians and the 'strange joy' of ministers are opposed to the socially-sanctioned masochism of Hester, who is taught by the letter of the law to forgo desire and accept a deathly life sentence as sombre Puritan subject.

MRS HUTCHINSON, FRIENDS AND THE PENITENTIARY SYSTEM

The rehabilitation of Mistress Prynne was by no means guaranteed. Hawthorne stresses the precariousness of her situation by drawing an analogy between Hester and an infamous contemporary. Tracing the history of the wild rose-bush that Hester passes on leaving the prison, Hawthorne refers to local legend: 'it had sprung up under the footsteps of the sainted Ann Hutchinson as she entered the prison-door' (p.52). This comparison is repeated when the narrator remarks that motherhood has saved his heroine from following in Hutchinson's footsteps. If not for Pearl, Hester may have blossomed into a religious and political radical and suffered 'death from the stern tribunals of the period, for attempting to undermine the foundations of the Puritan establishment' (p.134). Ann Hutchinson escaped execution, but she was excommunicated and banished for her role in the Antinomian controversy (1636–38). As Hawthorne explains in his sketch of 'Mrs. Hutchinson', she challenged the church by drawing a distinction between the 'chosen of man' and the 'sealed of heaven'.[34] In Puritan theocracy this was no minor matter of exegesis, but a major challenge to social and political authority. This is the pivotal point in Hawthorne's apology for the Puritan's treatment of Hutchinson:

These proceedings of Mrs. Hutchinson could not long be endured by the provincial government. The present was a most remarkable case, in which religious freedom was wholly inconsistent with public safety ... Unity of faith was the star that had guided these people over the deep, and a diversity of sects would either have scattered them from the land to which they had as yet so few attachments, or perhaps have excited a diminutive civil war among those who had come so far to worship together.[35]

The punishment of Hutchinson and the Antinomians proved to be the overture to a more widespread offensive against the Quakers. In the 'Custom House' essay, Hawthorne describes one of his ancestors, William Hathorne, as 'a bitter persecutor; as witness the Quakers, who have remembered him in their histories, and relate an incident of his hard severity toward a woman of their sect' (p.27). Hawthorne is conveniently silent on the precise nature of this incident (as he is on family involvement in the witch trials) and on a history of violent persecution that lasted almost a decade (1656–65) and included four executions.[36] The punishment that greeted the Quakers in the New World sustained a tradition. George Fox, the founder of the Friends, was imprisoned for his beliefs, only to transform his prison into a recruiting base. Converts served their sentence and left to recruit new followers, who in turn, like William Dewsbury, 'joyfully entered prisons as palaces, telling mine enemies to hold me there as long as they could; and in the prison house I sung praises to my God and esteemed the bolts and locks put upon me as jewels'.[37] When the first Quaker proselytisers arrived in the New World, in Boston in 1656, it seems that the Puritans had learned little from the English experience. Quakerism was outlawed, captains who transported Friends and sympathisers who sheltered them faced fines and whipping. Quakers who returned after banishment were mutilated and placed in Houses of Correction. Inevitably, with the prospect of martyrdom assured, Quaker migration to the New World swelled. When the Puritan authorities responded by introducing more severe penalties, the Quakers only sought their punishment with increased vigour. As New England prisons overflowed and sympathy for the Friends grew on both sides of the Atlantic, the Puritan elite eventually tried to diffuse the crisis by introducing less draconian penalties.

The Quakers managed to survive this reign of terror, and even its removal, and in 1682 William Penn was granted a royal charter to found a new state. Given their own intimate familiarity with punishment it was unsurprising that Pennsylvania pioneered an innovative disciplinary code. Penal reform was the flagship for the 'Holy Experiment' of Philadelphia. This experiment began with a shift away from execution, torture and the sanguinary punishments the Quakers had themselves endured and towards new styles of imprisonment. The Philadelphia Society for Alleviating the Miseries of Public Prisons was founded in 1776, and in the wake of revolution Pennsylvania continued to lead the way in those penal reforms that were to become an essential signature of the fledgling Republic's national identity. The development of the penitentiary was central to this process. It initiated a transition that would profoundly reshape penal institutions and ideology throughout the western world. As Foucault argues, the birth of the penitentiary was pivotal to the shift from classical punishment to modern discipline. The new system dispensed with public rituals focusing on the body in favour of private regimes geared towards psychological correction. This transposition began with the remodelling, in 1790, of the Walnut Street prison in Philadelphia. The main architectural innovation at the new 'Penitentiary House' was the establishment of 16 cells designed specifically for the solitary confinement of inmates. There were strict controls introduced governing prisoner communication and appearance: inmates were penalised for breaking silence, dressed in standardised uniforms and ordered to bathe and shave regularly. The redesign of Walnut Street was inspired both by the Quaker belief that no individual was beyond redemption and reformist thinking currently circulating in Europe.[38] The penitentiary sought to achieve rehabilitation through penitence (its lexical root) and to instil self-discipline by isolating the inmate from corrupting influences.

In 1829, at Cherry Hill on the outskirts of Philadelphia, the Eastern State Penitentiary was built with the intention of perfecting the Walnut Street model. At the time of its completion, Eastern was the most expensive public building in America. The architecture was inspired by the design of a gothic monastery: corridors and cells of stone were isolated from the world by a wall 30 feet high. Whilst Walnut Street and other institutions isolated prisoners at night, Eastern aimed to cloister them during the day as well. On arrival all prisoners were hooded until they reached their cell. Staff boasted that they could detain best friends in adjacent cells without them ever discovering the identity of their neighbour. Eastern allotted prisoners numbers, a uniform, cropped their hair and instigated near total bans on communication within the prison or with the outside world. The running tap-water and flush-toilet in each cell enhanced sanitation but was primarily a means of reducing prisoner contact. Cell doors included a feeding drawer and a peephole for the same purpose. The only source of light was an eight-inch-diameter hole in the ceiling, which would be closed for infraction of prison rules.

Eastern shaped prison design first in America, and then the western world. When de Tocqueville and de Beaumont visited Eastern for twelve days in 1831, they reported that 'this perfect isolation secures the prisoner from all fatal contamination', but they were also appalled by the 'silence of death': 'We have often trod during night those monotonous and dim galleries, where a lamp is always burning: we felt as if we traversed catacombs; there were a thousand living beings, and yet it was a desert solitude.'[39] Amongst his interviewees, de Tocqueville met an inmate who kept as companions all of the insects that entered his cell. Following his visit to Eastern a decade later in 1842, Charles Dickens responded with a similar mixture of admiration and horror. The penitentiary possessed a 'perfect order', but had 'cruel and wrong' effects on the prisoners.[40] Dickens met a prisoner addicted to peeling the skin from his fingers. Like de Tocqueville and Dickens, Hawthorne had major reservations about the penitentiary system, and these are articulated in *The Scarlet Letter*. The historical setting of Hester's story in the seventeenth century serves to cloak its commentary on contemporary punishment practices. The ideological imperative of *The Scarlet Letter* is to undermine the efficacy of the new penal regime, and encourage respect for the strengths of the *ancien régime*. To achieve this, however, Hawthorne ignores critical continuities between these systems.

Foucault notes that the birth of the penitentiary system spawned a 'network of writing', a prodigious 'documentary accumulation'.[41] Hester's scarlet letter is an example of the Puritan letter penalty, but Hawthorne's claim to have discovered it amongst 'bundles of official documents' also signposts an increasingly bureaucratised penal system. Hester's relation to her letter similarly resonates in separate time frames:

'It lies not in the pleasure of the magistrates to take off this badge', calmly replied Hester. 'Were I worthy to be quit of it, it would fall away of its own nature, or be transformed into something that should speak a different purport'. (p.136)

Whilst this appears to echo the Antinomian challenge to Puritan penal authority, it also anticipates the introjection of discipline to which the penitentiary system aspired. The new regime's model prisoners were to become their own jailers. Eastern was an impressive edifice and was also the site of ongoing construction as the penitentiary aimed at nothing less than the rebuilding of prisoner subjectivity. Reinforcing the superego would erect a prison within each inmate. In the process, by transforming punishment into self-punishment, and surveillance into self-scrutiny, the state would be relieved of the ethical burden of discipline. In Hester's case this reconstruction appears to have been exemplary. Hawthorne's heroine chooses a life sentence in the New World over liberty in the Old:

> Here had been her sin; here, her sorrow; and here was yet to be her *penitence*. She had returned, therefore, and resumed, – of her own free will, for not the sternest magistrate of that iron period would have imposed it, – resumed the symbol of which we have related so dark a tale. Never afterwards did it quit her bosom. (p.200. My italics)

Although the penitentiary system was founded on Quaker innovations, it was simultaneously allied with aspects of the Puritan ideal. Foucault characterises the notion of perpetual penality as intrinsically modern, but this was also the grail of Puritan theocracy. The continual self-regulation fostered by the Puritan code pre-empted the disciplinary tactics of the penitentiary. Hester's fate exemplifies these continuities: she is banished to a 'lonesome cottage' to contemplate her crime and perform mundane labours; she is isolated from the community, wears a drab uniform and loses her name to a state-imposed symbol. Hawthorne insists that solitary confinement continues even after Hester leaves her cell, since the scarlet letter has 'the effect of a spell, taking her out of the ordinary relations with humanity, and enclosing her in a sphere by herself' (p.58). Hester is alone in this sphere but still feels herself to be under constant surveillance. In a manner comparable to the situation of the prisoners at Eastern, whose spokes-and-wheel design was inspired by Bentham's panopticon, Hester feels that all eyes are 'intently fastened' on her, and consequently internalises the disciplinary gaze (pp.54–5). Visual modalities connect theatricality within classical punishment to the panopticism of modern discipline. In both modes the subject is to be transformed through the optic. On the platform of the scaffold Hester is subjected to 'the heavy weight of a thousand unrelenting eyes, all fastened upon her ... [an] intense consciousness of being the object of severe and universal observation' (pp.60–2). Surveillance produces the introspection desired by the pioneers of the penitentiary: 'the scaffold of the pillory was a point of view that revealed to Hester Prynne the entire track along which she had been treading, since her happy infancy' (p.61). This gaze pursues her beyond the scaffold until, as in the panopticon, an actual disciplinary presence becomes redundant.

Foucault reads the progression from public torture to private surveillance as an epochal rupture, but continuities can be drawn between seventeenth-century Puritanism and nineteenth-century panopticism. The Puritans believed they were under constant surveillance: 'we must Consider that we shall be as a City upon a Hill, the eyes of all people are upon us'.[42] God's gaze was similarly fixed and within the City the Puritan faithful were regularly exhorted to watch over each other. Puritan courts relied heavily on informants. To report the crimes of others was less a civic than a spiritual imperative.

> Puritan discipline was largely a matter of community vigilance, and each citizen, no matter what his official function in the control apparatus, was expected to guard the public peace as carefully as he would the peace of his own household. This meant that he had license to watch over his neighbours or even to spy on them, to inquire about their business or disrupt their privacy, so long as his main purpose was to protect the morality of the community.[43]

Incidents of family members reporting each other for crimes such as blasphemy indicate that the habits of surveillance extended into the Puritan home. Puritan panopticism was perfected by constant self-scrutiny: only those who monitored their every deed and desire could discover if God's presence was with them. The stratagems of surveillance deployed by the Puritans to detect the shapes of the Devil established the institutional and ideological groundwork for nineteenth-century panopticism. Writing in response to this legacy, Hawthorne does not share his ancestors' confidence: 'The scarlet letter had not done its office' (p.134). The confinement and surveillance of Hester Prynne may have curbed her wildness, but this success is only partial: 'it is to be feared, no genuine and steadfast *penitence*, but something doubtful, something that might be deeply wrong, beneath' (p.78, my italics). Hester performs the role of the penitent, but Hawthorne fears that it may *only* be a performance, that theatricality remains as integral to modern discipline as it was to the classical regime.

The reservations that Hawthorne expresses concerning the penitentiary system are even more marked in *The Scarlet Letter*'s second punitive drama. The relationship between Chillingworth and Dimmesdale can be read as an allegory of emergent relations of power and social control. Chillingworth's disguise is doubled: he is a warden, pretending to be a scholar, pretending to be a doctor. As a 'man of thought' and a medic he is affiliated with burgeoning discourses in the field of corrections (p.71). Chillingworth's claim to be a 'Physician of the soul' echoes Theodore Parker's tropes in 'Sermon on the Dangerous Classes': 'A jail ought to be a moral hospital where the offender is kept till he is cured.'[44] Although Chillingworth's lust for vengeance aligns him with the *ancien régime*, his tactics are those of the 'moral hospital'. Dimmesdale suspects that 'an eye was looking curiously into him', he has 'constantly a dim perception of some evil influence watching over him, [but can] never gain a knowledge of its actual nature' (p.117). These fears are well-founded, since Dimmesdale is almost continually subject to the 'gaze of Roger Chillingworth' (p.156). Fear of surveillance, as in Hester's case, results in the internalisation of the disciplinary gaze: '[Dimmesdale] kept vigils, likewise, night after night ... viewing his own face in a looking-glass, by the most powerful light he could throw upon it. He thus typified the constant introspection wherewith he tortured, but could not purify, himself' (p.120). Dimmesdale's performance as ideal penitentiary inmate recalls the institutional symbiosis between monastery and prison that provided rhetorical sanction for the new disciplinary practices.

For his part in this performance, the 'Physician of the soul' monitors, interviews and takes notes. Chillingworth wants 'to know all' (p.114). '[He] scrutinised his patient carefully ... he deemed it essential, it would seem, to know the man, before attempting to do him good' (p.105). Chillingworth's subterfuge confirms Foucault's contention that knowledge and power coalesce within modern disciplinary technology. Chillingworth, the new jailer, is 'strongly moved to look into the character and qualities of the patient'; emphasis is placed not on physical but psychological correction through proximity, disclosure and access to the soul (p.104). Hawthorne's account also concurs with Foucault's sense that the rhetoric of benevolent rehabilitation screens sadistic retribution: 'a secret enemy had been continually by his side, under the semblance of a friend and helper, and had availed himself of the opportunities thus afforded for tampering with the delicate springs of Mr Dimmesdale's nature' (p.135). Dimmesdale twice seeks to escape to the scaffold and the curative powers of public humiliation, but each time Chillingworth drags him back into the privatised sphere of deadly disciplinary intimacy. What masquerades as 'humanity, or principle' is really a 'refined cruelty' (p.71). *The Scarlet Letter* thus questions the efficacy and ethical superiority claimed by proponents of the penitentiary model:

> 'Is there no reality in the *penitence* thus sealed and witnessed by good works? And wherefore should it not bring you peace?'
>
> 'No, Hester, no! ... There is no substance in it! It is cold and dead, and can do nothing for me! Of penance I have had enough! Of *penitence* there has been none! ... Happy are you, Hester, that wear the scarlet letter openly upon your bosom! Mine burns in secret!' (p.152. My italics)

Foregrounding the key word in the new penal system, Hawthorne proclaims that there can be no closure without the public retribution that Dimmesdale finally embraces on the scaffold.

The Scarlet Letter insists on the absence of penitence within the secret spaces of the penitentiary, and further discredits the privatisation of punishment by associating the 'hidden practices of [Chillingworth's] revenge' with 'dark passion' (p.140). Advocates of the 'penitentiary house' in the North worked hard to distance themselves from analogies with the 'domestic institution' in the South. Abolitionist propaganda equated discipline within the plantation prison with sexual degeneracy. To avoid similar charges being levelled at Northern prisons, strict regulations were introduced enforcing sexual abstinence. Before the birth of the penitentiary, prisons had not been segregated, sexual assaults were commonplace and male prisoners could purchase 'visits' by wives or prostitutes. Under the new regime, all contact, even between family members during supervised visits, was drastically curtailed.[45]

The control of sexuality in penitentiaries, which was modelled on monastic vows of chastity, enjoyed more success with intercourse than with the 'secret vice' of masturbation. Puritan benefaction to the penitentiary system is once again evident, with the opposition between flesh and spirit reconfigured in pseudo-scientific terminology. Contemporary medical and psychiatric discourses now insisted on the dangers posed by desire to mental and physical health. The prison physician at Eastern cited masturbation as the cause of insanity, suicide, pleurisy and pulmonary tuberculosis. Although the penitentiaries did not go as far as the New Haven Puritans in classifying masturbation as a capital offence, they did follow their forebears in devising punishments that, rather than being purely prophylactic, appeared to repeat the 'dark passion' they were supposed to prevent. For a first offence prisoners might simply be starved of food, but recidivism was treated with callous and humiliating rituals. The 'shower bath', for example, involved ice-cold water being dumped from above onto naked prisoners. This cure sometimes resulted in hypothermia and even, after repeated implementation, mental breakdown (which of course confirmed the dangers of masturbation). The wardrobe associated with the shower bath included straitjackets, gags, bits and leather gloves. The unrepentant onanist might also be treated to extended bondage in the 'mad chair', devised by Dr Benjamin Rush, the 'Father of American Psychiatry'.

In one deft manoeuvre *The Scarlet Letter* publicises 'dark passions' hidden within the penitentiary system, whilst concealing the sadistic excesses of Puritan punishment. The rewards of Hester's public ordeal are juxtaposed with the excrescence of covert discipline. Hester, although far from rehabilitated, still manages to thrive after accepting public discipline. Conversely, behind closed doors, Chillingworth and Dimmesdale undergo dramatic physical and spiritual decline. Chillingworth, as representative of the penitentiary jailer, is charged with a far greater crime than adultery: 'He has violated, in cold blood, the sanctity of a human heart' (p.154). In this respect, Hawthorne's anxious repudiation of a pathogenic penitentiary system anticipates Dickens' condemnation of Eastern (which itself seems to prophesise the polemic of *Discipline and Punish*):

I hold this slow and daily tampering with the mysteries of the brain, to be measurably worse than any torture of the body, and because its ghastly signs and tokens are not so palpable to the eye and sense of touch as scars upon the flesh; because its wounds are not upon the surface, and it exhorts few cries that human ears can hear; therefore I the more denounce it, as a secret punishment which slumbering humanity is not roused up to stay.[46]

THE HEADLESS HAWTHORNE ON THE GENTLE SEX

Hawthorne's neo-puritanical response to new punishment practices is given added urgency by contemporary developments which suggested the imminence of radical social change and challenges to the rule of law. *The Scarlet Letter*, as various critics have noted, is haunted by the spectre of revolution.[47] When Dimmesdale contemplates flouting the law and escaping punishment on his return from the dark forest he undergoes a 'revolution in the sphere of thought and feeling' (p.169). At approximately this time, Henry David Thoreau had taken up residence in the woods at Walden Pond. From this retreat he called for programmes of civil disobedience that flouted unjust laws and profound revolutions in 'thought and feeling'. A few years later, Thoreau's transcendentalist contemporary Walt Whitman offered an even more radical clarion-call for revolutions within self and society, rooted in a profoundly anti-puritanical celebration of the body. Transcendentalism constituted a literary analogue to revolutionary stirrings at home and abroad. In this climate, Hawthorne's Puritan fable intervened as a salutary lesson on the necessity for repression and respect for the law.

Hawthorne started work on *The Scarlet Letter* in 1849, immediately after a spate of revolutionary uprisings in Europe. Zachary Taylor's election to the presidency in the same year was seen by some as an augury of revolution in the New World. Following the defeat of his party, Hawthorne was ousted as Inspector of the Revenue for the Port of Salem. In the 'Custom House' essay, the ex-Inspector uses punitive metaphors, suggestive of revolution, to describe both his inauguration and dethronement:

> According to the received code in such matters, it would have been nothing short of duty, in a politician, to bring every one of those white heads under the axe of the guillotine ... It pained, and at the same time amused me, to behold the terrors that attended my advent ... There are few uglier traits of human nature than this tendency ... to grow cruel, merely because they possessed the power of inflicting harm. If the guillotine, as applied to office-holders, were a literal fact, instead of one of the most apt of metaphors, it is my sincere belief, that the active members of the victorious party were sufficiently excited to have chopped off all our heads, and have thanked Heaven for the opportunity! (pp.30, 50)

Having been mistaken for a Jacobin by his Whig opponents, Hawthorne is then subjected to a political reign of terror. 'The Custom House' glides over the barbarous punishment of Quakers and witches by Hawthorne's ancestors, but relishes the opportunity to decry the cruelty of his political opponents.

The spectre of continental revolution creeps into the scenes that follow the 'Custom House'. The scaffold on which Hester is exposed to ridicule by the mob is described as 'effectual an agent in the promotion of good citizenship, as ever was the guillotine among the terrorists of France' (p.59). However, although the Puritans utilised the gallows, the whipping post, the stocks and the pillory, they did not employ the scaffold:

> The Puritans occasionally sentenced a malefactor to stand upon a shoulder-high block or upon the ladder of the gallows (at times with a halter about the neck), but in none of the New England histories Hawthorne used as sources (viz., Felt, Snow, Mather, Hutchinson, and Winthrop) are these structures called scaffolds.[48]

Scaffold, in antebellum America, was a synonym for Dr Guillotin's invention. This historical sleight-of-hand, reinforced by references to Hester's family heraldry and aristocratic forbearance, underscores Hawthorne's aversion to radicalism. A conservative deference to law and natural authority is apparent from the outset of *The Scarlet Letter*. The narrative opens with the act of punishment, and this timing is crucial: to ignore the 'crime' is to sanction implicitly the dominant culture's definitions; to ignore the trial is to sanction implicitly the guilty verdict. Adultery was invariably tried by jury, but this institution is replaced by Hawthorne's vision of benevolent patriarchs calmly administering justice in the best interests of Hester and the community.

A second historical anachronism in this opening sequence further testifies to the impact of contemporary developments on this colonial drama. As Hester walks towards the scaffold Hawthorne refers to the mainstay of Puritan discipline, the whip, listing the various groups who might expect to encounter it: 'sluggish bond-servant, or an undutiful child … an Antinomian, a Quaker, or other heterodox religionist … or an idle and vagrant Indian' (p.54). Puritan whippings were often bloody. The Quaker William Brend, for example, received 117 lashes with a corded whip:

his flesh was beaten black and as into jelly, and under his arms the bruised flesh and blood hung down, clotted as it were into bags; and it was so beaten into one mass, that the signs of one particular blow could not be seen.[49]

Hawthorne ignores such cruelties, and his list of crimes that led to the whipping post – laziness, disobedience, drunkenness, unorthodox faith – omits adultery despite the fact that, like all sex crimes, it was routinely treated with the scourge. That the only whipping in *The Scarlet Letter* is self-administered by a guilt-ridden flagellant is attributable to the fact that, in 1850, the whip signified slavery in the same way that the scaffold signified the French revolution. For Hester to have gone under the lash would have been to associate her symbolically with the oppressed slave. Hawthorne admires his heroine's noble endurance of pain, but he does not wish to challenge the justice of her sentence, nor confuse her class identity.

Published alongside the 1850 Compromise, *The Scarlet Letter* offers a corrective to abolitionist propaganda, insisting on the necessity of accepting suffering and forgoing vigilantism in the interest of social stability. Although Hawthorne removes the whip from Hester's back, his heroine still displays characteristics that align her with a slave. Her 'dark and abundant hair … richness of complexion … [and] a marked brow and deep black eyes' were familiar ciphers in the discourses of 'passing'. These features are inherited by Pearl, the dark lady's daughter: 'black eyes … hair already of a deep, glossy brown, and which, in after years, would be nearly akin to black' (p.90). The artefact which connects mother and daughter and sutures the narrative, a 'scarlet rag of cloth', is suggestive of two 'curses' associated with blood: menstruation and miscegenation. Hester is marked stigmatically by Puritan judges, but also by patriarchy and white racial hegemony. Her body bears the signs of bad blood. 'A', perhaps, is for 'Africa' and the figure of the tragic mulatto, who in antebellum literature is often tricked into marriage, flees the Old World (which we might read as the South in this coded slave narrative) for the Northern star, only to be pursued by her master.

In Puritan demonology the adulterer's master was the 'Black Man', roaming the forest with a book which he invited his followers to sign. In *The Scarlet Letter* only Mistress Hibbins has accepted this invitation, and coincidentally, in the North at this time, it was often wealthy white women who placed their authorising signatures on fugitive slave narratives. In antebellum New England especially, there was a productive synthesis between abolitionism and the women's rights movement. One of the leading figures in this alliance, Angelina Grimké, noted that 'analysis of the condition of slaves has led to a greater awareness of my own'.[50] The year before Hawthorne began writing *The Scarlet Letter*, Grimké and her sisters helped draft the 'Declaration of Sentiments', issued at Seneca Falls by the first national convention of women's groups. In his sketch of Anne Hutchinson, Hester's prototype, Hawthorne saw the Antinomian radical as a forerunner of a new generation of women: 'there are portentous indications, changes taking place in the habits and feelings of the gentle sex, which seem to threaten our posterity with many of these public women, whereof one was a burthen too grievous for our fathers'.[51] Hutchinson's punishment was motivated as much by her challenge to patriarchal authority as to religious orthodoxy. At her trial she was accused of 'masculine' behaviour: 'You have stepped out of your place. You have rather been a Husband than a Wife and a preacher than a Hearer; and a Magistrate than a Subject.'[52] According to Hawthorne, Hutchinson articulated 'strange and dangerous opinions ... doctrines productive of change and tumult'.[53] These are the opinions that Hester secretly harbours, but which increasing numbers of American women were voicing in the antebellum North. Hawthorne's target in *The Scarlet Letter* is not wayward Puritans so much as his wayward contemporaries, and especially radical women.

It has been speculated that one of the possible role models for Hester Prynne was Margaret Fuller, who died in the year of *The Scarlet Letter*'s publication. Dismissed by Hawthorne as a 'great humbug', Fuller was at the forefront of women's rights activism, abolitionism and support for revolutions in Europe. She was also involved in contemporary debates on prison reform. As part of her support for the Women's Prison Association, Fuller visited a number of institutions, wrote on the incarceration of female offenders and campaigned against the death penalty. She was joined in these efforts by the Grimké sisters, Juliana Tappan, Dorothea Dix, Eliza Farnham and members of the Female Moral Reform Society, for whom changes to the penal system were a priority. American women, especially in the hotbed of New England radicalism, were at the forefront of calls to replace corporal and capital punishment with new rehabilitative methods. From 1844 to 1847 Eliza Farnham managed America's first women-only prison, at Mount Pleasant in New York. As the country's inaugural female governor she encouraged a general relaxation of regulations, educational programmes and a variety of social events. Conversely, in *The Scarlet Letter*, Hawthorne offers a contrast between benevolent patriarchs looking to Hester's spiritual well-being and an angry mob of women baying for her blood: 'the women ... appeared to take a peculiar interest in whatever penal infliction might be expected to ensue' (p.55). A succession of women, whose husbands are significantly absent or silent, call for Hester's punishment to be handed over to them with the promise of branding and execution. At this point in the proceedings a solitary male figure intercedes to inquire whether there is 'no virtue in woman, save what springs from a wholesome fear of the gallows' (p.56). Definitions of female virtue in the nineteenth century were formulated in accordance with the cult of True Womanhood. This hegemonic formulation, centred on the archetypal 'Angel in the House', was geared towards the disciplining of women, and the control, in particular, of their sexuality. In *The Scarlet Letter*, Hawthorne offers a conservative fantasy of correction whereby a wild woman is transformed into an Angel: 'She never battled with the public, but submitted uncomplainingly to its worse usage; she made no claim upon it, in requital for what she suffered; she did not weigh upon its sympathies' (p.130).

Hester's daughter undergoes a similar transformation. Pearl's unruliness is tamed on the scaffold by a father's kiss that ensures she will 'never do battle with the world, but be a woman in it' (p.196). This metamorphosis from wayward child to dutiful daughter offers another intervention by Hawthorne in contemporary debates on punishment, one concerned specifically with developments in domestic discipline. Attitudes towards discipline within the home underwent significant changes in the antebellum North. The 1830s and '40s saw a proliferation of domestic manuals, child-rearing guidebooks and pedagogical primers where discipline was a central concern. The coalition of Northern women calling for the abolition of violence on the plantation and in the penal system also demanded its abrogation within the home and school. In Lydia Sigourney's *Letters to Mothers* (1839), Catherine Beecher's *Treatise on Domestic Economy* (1841) and Mary Peabody Mann's *Moral Culture of Infancy* (1841), emphasis was placed on affection rather than authority. To secure a child's devotion was the most effective means of controlling his or her behaviour. Love, in other words, could be utilised as a disciplinary tool to enforce the child's internalisation of parental norms. Lyman Cobb advised that a 'child or pupil, who obeys his parent or teacher from LOVE purely, can be relied on when *absent*, as well as when *present*.[54] Richard Brodhead defines these new tactics, adopted by the American middle class, as forms of 'disciplinary intimacy'.[55] The transition from visible forms of corporeal violence to the covert stratagems of *surveillir* was evident both in the penitentiary system and the bourgeois home.

Hester experiments with disciplinary intimacy: 'she early sought to impose a tender, but strict, control … both smiles and frowns' (p.83). Her failure to impose authority on Pearl hints at Hawthorne's scepticism about progressive modes of domestic discipline and his nostalgia, once again, for more traditional methods. As early as 1628 the Puritans had been warned, in John Robinson's child-rearing manual, against the discipline of love:

> it is wisdom [for parents] to conceal … their inordinate affection … from the children … as the ape is said, many times to kill her young ones by too strict embracing them … there is in all children, though not alike, a stubbornness, and stoutness of mind arising from their natural pride, which must in the first place be broken and beaten down.[56]

The Scarlet Letter seems to endorse Robinson's judgement: 'the harsh rebuke, the frequent application of the rod, enjoined by Scriptural authority, were used, not merely in the way of punishment for actual offences, but as a wholesome regimen for the growth and promotion of all childish virtues' (p.83). However, when Hester resorts to '[p]hysical compulsion or restraint' it has only limited effect, and she is forced to recognise that 'the task was beyond her skill' (p.83). This may be a problem with personnel, however, rather than regimen. Hester's double bind is that she cannot impose discipline on that which embodies her own lawlessness. The 'Declaration of Sentiments' had insisted that 'all men and women … are endowed by their Creator with certain inalienable rights'.[57] In Hester Prynne, Hawthorne offered an alternative vision of the inalienable rights associated with unruly women. The daughter's inheritance from her mother can only be exorcised once the father's law and love have been reinstated on the scaffold. *The Scarlet Letter* thus preaches a neo-Puritan parable on the ineffectiveness of emergent modes of discipline associated with the feminine, and valorises the authority of the *ancien régime*.

MS PRYNNE AND THE NEW PURITANS

According to the Foucault model, penal styles in France underwent an irrevocable rupture in the nineteenth century, with the *ancien régime* dislodged by new technologies of *surveillir*. Transplanted to American soil, this break is far less distinct. *The Scarlet Letter* has been read as an intervention in the conflicts between emergent and residual modes of punishment in the antebellum North. These conflicts were not resolved in Hawthorne's time, and continue to characterise the American penal machine. In 1850, Hawthorne's nostalgia for the *ancien régime* could easily have been sated by looking beyond his native Boston to those states below the Mason-Dixon line. As we shall see (in Chapter 4), semi-feudal practices thrived in the South both before and after the Civil War. Closer to home, Hawthorne might also have taken comfort from fundamental conflicts within the penitentiary system itself. Eastern penitentiary provided a blueprint for prison design across America, but it also faced competition from a second influential institution, built in 1817 at Auburn in New York. Although inmates at Auburn were segregated at night, they congregated during the day in workshops and outside the prison in work teams. Auburn prisoners were subjected to heavy labour and routine whippings by the guards. This system helped significantly to reduce costs, and instructed inmates in the discipline of industrial labour. Auburn's first governor, Elam Lynds, was an ex-army captain who had little faith in the concept of reform, and believed instead in regular flogging to 'break the prisoner into a state of *passive obedience*'.[58] Lynds used prison labour to build a new facility at Ossining (nicknamed Sing Sing) and pioneered a regime that fused military and industrial discipline.

An intense rivalry was established between the Eastern and Auburn models, with each claiming ethical and economic advantages. In their report *On the Penitentiary System in the United States*, de Tocqueville and de Beaumont noted that 'the Philadelphia system produces more honest men, and that of New York more obedient citizens'.[59] Kai Erikson notes the continuity between these two systems and the nation's religious ancestry. Whilst Eastern was founded on the Quaker faith in the possibility of redemption through penitence, Auburn reflected the Puritan insistence on harsh discipline: 'Philadelphia provided a setting in which a man's natural grace could emerge, Auburn offered a setting in which his inherent wickedness could at least be curbed and bent to the needs of society.'[60] Due to greater costs and persistent criticisms concerning the high incidence of mental health problems, Eastern was ultimately less influential than Auburn, and the 'congregate system' eclipsed the Quakers' preferred 'segregate model'. By the appearance of *The Scarlet Letter*, however, both models were in crisis. 'By the 1850s, penitentiaries generally fell into a pattern of stagnation, growing debt, corruption, and endemic disorder. The cycles of reform, stagnation, and repression would continue throughout the penitentiary's history.'[61]

The next cycle of reform was given initial impetus in 1867 by a *Report on the Prisons and Reformatories of the United States and Canada*. Commissioned by the Prison Association of New York and produced by Theodore Dwight and Enoch Wines, this report offered severe criticisms of the malaise affecting the system, and encouraged a return to rehabilitative ideals. The National Congress on Penitentiary and Reformatory Discipline met in 1870 and endorsed a 'Declaration of Principles'. This document expressed the belief that 'the supreme aim of prison discipline is the reformation of criminals, not the infliction of vindictive suffering'.[62] To this end the 'Declaration of Principles' encouraged improvements in sanitation, reforms in prison administration that included the removal of political appointments and increased involvement by women, a new system of prisoner classification based on behaviour rather than criminal record, and a greater emphasis on literacy, learning and work skills. This landmark document established a blueprint that helped shape prison management for much of the next 100 years. The immediate aftermath of the 1870 conference witnessed a steady increase in the number of 'reformatory' prisons, specifically for young adults and women, in which religious and vocational training was prioritised. Zebulon Brockway, the superintendent at Elmira reformatory, epitomised this renaissance in the rehabilitative ethos, viewing his role as a 'scientist of penology' and his charges less as convicts than 'patients'.

The most significant subsequent phases of reform, and a cyclical rekindling of enthusiasm for the ideals of the penitentiary system took place during the progressive era and the 1960s (in conjunction with the civil rights movement). The history of the penitentiary in its native country has seen constant swings between 'Quaker' faith and 'Puritan' scepticism in the possibility of amelioration. Since 1970 the penitentiary system has witnessed the most sustained assault on the rehabilitative credo in its history. The American penal system has been reshaped by a renaissance in Puritan thinking. In 1995, in

California, a 27-year-old African-American with two prior convictions for robbery was given a sentence of 25 years to life for stealing a pizza. This might be read as an emblematic moment in the recovery of Puritanical zeal for punishment in the post-Vietnam era. A new Puritanism in punishment practice played a crucial role in the rise to politico-cultural hegemony of the New Right in the 1970s and '80s, and has shown few signs of abating in the twenty-first century. In the realm of corrections, the politics of return have not simply tried to circumvent progressive reforms of the 1960s. The Justice Juggernaut has sought to bypass the rehabilitative ideal, which dates back to the founding of the Republic, and return to the draconian simplicities of Puritan retribution. Punishment has returned to the heart of the political agenda, to a position of prominence it has not enjoyed since the early colonial period. Post-Vietnam America has witnessed a massive upsurge in the practice of punishment as part of an ambitious attempt to perfect the re-integration of religion and law, church and state.

One of the key legal developments accelerating this attempt is the transformation of sentencing policy. Indeterminate sentences, the bedrock of criminal justice since the 1870s, have been eroded by a dramatic rise in determinate, mandatory and presumptive sentencing. The most notorious example of this is the 'three strikes and you're out' law which recasts recidivism as innate depravity and enforces a life sentence for the theft of a pizza. These developments reflect both a renunciation of the rehabilitative ideal and a nostalgia for notions of crime as sin that have their ideological ancestry in Puritan criminology. This nostalgia is evident in the rhetoric of those self-appointed guardians of public ethics who claim to speak on behalf of a 'moral majority'. The so-called 'war on drugs', so pivotal to law and order debates, has established a demonology every bit as hysterical and virulently viral as the Puritan war on witchcraft. Drug dealers and users are automatically associated with sexual degeneracy, violence and social breakdown. For the new Puritans, the Devil's Mark has metastasised. The 'Black Man' has moved from the forest to the city and is now easily identifiable in the form of African-American and Hispanic youths. The media construction of this cohort as folk devil has exacerbated increasing racial imbalances in the prison population: currently over half of all prison inmates are African-American, and one fifth Hispanic.

As the conservative counter-revolution gained momentum in the late 1970s and early '80s, it became apparent that the celebrated 'revolt against the state' was a misnomer in the field of corrections. The New Right was highly committed to an unprecedented expansion of penal machinery at both local and federal levels. An almost exponential rise in prison numbers underlines the rekindling of a Puritan appetite for punishment in contemporary America. When the US government first started to compile annual statistics on corrections, in the mid 1920s, it recorded around 100,000 prisoners. Between the 1920s and the 1960s this figure doubled and, aside from a slight dip during the Second World War and Vietnam, remained roughly constant at around 200,000 inmates. This figure started to climb in the 1970s and swelled during the Reagan presidency to 800,000. The 1 million and 2 million marks were surpassed in 1994 and 2000, respectively. Having remained relatively constant for the first half of the twentieth century, the American prison population grew tenfold, from 200,000 to 2 million, in under 30 years. It is important to note that the prison population represents only one-third of those persons undergoing some form of correctional supervision. In 1997 a demographic of 5.7 million included approximately 10 per cent in jail, 21 per cent in prison, 12 per cent on parole and 57 per cent on probation. In the same year, the budget for corrections exceeded $30 billion, having been a relatively meagre $4 billion in 1980. In California, one of the boom states for a burgeoning prison industry, $4 billion is now the annual budget for corrections:

> Before 1970, a state might operate four to six prisons; by 1996 the state and federal systems were averaging twenty-nine correctional institutions, with some states operating about 100 prisons. Nation-wide in 1996 the total number of correctional institutions was about 1500 ... To keep up with the flood of new commitments, we need to add one 1,000-person-capacity prison every week for the next decade.[63]

Ironically, the prison-building bonanza has seen a return to the architectural blueprint established at Eastern, but devoid of any rehabilitative aspirations. The new breed of 'SuperMax' facilities house their inmates in cells that measure six feet by eight, for an average of 23 hours per day. Prisoners, as at Eastern, are segregated during meals, exercise and religious services. Hoods are used routinely, not to protect the prisoner from corrupting influences, but to protect the staff from being attacked. The SuperMax and control units in other prisons have improved on the Quakers' segregationist model: remote control doors ensure that prison officers can achieve almost no contact with their charges.

The rejuvenation of Puritan penality is particularly stark on death row. During the Depression there had been an average of 200 executions each year, but this number declined markedly after the Second World War. Between 1965 and 1967 there were only ten executions, and in the next four years they ceased altogether. In 1972, following *Furman v. Georgia*, the Supreme Court decreed, by a five-to-four majority, that capital punishment as it was currently practised constituted 'cruel and unusual punishment'. The consequence of this ruling was a further five years of *de facto* abolition. Crucially, however, only three of the judges had believed that the modifier, 'as currently practised', was unnecessary, thus leaving the door to the death house ajar. As the renaissance in Puritan punishment has escalated, executions have once again become routine. From one execution in the year of Reagan's inauguration, the figure rose to an average of 23 between 1984 and 1994, and around 80 each year from 1997 to 2000. During this period the number of prisoners diagnosed with AIDS rose from 14,519 in 1985 to just under 250,000 in 1992. Amongst some factions in the moral majority, this was read in much the same way that their Puritan ancestors responded to plagues amongst the savages: a divine death sentence delivered on the depraved.[64]

In 1995, in the midst of this Puritan revival, Hollywood offered a rather limp adaptation of *The Scarlet Letter*. Hawthorne's tale was bowdlerised by director Roland Joffé to conform to the clichés of romantic formula and liberal feminism. Alongside the New Sodom of MTV, Hollywood had been repeatedly targeted by factions within the moral majority as a site and cause of decadence and spiritual decay. The resurgence in Puritan penality in contemporary America is not restricted to the arena of corrections. As in the colonial era, there has been an audacious effort to label and discipline groups that threaten social stability on both sides of the prison walls. One of the main folk devils targeted in this respect was the single mother. When Demi Moore appeared in Joffé's *The Scarlet Letter*, Hester Prynne was closer to the norm than the exception: in 1995 around half of all American children were spending significant periods in mother-only households. The numbers of single parents raising children rose from 9 per cent in 1960 to 30 per cent in 1992. The causes of this development are, of course, complex. For the new Puritan, however, this was simply further evidence of moral decline and social breakdown. The roots of this crisis were traced to 1960s radicalism and permissiveness, when women's traditional role was undermined and sex was separated from reproduction by the pill. In some states, in the early 1960s, there were laws against the sale and use of contraception. Doctors could be punished for giving contraceptive advice even to married couples. In 1964, over three centuries after Hester's ordeal, the Supreme Court ruled that Massachusetts law still 'prescribed pregnancy and the birth of an unwanted child as punishment for fornication'.[65] The Supreme Court overturned the legislation in question, insisting that the state and the church must be disassociated, but the rise of the New Right has seen numerous attempts to drag single mothers back to the scaffold.

In the wake of urban insurrection in Los Angeles in 1992, Dan Quayle offered his verdict on the root causes of the problem. Omitting any reference to the punishment beating of Rodney King and the subsequent acquittal of four white police officers, the vice-president pinpointed the inner cities 'filled with children having children'.[66] Quayle accused single mothers of being unable to control their children (and implied that their poverty was a product of an inability to control their sexuality). The liberal media were also castigated for 'sending out the wrong signals' in popular sitcoms such as *Murphy Brown*, where a single woman was shown raising a child and enjoying a successful career. Quayle's 'analysis' converged with a spate of right-wing, fundamentalist harangues against single mothers and sex out of wedlock. During the Congressional elections a few years later, this hostility was given a focal point by Newt Gingrich, another aspiring Puritan patriarch. One of the central planks to Gingrich's 'Contract with America' was a proposal to cut welfare support to single mothers after specific periods and place all dependent children in orphanages. In a disturbing echo of Hester's interrogation on the scaffold, AFDC (Aid to Families with Dependent Children) was also to be made dependent upon the mother publicly identifying and being married to the father of the child. The Welfare Reform Bill subsequently passed by Congress was less draconian than Gingrich's propaganda exercise, but still essentially punitive in spirit and design. Single mothers, or 'welfare queens' as they were labelled by the media, had their entitlement to assistance restricted to two years at a time, and no more than five years in total. The soaring bill for corrections has been partly financed by a $9 billion cut, between 1992 and 1998, in the welfare budget, as part of an attempt to discipline the new Ms Prynnes. The conservative counter-revolution, with its zealous integration of religious morality and law, continues to persecute single mothers, especially those with complexions even darker than Hawthorne's dark lady. Puritan ghosts continue to haunt the American penal machine. The post-Vietnam era provides the most recent example of this haunting, but one of the most spectacular reversions to Puritan penality occurred in the Cold War preliminaries to imperialist aggression in South-East Asia. It is the Communist witch-hunts of this period which will now be interrogated.

3
Reading the Rosenbergs:
The Public Burning and
The Book of Daniel

> ... it's almost as though there is something critical about the elec-
> trocutions themselves, something down deep inside, a form.
>
> *The Public Burning*, Robert Coover[1]

In Robert Coover's *The Public Burning*, Ethel Rosenberg wears a scarlet letter. Vice-president Richard Nixon, as he becomes more deeply involved in their case, begins to fantasise about the Rosenbergs' past and imagines 'little Ethel ... wearing an "A" on her chest' (p.266). Ethel's badge of shame, also of a cardinal hue, signifies a secret crime far greater than Hester's adultery. 'A' is for the atom bomb, whose secret the Rosenbergs allegedly gave to the Soviet Union. In the extensive media coverage that their trial received, the Rosenbergs were accused of having committed nothing less than the 'Crime of the Century'. Congressional records from this period include statements blaming the Rosenbergs for the deaths of thousands of US soldiers in Korea. In his judgement, Judge Irving Kaufman stated that the accused were guilty of an act 'worse than murder'.[2] He charged the Rosenbergs with the loss of at least 50,000 lives in Korea, and added, 'who knows but that millions more of innocent people may pay the price [of] your treason'.[3] Not to be outdone by the legislature and judiciary, the executive branch of the US government consummated this hyperbole in his explanation for not granting clemency:

> The nature of the crime for which they have been found guilty
> and sentenced far exceeds that of the taking of the life of another
> citizen; it involves the deliberate betrayal of the entire nation and
> could very well result in the death of many, many thousands of
> innocent citizens ... By immeasurably increasing the chances of
> atomic war, the Rosenbergs may have condemned to death tens of
> millions of innocent people all over the world.[4]

As Eisenhower sent them to the chair, the Rosenbergs' supporters felt that they had been the victims rather than the perpetrators of the 'Crime of the Century'. Jean-Paul Sartre described their deaths as a 'legal lynching' and accused America of being 'afraid of the shadow of your own bomb. Magic, witch hunts, *autos-da-fe*, sacrifices; your country is sick with fear.'[5] Whichever definition of the 'Crime of the Century' is accepted, the execution of the Rosenbergs, in Sing Sing on June 19, 1953, is a critical moment in the history of punishment in the US.

One of the Rosenbergs' supporters, Arthur Miller, described their execution as a 'blood sacrifice' at the altar of Cold War politics. In *The Public Burning*, Miller is left alone watching *The Crucible* on a deserted Broadway whilst millions are massed in Times Square to witness the execution spectacular: 'Art, less deadly than we had hoped' (p.473). Both Miller and Coover recognised the Puritan cast to Cold War politics. Although the Rosenbergs were tried in accordance with the Espionage Act of 1917, the charge was not treason but *conspiracy* to commit treason: the thought was as sinful as the deed. This crime was compounded by their stubborn refusal, like Hester on the scaffold or the witches executed at Salem, to confess their guilt. From the opening paragraph of *The Public Burning*, Coover establishes the execution as a haunting return of the witch trials:

> thieves of light to be burned by light – in the electric chair, for it is written that 'any man who is dominated by demonic spirits to the extent that he gives voice to apostasy is to be subject to the judgement upon sorcerers and wizards'. (p.3)

The 'thieves of light' are deemed possessed by 'the Phantom'. Coover's personification of the Red Menace is both a contemporary comic book invention and a reincarnation of the Puritan Devil: devious, legion, masked. 'The Phantom's dark gospel has spread throughout the world, he has acquired dozens of new disguises and devices' (p.14). Traced through the stencil of comic book Cotton Mather, the execution is figured as a 'fierce public exorcism', an *auto da fé* to 'cleanse their souls of the Phantom's taint' and 'force him to materialise' (pp.3–4). As Uncle Sam explains to his votary, Richard Nixon, the true nature of the Rosenbergs' crime is siding with the '*Sons of Darkness*', a horde of heretics and fanatics working against the '*Sons of Light*' (p.88). The discursive strategies that sentence the Rosenbergs to death and transform the chair into an altar are historicised by Coover: Red-scare-mongering is linked to a classical Manichean vision through Puritan demonology. Eisenhower's speeches from this period confirm Uncle Sam's teachings in chiaroscuro imagery: '*Freedom is pitted against slavery; lightness against the dark* ... It is, friends, a spiritual struggle' (pp.150, 152). As Eisenhower becomes Uncle Sam's mouthpiece, an instrument of His Will, his enemies are bewitched by the Phantom of 'demon-possessed Communism' (p.12). *The Public Burning* thus ambitiously reworks Puritan notions of subjectivity, historical process and instrumentality; or rather, Coover underscores the extent to which such notions were resurrected in Cold War political rhetoric and popular culture.

Moments before the execution that will signal the resolve of the Sons of Light, there is a blackout in Times Square. What follows is

> widespread madness, dissipation, and fever, an inelegant display of general indiscretion and destruction, corruption, sacrilege and sodomy, twisted camera booms, base iniquity, smashed klieg lights and shredded trousseaus, tipped and scattered chairs and pews, incest, desecration, tangled bodies, rampant nihilism, bestiality, liberated freak shows, careless love and cheating hearts, drunkenness, cock-sucking, and other fearsomely unclean abominations, all of it liberally sprinkled with soot, snot, and pigeon shit – not exactly Cotton Mather's vision of Theopolis Americana! (p.495)

The power cut in fact produces a darkened mirror image of Mather's Edenic vision, the orgiastic dystopia that Puritan law was designed to contain. The Manichean dualism informing *The Scarlet Letter*, in which light (law) is opposed to darkness (desire), is sustained by Coover: the electricity that brings enlightenment also powers the chair in a ritual that symbolically purges the shadow from the land. Coover parodies pseudo-spiritual rhetoric by resurrecting the Puritan tradition of the execution sermon and conflating the rituals of state murder with baptism:

> 'Thou anointest my head with oil', says the rabbi gravely, as indeed one of the guards dips his finger into a jar and slaps a dab of conductive paste on the little bald patch, freshly shaved, at the back of the condemned man's head. (p.508)

As the electricity courses through Julius Rosenberg, the parodic register is sustained through images of mock exorcism: 'Greasy yellow-grey smoke plumes from the top of his head like a cast-out devil' (p.510). Paul Maltby has argued that the focus on religious and mythological meanings in most readings of *The Public Burning* has dehistoricised the text.[6] A mythological approach denies Coover's dissident deconstruction of the discourses through which the Rosenberg executions were legitimated. Religious and mythological homilies were utilised to translate state murder into spiritual necessity and superpower rivalry into a 'conflict between Good and Evil, Light and Darkness, Gods and Godlessness, Freedom and Slavery'.[7] What follows will be an attempt to underline Maltby's insistence on reading the Rosenbergs in relation to the history of Cold War politics and economics. In particular, their execution can be seen as a key link in a chain of post-war developments in consumerism, media, the permanent arms economy and panopticism.

PLAGUES, PANOPTICONS AND
THE PERMANENT ARMS ECONOMY

Rulers dreamt of the state of plague.

Discipline and Punish, Michel Foucault[8]

In *Discipline and Punish*, Foucault both comments on and contributes to the 'documentary accumulation', the 'network of writing', that has become increasingly integral to the penal process (p.189). In the Rosenberg case, the state death sentence itself generated an explosive proliferation of texts: the couple's 'Death House' letters, legal documents, historical essays, journalistic assessments and numerous artistic interventions. *The Public Burning* was written a few years after E. L Doctorow's *The Book of Daniel* (1971), another ambitiously dissident contribution to the network of writing surrounding the Rosenbergs. Whilst Coover offers a polyvocal approach to his subject, including the dissonant voices of Uncle Sam and Richard Nixon alongside the Rosenbergs, *The Book of Daniel* is focalised through a single figure, Daniel Isaacson, trying to piece together a history that includes the execution of his parents, Paul and Rochelle.

Doctorow's reading of the Rosenberg execution is roughly con-temporary with, and bears an interesting relation to, Foucault's history of the birth of the prison. *Discipline and Punish* opens with the stunning juxtaposition of the public torture and execution of Damiens the regicide in 1757 with Leon Faucher's rules for 'the House of young prisoners in Paris', published in 1838 (p.6). Doctorow's narrator employs a similar technique. Daniel is a postgraduate student working on a history of punishment. His account of the trial and execution of his parents is juxtaposed with a range of references to punishment practices, including burning at the stake, smoking over sulphur fires, hanging, drawing and quartering, and finally, inevitably, electrocution. Although historiographic technique here is comparable, Foucault's juxtapositions are intended to establish a rupture in the history of punishment, whilst Daniel's are designed to display profound continuity.

Despite this deviation there are many other points at which these texts converge. Both Doctorow and Foucault flamboyantly traverse the conventional opposition of creative and critical. *The Book of Daniel* includes lengthy passages of 'history'; *Discipline and Punish* deploys 'literary' devices. Part of the logic to this traversal can be traced to a mutual recognition of the aesthetics of punishment. According to Foucault punishment is 'an art of conflicting energies, an art of images linked by association, the forging of stable connections that defy time' (p.104). Haunted by images, connections and (especially electrical) energies, Doctorow's narrator reaches the same conclusion. Although his parents may have been killed by electricity, Daniel knows they were strapped in with stories. The Isaacsons read their own lives according to the Marxist narrative of history and were killed by the Cold War fable of international communist conspiracy. J. Edgar Hoover was an avid reader and sometimes writer of mystery stories. The Rosenbergs might be read as his masterpiece. In *The Public Burning*, Nixon sums up the case against the Rosenbergs as 'The Crime of the Century, by J. Edgar Hoover' (p.131). Richard Godden has analysed the development of a 'poetics of persecution' within the Cold War disciplinary apparatus headed by Hoover.[9] The communist witch-hunt, like its Puritan predecessor, relied heavily upon the allegorical imagination to enforce its binary brandings: American/Red, safe/dangerous, normal/abnormal. In *The Public Burning*, McCarthy's 'metaphors grip the national imagination utterly' (p.10). In *The Book of Daniel*, the eponymous narrator recognises that to save his parents and himself he must challenge the state's narrative with one of his own.

Alongside a mutual recognition of the conjunctions between punitive power and narrative, both Doctorow and Foucault also see punishment primarily as a 'political tactic', centred on the body and connected to 'other ways of exercising power' (p.23). Daniel's alternative history reads his parents' execution as an admonitory archetype in which the Isaacsons' bodies are central to the development of new disciplinary tactics within Cold War society. Similarly, Foucault's thesis hinges on the contention that the modern prison can be seen as a template for other institutions, a model for new power relations and forms of social control based on knowledge, surveillance and discipline: 'Is it surprising that prisons resemble factories, schools, barracks, hospitals, which all resemble prison?' (p.228). Foucault dates the completion of the carceral continuum by describing the regime at a home for young offenders at Mettray in 1840. Daniel parallels the Isaacsons' imprisonment with his own incarceration in a children's home. In *The Public Burning*, a movie-goer forgets to remove his 3-D specs on leaving the cinema, and is afflicted with a bizarre double vision of Times Square: 'the exercise yard of a federal prison, if his left eye is to be trusted, or else the New Jerusalem' (p.286). Foucault, Doctorow and Coover converge in their respective doubled visions of a carceral society.

In *Discipline and Punish* the genealogy of this society is traced to the plague. From the middle ages through to the seventeenth century, during a plague outbreak there was constant surveillance: watchmen, sentinels, observation posts. This increase in the presence of authority increased the threat of punishment for the breaking of plague rules, so that fear and paranoia were rife. Foucault suggests that 'rulers dreamt of the state of plague', that epidemics were pathogens for political phantasies of increased social control. Throughout the modern carceral society one can, he argues, 'read the haunting memory of "contagions"' (p.198). The model of surveillance and segregation provided by plague conditions is a palimpsest beneath the development of the prison and the prison society; the political and architectural form taken by this development is the panopticon.

Rulers in Cold War America also dreamt of the state of plague, and their dreams were themselves contagious. Political intolerance was often articulated through viral metaphors. Truman's Attorney General, J. Howard McGrath, claimed that 'Communists are everywhere – in factories, offices, butcher shops, in private businesses, and each carries in himself the germs of death for society'.[10] In *The Public Burning*, Hoover delivers 'firm advice' to parents about the vulnerability of American youth:

Whether you know it or not, your child is a target. His mind is the fertile plot in which the Communist hopes to implant his Red virus and to secure a deadly culture which will spread to others. When enough are infected the Red Pied Piper hopes to call the tune. (p.106)

Even vice-president Nixon is not immune to contamination by the 'Marxist Virus': 'It was as though something had got into me last night, like an alien gene, and I'd lacked the strength to fend it off' (p.174). In Cold War demonology, communism is traced through the metaphoric stencil of the plague. Accordingly, merely being in the company of a radical constitutes a threat to personal and civic health. The allegorical fertility of Cold War aesthetics defined a fellow traveller as complicit in the murder of thousands of American soldiers in Korea. Mass lockdown became legitimate quarantine to contain the deadly contagion of political dissidence. The myth of the Red Death, like any plague, generated mass hysteria that exceeded mere facts. Despite the statistic that membership of the Communist Party peaked at around 40,000, the fear was that 'They' were everywhere.

Paranoia was exacerbated by a development in the figure of the plague carrier. Whilst pre-war communists displayed clear signs of their disease – they were working-class, immigrant and visibly alien – their post-war variants were often indistinguishable from a healthy American citizen. The aliens of Cold War science-fiction cinema offered allegories of state allegory. Don Siegel's *Invasion of the Body Snatchers* (1956) held up a cracked mirror to the McCarthyite fantasy of reverse colonisation, of imperial America being taken over from within by a covert army. Conquest by aliens and atomic mutants appeared on screens across America during the trial and execution of the Rosenbergs, in, for example, *Invasion USA* (1952), *Them!* (1953) and *The War of the Worlds* (1953). In *The Public Burning*, Coover mimics these elisions between popular culture and the manufacture of political paranoia. The shapes of the Phantom are sketched in comic book hyperbole by Hoover and McCarthy:

the Rosenbergs, grown monstrous, octopuslike as Irving Saypol depicted them, breaking out of their cells, smashing down the walls of Sing Sing with their tentacles, and descending upon the city like the Beast from 20,000 Fathoms. They knock over buildings, crush automobiles under their bodies, swallow policemen whole, get tangled in a Coney Island roller coaster. Bullets do not stop them. (p.107)

The reverse colonisation fantasy is completed by a gallery of villains who join forces with the Rosenberg monster: 'Super Mau Mau', Fu Manchu (played by Chairman Mau) and an army of zombies, 'blinded, their flesh eaten away, from Hiroshima and Nagasaki' (p.107).

Alongside science-fiction cinema and comic books, paranoia fed and was fed by a proliferation in espionage narratives. *Casino Royale*, the first Bond novel, was published and quickly sold out in the same year that the Rosenbergs were executed. Their trial revolved around 'a lot of pretty fair spy stories ... secret codenames, recognition signals, covert drop sites, escape plans, cover stories, payoffs, cat-and-mouse games with FBI surveillance teams, border intrigues' (p.117). The ideological mission of the spy as a Cold War icon, as Bruce Robbins has argued, was to convert the 'fund of international wartime knowledge' that created the bomb into 'national secrets'.[11] The big secret was that there was no secret. The figure of the spy, however, corroborated the myth that the atom bomb was based on a confidential formula that could be stolen and given away.

The 'Soviet spy network', the 'imminent invasion' and the 'secret' were Cold War chimeras which served the interests of an emergent surveillance state. The assiduous manufacture of paranoia justified massive increases in state and police power. The idea that there was 'a Red under every bed' legitimated increases in funding to place 'an FBI agent behind every mailbox'.

> After all, the FBI *had* to win this one – their whole reputation depended on it, as well as their budget and a lot of jobs. Including Hoover's ... Each division had to justify its budget and salaries, come up with the goods when pressed. (pp.133, 135)

Alongside the FBI, cash injections were guaranteed for all those (anti-) bodies that promised to cure the contagion of communism: CIA, HUAC, NSA, the Attorney General's Office, the Department of Justice, the Subversive Activities Control Board. The extension of surveillance both was justified by and helped to legitimate paranoia as cultural pathology. Doctorow's Daniel knows that there are files on him, and he remembers when they came for his parents, there [was] a slight oddness in the way they reacted to the knock on the door – as if they knew what was coming. But they did know what was coming. And so did everyone else who lived with some awareness into that time.[12]

The Book of Daniel connects the dilation of the panoptic gaze to the installation of a permanent arms economy. Searching for answers to the questions surrounding his parents' execution, Daniel travels to California and is confronted by an escalation in the technology of death:

> On the Freeway we pass a convoy of army trucks. Helicopters cross the highway overhead. Gnatty jets loop in the sun high over the ocean. Electronic plants nestle in their landscaping. A highly visible military-industrial complex ... It was the country of strontium children. (p.269)

In the wake of the Second World War, ruling interests in the military-industrial complex were unwilling to downsize to pre-war levels. War had been good for business, so a new war, a new enemy had to be found. That enemy, the Soviet Union, justified not only huge increases in expenditure on surveillance, but also sustained levels of expenditure on the machinery of war. Ironically, Eisenhower's injunction to preparedness appropriated penal imagery from *The Communist Manifesto*: 'It is up to every American ... they must, at any cost, remain armed, strong, and ready fir [*sic*] the risk of war! ... in the final choice, a soldier's pack is not so heavy a burden as a prisoner's chains' (p.154).

The Warfare State is verso to the recto of the Rosenberg trial. The panopticon and the permanent arms economy are structurally integrated and the Rosenbergs can be read at their interface. Joyce Nelson proposes that the 'anti-communist hysteria sweeping the continent in the late 1940s was a corollary of the sanitised publicity campaign simultaneously being conducted around the burgeoning nuclear industry'.[13] Whilst the public gaze was captured by the atom spies, the dangers of nuclear power were conveniently obscured. Simultaneously, the preoccupation with the secret the Rosenbergs had allegedly stolen deflected from the secret activities of the Army, the Public Health Service, the Atomic Commission and other organisations, activities that included radiation testing on prisoners, mental patients and orphans. Focusing attention on the figure of the traitorous spy also helped to cover up complicity between American business and Nazi Germany before and during the war. As Robert Proctor notes: 'Ignorance, like knowledge, is a manufactured product.'[14]

THEME PARKS, CONCENTRATION CAMPS AND CARNIVALS OF CRUELTY

To repeat the question: to what extent can suffering compensate for 'debt'? To the extent that *inflicting* pain occasions the greatest pleasure, to the extent that the injured party exchanges for the damage done, together with the displeasure it causes, an extraordinary pleasure which offsets it: the opportunity to *inflict* suffering – an actual *festivity* ... No festivity without cruelty: such is the lesson of the earliest, longest period in the history of mankind – and even in punishment there is so much that is *festive*!

The Genealogy of Morals, Friedrich Nietzsche[15]

... so many sparks of the carnival bonfire which renews the world.

The World Turned Upside Down, Mikhail Bakhtin[16]

Discipline and Punish suggests that, between the eighteenth and nineteenth centuries, punishment went inside from the public to the private sphere. In the process of this relocation the function of punishment as spectacle was minimised, 'it survived only as a new legal or administrative practice' (p.8). The elaborate theatricality of the Rosenberg show-trial would seem to confirm Foucault. The mass media has played an increasingly central role in reinventing the spectacle of punishment. The coverage of the Rosenberg trial and the McCarthy hearings might even be read as a pilot for a deluge of legal dramas which have followed and shifted the locus of theatrics into the courtroom. In *The Book of Daniel*, a 1960s radical proposes that, had the New Left been present at the Isaacson trial, they would have turned it into theatre and countered the state's spectacle of power with a counter-insurgent carnival of images. Artie Sternlicht's critique, however, ignores the extent to which not only the trial, but also the execution were already the product of elaborate stagecraft: 'Frying, in five (covert) acts' (p.146). In *The Public Burning*, Nixon similarly speculates on the dramaturgy of the Rosenberg trial: the scripts (from legal documents to love letters), the actors (from the accused to the president), the sets (from Los Alamos to the Sing Sing Death House), the props (from a torn box of Jell-O to the electric chair), the many directors involved in this production (Hoover, Kaufman, McCarthy, Eisenhower) and even a full-scale dress rehearsal (the Brothman–Moskowitz trial).

> Maybe it was nothing more than an exemplary entertainment of sorts ... everybody in this case from the Judge on down ... myself included – [were] behaving like actors caught up in a play ... Even the Rosenbergs seemed to be swept up in this sense of an embracing and compelling drama, speaking in their letters of sinister 'plots' and worldwide 'themes' and 'setting the stage' and playing the parts they had been – rightly or wrongly – cast for 'with honour and with dignity' ... and this thought hit me now like a revelation – *it was like a little morality play for our generation!* ... in order that my generation might witness in dramatic form the fundamental controversy of our time! (pp.117–20)

Whilst the live audience for the execution itself was relatively modest, millions followed the coverage on television, radio and in the newspapers, thus problematising Foucault's suggestion that punishment itself has become the 'most hidden part of the penal process' (p.9). Immediately after the execution the public was treated to grisly details, including the high drama when Ethel, in a 'cheap prison dress', failed to follow the state script: it took three 'doses' to complete the death scene. One of the characteristics of the *ancien régime* is the public exposure of the body of the condemned following the execution. After their botched electrocution, a photograph of the corpses of Julius and Ethel Rosenberg, side by side in open caskets, appeared in several newspapers and *Time* magazine. Sylvia Plath chose to open her semi-autobiographical account of growing up in the Cold War with the Rosenbergs and the obscene visibility of their punishment:

> That's all there was to read about in the papers – goggle-eyed headlines staring up at me on every street corner and at the fusty, peanut-smelling mouth of every subway ... I kept hearing about the Rosenbergs over the radio and at the office.[17]

The Bell Jar casts the Rosenbergs as the stars in a theatre of cruelty and in her journals Plath ironically bemoaned that the dramatic climax itself 'could not be televised ... so much more realistic and beneficial than the run-of-the-mill crime program. Two real people being executed.'[18]

Extrapolating from the media coverage of the Rosenberg case, Coover chooses to stage his account of the execution in Times Square as a big budget spectacular: 'What is it? It appears to be a stage with an electric chair. Or else a movie lobby with sawdust on the floor' (p.286). Coover caricatures the theatricality of the execution with a full-scale replica of the Sing Sing death house built in Times Square, complete with '[s]pecial seating sections ... camera platforms ... VIP passageways, wedding altars, sideshows, special light and sound systems' (p.5). In a metafictional moment, the chair of the Entertainment Committee, Cecil B. De Mille, explains to warden Denno why artifice is necessary to produce the illusion of the real at such events:

> 'See, life and the real stuff of life aren't always the same thing, Warden – like one don't always give you the other, you follow? So sometimes, to get your story across, you gotta work a different angle or two, use a few tricks, zap it up with a bit of spectacle – I mean, what's spectacle? It's a kind of *vision*, am I right?' (p.281)

One of the 'tricks' De Mille devises involves the recreation of the set design of *The Valiant* on the Times Square stage. This simulation within a simulation is designed to surprise Ethel with 'a little jolt of deja vu' since, in one of the multiple ironies Coover is so finely attuned to, she had starred in a death row drama as an aspiring 16-year-old actress.

Although Ethel and Julius may have been centre-stage during this punitive performance, they were not its focal point. The Rosenberg case may undermine Foucault's sense of the disappearance of theatricality from the punitive act itself, but it reinforces his insight that punishment is not only, and sometimes not even, about preventing crime. *Discipline and Punish* proposes that 'the guilty person is only one of the targets of punishment. For punishment is directed above all at others, at all the potentially guilty' (p.108). In the case of the Rosenbergs, although the specified crime was conspiracy to commit treason, the a priori offence was political radicalism. The investigation, trial and execution targeted those who might be similarly guilty of radical sympathies. Consequently, from the state's perspective, the Rosenbergs' bodies were less significant as the subject of pain than as 'the object of a representation'; their bodies were punished in an effort to 'correct, reclaim, "cure" radical strains within the national body' (p.94, p.10). In the *ancien régime*, the execution aimed to foreground the power of the state, 'by manifesting it at its most spectacular ... to make everyone aware, through the body of the criminal, of the unrestrained presence of the sovereign' (pp.48–9). The Rosenberg execution similarly displayed state power to the public as both consolation (against the fear of communism) and caution (against those who did not fear communism).

The political education implicit in the state slaughter of the Rosenbergs included instruction on ethnicity, family and gender identity. A CIA memo published in the early 1990s revealed for the first time that the Rosenbergs were offered a deal only a few months prior to the execution. Their sentence would have been commuted to life imprisonment if they were willing to 'appeal to Jews in all countries to get out of the communist movement and seek to destroy it'.[19] The Rosenberg's ethnic identity was intended to be utilised as a resource against communism, and although the state failed here it was successful in other respects. Jews were already associated with conspiracy in WASP demonology, and this was grafted onto anxieties about communism. In *The Public Burning*, the 'groun'-hog hunt' for atom bomb spies provides an alibi for the infiltration and intimidation of ethnic communities. FBI agents disguise themselves as tourists and

> slip catlike through the ghettos of the nation's cities, in deep where the unassimilated live, speaking alien tongues, eating weird shit... 90 percent of all Commies in this country, as every G-man knows, are foreign-born or were dropped by foreign-born parents. (p.17)

Perversely, as Jews who did not practise Judaism, the Rosenbergs' punishment could also be directed at apostasy, reinforcing the sense that the permanent war was also a *jihad*: 'Atheism, as J. Edgar Hoover of the FBI has so often reminded us, is the first step toward Communism' (p.104).

Attacks on the Rosenbergs' beliefs served to discredit their politics, their ethnicity and their 'dysfunctional' family life. The judge, attourneys, the media and even Eisenhower accused them of loving the Party more than their own children. This was part of a more general assault upon Ethel Rosenberg that enforced ruling notions of appropriate female behaviour. Ethel was castigated for her lack of maternal feeling, and her general demeanour was repeatedly referred to as 'unfeminine'. Her strength was used against her; a persistent failure to break down in public became *de facto* evidence of her deviant nature. Although she was initially arrested with the intention of forcing her husband to confess, towards the end of the trial many believed that she was the 'mastermind', the older woman (by three years) who dominated a 'feminised' 'Julie' (Ethel's nickname for Julius). This persecution on the grounds of inappropriate gender behaviour was led by public queer-bashers including Cohn, Hoover and McCarthy who were, or were rumoured to be, closet homosexuals.

The Rosenbergs were found guilty on several counts: their crime, their politics (one was seen to entail the other), their ethnicity, their family life and gender identity. Punishment thus served the function of underlining hegemonic norms; it became, in Foucault's terms, a means of 'defining an individual' (p.18). *Discipline and Punish* diagnoses this imperative as the driving force beneath modern punishment practices: 'The power of the Norm appears through the disciplines ... so that they might all be like one another' (pp.182, 184). Coover's Nixon similarly recognises that the Rosenbergs were being punished for failure to respect the Norm:

> In a very real sense, Julius Rosenberg was going to the electric chair because he went to City College of New York and joined the American Students Union when he was sixteen. If he'd come to Whittier instead and joined my Square Shooters, worn slouch sweaters and open collars with the rest of us, it wouldn't be happening. Simple as that. (pp.185–6)

As the electricity surges through Julius' body 'the picture is one of a general release from tension with each successive charge, a return, in the words of Warren Harding, to normalcy' (p.510). This process is accented subsequently by Uncle Sam in his Durkheimian alibi for the public burning: 'It ain't easy holdin' a community together, order ain't what comes natural, you know that, boy, and a lotta people gotta get killt tryin' to pretend it is' (p.531). Coover recognises that the state is less concerned with the criminal act than its agent, and will use definitions of the criminal to standardise and stabilise behaviour elsewhere. The Rosenbergs resisted this process by refusing to apologise for their politics or their personalities. Thus, as well as being accused of being 'Commies', bad parents and of potentially suspect sexuality, butch Ethel and 'mousy' Julie were to be found guilty of not finding themselves guilty. They resisted the strategy, in modern punishment practice, described by Foucault, of encouraging the criminal to become a 'voluntary partner in the procedure ... It is not enough that wrong-doers be justly punished. They must if possible judge and condemn themselves' (p.38).

Although *The Public Burning* shares the recognition in *Discipline and Punish* that modern punishment serves a variety of functions, Coover departs from Foucault's periodisation. The Cold War saw a classical 'country of tortures' erupting in the heart of the modern carceral city. Coover depicts the public burning as both a modern media spectacle and a medieval carnival. Bakhtin divided the carnivalesque into three categories – comic verbal compositions, billingsgate, and ritual spectacles – and each of these is evident in Coover's work. Carnivalesque verbal compositions offered comic subversions of official ideology, ritual, religion and language. These texts, both written and oral, would often mock Latin learnedness and revel in bawdy licentiousness. *The Public Burning* combines parodic pedantry and vernacular vulgarity alongside its assaults on the sacred and secular rituals of the dominant culture. Bakhtin described the tone and rhetorical devices of these compositions in terms which are also applicable to Coover. The 'atmosphere of the fair' is apparent throughout the Times Square execution spectacular, with endless speeches indulging in the 'comparative and the superlative'.[20] Uncle Sam, in particular, 'speechifies' in the

> tone and style of the fair ... [with] the cry of the quack and druggist ... the enormous accumulation of superlatives, typical of marketplace advertising ... After words of praise [Uncle Sam] turns to curses ... These pejoratives were especially applied to persons accused of heresy, doomed to the stake. (pp.214–15)

Uncle Sam is as excessive in his billingsgate against the Rosenbergs and their master the Phantom as he is in his panegyric to the American people.

The other major manifestation of the carnivalesque tradition in *The Public Burning* centres upon the ritual spectacle of the execution itself, a three-day pageant in the marketplace involving numerous comic side-shows. The burning of the Rosenbergs, in Bakhtinian terms, might be understood as an official feast, a ritual that sanctioned the existing pattern of things and reinforced it ... it asserted that all was stable ... the existing religious, political, and moral values, norms, and prohibitions. It was the triumph of the already established, the predominant truth that was put forward as eternal and indisputable. This is why the tone of the official feast was monolithically serious and why the element of laughter was alien to it. (p.199)

The official feast involved elaborate displays of hierarchical precedence: 'everyone was expected to appear in the full regalia of his calling, rank, and merits and to take the place corresponding to his position' (p.196). At the public burning, dress codes and hierarchies are strictly observed (in the order of the speeches and seating arrangements). The carnival often included the miming and mocking of 'civil and social ceremonies and rituals', the presence of 'open-air amusements ... giants, dwarfs, monsters, and trained animals' and the staging of 'mock beatings' (p.209). The Times Square spectacular involves a sustained lampooning of the ritual of execution in which Walt Disney provides the amusements, giants and monsters are in attendance (Uncle Sam and the Phantom), along with trained animals (a donkey and the elephant who copulate and defecate copiously) and mock beatings are performed on stage as part of the pre-execution festivities.

Bakhtin submitted that 'one of the indispensable accessories of carnival was the set called "hell". This "hell" was solemnly burned at the peak of the festivities' (p.197). In *The Public Burning*, the death house set is the scene of a climactic conflagration, the ritual burning, in the form of the Rosenbergs, of the hell presided over by the Phantom. Coover's carnival, as well as mocking official ceremonials, also frequently 'parod[ies] the Church's cult' (p.200). This mimicry has particular significance, given that *The Public Burning* appeared on the dawn of a fundamentalist revival amongst the new Puritans. In place of ecclesiastical authority, Coover sends in the clowns who were indispensable to carnival spectacle. Bakhtin's description of carnival logic as 'a continual shifting from top to bottom, from front to rear, of numerous parodies and travesties, humiliations' is realised by Nixon's slapstick antics on the Times Square stage (p.200). The vice-president is literally caught with his pants down, backing onto the stage with 'I AM A SCAMP' written on his buttocks in lipstick. Nixon's attempt to save face by getting everyone to disrobe threatens to upstage official ceremony with a spontaneous 'feast of the ass'.

According to Bakhtin, the carnivalesque is characterised by a grotesque realism that revels in the unruly materialism of the body. Coover's preoccupation with bodily protuberances, digestion, waste, beatings and various debasements reaches a sublimely grotesque conclusion as Nixon takes to the stage:

> pants in a tangle around my ankles, my poor butt on fire from its Dance Hall skid, my shoulder aching, face stinging, stomach rumbling, sweating hands clutching my still-enflamed though fastly shrivelling pecker … and a pervasive odour of excrement in the air which I was afraid was my own. (p.470)

As the vice-president attempts to restore some dignity by leading the crowd in prayer he trips over, 'crack[s] a stupendous fart' and mistakes the lipstick on his arse for rectal haemorrhaging (p.473). 'The essential principle of grotesque realism is degradation, that is, the lowering of all that is high, spiritual, ideal, abstract' (p.205). From the ceaseless humiliations of the vice-president to images of the Supreme Court justices unable to extricate themselves from a mound of elephant faeces, grotesque realism in *The Public Burning* is designed to ridicule the punitive authority that ordered the Rosenbergs' execution. The state attempted to represent the execution in relation to an ideal – a necessary step in the war of light against dark – but, in carnival mode, Coover 'turn[s] their subject into flesh' (p.199).

In the carnival tradition the grotesque body is debased, beaten and killed, but only to be reborn. Coover both invokes and undermines this dynamic when, in the scene following the burning of the Rosenbergs, Nixon is sodomised by Uncle Sam. This burlesque climax realises the vice-president's ambition to be entered by the 'Incarnation', albeit in a manner more literal than he may have anticipated. But it also suggests a certain distance between Coover and the utopian yearning of the carnival imagination. The ambivalence of carnival laughter, the dialectic between debasement and celebration, death and birth, is largely absent from *The Public Burning*. The marketplace is not a sanctuary from official culture, but its heartland, and the people who throng here receive as much hostility as their rulers. For Bakhtin the pagan festivities that lie at the roots of medieval carnival were 'linked to moments of crisis, of breaking points in the cycle of nature or in the life of society and man. Moments of death and revival, of change and renewal always led to a festive perception of the world' (p.199). *The Public Burning* recognises the execution as a key 'moment of crisis' in Cold War history, but this is a breaking point without renewal: the dead are not reborn. Finally, Coover's ridicule is not redemptive and carnivalesque affirmation is eclipsed by apocalypse.

FROM THE CHAIR TO THE BOMB (AND BACK)

'Jack Rockefeller – hullo, Junior! Give the folks a wave there – can you put a spot on him? We wouldn't be here without him! Jack Rockefeller, everybody!'

The Public Burning, Robert Coover (p.420)

Coover's partial invocation of the carnivalesque tradition reflects the resurgence of residual punishment practices in Cold War America. In the colonial regime being accused was one of the proofs that justified judicial torture. The assumption was that one could not be the object of suspicion and be entirely innocent. This legal (il)logic resurfaced in the communist witch-hunts, where investigation became a mode of punishment involving harassment, discrimination and ostracism. There was, as in Foucault's analysis of the feudal code, a conflation of 'the ritual that produced the truth' and the 'ritual that imposed the punishment' (p.42). Cold War persecution saw a revival in the Wonderland logic of verdict first, trial later. In *The Book of Daniel* there are references to Lewis Carroll during the narrator's excursion to Disneyland. This theme park is described ominously by Doctorow as 'a town somewhere between Buchenwald and Belsen' (p.291). Andrew Ross has suggested that the dawn of the Cold War witnessed a contest taking place 'over the soul and shape of modernity itself – what was it going to look like? Auschwitz? ... Disneyland?'[21] In a similar vein, Alice Jardine asks 'how did [the US] get from Hiroshima and Nagasaki to Disneyland in ten years?'[22] Daniel offers answers to these questions, answers that challenge the polarities assumed by Ross and Jardine. The Disneyland aesthetic, with its profitable synthesis of social control, spectacle and surveillance, can be read as a species of Cold War panopticism. Daniel notes that the crowd-handling skills at the theme park would light up the eyes of an SS officer. Rather than opposing spaces devoted to pleasure and punishment, *The Book of Daniel* encourages recognition of both as key locations in the development of discipline.

Daniel's reading of Disneyland is founded on an unmasking of the commodity logic connecting theme parks, the panopticon and the permanent arms economy. Disneyland was being designed at the time of the Rosenbergs' execution and, as Richard Godden has argued, one should not underestimate the extent to which 1950s affluence, symbolised by this theme park, was built on 'the federal funding of the technology of destruction (the permanent arms economy)'.[23] Daniel's critique synthesises the old left preoccupation with capital and class power and the New Left's interest in media and image. Disneyland is recognised both as a symbol of capitalism and the capital of symbolism. In a dialectical pattern, Disneyland is figured as a prison house of signs, a space of social control, but Daniel also appreciates the Disneyfication of punishment in the spectacle surrounding his parents' trial and execution.

Coover makes similar connections in *The Public Burning*. Walt Disney is prominent among those on the Entertainment Committee organising the Times Square spectacular, and is responsible for side-show events.

> [H]e and his Disney Imagineers have reserved a number of key corner locations for their own Mouse Factory specials ... He has also built a scale model of Sing Sing prison, using all the little braying schoolboy truants from *Pinocchio* for the prisoners, and an imaginative simulation, using life-sized models with moving eyeballs, of Harry Gold's complicated fantasy life. (pp.281–2)

The Disney Rat Pack provide security at the main event and are led by Mickey Mouse, whose career is exactly contemporaneous with that of Herbert Hoover. Over and above this cute coincidence, Coover intimates couplings between Disney and American fascism that recall Doctorow locating death camps on the west coast. Uncle Sam associates the Rosenbergs with the American desire for '*elbow-room* – the continent – the *whole* continent – and nothin' *but* the continent!' (p.8). Imperialist expansion in Korea, 'brought about' by the Rosenbergs and hugely profitable to the burgeoning permanent arms economy, was justified politically with coded reference to manifest destiny, but the italicised '*elbow-room*' also clearly echoes *Lebensraum* and National Socialist polemic. The second aural echo here, of legal procedure ('the truth, the whole truth and nothing but the truth'), parallels capitalist aggression overseas with coercion at home. The Rosenbergs were connected to the war in Korea, though not in the sense proposed by Judge Kaufman.

In the Disneyland section of *The Book of Daniel*, the narrator makes another startling connection, by juxtaposing the chair that killed his parents with a theme park ride:

> What Disneyland proposes is a technique of abbreviated shorthand culture for the masses, a mindless thrill, like an electric shock, that insists at the same time on the recipient's rich psychic relation to his country's history and language and literature ... This technique may be extremely useful both as a substitute for education and, eventually, as a substitute for experience. (p.295)

Daniel recognises the real achievement of Disneyland as the manipulation of history and the control of crowds for economic gains, a combination precisely analogous to the state stage-crafting of his parents' trial and execution. Daniel's reading also anticipates Baudrillard's description of Disneyland as a site that signifies the end of the real and which exists to disguise the fact that the rest of America *is* Disneyland. The electricity that runs the theme park and murders the Isaacsons flows through the circuitry of capital. Godden suggests that Daniel's critique hinges on the revelation

> that Corporate Capital tortures the consumer's body, in order to ensure a money flow. For Daniel, more generally, electricity is everywhere, and everywhere a double synonym, standing for that which killed his parents, and that which fuels his culture's growth economy – hence his gnomic gloss, 'The electric chair as methodology of capitalist economics.'[24]

This gloss provides the link between capital and punishment but, surprisingly, Doctorow fails to explore the evolution of the chair, a history that testifies to the accuracy of Daniel's aphorism.

The chair was born in a business feud between two utility companies: the Edison Corporation and Westinghouse Electrical and Manufacturing Company. Thomas Edison was obsessively committed to direct current. His main competitor, George Westinghouse, was equally committed to the alternating variety. In 1887, 'the Battle of the Currents' began with Westinghouse challenging Edison's virtual monopoly in New York City. Edison's response to this competition was to launch a vigorous campaign of negative publicity against his rival's product, trying to persuade the public that AC was far too dangerous for domestic use. Edison's publicity team tried to introduce the term 'Westinghoused', meaning 'to kill by electricity', into American vernacular. In 1887 Edison went on the road, inviting journalists and members of the public to exhibitions at which cats and dogs, calves and horses were electrocuted using AC. Coover offers an implicit homage to these infamous exhibitions during the pre-execution warm-up, when the executioners 'test out the chair by burning six or seven chimpanzees in it' (p.172). When the Electrical Death Act, permitting capital punishment by electrocution, was passed in June 1888, Edison's publicity offensive switched tactics with an audacious attempt to get all prisons in New York state to use AC dynamos to power the electric chair. The ironies here were multiple. The electric chair was, after all, an Edison invention and Westinghouse was a staunch opponent of the death penalty. Unperturbed by such ethical niceties, Edison arranged to buy a Westinghouse dynamo through a dealer in South America and had it shipped to New York. Here it was used, on August 6, 1890, to electrocute William Kemmler, the first victim of the modern and 'civilised' form of execution. It was, however, anything but the efficient operation its proponents had hoped for. Kemmler, like Ethel Rosenberg 60 years later, had to be electrocuted several times. Subsequently, his body was so badly burnt it could not be identified by the next of kin.

In his critique of Disneyland, Daniel notes the prominence, in a list of corporate sponsors, of General Electric, whose product runs all of the rides. In the late 1880s Edison merged his company into General Electric partly to increase his chances of squeezing Westinghouse out of the market. Both General Electric and the Westinghouse Corporation were involved in the nuclear industry at its inception, and were part of the decision-making process, in 1941, to undertake the building of the atomic bomb. Representatives from both corporations were included on a committee of scientists who submitted the report to the US Uranium Committee that was behind the initiation of the Manhattan Project. These developments were of course hugely profitable for both corporations. 'G.E. entered World War II doing $340 million of business a year and emerged doing $1.3 billion.'[25] A circuit of connections, powered by the dynamo of capital, emerges here between the history of the electric chair and the permanent arms economy. The same utility companies that pioneered the technology that killed the Rosenbergs were also heavily involved in the development of the technology that the Rosenbergs were executed for conspiring to steal. One of the most powerful lobbies against clemency for the Rosenbergs was the Holy Six, lead by 'Electric Charlie' Wilson, ex-president of GE. The alleged theft of the A-bomb resulted in lucrative contracts for refinements in the technology of death. As Coover succinctly puts it: 'TRUMAN ORDERS HELL BOMB BUILT ... Du Pont gets the H-bomb contract, cash on the line' (p.17). Although it may not have fulfilled the Bakhtinian definition of carnival ambivalence, something was being born whilst the Rosenbergs were burned: a permanent arms economy that was structurally integrated with consumer culture. In the year the Rosenbergs were arrested, Diner's Club issued the first credit cards.

Throughout *Discipline and Punish*, Foucault's tropes for describing punitive power, such as 'network' and 'resistance', have an electrical resonance. Coover's Nixon uses the same register: 'Power, I knew, was something that existed in the universe like electricity' (p.175). Despite Nixon's naturalisation, *The Public Burning* tends to follow *The Book of Daniel*, whose narrator sees electricity less as a natural force than a synonym for capital and punishment. Times Square is chosen as the site of the burning because it is the 'Electrical Street of Dreams': 'The United States is the first electric nation of the world, and this is its luminous navel' (p.164). The shining jewel in this navel is the death house mock-up. The stage is

> spotlit; the VIP area, empty still, is bright as a ballpark; newsmen's flashguns pop like Fourth of July fireworks; multicolored electric arrows dart relentlessly at floodlit theatres and hotels; and vast neon spectaculars hawk everything from Planters Peanuts to patriotism, campaign quips to Kleenex: all direct and glaring evidence of the sheer *power* of Uncle Sam and his Legions of Light ... The Paramount Building has spread an all-electric United States flag across its broad facade ... while over the Elpine Drinks counter on Forty-sixth Street, a gigantic flashlight, powered with Evereadies – 'the battery with Nine Lives' – shines on a Kodak ad that says: 'You press the button, we do the rest!' (p.398)

The electricity that powers capital punishment also runs the post-industrial revolution; the technology of reproduction (the camera and the advertising image) is integrated with the technology of death (the chair and the bomb). 'You press the button, we do the rest!' Robert Lowell's war poem, 'For the Union Dead', recalls an advertising image used by the Mosler safe company that showed its product unscathed in the post-apocalyptic wasteland of Hiroshima. In Coover's Cold War carnival, consumer capitalism and war are similarly fused, as peddlers in Times Square hawk 'Cherry-Oonilla ice cream and miniature A-bombs that produce edible mushroom clouds' (p.287).

In chapter ten of *The Public Burning*, 'Pilgrimage to the *New York Times*', Coover explains how urgent links are erased by the media:

> There are sequences but no causes, contiguities but no connections ... The execution of an unemployed housepainter in Berlin takes shape beside the report that a new collection of wallcoverings and shower curtains offers a variety of choices to housemakers who wish to decorate the bathroom: BATH WALLPAPERS / ARE EASY TO CLEAN. (p.190)

Coover's method involves the juxtaposition of images to encourage precisely those connections suppressed elsewhere in Cold War culture. One of the most illuminating sequences offered in this respect begins with Walt Disney

> studying the Death House set and dreaming up further novelties ... New York state troopers deploy themselves in a concentric series of barricades and roadblocks to defend the Square against protest matches ... Newsreel cameramen move cameras and klieg lights into position and TV generator trucks are brought in ... the crowds are already pushing north into the Park, east and west towards the rivers, south to Macy's which is jammed to the walls this afternoon with shoppers seeking those novel 'Dr. T Caps' with five rubbery fingers sticking up on top, inspired by the new Dr. Seuss movie premiering this afternoon at the Criterion. (p.282)

A sequence that includes capital punishment, death house sets, entertainment and shopping may appear implausible, but in a retrospective on the Rosenbergs, Karl Klare recalls an outing to the new Cross County Shopping Centre in Westchester, taken by his family shortly after the execution:

> The FBI used to sponsor a mobile exhibit on its achievements built into a custom-modelled trailer truck complete with an authentic replica of a death chamber containing an electric chair. The exhibit was rolled out to shopping malls – perfect family entertainment for Sunday afternoons.[26]

4
Punishment, Resistance and the African-American Experience

This time, although he couldn't cipher but one word, he believed he knew who spoke them. The people of the broken necks, of fire-cooked blood and black girls who had lost their ribbons. What a roaring.

Beloved, Toni Morrison[1]

The incorporation of capital and punishment, of course, significantly predates the Cold War era. Nowhere is this more disturbingly illustrated than in African-American history. When did 'America' first signify punishment in black consciousness? A black youth, press-ganged in the Canaries, was part of Columbus' crew during the expedition that launched the European colonisation of the Americas. For the impressed sailor the *Santa María* would have been a floating prison on which he would have been routinely subjected to flogging and assorted naval tortures. Subsequently, of course, black people arrived in the New World not as crew but cargo. Capturing the essentially punitive nature of their experience and that of those who followed, John Edgar Wideman, author of *The Lynchers*, described himself as 'a descendant of a special class of immigrants – Africans – for whom arrival in America was a life sentence in the prison of slavery'.[2]

This sentence began in Jamestown, 1619, when a Dutch man-of-war sold around 20 slaves to the colony. Over three centuries later, writing from Soledad prison, George Jackson pin-pointed the precise moment when he first felt the punitive presence of the white man. In 1941, 'early on a rainy Wednesday morning, late September', a white doctor was in attendance at Jackson's birth:

The first motion that my eyes focused on was this pink hand swinging in a wide arc in the general direction of my black ass. I stopped that hand, the left downward block, and countered the right needle finger to the eye. I was born with my defence mechanisms well developed.[3]

Soledad Brother exemplifies the effort in African-American prison writing, during its renaissance in the 1960s and early '70s, to draw critical analogies between individual and collective experience, between specific punitive acts and a long history of white oppression. For Jackson this was never simply an intellectual exercise; it was a race memory encoded in a body confined to a cell for 23½ hours each day:

> My recall is nearly perfect, time has faded nothing. I recall the very first kidnap. I've lived through the passage, died on the passage, lain in the unmarked, shallow graves of the millions who fertilised the Amerikan soil with their corpses; cotton and corn growing out of my chest, 'unto the third and fourth generation', the tenth, the hundredth ... They've been 'killing all the niggers' for nearly half a millennium now, but I am still alive. I might be the most resilient dead man in the universe.[4]

As Elaine Scarry contends, '[w]hat is "remembered" in the body is well remembered'.[5] This chapter will examine the ways in which these memories have conflated the meanings of 'America', 'capital' and 'punishment' for many African-Americans, from the middle passage to the new slave ship. I will conclude by considering the defence mechanisms with which the nexus of white punitive and economic power has been met.

FROM THE PASSAGE TO THE PLANTATION PRISON

> Of course black people were 'guilty' of being black. Slavery was punishment for their 'crime.'
>
> *Women, Race and Class*, Angela Davis[6]

Before the prison doors opened there was the middle passage. In excess of 10 million Africans were kidnapped, chained, beaten and branded before being shipped to the New World. Initial interaction between black and white in America established a punitive dynamic whose legacy is still evident in contemporary race relations. The dream of white punishment has always been the destruction of black subjectivity. Isolation from family, friends, community, history and language was the first stage in coercing the black subjects' consciousness of their status as property rather than people. This process was consolidated by confinement on a slave ship, a sentence that could last from three weeks to a year. As many as 400 captives were placed in heavy iron chains and packed into spaces often allowing them less room than a coffin. Light, air, food and water were in short supply. Sanitation was practically non-existent and disease rampant. Those who complained or sought to escape were flogged or worse. A not uncommon practice was the dismemberment of the least compliant captives as a warning to the rest of the cargo.

In his autobiography, Olaudah Equiano stresses the impossibility of expressing his experience of the middle passage: 'I am yet at a loss to describe ... the feelings of my mind', it was 'a scene of horror almost inconceivable'.[7] *The Interesting Narrative* introduces a double bind that Kali Tal has identified as integral to the 'literature of trauma', and which surfaces repeatedly in representations of punishment within African-American writing: one is compelled to speak the unspeakable, the experience that must and cannot be communicated.[8] Equiano attempts to loosen the bind by concentrating on the material conditions of his confinement: 'so crowded that each had scarcely room to turn himself ... The foul and poisonous air of the hold, extreme heat, men lying for hours in their own defecation, with blood and mucus on the floor.'[9] Equiano's references to other captives as 'fellow prisoners' underlines the punitive nature of his experience. When he responds to incarceration with a hunger strike Equiano is brutally flogged. Refusing to eat was one of the more serious offences that the slave-ship prisoner could commit, since it was equivalent to the wilful damage of cargo. To protect their investment, captains resorted both to the whip and force-feeding: 'the guards held them down and inserted metal bars between their teeth. The device was screwed until their jaws were pried open, sometimes crunching teeth in the process.'[10] When he sees a huge pot boiling on deck, Equiano fears that the prisoners are about to be eaten by their captors. This neat inversion of colonialist demonology is accentuated with gothic tropes: 'I was now persuaded that I had gotten into a world of bad spirits, and that they were going to kill me.'[11] Toni Morrison's account of the middle passage develops Equiano's metaphor. The crossing in *Beloved* is traced through the inchoate 'rememories' of a revenant child who conflates the slave ship with the underworld and her captors with white demons, 'men without skin':

I am always crouching ... someone is thrashing but there is no room to do it in ... if we had more water we could make tears ...

I cannot fall because there is no room to ... some who eat nasty themselves ... small rats do not wait for us to sleep ... daylight comes through the cracks... the iron circle is around our neck. (pp.210–12)

For many, the middle passage was a death sentence. Many of those who made it through the passage died in the first year of their arrival due to disease, starvation and over-work. For those who survived the first year and for their descendants, the system that held them was heterogeneous. Although slavery is a singular noun it assumed a variety of forms. Slavery in North America underwent major developments between the early colonial period and the Emancipation Proclamation. The nature of the slave system and the enslaved subject's experience varied dramatically according to region (rural or urban, Old South or New Territories), crop type (cotton, sugar, tobacco), size of unit (from smallholdings to vast plantation factories) and the practices of individual masters. Slavery was, to use Peter Parish's useful phrase, a 'system of many systems'.[12] This diversity must be respected, but it is equally crucial to recognise that, as Peter Kolchin insists, 'much more united the slaves than divided them'.[13] Arguably the most crucial common denominator in the lives of African-American slaves was the experience of punishment. Walvin insists that 'it is impossible to understand the realities of slave life without confronting the ubiquity, the inescapability, of physical punishment'.[14] That slavery was founded on a punitive ethos is axiomatic, but the extent to which it saturated all aspects of social and economic life can still be underestimated. Punishment was not an unfortunate by-product of a means of production; economic and punitive imperatives were irrevocably integrated. The sheer range of punishments inflicted on slaves is terrifying. The withholding of provisions, clothing, passes and free time all constituted relatively minor penalties imposed for misdemeanours. At the other end of the spectrum lie various modes of torture and execution: castration, branding, maiming, being forced to drink piss or eat a raw chicken. One case documents a slaveowner who 'made de overseer tie dat dead Nigger to de one what killed him, and de killer had to drag de corpse 'round 'til he died too'.[15] In the middle of this punitive spectrum there lies the routine usage of chains, incarceration and the whip. For those slaves fortunate enough to elude this disciplinary arsenal the threat of punishment was still pervasive. If, as Foucault suggests, torture begins with the sight of the instruments, then slaves' profound insecurity would have been compounded by the visibility of the scourge, the whipping-post, the prison, the fist and the boot of their masters.

According to Scarry's analysis of the torture scenario, the display of weaponry is designed to 'convert the prisoner's pain into the torturer's power'.[16] Punishment was pivotal to the slave's experience and to the subjectivity of the master. Its primacy is confirmed repeatedly in the rhetoric of the planter class: 'The fear of punishment is the principle to which we must and do appeal, to keep them in awe and order.'[17] The centrality of punishment to the power-base and self-image of the slaveocracy is also confirmed by the specially severe treatment of slaves who sought to avoid it. Frederick Douglass recounts the execution of Demby, a slave who ran away from a flogging. The overseer resorted to summary execution and offered the following justification to Demby's master:

> [Demby] was setting a dangerous example to the other slaves, one which, if suffered to pass without some demonstration on his part, would finally lead to the total subversion of all rule and order upon the plantation. [The overseer] argued that if one slave refused to be corrected, and escaped with his life, the other slaves would soon copy the example; the result of which would be, the freedom of the slaves, and the enslavement of the whites.[18]

On the plantation, pain was a branch of pedagogy. In Morrison's *Beloved*, Schoolteacher is master. Any failure to attend to lessons went to the heart of slavery's power relations and was countered with utmost force.

The degree to which slavery and punishment were synonymous cannot be realised simply by documenting the range and severity of tortures practised on the slave. Irrespective of the frequency of floggings and executions, slavery was essentially punitive in its structure. Slaves were sentenced to a life of hard labour in plantation prisons, with almost no prospect of release. Several historians of slavery have recognised that the plantation was, in effect, 'a prison without walls: self-contained, stratified, paternalistic, coercive'.[19] The plantation system in the antebellum South can be compared with the penitentiary system evolving in the North. The master performed a role analogous to the warden, whilst the overseers and drivers were his guards, maintaining discipline and surveillance. In both plantation and prison a systematic assault on identity was initiated by assigning new names or numbers and inflicting humiliating physical inspections. In terms of size there was little to choose between a cell in the new penitentiaries and standard slave accommodation. The choices facing the slave and the prisoner were also comparable. Each could serve their time as painlessly as possible, following orders and seeking to steer clear of additional punishment, they could practise daily subversions of the system designed to keep them as docile subjects, or they could attempt to escape. In both institutions there were hierarchies and prisons within prisons. Some captives received less physically demanding details in the Big House, whilst others were sentenced to hard labour outdoors.

The figure of slavery as prison is central to the slave narrative. Harriet Jacobs' *Incidents in the Life of a Slave Girl* offers a series of analogies between bondage and penal imprisonment which focus on the relative advantages of the latter condition. Jacobs declares that she would rather 'live and die in jail, than drag on, from day to day' in slavery's 'cage of obscene birds'.[20] Highlighting obscenity, the sexual abuse endemic to slavery, was crucial to the abolitionist agenda. Jacobs reminds her readers that '[s]lavery is terrible for men; but it is far more terrible for women ... *they* have wrongs, and sufferings, and mortifications peculiarly their own' (p.77). *Incidents* sketches the concentric circles of confinement surrounding the African-American woman, and underlines the extent to which patriarchy, as well as the plantation economy, was experienced as a carceral institution. From its nucleus inside the master's house the locus extends to Lincoln's 'House Divided'. In the wake of the Fugitive Slave Act of 1850, Jacobs insists that since her liberty is not guaranteed anywhere the entire nation has become her prison.

Incidents delivers a formidable critique of the unpardonable prison sentence imposed on African-Americans. The climax to a chapter devoted to the cruelties practised on neighbouring plantations tells of a master who considered 'punishment in jail, on bread and water, after receiving hundreds of lashes', to be too mild for the offence of trying to escape (p.48). Accordingly, he had a recaptured slave placed in a cotton gin, 'which was screwed down, only allowing him room to turn on his side when he could not lie on his back' (p.49). He was found dead, eaten alive by vermin, five days later. In flight from her master, Jacobs repeatedly retreats to confined spaces – dens, dark holes, cavities under floorboards – which prove, paradoxically, to be both representative of, and temporary sanctuaries from, the prison house of slavery. The most significant of these is her 'loophole of retreat', a small garret in a shed adjoining her grandmother's house (p.113). This space is identified as her 'prison' and 'cell': 'I lived in that dismal hole, almost deprived of light and air, and with no space to move my limbs, for nearly seven years ... my body still suffers from the effects of that long imprisonment, to say nothing of my soul' (p.148). Jacobs documents the sufferings endured during this long sentence: the cramped conditions, attacks by vermin, the absence of companionship and communication. In this respect, *Incidents* typifies the formal and thematic bonds that bind slave narratives and prison literature.

PLANTATION PUNISHMENTS

None but those who resided in the South during the time of slavery can realise the terrible punishments that were visited upon the slaves.

The House of Bondage, or Charlotte Brooks and Other Slaves,
Octavia V. Rogers Albert[21]

Jacobs insists that the suffering she endured during her seven-year term of self-incarceration was still preferable to her 'lot as a slave', and this despite the fact that she

was never lacerated with the whip from head to foot; I was never so beaten and bruised that I could not turn from one side to the other; I never had my heel-strings cut to prevent my running away; I was never chained to a log and forced to drag it about, while I toiled in the fields from morning to night; I was never branded with hot iron, or torn by bloodhounds. (p.115)

This litany of 'privileges' is double-edged: the punishments Jacobs has evaded alert the reader to suffering inflicted elsewhere. Alongside her own story, Jacobs documents tyrannical regimes on neighbouring plantations and traces contiguities between the individual and the social body. These passages, as Mary Titus notes, revolve around 'multiple, graphically described incidents of the abuse of bodies – whipped, scalded, starved, clubbed, torn apart, and devoured by vermin'.[22] Mr Litch, for example, owns 600 slaves on a plantation so extensive that it has its own jail and whipping post, therefore 'whatever cruelties were perpetrated there, they passed without comment' (p.46).

Various were the punishments resorted to. A favourite one was to tie a rope round a man's body, and suspend him from the ground. A fire was kindled over him, from which was suspended a piece of fat pork. As this cooked, the scalding drops of fat continually fell on the bare flesh. (p.46)

Deborah Garfield notes how food and torture are blended by Jacobs to intimate a perversion of the cult of domesticity.[23] Planter propaganda, which sought to represent slavery as a domestic institution, is compromised by recollections in *Incidents* of a cook, accused of a lack of culinary finesse, being force-fed dog food. The undermining of Southern hegemonic fables is similarly apparent when a runaway slave is locked in a cotton gin. Whilst elsewhere slavery is termed 'slow murder', the grisly death of this fugitive is speeded up in a gothic image that visualises slavery's consumption of human bodies. Inside the technological centrepiece of the plantation economy, Jacobs unveils the abject black corpse that feeds the domestic institution.

Jacobs suggests that the power to punish can be deadly for masters as well as slaves: 'It makes the white fathers cruel and sensual' (p.52). Although she recites this axiom of abolitionist propaganda, one that appeared compulsorily in slave narratives, elsewhere in *Incidents* the emphasis is less on the ethical dangers and more on the social advantages that accrue to those who wield the whip. Sandra Gunning argues convincingly that Jacobs is interested not only in 'brutalised slave bodies, but [in] the nature of the victimisation process developed and sustained as part of the means of constructing white privacy'.[24] Perversely, the punishment of black bodies averted attention from white culpability. Flint beats Jacobs to deflect attention from his desire for her, and exiles black women he has impregnated to safeguard his private identity and public position: 'Indeed the protection of Flint's life as father and husband is predicated on the exposure and punishment of black female bodies; they become criminalised, while white paternity is replaced by irresponsible, immoral black maternity.'[25]

Jacobs' attestation to the primacy of punishment within the social relations of slavery is echoed throughout the literature of slavery. In his *Interesting Narrative*, Equiano compiles an inventory of the 'instruments of torture used in the slave trade' and documents their usage: 'neck-yokes, collars, chains, hand-cuffs, leg-bolts, drags, thumb-screws, iron-muzzles, and coffins; cats, scourges'.[26] *The Narrative of the Life of Frederick Douglass* is set in Maryland, where 'it is generally conceded that [slaves] are less cruelly treated than in Georgia, Alabama, or Louisiana' (p.32). Despite this conventional disclaimer, Douglass' autobiography is structured around a series of confrontations with a white punitive power that is often total and unregulated.

> The plantation is a little nation of its own … The law and institutions of the state, apparently touch it nowhere. The troubles arising here, are not settled by the civil power of the state. The overseer is generally accuser, judge, jury, advocate and executioner. The criminal is always dumb.[27]

There were very few legal limitations on the punishment of slaves: whipping, maiming, incarceration, shackling and starvation were all judicially sanctioned. The slave community was subjected to discipline that was localised, private and informal. Summary justice, outside the courts, was the 'cornerstone of the system'.[28] The micro-systems of discipline constructed by individual slave owners interlocked to form a penal sub-system. This system was itself underpinned by a public disciplinary apparatus operating within and between states. On a day-to-day basis the slave could be subjected to discipline by the driver, the overseer, the master or members of his family, but the system did not finish with the boundaries of the plantation. Once the estate's margins were crossed the slave was confronted by local law enforcement: justices of the peace, constables and sheriffs, slave patrols and vigilante groups.

If the offence were deemed serious enough, punitive authority passed to a formal hearing in magistrate's court, superior court, and on rare occasions the state supreme court. Whilst there were very few laws prohibiting cruelty against them, the law codified a large number of crimes as capital offences when committed by slaves. Virginia's slave codes included 71 capital offences for blacks that did not apply to whites. Since execution and long-term imprisonment robbed the master of labour power, sentences were often commuted to punishments that, as in the 'little nations', focused on the body, such as flogging, branding and cropping. When a slave was sentenced to capital punishment the authorities exploited the spectacle to the full and insisted on attendance by the black community. Executions were made especially brutal. The execution of slaves would involve castration, disembowelment, decapitation or the use of fire, to serve as an instrument of terror against the captive audience. Given the immanence of the disciplinary apparatus already confronting the slave community, the excess of these spectacles might appear unwarranted. However, these punitive performances may have been staged primarily for the benefit of their white directors, having less to do with suppressing rebellion than with suppressing anxieties amongst the planter class about the possibility of challenges to its omnipotence.

Whilst execution was a relatively rare display of disciplinary potency, the whip was a permanent presence. As Douglass stated epigrammatically: 'The whip is all in all.'[29] Flogging assumed a variety of forms: there were variations in instrument (types of whip, rod, scourge and paddle), in personnel (it could be applied by master, mistress or child, driver or overseer, constable or patroller) and in method (ranging from a swift tap on the way to the fields to being tied naked to a public whipping post to receive 100 lashes). Various groups in Southern society sought to regulate the practice of flogging. Local laws often prescribed a number of lashes for specific offences, but these were almost impossible to enforce in the 'little nations'. Some churches investigated allegations of excessive usage, and even excommunicated masters who refused to restrain their use of the scourge. Despite the exhortations, however, there is evidence to suggest that restraint was rarely practised, and mixed messages were delivered from the Southern pulpit. Whilst a minority recommended New Testament self-discipline, the majority regurgitated Old Testament precedents to establish the master's divine right to punish: 'We esteem it the duty of Christian masters to feed and clothe well, and in the case of disobedience to *whip well*.'[30] Slaves were also subjected to sermons and admonished to recognise their masters as 'GOD'S OVERSEERS ... if you are faulty towards them, God himself will punish you severely for it in the next world'.[31]

Another source of largely ineffective regulation for flogging was the management manual that warned of the economic pitfalls of over-reliance on the whip. However, whilst suggesting fiscal disincentives against cruelty, the management manual would also propose refinements in sadism. A pseudo-science of the scourge evolved, including technical advice on the optimum length and width for this instrument. Masters were advised to whip a slave on their legs if welts had developed on their back, not due to compassion, but because scar tissue deadened sensation. Manuals may have recommended selective scourging, but they also offered ways of maximising returns, such as enforcing attendance by slave children.

Used sparingly, it was urged, the whip could be an even more effective disciplinary tool. As a planter in North Carolina explained in his *Instructions to Managers*:

> Whip a dog every time he enters your parlour and kitchen and you will soon be unable to coax him to put his nose inside the door. But if he is sometimes allowed to lie by the fire and sometimes severely lashed, he will take ten thousand stripes and be a house dog in spite of them.[32]

The existence of documents recommending selective scourging does not, of course, prove that restraint was endemic to the system. In fact, it could easily be read as evidence of widespread malpractice. Although statistical evidence is equivocal, existing archival records, posters for runaways specifying the number of their 'stripes' and newspaper reports often testify to the frequency of flogging. This was not exclusive to the 'little nations':

> The public punishment of slaves and free blacks by city authorities was a common sight in the urban South. A Richmond newspaper laconically described a city court's business: 'There was nothing of moment before 'His Honour' yesterday. An average amount of niggerdom was ordered to be thrashed … for violations of the police regulations and city ordinances of so slight a character that it is hardly worthwhile publishing them in a newspaper.'[33]

Slave narratives and abolitionist rhetoric advertised the pre-eminence of the whip, and aimed to convert it into a synecdoche for the ineffable sufferings of slavery. Abby Kelley swore that 'when my flesh quivers beneath the lash … the English language is not adequate'.[34] Despite the inarticulateness they produce, floggings function as primary, and on occasion primal scenes in the discourses of anti-slavery. The biographies of Frederick Douglass, Charles Ball and William Wells Brown either open with or hinge upon the moment in which the authors witnessed the whipping of their mother or a female relation by their master. The eroticised punishment of black mothers by white father figures forms the crucible in which the narrator's conception of slavery and subjectivity is formed. Similarly, narratives by Harriet Jacobs, J. H. Banks and Solomon Northrup each offer a flogging scene as their introduction to the slave's experience, or as a turning-point in relations with white power. The slaveocracy attempted to fix an image of the plantation as consummate fusion of the commercial and the domestic. The slave narrative challenged this proscriptive parable by converging on the whip. The genre wrenched slavery from the realms of economic and paternalistic discourse and positioned it in a disciplinary context. The moment the whip was cracked may have produced pain that was beyond articulation, but it was also the point at which pro-slavery propaganda could be most effectively silenced.

In the opening chapter of his *Narrative*, the child-narrator Douglass watches in mute terror from a closet whilst his master flogs Aunt Hester. Captain Anthony is the first in a succession of master-father figures (Hopkins, Gore and Covey) armed with the phallic scourge that Douglass encounters. The imagery associated with this initial meeting crosses the religious and the gynaecological, as Douglass describes the Captain's beating of Aunt Hester as 'the bloodstained gate, the entrance to the hell of slavery, through which I was about to pass' (p.28). Jenny Franchot's reading of this scene confirms its importance as the narrative's 'originating moment', the moment in which the young Douglass is 'stunned into commodity status'.[35] Franchot goes on to assert that the image of the 'victimised – often "whipped" – female body' establishes an opposition between passive black femininity and a powerful white patriarchy that problematises Douglass' *Narrative*.[36] This critique might seem to be reinforced by the correlation between the *Narrative*'s primal scene and Freud's 'A Child is Being Beaten'. Captain Anthony is Hester's figurative father, and possibly Douglass' biological parent. The potent admixture of voyeurism, guilt and desire evident within this triangle echoes the classical psychoanalytical account of sadistic fantasy. Douglass' pre-occupation with the whip, the root and the 'rod of the oppressor' might also seem to strengthen the charge of a problematic phallocentricism in the *Narrative*. At the same time, the rather tidy oppositions underlying Franchot's critique threaten to erase the tangled skein of blood, capital and genealogy that is evident in the slave narrative. The erotic undercurrent in the imagery does not automatically entail a symbolic siding with white punitive power, nor a rejection of black femininity. The slave narrative typically elides the binary logic of the plantation economy in favour of crossings between white and black, masculine and feminine, power and passivity. The graphic nature of Douglass' opening chapter is itself partly attributable to a gendered crossing between the genres of slave autobiography, the sentimental novel and sensationalist fiction.

Despite the pre-eminence assigned to the whip in the slave narrative there is less consensus concerning its role amongst some historians. Fogel and Engerman, for example, agree that whipping was 'probably the most common punishment meted out against errant slaves', but go on to argue that, in general terms, it was used sparingly and was often 'as mildly applied as the corporal punishment practised within families today'.[37] In their controversial study, *Time on the Cross*, Fogel and Engerman repeat the message from plantation manuals concerning the ineffectiveness of excessive flogging in comparison with alternative tools of labour control (such as bonuses and profit-sharing schemes). Whilst attesting that '[r]eliable data on the frequency of whipping is extremely sparse', they also offer the records kept by a Louisiana planter, alongside census data and account books, as statistical support for their claims.[38] Fogel and Engerman's assertion that flogging was the most prevalent form of punishment inflicted by slaveowners ignores the essentially punitive nature of slavery itself, with its profound and incessant deprivations of liberty. As Douglass stated: 'Work, work, work, was scarcely more than the order of the day than of the night … I was somewhat unmanageable when I first went there, but a few months of this discipline tamed me' (p.85). The assumption made in *Time on the Cross* that only 'errant slaves' were whipped and that they typically experienced only a 'mild whipping' also seems wildly incongruous alongside Douglass' *Narrative*: 'It seems as though I should not forget this flogging when I die; it grieved my soul beyond the power of time to cure' (p.143).

To declare that 'reliable data is extremely sparse', of course, is to reject the authority of literature by and about slaves. It is undoubtedly important to recognise that slave narratives were political literature offering a representation of slavery that was least favourable to the institution. However, one must apply equally rigorous standards of scepticism towards the official records of the slaveholding class, especially those produced by an order under siege and desperate not to provide evidence of disharmony. Fogel and Engerman's understanding of the whip is representative of the general model of punishment that they offer in *Time on the Cross*. They contend that slavery maintained structural stability not by physical force but through forms of hegemonic assimilation. This account reads slavery as America's 'time on the cross', but the body has been taken down. Slavery becomes a figurative punishment for the nation as a whole, rather than a series of material practices brought to bear on the black body.

Strictly quantitative approaches to slavery are also questionable due to their inability to account for contradictions within the system, and as Blassingame reminds us, '[n]owhere does the irrationality of slavery appear as clearly as in the way that slaves were punished'.[39] Masters often acted in ways that were not to their economic advantage: 'Sometimes they would catch Richard and drive four stakes in the ground, and they would tie his feet and hands to each one and beat him half to death. I tell you, sometimes he could not work.'[40] Contrary to the assertion that slaves were kept in place through hegemonic manipulation and the promise of economic reward, Douglass offers the following:

> I have observed this in my experience of slavery, – that whenever my condition is improved, instead of increasing my contentment, it only increased my desire to be free ... I have found that, to make a contented slave, it is necessary to make a thoughtless one. (p.126)

One of the crucial lacunae produced by a quantitative methodology is the erotic economy of slavery: forms of libidinal interest accrued alongside the (im)purely pecuniary. The whipping of Aunt Hester introduces a gallery of sadists who brutalise black women in Douglass' *Narrative*. These figures, like Dr Flint in Jacobs' *Incidents*, 'loved money, but [they] loved power more' (p.80). Despite warnings from her white editor, Jacobs chose to foreground slavery's marriage of erotic and punitive power. She further challenged propriety by hinting that this union was not confined to heterosexual relations. Jacobs recalls waking at night in her room to find her mistress looming over her, and the case of a young male slave forced to attend to a sick master:

> As he lay there on his bed, a mere degraded wreck of manhood, he took into his head the strangest freaks of despotism; and if Luke hesitated to submit to his orders, the constable was immediately sent for. Some of these freaks were of a nature too filthy to be repeated. I left poor Luke still chained to the bedside of this cruel and disgusting wretch. (p.74)

Only by moving beyond the account books of the master can one begin to gauge the extent to which African-Americans experienced the system of slavery as inherently punitive. From the perspective of the slave community, the plantation economy's primary product was not cotton, or tobacco, or sugar, but pain. This pain often followed the ex-slave to the North. In the narratives of Equiano, Douglass, Jacobs and others, the authors are plagued both by the memory of punishment and by the possibility of its return. The insecurity of ex-slaves is compounded by the racism and institutional discrimination they encounter in the nominally 'Free' states. The slave narrative proposes that the prison walls did not end at the plantation's boundary. In place of liberty, the slave encountered only degrees of imprisonment in the Land of the Free.

'A SMALL PIECE OF HELL': CHAIN GANGS, LYNCHING AND THE RECONSTRUCTION OF SLAVERY

Eighteen seventy-four and whitefolks were still on the loose. Whole towns wiped clean of Negroes; eighty-seven lynchings in one year alone in Kentucky ... grown men whipped like children; children whipped like adults; black women raped by the crew; property taken; necks broken.

Beloved, Toni Morrison (p.180)

In an autobiography dictated to a reporter on the South Carolina *Independent*, an anonymous African-American from Georgia offered a story that repeated the familiar formula of the slave narrative. The transcript began with obscure genealogy, enforced illiteracy, family break-up, routine whippings and the sexual abuse of black women. Although formally undistinguished, the noteworthy feature of this narrative is that it documented life *after* the Civil War. 'Autobiography by a Georgia Negro Peon' was first published in 1904 and its subtitle, 'The New Slavery in the South', highlighted fundamental continuities in the African-American experience following emancipation. H. Bruce Franklin includes this text in his anthology of twentieth-century prison writing and prefaces it with a cogent reminder that whilst the Thirteenth Amendment formally abolished chattel slavery, it also lay the legal groundwork for new forms of penal slavery: 'Neither slavery nor involuntary servitude, *except as a punishment for crime whereof the party shall have been duly convicted*, shall exist within the United States, or any place subject to their jurisdiction.'[41] This punishment clause was part of a strategy by which white power maintained the punitive oppression of

African-Americans. A massive expansion of penal machinery, combined with debt peonage and black codes, convict leasing and contract labour, chain gangs and lynching, ensured that, although the walls of the plantation prison had been pulled down, liberty remained little more than a legal fiction. The postbellum period saw a legal redrafting of slavery which was far more than a paper exercise. The labour contracts of debt peonage, Jim Crow segregation laws and literacy tests enforcing disenfranchisement were underwritten by the pervasive promise of punitive violence.

In his autobiography, the anonymous Georgia peon records some of the stratagems by which, for many African-Americans, reconstruction was translated into the reconstruction of slavery. The change of regime occurring nationally in the wake of war is echoed in microcosm on the plantation, as the old master dies and the son, a powerful politician, takes over. The Senator increases productivity by concretising the plantation's status as a *de facto* prison. First, he coerces his illiterate workforce into signing ten-year contracts that prohibit them from leaving the plantation:

> ... if we got mad and ran away, we could be run down by bloodhounds, arrested without process of law, and be returned to our employer, who according to the contract, might beat us brutally or administer any other kind of punishment that he thought proper. In other words, we had sold ourselves into slavery – and what could we do about it?[42]

Following the completion of their ten-year terms, the workforce discover that they are in debt to the Senator for use of the local store, from which they were compelled to purchase their supplies. Once their status changes, from 'free' labourer to debt peon, they are held in a stockade and sentenced to further hard labour to settle the arrears. The imprisonment of the current workforce, however, is only half of the Senator's strategy, as he also recruits additional labourers: 'This was the beginning of the Senator's convict camp. These men were prisoners who had been leased to the Senator from the State of Georgia at about $200 each per year.'[43] Over the next two years the number of convict labourers swells from 40 to 200, and distinctions are lost between worker, prisoner and slave. Convict leasing had been practised on a small scale before the war, but in the postbellum period it became a key tactic in the reconstruction of slavery. The formal abolition of slavery left the plantocracy facing a crisis in social control and agricultural labour supply. Given its centrality to the previous regime, it is unsurprising that punishment was resorted to as the solution to this crisis.

The new regime was initiated by the black codes that both replaced and repeated antebellum slave codes. Until they were themselves replaced by relatively more sophisticated Jim Crow legislation, the codes were crudely discriminatory. The majority of these statutes only related to African-Americans and included a vast array of nebulous offences including 'insulting gestures' and 'mischief'. The codes operated alongside equally obscure vagrancy laws hurriedly drafted by Southern legislatures to discipline the ranks of the black unemployed. 'Free negroes' were compelled to obtain written proof of employment on an annual basis. If they were found roaming without such proof they could be arrested for vagrancy, but if they chose to stay put they could be imprisoned for loitering. Before the Civil War there had been hardly any black prisoners. Following the war, the codes ensured that in some Southern states African-Americans accounted for more than 90 per cent of the prison population.

The fee system played a pivotal role in the manufacture of a labour pool of licit slaves. Law enforcement officials, magistrates and judges received a fee for arrests and convictions and this, along with the costs incurred during the judicial process, was passed on to the prisoner. Often the sentence for a misdemeanour would be no more than a few days, but the costs would entail several further months of hard labour. When Milly Lee was convicted of using 'abusive language' she was fined one dollar. This penalty was worked off after two days but 'it required nearly a year of labour to satisfy the "costs" consisting of fees to judge, sheriff, clerks and witnesses, totalling $132'.[44] As poverty was implicitly criminalised, African-American defendants found themselves sentenced, in the words of a New Orleans black newspaper, to 'three days for stealing, and eighty-seven for being coloured'.[45] After the imposition of fines they were unable to pay, African-Americans were sent to prisons which became, in effect, the new slave warehouses. From this location former masters, private companies and the state could select prisoners and contract their labour by assuming responsibility for their fine. The state profited in various ways from the new penal system. Emptying the prisons cut expenditures and raised revenue. The state also put prisoners to work at tasks such as road maintenance. Road gangs saved money and indirectly increased the attractiveness of agricultural labour to the black workforce. Also, by making their punishment highly visible, the road gang reinforced the racist code that equated blacks and criminality. Chain gangs and convict leasing ensured that, for the state, crime began to pay.

Black prisoners, as well as being put to work by the state, were also exploited by private capital. This could mean, as in 'Autobiography by a Georgia Negro Peon', a return to the plantation, or to work in mines and mills and on railroads and canals. The material conditions endured here were often even worse than those endured under chattel slavery, since the companies leasing convict labour did not have the financial incentive to maintain their 'property'. It was cheaper to replace slave labour than provide properly for it, and consequently death rates for black convicts soared. In 1870 the mortality rate amongst black prisoners in Alabama reached 41 per cent. Life expectancy for most convicts varied from between three and seven years, and could be shorter than the average sentence. This statistic also fails to account for the large numbers of prisoners compassionately pardoned when they were about to die. Franklin observes that the value of black prisoners sometimes did not end with their death: 'the bodies of convicts leased to the mines and railroads of Tennessee were sold to the Medical School at Nashville'.[46]

The conditions that translated prison sentences into death sentences make this arguably the most brutal punishment regime in American history. On the railroads prisoners were kept in rolling cages and shackled even in their sleep:

They relieved themselves in a single bucket and bathed in the same filthy tub of water. With no screens on the cages, insects swarmed everywhere. It was like a small piece of hell, an observer noted – the stench, the chains, the sickness, and the heat.[47]

A railroad company building a line through the Canay Swamps had convicts working in water

ranging to their knees, and in almost nude state they spaded caney and rooty ground, their bare feet chained together by chains that fretted the flesh. They were compelled to attend to the calls of nature in line as they stood day in and day out, their thirst compelling them to drink the water in which they were compelled to deposit their excrement.[48]

Working hours were from around 4.30 a.m. for 'as long as it is light enough for a guard to see how to shoot'.[49] Work and punishment practices in the convict lease system borrowed from antebellum traditions. In the mines, for example, a task system based on the plantation model was employed, according to which groups would be flogged for failing to achieve a day's quota. Oshinsky and Colvin document cases of prisoners being hung from crucifixes, stretched on racks and crammed into coffin-sized sweatboxes for minor infractions of discipline.[50] Summary executions were routine. Another spectre from the days of slavery was the institutionalisation of sexual abuse: 'Sexual assaults in convict lease camps were also numerous.'[51] Far more African-Americans attempted to escape penal than chattel slavery. The chances of success were quite high, given that recapturing fugitives was a low priority for the state and private companies. 'In the mid-1870s a Georgia legislative committee reported that nearly half of the state's convicts had escaped.'[52] The lack of commitment to recapturing runaways indicates the extent to which economics, rather than public safety, was the primary consideration within the postbellum penal system. Punishment in this system was devoid of penological rhetoric concerning rehabilitation, common in the North, and was stripped bare of the paternalist vesture which had cloaked the plantation economy. The abolition of chattel slavery prefigured the perfection of new forms of nakedly penal slavery, in which capital and punishment became fully integrated.

Morrison's *Beloved* attempts to recreate this 'small piece of hell' in the career of Paul D. After the 'short, flashy results' of the Civil War, Paul D finds himself on the run alongside thousands of emancipated slaves

> [w]ho, like him, had hidden in caves ... slept in trees in the day and walked by night ... buried themselves in slop and jumped in wells to avoid regulators, raiders, patrollers, veterans, hill men, posses and merrymakers ... Move. Walk. Run. Hide. (pp.171, 66)

After a stint as a bond slave, Paul D attempts to murder his owner and is sent to a prison camp in Alfred, Georgia (in 1866 the first state to utilise chain gangs). Here he sleeps 'underground and crawled into sunlight for the sole purpose of breaking rock' (p.40). Alongside the hard labour, poor food and lack of hygiene, the prisoners are also at constant risk of sexual assault:

Chain-up completed, they knelt down ... Kneeling in the mist they waited for the whim of a guard, or two, or three. Or maybe all of them wanted it ... 'Breakfast ? Want some breakfast, nigger?' ... Occasionally a kneeling man chose gunshot in his head as the price, maybe, of taking a bit of foreskin with him to Jesus. (p.108)

In confirmation of the Georgia legislative committee's report on lax security, all 46 prisoners manage to escape the camp during a storm, after which Paul D is 'purchased by Northpoint Bank and Railroad Company' (p.141). These experiences crystallise the transition from chattel to penal to wage slavery and demonstrate that, although the terminology changed, the essentially punitive nature of the experience of many African-Americans at this time remained disturbingly constant.

As the reconstruction era was eclipsed by the New South another change of terminology had little discernible impact. A combination of the state and Southern and Northern capital continued to exploit black prison labour. The primary industries (forestry and mining) and the transport infrastructure (roads, railroads and canals) that fuelled the industrialisation of the South were often dependent on the profitable punishment of African-Americans. Industrialisation was not accompanied by a transition to modern punishment practices centred on psychological correction: the black body remained the target of torture. The semi-feudal plantation economy had of course been founded on the punitive regulation of black bodies. What is less well recognised is the extent to which the industrialisation of the New South was similarly inspired.

The new synthesis of capital and punishment thrived until the 1890s, when it was forced to adapt to changes in demographics, labour relations and law. The Great Migration to Northern cities had a massive impact on convict labour supply. Simultaneously, the system was under fire from workers who refused migration. The penalised black body had been deployed successfully as a disciplinary tool in labour relations with 'free' workers. A steady supply of black convict labour kept wages low, working conditions poor and undermined the effectiveness of organised revolt. However, organised resistance, from groups such as the Knights of Labour and the Farmers' Alliance, was beginning to increase the costs of convict labour. The state initially responded to these twin threats by tightening up on already strict vagrancy and contract evasion legislation, whilst judicial decision-making responded to local labour needs by sending convicts to areas of shortage. Alongside these short-term measures, a new model of prison labour emerged, gradually replacing the convict lease: the state-owned prison farm. In Mississippi, Texas, Tennessee and Arkansas, some of these developed into super-plantations, agricultural factories for cotton manufacture that dwarfed their antebellum predecessors. Parchman Farm in Mississippi covered 16,000 acres and was the state's chief source of revenue.

Although only two Southern states abolished the lease system in the nineteenth century, and it was still functioning in Alabama into the 1920s, its value as a system of social control had been significantly undermined by legal developments. The case of *Plessy v. Ferguson* in 1896 established the 'separate but equal' ruling. This doctrine paved the way for a catalogue of Jim Crow laws which, alongside the systematic disenfranchisement of African-Americans, provided an alternative means of race oppression: 'As legalised segregation became entrenched and its coerciveness affected all race relations, the punishment system (both official and unofficial) receded.'[53] The unofficial punishment system mentioned here refers primarily to lynching. The massive expansion in state-sponsored punishment after the Civil War did not displace the private criminal justice system that dominated the plantation economy. In fact, punishment continued to thrive at the local level, especially in the form of lynch law. A vibrant tradition of extra-legal punishments was maintained by various white supremacist groups. The night rides of the Klan were routine in every Southern state by 1870. The Klan cultivated the image of an unofficial police force, honourable opponents of the rampant black criminality which had been unleashed, allegedly, by emancipation. Their rationale was that punishment for blacks and whites ought to be separate and unequal:

The white man's law, said many racists, was unsuited to Negroes, who were adapted by racial experience to the ways of the jungle. *Due process, trial by jury*, even imprisonment, were meaningless to them, for they saw no connection between crime and punishment unless one was *immediately* followed by the other.[54]

Alongside smaller vigilante groups, such as the White Cohort and the Knights of the White Camellia, the Klan filled the holes left by the formal dismantling of slavery's punitive apparatus: 'Where convict leasing was used as punishment in more settled areas, lynching was used in more sparsely populated areas.'[55] Lynching had an established place in Southern rituals of violence over half a century before its post-Civil War renaissance. The term itself dates to the 1780s and memorialises Colonel Charles Lynch of Bedford County, Virginia. Lynch responded to what he perceived as a local crime wave by taking the law into his own hands and punishing offenders summarily beneath a huge oak tree on his land. Douglass, in his *Narrative*, supplies an indication of the ubiquity of lynch law in the antebellum period, when he remarks, after a fight with a group of white carpenters in a Baltimore dockyard, that 'to strike a white man is death by Lynch law, – and that was the law in Mr Gardner's ship-yard; nor is there much of any other out of Mr Gardner's ship-yard' (p.143).

Once the market value of black life was reduced by the Thirteenth Amendment, lynch law became a veritable industry. In *A Red Record*, Ida B. Wells estimated that over 10,000 lynchings took place between 1865 and 1895.[56] The extent to which this practice was informally sanctioned is indicated by the fact that during the same period only three white men were executed for taking part in a lynching, and there were no federal prosecutions until 1942. There were also many instances when lynching was officially sanctioned. When George Hughes was lynched in Sherman, Texas, a mob burnt down the jail he was in, dragged his dead body to the black part of town and set fire to it. Local law enforcement assisted by redirecting traffic. In his *Autobiography*, Malcolm X reports how, after discovering his father severely beaten around the head and run over by a tram, the police entered a verdict of 'suicide'. The extent of collusion between vigilante violence and the police is evident in the large number of lynchings that did not conform to the mythological fable of a surreptitious, nocturnal ceremony. In 1899, for example, Sam Holt was mutilated, tortured and burnt at the stake in broad daylight whilst an audience of 2,000 people cheered. At some lynchings, photographs were sold as picture postcards, and there was a profitable trade in souvenirs amongst collectors of curios, such as clothing and even body parts of the victims.

The defenders of lynch law argued that it was an honourable response to the 'New Negro Crime': the rape of defenceless white women. The frequency with which honourable responses were called for testifies in part to the conveniently nebulous definitions offered of this crime: 'rape was a very loosely defined term that could apply to any contact between a white female and a black male'. Rape did not have to involve penetration or even physical intimacy, sometimes a gesture, or even proximity in a private space was apparently enough to justify the charge. The Southern novelist Clinton Dangerfield explained as follows: 'there was no such thing as an innocent black, the "racial attitudes" of blacks merited "racial punishment", and the virtue of one white woman outweighed "in value" the lives of a hundred Negro men'.[57] Frederick Douglass noted that in the immediate aftermath of Civil War this punishment was rarely practised with reference to the virtue of white womanhood: 'During this time the justification for the murder of Negroes was said to be Negro conspiracies, Negro insurrections, Negro schemes to murder all white people, Negro plots to burn the town and to commit violence generally.'[58] The legitimation of lynching in relation to race war became increasingly difficult following reconstruction and the wholesale disenfranchisement of African-Americans. Accordingly, a new strategy was devised, one that was emotively charged and largely free of the necessity of providing material evidence. Although rape was still only the official charge in around 20 per cent of lynchings, it was the essential background against which the practice continued. As Clarence Poe explained: 'it is only because lynching for rape is excused that lynching for any other crime is ever attempted'.[59]

Lynching served a variety of functions: it was a diversionary measure, it fed and was fed by media legend, it helped foster social solidity in the white community, and it responded to economic developments. As a diversionary measure the lynching of black men for alleged outrages against white womanhood deflected from the long history of sexual assaults on black women by white men. As Angela Davis argued:

> Slavery relied as much on routine sexual abuse as it relied on the whip and the lash ... [it was] a savage punishment ... Together with flogging, rape was a terribly efficient method of keeping Black women and men alike in check. It was a routine arm of repression.[60]

The rape of black women within slavery was institutionalised. It could not be legally challenged since the slave was defined as property, and punishment for damaging one's own property was a *non sequitur* in Southern law. In antebellum Missouri, if a white man other than the master committed a sexual assault on a slave he could be found guilty of 'trespass'. These legal fetters were reinforced by fables of black sexual licentiousness. In the antebellum South the myth of the black whore became an alibi for rape; in the postbellum South the myth of the black rapist was similarly circulated to justify lynching. The news media played a vital role in pedalling the figure of the black rapist and assorted 'Bad Nigger' stereotypes. In generating paranoid fantasies of rampant black criminality, a burgeoning print media laid the groundwork for developments in the coverage of crime that subsequently sought to make the signifiers 'black' and 'crime' synonymous. In the postbellum South, lurid reportage of unchecked black crime-waves also served as a focal point for social solidarity amongst a white community where economic and political consensus was being unravelled by rapid industrialisation. Resurrecting the social symbolism of slavery, the ritual demonisation and punishment of the black body as 'lazy', 'dangerous', 'dirty' and 'unruly', offered a point of convergence for a disparate and potentially disunified white community.

The close correlation between upsurges in lynching and unemployment establishes the importance of economic determinants. The highpoint in lynching (and also in convict leasing) occurred during a severe economic downturn between 1889 and 1993, which increased inter-racial competition in the labour market. That the intricate connectivity between punishment and economics was sustained into the twentieth century is illustrated by an infamous lynching that took place in Waco in 1916. Jesse Washington, a 17-year-old illiterate cotton picker, was mutilated, castrated, chained to a car and stoned by a mob before being burnt alive and hung from a tree beside the mayor's office. In *The Crisis*, the NAACP newspaper, DuBois explained why this act had to be read not simply in racial terms, but in relation to capitalism, as 'an incident of terror within the political economy of peonage'.[61] DuBois linked Washington's lynching at the hands of almost 10,000 whites to the Tulsa Inferno of 1921. A bootblack, Diamond Dick Rowland, accidentally stepped on the foot of a young white woman in an elevator. She reported the incident to the police and Rowland was arrested, tried and prosecuted for rape. With the newspapers calling for the death penalty, the large black population of Tulsa – 15,000-strong and known as 'Little Africa' – took to the streets to call for Rowland's release. They were met by a coalition of police, the National Guard and the Klan, who laid siege to Little Africa, destroying 1,000 homes and killing over 200 people. Dynamite was dropped from planes and over 6,000 black citizens were held in concentration camps. DuBois linked these individual

(Washington, Rowland) and collective (Waco, Tulsa) acts of punitive repression to the Red Scare, suggesting a continuum between race discrimination and attacks on Wobblies. Peter Linebaugh summarises DuBois' critique as follows:

> The Tulsa inferno was the climax to a cycle of repression that began a few years earlier when seventeen Oklahoma Wobblies with the Oil Field Workers Union were stripped, tied, whipped, tarred, feathered and threatened with hanging. The NAACP detailed how the inferno re-established a new basis for labour 'peace' in the mid-continental oil fields. The cheap oil thus provided was the precondition of 'Fordism' and the gasoline culture of twentieth-century America.[62]

Punishment had been pivotal to the profits of the plantation economy. DuBois' critique suggests the extent to which it continued to play a critical role within urban-industrial capitalism.

BEATING THE BAD NIGGER:
FROM BIGGER THOMAS TO RODNEY KING

> ... it seems sort of natural-like, me being here facing the death chair. Now I come to think of it, it seems like something like this just had to be.
>
> *Native Son*, Richard Wright[63]

Although they rarely appeared in movies, comic strips and radio shows during the 1920s and '30s, the prominence of the Bad Nigger folk devil in print media helped to maintain the equation between African-Americans and crime. Sociological studies conducted in the South at this time revealed that many whites believed all crime was committed by the black community. Statistics would suggest that similar sentiments were in operation in the justice system. African-Americans were far more likely to be imprisoned for an offence than whites, and then received disproportionately severe sentences. In the 1920s, African-Americans represented around 9 per cent of the national population, but over 30 per cent of the prison population. This situation deteriorated further during the Depression, when a rise in the national imprisonment rate, from 79 to 137 per 100,000, was produced almost exclusively by increases in the incarceration of African-Americans.

Growing up in Mississippi and Tennessee during this period, Richard Wright routinely encountered discrimination and punishment at the hands of white America. In his autobiography, *Black Boy*, and essays such as 'The Ethics of Living Jim Crow', Wright recalls memories of police harassment, punishment beatings and lynchings that intimate how little had changed in the half-century after abolition: 'In me was shaping a yearning for a kind of consciousness, a mode of being that the way of life about me had said could not be, must not be and upon which the penalty of death had been placed.'[64] The title of Wright's collection of short stories, *Uncle Tom's Children*, suggests the extent to which slavery's legacy of punitive violence continued to dominate African-American life. Set in the early decades of the twentieth century, four of the five neoslave narratives in this collection climax with execution, and each of them documents the brutalisation of the black body.

The opening story in *Uncle Tom's Children*, 'Big Boy Leaves Home', suggests the continued vibrancy of lynching in Southern ritual. A group of black youths trespass onto white property to swim in a creek. When a white woman stumbles across them, her soldier boyfriend starts shooting and in the confrontation that follows two of the youths and the white man are killed. In a pattern repeated in each of the other tales in the collection, black transgression accelerates accidentally and incrementally: it starts with a minor trespass on white land, then proximity to white womanhood, and culminates with murder. Big Boy's first instinct is to run, because '[t]heys gonna lynch us'.[65] Big Boy, in a mirror-image of the slave narrative, takes flight. His route along a railroad track echoes other fugitive escapes, as does his discovery that leaving home leads initially only to greater levels of confinement (an underground kiln and a secret compartment in a truck). In the slave narrative the act of witnessing punishment was a rite of passage. 'Big Boy Leaves Home' similarly hinges upon such a spectacle as the main figure sees his friend caught by the mob: 'a tar-drenched body glistening and turning in the crowd of white people and dogs'.[66] The mob sing songs and take 'SOURVINEERS' from the victim's body, whilst justifying their actions with the familiar alibi: 'Ef they git erway notta woman in this town would be safe.'[67] However, by tracing the sequence of events to a trespass on land, another form of patriarchal property, Wright hints at an alternative explanation involving the fusion of sexual and economic imperatives underlying Southern punitive practice.

Big Boy was a forerunner of Bigger Thomas, Wright's archetypal embodiment of the Bad Nigger folk devil. In his prefatory essay to *Native Son*, Wright explains that Bigger represents a condensation of those rebellious African-Americans who

> consistently violated the Jim Crow laws of the South and got away with it, at least for a sweet brief spell. Eventually, the whites who restricted their lives made them pay a terrible price. They were shot, hanged, maimed, lynched, and generally hounded until they were either dead or their spirits were broken. (p.xi)

The plot trajectory of the tales in *Uncle Tom's Children* is repeated in Bigger's story. A young black man goes on the run after the accidental manslaughter of a white heiress, and is eventually caught, tried and sentenced to death. Although the crime is murder, Bigger realises that the trial and press coverage will be dominated by the issue of rape, as he is used to confirm racist fables of the predatory black male lusting after white flesh.

Native Son is a prison novel long before Bigger reaches the state penitentiary in Book Three. Books One and Two, traced through the generic stencil of the slave narrative, underline the extent to which Bigger's experience has been intrinsically carceral: 'He was their property, heart and soul, body and blood; what they did claimed every atom of him, sleeping and waking; it coloured life and dictated the terms of death' (p.307). *Native Son* offers a picture of black captivity in some respects more total than that encountered in nineteenth-century slave narratives. The concentric circles of confinement that ring Bigger begin in a 'tiny one-room apartment', a rat trap in the segregated housing district of Chicago's black belt (p.8). The Thomas family came to Chicago in the Great Migration seeking emancipation, but, as Rosenblatt notes, they instead encounter 'a different form of enclosure. They escaped out of one house of bondage into a smaller and more cramped house where the story begins.'[68] Whilst *Uncle Tom's Children* focused on the rural South, *Native Son* moves to a setting in the urban North, to figure the ghettos forcefully as a new plantation prison.

As he leaves his cramped accommodation each day Bigger is greeted by an overseer in the shape of a huge image of the state's attorney:

> … one hand was uplifted and its index finger pointed straight out into the street at each passer-by. The poster showed one of those

faces that looked straight at you when you looked at it and all the while you were walking and turning your head to look at it it kept looking unblinkingly back at you ... Above the top of the poster were tall red letters: IF YOU BREAK THE LAW, YOU CAN'T WIN! (p.16)

In Foucault's terms this poster is both a punitive sign and a sentinel encouraging communal self-vigilance. Bigger's position beneath the gaze of this sentinel can be traced back to the surveillance tactics which were integral to plantation discipline. Slave management manuals insisted on constant monitoring: 'watch all their motions with a careful eye ... to save us from catastrophe which at all times threatens us'.[69] To enhance their visibility slaves, like prisoners, were limited in their choice of clothing. South Carolina, for example, passed statutes determining legitimate materials for 'negro apparel'. Drivers and overseers operated as the master's eyes in the field. Masters also encouraged slave children to spy on their parents, and domestic slaves to monitor field slaves in return for rewards. Douglass' *Narrative* documents the lengths to which Mr Covey and other overseers would go to maintain a constant disciplinary gaze: 'He appeared to us as being ever at hand. He was under every tree, behind every stump, in every bush, and at every window, on the plantation' (p.71). As Douglass discovers when attempting escape, the master's glare extended beyond the plantation: 'At every gate through which we were to pass, we saw a watchman – at every ferry a guard – on every bridge a sentinel – and in every wood a patrol' (p.95). That the Jehovan fantasies of white slaveocracy did not disappear with abolition is testified to by the surveillance technologies being deployed in inner cities around black neighbourhoods. Mike Davis reports that Ed Davis, former LAPD chief and then state senator, proposed the installation of a geo-synchronous satellite above the city, a high-tech overseer allowing a panoptic purity that Mr Covey could never have dreamt of.[70]

On the city streets, beyond the panoptic gaze of the state attorney, Bigger's sense of confinement is exacerbated by the sight of white people moving freely whilst he remains fixed in place:

Goddammit, look! We live here and they live there. We black and they white. They got things and we ain't. They do things and we can't. It's just like living in jail. Half the time I feel like I'm on the outside of the world peeping in through a knot-hole in the fence. (p.23)

At every turn in the prison city, Bigger's movements are restricted by fences, gates, walls, locked doors and windows, and the police. When he is captured and sent to prison Bigger does not experience a loss of liberty so much as an escalation in his sense of confinement. *Native Son* sustains the challenge made in the slave narrative to any straightforward opposition of freedom and bondage, and the carceral vision in *Native Son* grows more acute as Bigger's plight worsens. On the run from an 8,000-strong lynch mob, Bigger retreats to ever-smaller spaces, and the carceral net seems to extend beyond the city to nature itself:

His eyes jerked upward as a huge, sharp beam of light shot into the sky. Then another. Soon the sky was full of them. They circled slowly, hemming him in; bars in light forming a prison, a wall between him and the rest of the world; bars weaving a shifting wall of light into which he dared not go. (pp.241–2)

On arrival in his cell, this carceral cartography escalates to meta-physical proportions:

Standing trembling in his cell, he saw a dark vast fluid image rise and float; he saw a black sprawling prison full of tiny black cells in which people lived … no one could go from cell to cell and there were screams and curses and yells of suffering and nobody heard them, for the walls were thick and darkness was everywhere. Why were there so many cells in the world? (p.335)

Native Son concludes with Bigger in his cell awaiting execution, and in this respect Wright's description of him as a 'meaningful and prophetic symbol' is precise (p.vii). Bigger can be read as a forerunner of the massive lockdown of African-Americans in the post-war period. This process established momentum during the 1950s and '60s with the mass detention of black militants. In the slave narrative, punishment had been a catalyst to writing and political conscious-ness. In *Native Son*, Bigger's imprisonment similarly sparks new levels of articulation and awareness. This tradition is continued in the post-war proliferation of prison writings by African-Americans. Much of this writing hinges upon a sense of indistinct boundaries – specifically, that '[t]he prison is the street, the street is the prison'.[71] Or, as prison poet Etheridge Knight writes in 'The Warden Said to Me the Other Day':

> 'Say, etheridge,
> why come the black boys don't run off
> like the white boys do?'
> I lowered my jaw and scratched my head
> and said (innocently, I think), 'Well, suh,
> I ain't for sure, but I reckon it's 'cause
> we ain't got nowheres to run to.'[72]

One of the earliest contributions to this burgeoning genre was *The Autobiography of Malcolm X*. The *Autobiography* pinpoints imprisonment as Malcolm X's formative experience, a catalyst to his faith and the source of his political and historical recognition that 'America' was synonymous with 'prison'. The *Autobiography* cites systematic assaults on the bodies and identities of African-Americans on both sides of the prison walls during the early stages of the Cold War. Officials at this time were generally keen to empty their prisons of religious and political radicals because of the impact of their teachings on fellow inmates. However, from around the time of the Rosenberg executions to the early 1970s, there was a turnaround in strategy. Thousands of Muslims and black militants were targeted, and prison was used overtly as an instrument of political repression. Eldridge Cleaver explained how Malcolm X's 'merciless and damning indictment of prevailing penology' appealed to this generation of black political prisoners.[73] *Soul on Ice* confirmed and extended X's critique of prison as 'a continuation of slavery on a higher plane'.[74] For many African-Americans, 100 years after slavery, the Land of the Free was still the site of 'blood and guns and knives, whips, ropes and chains and trees, screams, night riders, fear, nightsticks, police dogs and firehoses, fire, wounds and bombs'.[75] Cleaver, like Bigger Thomas, was sentenced as an exemplary embodiment of the black rapist folk devil. Although he went on to repudiate this position, *Soul on Ice* outlines how, as an adolescent, Cleaver came to feel that rape could be an 'insurrectionary act'.[76] Seduced by the allegorical fertility of white racism, Cleaver came to view his victims as embodiments of a collective White Woman, an archetype who herself signified the punitive power of the dominant culture:

> You're my Moby-Dick,
> White Witch,
> Symbol of the rope and hanging tree,
> Of the burning cross.[77]

Cleaver, performing as the self-fulfilling prophecy of white racism and patriarchal misogyny, claimed to see white women as symbols of the violence inflicted upon the black body. *Soul on Ice* does not seek to excuse sexual assault, but it does explain how a young man, miming the myth of the black rapist, might articulate his aggression in terms of the punishment of punishment.

Alongside *Soul on Ice*, George Jackson's *Soledad Brother* continued the legacy of Malcolm X's *Autobiography* by insisting on a brutal lack of distinction between life inside and outside the corrections system:

> Black men born in the US and fortunate enough to live past the age of eighteen are conditioned to accept the inevitability of prison. For most of us, it simply looms as the next phase in a sequence of humiliations ... I was prepared for prison. It required only minor psychic adjustments.[78]

Jackson's critique offers incisive analogies between modern prison and the antebellum plantation. Within slavery the practice of punishment required that the slave perform the role of willing victim, both of day-to-day degradations (lack of liberty, food, clothing) and more direct forms of punitive oppression (whippings and beatings). Indeterminate sentencing made a similar performance imperative for the African-American prisoner. The official rationale behind indeterminate sentencing was the devolution of punitive authority from judges to the prison officials who could best assess the extent of a prisoner's rehabilitation. In practice, however, this became a powerful disciplinary tool that extended punishment indefinitely for prisoners unwilling to play the role of willing victim. George Jackson was given an indeterminate sentence (one year to life) for a robbery involving goods worth around $70. By the time of his murder, in 1971, he had spent over ten years in prison, and almost eight years in solitary confinement, for refusing to submit to the authority of his keepers:

> The attitude of the staff toward the convicts is both defensive and hostile. Until the convict gives in completely it will continue

to be so. By giving in, I mean prostrating oneself at their feet. Only then does their attitude alter itself to one of paternalistic condescension.[79]

Jackson highlights the psychological corrections required of the African-American prisoner, but also insists on the persistent physicality of their punishment. Thomas Cobb, an expert on the law of slavery in the antebellum South, advised that 'the slave can be reached only through his body'.[80] Contemporary US prison authorities appear to have heeded this advice. Whilst *Discipline and Punish* suggests that the modern prison has progressed from the body to the soul as the locus of its interest, *Soledad Brother* records more than a residual concern for the corporeal. On the plantation, one of the punishments felt most keenly was restrictions on food. Jackson similarly records the misery of the prison 'punishment diet': 'two small patties of food mixed together, like dog food'.[81] At the same time, guards are trained in a 'full range of anti-body tactics' to facilitate the routine beatings inflicted on non-compliant prisoners: 'starve his body, expose it to the elements, chain his body, jail it, club it, rip it, hang it, electrify it, and poison-gas it'.[82]

Soledad Brother concludes with Jackson's response to the death of his brother, who was shot whilst trying to free Angela Davis from a California courtroom. Davis' own writings in and on prison offer some of the most historically informed and critically adept critiques of the continuities between the plantation and America's burgeoning prison-industrial complex. Davis insisted that prison be seen as one part of a pervasive 'law enforcement–judicial–penal network' that punished African-Americans on the streets and in the courts before they were found guilty. Davis also accentuated the longevity of this network:

> Black people have become more thoroughly acquainted with America's jails and prisons than any other group of people in this country. Few of us indeed have been able to escape some form of contact – direct or indirect – with these institutions at some point in our lives … Historically the prison system has been an integral part of our lives. Black people emerged from slavery only to encounter the prison labour system.[83]

As Jacobs had helped to foreground the distinctive nature of the slave woman's experience, Davis drew attention to the particular sufferings of the black woman prisoner: 'sufficient attention has not been devoted to women in prison. I have often heard the rumour that as compared to men's prisons, women's institutions are humanely benign ... This is a myth which must be immediately smashed.'[84] In her autobiography, Assata Shakur offered assistance to Davis in demolishing this myth and echoed *Incidents in the Life of a Slave Girl* by documenting abuse, ritual infantilisation and the use of prisoners' children as a disciplinary tool against African-American mothers.[85]

Jackson, Davis and Shakur, as Marxists in the late 1960s and early '70s, were each convinced that they were witnessing the collapse of capitalism. As imperialist aggression was beaten back in South-East Asia and political radicalism swelled on the homefront, the explosion in the prison population, to the extent that sports stadia in some states were used as temporary detention centres, was seen as a symptom of the death throes of the dominant social structures: 'the entire apparatus of the *bourgeois democratic* state – especially its judicial system and its prisons – is disintegrating'.[86] In retrospect, given the rise and rise of the prison-industrial complex, these death throes now appear like the birth pangs of a devastatingly durable and massively extended political economy of punishment. African-Americans have borne the brunt of the post-Vietnam renaissance in Puritan punishment. Having all but disappeared by the 1960s, the chain gang has come back into fashion as one of the most potent symbols of this revival. Up until the late 1970s, the rise in the black prison population mirrored the overall rise in the prison population. However, since the first Reagan administration the rate of imprisonment for African-Americans has accelerated almost exponentially. By 1994, despite constituting only 12 per cent of the national population, there were more African-Americans than white Americans in prison. One in four black men aged between 20 and 29 was either in jail or on bail, probation or parole. The disproportionate number of African-Americans in prison reinforces racist assumptions about criminality and results in African-Americans being more likely to be arrested than white Americans. Once they are arrested they are less likely to receive bail, more likely to be indicted, less likely to have their case dismissed, more likely to be convicted, less likely to be given noncustodial sentences, more likely to serve the full term on their sentences, and consequently less likely to receive parole. The consequence of this vicious circle is a prison industry run almost exclusively by whites for ever-increasing numbers of African-Americans.

In part these statistics can be attributed to economic developments. The shrinkage of the manufacturing base within the American economy, the main source of labour for African-American males, has generated high levels of unemployment. Incarceration is an effective means of prohibiting this group from competing in the labour market. Concurrently, media mythology and political rhetoric have combined to manufacture hysteria around the subject of crime. Despite the fact that African-Americans are the main victims of crime, suburban white paranoia has been adroitly manipulated by images of habitual black criminality. Electioneering, news programmes and popular docu-soaps, such as *Cops*, *Emergency 911* and *LA Law*, have fabricated a regime of truth that compounds the key signifiers 'crime', 'black', 'urban' and 'crisis'. In a stunning inversion of progressive orthodoxies established in the 1960s, crime has been configured as a cause rather than a symptom of social collapse. Accordingly, the social programmes pioneered in the 1960s have been ditched in favour of an emphasis on punishment rather than prevention. Nancy Reagan, as she surveyed the aftermath of a SWAT raid on a rock house in a black neighbourhood in 1989, offered the following soundbite to the assembled media: 'These people in here are beyond the point of teaching and rehabilitating.'[87] This homily from the First Lady articulated the sensibility behind her husband's relocation of state resources from welfare to warfare on assorted undesirables, at home and abroad.

The so-called 'war on drugs', pioneered by Reagan, has been central to the contemporary renaissance in Puritan punishment. The toughening-up of sentencing policy for drug-related offences has been the primary cause of escalating rates of incarceration. In 1980, 27 per cent of the federal prison population were drug offenders. By 1990 this figure had risen to 47 per cent. The illicit drug industry and law enforcement have been locked in gainful dependency. Increased enforcement produces increased profit margins, which in turn feeds the prison industry and legitimates increased resources for enforcement. In the process it has proved difficult to distinguish between the war on drugs and a new witch-hunt targeted at the African-American community. Between 1986 and 1991 there was a 447-per-cent increase in the number of African-Americans imprisoned for drug-related offences. Studies have shown repeatedly that African-Americans are more likely to be charged and more likely to receive long sentences for narcotics offences. Urban black youths get substantially longer terms for smoking cheap crack cocaine than do white suburbanites for snorting the more expensive powdered variety.

> Under new federal statutes, defendants convicted of selling 5 grams or more of crack cocaine, worth perhaps $125, receive a mandatory minimum of five years in prison. However, it takes 500 grams of the powdered drug, nearly $50,000 worth of 'yuppie cocaine', to receive an equivalent sentence.[88]

The war on drugs is a highly selective and covertly racialised campaign. Given the hegemony of the prison-industrial complex, this war seems destined, like the permanent arms economy, to be perpetual. The contemporary dependency on prison in the US as the solution to social problems parallels the nineteenth-century dependency on slavery in the South. There is, however, a crucial distinction to be made here: the new slave ship is unopposed by any large-scale abolitionist effort. This is not to suggest that local endeavours are not being made. One of the most prodigious efforts in this respect has been made from the inside by Mumia Abu-Jamal, housed since 1983 on death row. Jamal's own case highlights the continuing use of punishment as a tool of political repression. Jamal was a Black Panther who moved into political journalism and became known in his native Philadelphia as 'the voice of the voiceless'. On December 9, 1981 he witnessed his brother being beaten by Daniel Faulkner, a police officer. In the struggle that ensued Faulkner was shot and killed and Abu-Jamal was also wounded. Despite the fact that several eyewitnesses claimed to have seen another man shoot Officer Faulkner and then flee the scene, Abu-Jamal was sentenced to death row. During the trial repeated references were made to Abu-Jamal's political affiliations, he was prohibited in his choice of counsel and was banned from the courtroom for lengthy periods. Subsequent investigation has cast major doubts on police evidence and witnesses. Abu-Jamal has since spent over 20 years on death row. Like many before him, he has used his confinement as an opportunity both to detail his personal experience of punishment and to denounce the larger punitive systems that operate on the African-American community.

In *Live from Death Row*, Abu-Jamal documents daily life in Pennsylvania's 'dead zone', where 60 per cent of those held are black. Death row represents a prison inside prison, and these concentric circles of confinement continue to spiral inwards, as Jamal spends most of his time under the stricter regime of DC (disciplinary custody) rather than AC (administrative custody). In a manner reminiscent of *Incidents in the Life of a Slave Girl*, *Live from Death Row* offers meticulous attention to the material conditions of African-American incarceration. Each day Abu-Jamal spends an average of 23 hours in a six-foot-by-ten cell with 'shatterproof glass, steel trim, and wire mesh'.[89] The privilege of being transferred outside involves relocation to the 'dog pen', 'a chain-linked fenced box, ringed by concertina razor wire, under the gaze of gun turrets' (p.6). Abu-Jamal recognises that privileges such as the dog pen, television, prison jobs and visits are designed to control inmate behaviour in much the same way that Frederick Douglass criticised the 'free time' allowed to slaves by their masters as a pacifying ruse. Alongside the manipulation of privileges, Jamal details the deployment of solitary confinement, around-the-clock lock-ins, beatings, harassment and the increasing use of drugs to tranquillise a prison population largely held on drug-related convictions. More potent than any of these disciplinary devices, however, is the waiting: 'the most profound horror of prisons lives in the day-to-day, banal occurrences that turn days into months, and months into years, and years into decades' (p.53). For those in the dead zone execution is a *fait accompli*, since prison life is structured around a systematic reduction of liberties which makes it, effectively, a taster of death.

Abu-Jamal's account of his personal experience on death row is integrated with a structural critique of contemporary punishment practice: 'We are in the midst of the Marionisation of US prisons, where the barest illusion of human rehabilitation is stripped from the mission, to be replaced by dehumanisation by design' (pp.73–4). Marion Federal penitentiary was a prototype for the SuperMax facilities (sometimes called SMUs, special management units, or RHUs, restricted housing units) that first evolved in Reagan's America. Almost all states now possess a SuperMax designed to hold their worst offenders within a regime based on permanent lockdown. In Pennsylvania's SuperMax, SCI Greene, Abu-Jamal undergoes solitary confinement for 24 hours a day, two days a week, and 23 hours a day for the remainder. This practice is almost identical to the regime developed and discredited as both inhumane and ineffective at Eastern Penitentiary over 150 years ago. Jamal makes it clear, however, that Marionisation has as much to do with economics as misplaced nostalgia. The Puritan revival has meant that in some states the costs of correction are now exceeding those for education. California leads the way in this shift of resources to punitive pedagogics, and can boast the largest prison-industrial complex in the western world – over 50 per cent bigger than the entire US federal system. Abu-Jamal notes that whilst 20 years of tough determinate sentencing (1973–93) in California had no significant impact upon crime rates, it did produce a 500 per cent increase in the prison population. This increase has been accelerated by the Clinton Crime Bill, which gave the appearance of responding to the manufactured hysteria surrounding crime, but also translated into a '\$30+ billion public employment program for predominantly white workers' (p.109):

> America enters the postindustrial age, when Japan produces the world's computer chips, Germany produces high performance autos; and America produces ... prisons. Prisons are where America's job programs, housing programs, and social control programs merge into a dark whole. (p.108)

According to John Edgar Wideman's Introduction, Abu-Jamal 'does not identify freedom with release from prison' (p.xxxii). In this respect he continues a tradition in African-American cartography of situating prison walls at the nation's borders. In the neoslave narratives of prison authors, as in the historical slave narrative, the black body can be subjected to discipline irrespective of location. The assault that led to Abu-Jamal's death sentence was not exceptional. *Live from Death Row* appeared a few years after the punishment beating of Rodney King. During coverage of the King trial, *The Justice Files*, a network television show, reported that 79,000 cases of police brutality had been recorded between 1981 and 1991. It failed to note, however, that the majority of these incidents involved black victims and white officers and that many more instances go unrecorded. Robert Gooding-Williams has argued that the 'aura of the extraordinary' surrounding the King beating must be dispelled.[90] Instead, it ought to be read as one instance of a continuous historical practice involving 'local reiterations of a national social agenda'.[91] The punishment beating of Rodney King also needs to be read in relation to the long history of the operation of white punitive power on the black body.

King received 56 baton blows, several blasts from stun-guns and a number of kicks and shoves. His leg was broken, but most of the injuries centred on his head and included multiple skull fractures, a broken cheek bone and a shattered eye-socket, resulting in long-term facial paralysis. After detailed examination of the video footage, however, a jury was not convinced that they had witnessed cruel or unusual force. Instead, they sided with the defence team which saw the black body less as the victim of punitive violence than the source of potential danger. This tactic belongs to a long history in the US of condoning white violence as retaliatory punishment for the imagined excesses of the black body. Each frame of the 81-second Holliday video was deconstructed so that King's flinching, his hand movements to ward off baton blows, every clumsy effort to rise, could be read as a sign of imminent attack. Repeated references to the prisoner's 'cocked' leg and the 'trigger position' of his arm lent subliminal credence to the possibility of a concealed weapon. The arresting officers had made racist references to King's 'animal' behaviour, 'bearlike' groans and to 'gorillas in the mist'. The defence case relied on similar iconography to conjure images of the bestial Bad Nigger coiled to spring at the great white hunter. Utilising what Toni Morrison has termed 'American-Africanism', the defence team fuelled the negrophobic paranoia of the almost all-white jury from suburban Simi Valley and released the video evidence's allegorical potential.[92] The images no longer depicted Rodney King being beaten by officers Koon, Wind, Powell and Briseno. Instead, they signified crime versus law, urban chaos versus suburban stability. In his closing argument defence attorney Paul de Pasquale completed this adaptation by referring to 'the *likes* of Rodney King': '[The defendant] was part of the line between society and chaos … This is not some orgy of violence. This is careful police work.'[93] According to this interpretation 'society' was of course synonymous with Simi Valley and white suburban America, whilst 'chaos' signified South Central and the urban jungle seething with black criminality.

In her analysis of the jurors' identifications Judith Butler uncovers a need to be persuaded that the ring of white officers – armed with batons, surrounding a lone black man – were in fact potential victims of black violence. This need was met by exploiting their own, media-fuelled, sense of vulnerability to black aggression. However, as well as identifying with the thin blue line of defence, the jury was also encouraged, perversely, to identify with a whitewashed version of Rodney King:

the blows he suffers are taken to be the blows they *would* suffer if the police were not protecting them from him. Thus, the physical danger in which King is recorded is transferred to them; they identify with that vulnerability, but construe it as their own, the vulnerability of whiteness, thus refiguring him as the threat.[94]

Butler pursues a circular dynamic of projection/introjection here that is familiar to postcolonial critiques of the imperialist imagination. By making the black victim the source of the violence they receive, white violence and culpability are disavowed. This is the cover-up that allows the overseer, the lynch mob and the cop to punish with impunity. As Scarry has contended in her commentary on the self-delusion of power: '[power] covers itself. It bases itself in another's pain and prevents all recognition that there is "another" by looped circles that ensure its own solipsism.'[95]

The historical continuities suggested by the King case were staged by the Black Student Union, at Amherst College, a few days after the trial verdict. They hung '40 black and faceless effigies' around the campus.

Accompanying each of the effigies was a copy of at least one newspaper article (some of them dating from the 1880s) reporting an act of violence – in most cases a lynching – performed by white Americans on the bodies of black Americans.[96]

This act received very little coverage, in part because the media were currently fixated on 'rioting' in inner cities. The failure to punish the police officers for their punishment of King had spectacular consequences. These repercussions, with perverse irony, were read less as a response to the injustice of the verdict than as a confirmation of its efficacy. As the media focused almost exclusively on images of black violence against whites and property (despite the fact that only 36 per cent of those arrested in the subsequent riots were African-Americans), police killings became additional instances of justifiable force, rather than of summary execution. Fifty-two people were killed in the uprising, and 2,383 injured. Only 20 law-enforcement and fire personnel were included in the latter figure, whilst the majority of the murder victims were unarmed black and Latino 'looters'.

As well as a rebellion against the Simi Valley verdict, the LA uprising can also be read as a prison insurrection. The carceral city in *Native Son*, itself a descendant of the plantation prison, has been massively consolidated in the postmodern urban landscape. Mike Davis has argued that LA is a paradigm for contemporary American cities, and that one of its most conspicuous features is the shift towards a carceral configuration: '[L.A. displays] an unprecedented tendency to merge urban design, architecture and the police apparatus into a single, comprehensive security effort.'[97] The pleasure dome is also a prison city. Ignoring its high-tech trappings, the postmodern prison city is strongly reminiscent of the plantation prison, with the luxurious mansions of the white masters strictly segregated from the slave quarters. In the old South, slaves were routinely stopped, searched and questioned, and black youths are singled out for identical treatment in the postmodern city, spread-eagled against a patrol car or forced to 'kiss the sidewalk'. Quarantines and curfews are imposed in black districts, with juveniles required to carry passes and proof of residence once they stray from their neighbourhood. The postmodern prison city is warranted by hysterical reference to drugs and gang warfare that echo antebellum fantasies of slave insurrection. Davis notes that sections of downtown LA are in danger of becoming a 'vast penal colony'.[98] This trope is conspicuous in non-Anglo representations of LA, from Singleton's South Central in *Boyz'n'the Hood* to Staci Rodriguez's projects poetry ('penal colonies/ with WW III helicopters/ flying over them').[99]

Alongside the informal application of carceral design to the urban landscape, LA has also seen a massive extension in its formal penal apparatus. In excess of 50,000 prisoners are being held in federal and county correctional facilities within a three-mile radius of city hall. To meet the objections of commercial interests, prison architects are attempting to merge their buildings with the existing environment:

> If buildings and homes are becoming more prison- or fortress-like in exterior appearance, then prisons ironically are becoming architecturally naturalised as aesthetic objects ... As an office glut in most parts of the country reduces commissions for corporate highrises, celebrity architects are rushing to design jails, prisons, and police stations.[100]

Davis argues that the carceral archisemiotics of postmodern LA need to be traced back to the urban insurrections of the 1960s and the resultant anxieties of white planners. In a similar vein, in *Soul on Ice*, Cleaver connected the National Guard's crushing of the Watts rebellion with contemporary military offensives in South-East Asia. Cleaver classified punishment as a key tool in a campaign of endocolonialisation, and drew repeated analogies between the plight of non-whites in America and overseas:

> The techniques of the enforcers are many: firing squads, gas chambers, electric chairs, torture chambers, the garrotte, the guillotine, the tightening rope around your throat ... The police do on the domestic level what the armed forces do on the international level: protect the way of life of those in power. The police patrol the city, cordon off communities, blockade neighbourhoods, invade homes, search for that which is hidden. The armed forces patrol the world, invade countries and continents, cordon off nations, blockade islands and whole peoples; they will also overrun villages, neighbourhoods, enter homes, huts, caves, searching for that which is hidden. The policeman and the soldier ... will shoot you, beat your head and body with sticks and clubs, with rifle butts, run you through with bayonets, shoot holes in your flesh, kill you.[101]

Given the proximity between the 1992 urban uprisings and Desert Storm, Cleaver's analysis of the contiguities between the exercise of punitive power on non-white subjects at home and imperialist aggression overseas seems as prescient as it is persuasive.

WHITE PUNISHMENT, BLACK RESISTANCE

> What I do feel is the urge to resist, resist, and never stop resisting or even think of stopping my resistance until victory falls to me.
>
> *Soledad Brother*, George Jackson[102]

A failure to recognise the defiance with which discipline has been met risks reducing African-Americans to passive victims and mere metonyms for white punishment. Any survey of the punishment of African-Americans is entirely inadequate unless it includes the long and vibrant traditions of resistance. These traditions begin, as Walvin notes, with slavery: 'The history of slavery is the story of enslaved resistance as much as slave-owning domination.'[103] The counter-culture of resistance took a variety of forms, both individual and collective. The diversity of punishment practices evolved by the slaveholders was met by equally varied forms of opposition. This subversion stretches back beyond the middle passage with bloody battles to avoid kidnap, struggles on the slave coast and insurrections on slave ships. Upon arrival in the New World resistance sometimes generated mass uprisings. In 1712 an African corps planned to burn New York to the ground. Charles Deslondes led a revolt in Louisiana in 1811, Denmark Vessey planned to storm Charleston in 1822, and Nat Turner led a bloody rebellion in 1831. Even though mass uprisings were relatively rare, the plantocracy lived in constant fear of having their own violence visited upon them. George Cruickshank offered the following maxim in his *Comic Almanac*:

> The planter's dream doth plainly seem
> To point a moral deep:
> If you choose to whack a nigger's back,
> You should never go to sleep.[104]

The planter's dreams were nourished by confrontations with slaves in which punishment was often the catalyst. In his autobiography, Douglass defines his decision to resist punishment and fight with the overseer as 'the turning-point in my career as a slave. It rekindled the few expiring embers of freedom, and revived within me a sense of my own manhood ... You have seen how a man was made a slave; you shall see how a slave was made a man' (p.112). Since slavery relied on violence to deprive slaves like Douglass of a conventional masculine subjectivity, it was predictable that they might associate acts of violence with the recovery of their 'humanity'. Violent struggles against punishment prove pivotal in the male slave narrative, from Douglass and Equiano to Wells Brown, William Green, Samuel Hall, Solomon Northup and Jermain Loguen. In Jacobs' *Incidents* there are references to her brother, Benjamin, fighting with his master to avoid a flogging. However, in literature by African-American women the emphasis falls less on individual acts of physical retaliation than on non-violent forms of familial and communal defiance.

Given the extreme punishments meted out to slaves who raised their hands against masters, physical confrontations often led to escape attempts. Some slaves made getaways for good, whilst others were habitual fugitives who ran away for short periods. Fugitive flights to the North constitute one of the most daring and fabled forms of resistance practised by slaves. From 1732 to 1782, out of a population of around 40,000, local newspapers carried 5,600 advertisements for runaway slaves. This figure represents only recorded instances from limited archival resources, and it is worth noting that both slaves and masters often had vested interests in not advertising successful escapes. Flight was facilitated by a supportive network, dubbed the 'underground railroad' by disgruntled slaveowners, which provided food, shelter, money, changes of clothing and vital information about local terrain and white patrols. The successful escape by a lone fugitive is central to the mythology of slavery, but there were occasions on which larger numbers set out for freedom. Because of the difficulties associated with organising successful mass escapes, however, alternative strategies were sometimes preferred, such as the establishment of semi-permanent sanctuaries in the mountains or swamps. Occasionally these 'maroon' communities forged alliances with Native Americans and poor whites. Collectively, these 'outlyers' repelled invasions from surrounding white communities and often 'engaged in guerrilla-like activities, plundering and burning plantations, stealing stock, and attacking, robbing, and murdering whites'.[105]

Rebels, runaways and outlyers practised open rebellion, but there were stratagems by which many more slaves practised covert resistance on a daily basis. Those that would never consider raising their hands to a master became highly skilled at threatening his life and livelihood through alternative means: poisoning, arson, theft, the deliberate destruction of crops, livestock, farm buildings and equipment. Another form of property utilised in resistance was the slave's own body. Feigning illness was a means of disrupting work routines and protesting the conditions of punitive labour. A Virginia planter complained as follows: 'I find it impossible to make a negro do his work well. No orders can engage it, no encouragement persuade it, nor no punishment oblige it.'[106] Many slaves perfected the pose of the 'eye servant' to appear productive and submissive before the disciplinary gaze:

> You may call me Raggedy Pat
> 'Cause I wear this raggedy hat,
> And you may think I'm a workin'
> But I ain't.[107]

The plantation was a conflicted site, both prison and community. In this space punishments were inflicted daily, but vibrant cultural forms (religion, music, dance and folk tales) also appeared. The songs sung in the field offered symbolic resistance – mocking the master, anticipating vengeance – and could also serve pragmatic purposes by supplying information about secret meetings or imminent danger: 'Sister, carry de news on,/ Master's in de field.'[108]

Resistance to white punitive power since abolition has continued the combination of direct and indirect assaults alongside modes of symbolic defiance. The flight of fugitive slaves was replicated by large numbers of prisoners escaping from convict camps throughout the nineteenth and early twentieth centuries and by spectacular flights by political prisoners in the 1960s, such as Assata Shakur and Angela Davis.[109] Bruce Jackson has tracked direct links between African-American worksongs in Texas prisons and songs sung on Southern plantations in the antebellum period.[110] In *Wake Up Dead Man* he notes that, as on the plantation, these songs served multiple functions: they constituted symbolic assaults on authority and offered protection against punishment, responding to guard movements and establishing a collective rhythm so that individuals could not be singled out for shirking.

Wright's *Uncle Tom's Children* chronicles an increasingly self-conscious resistance to punishment amongst the descendants of slavery. The collection begins with Big Boy's panicked flight from the lynch mob ('Big Boy Leaves Home'), but then progresses to Mann's self-defence ('Down by the Riverside'), Silas' outraged stand against injustice ('Bright and Morning Star'), Taylor's decision to march on City Hall in protest against a night of punishment beatings ('Fire and Cloud') and Sue's decision to shoot a white man and sacrifice herself in the interest of others ('Long Black Song'). *Uncle Tom's Children* progresses from the individual to the collective, from survival instinct to self-immolation, from protecting oneself from punishment to protecting one's family, community and comrades. The titular reference to Stowe suggests that the children of slavery are still in bondage, but the collection insists that they are no longer meekly willing to accept the master's lashes. Following the trajectory of *Uncle Tom's Children*, *Native Son* moves inexorably towards, without succumbing to, fatalism. For Bigger, punishment prefigures an awakening. As he confronts white punitive power in its most naked form, he achieves some degree of liberty – from fear – that was not possible outside his cell. Prison becomes a relative sanctuary and a space of knowledge, of self and society.

In this respect Bigger occupies a position in a long history of figures in African-American art and history who have subverted white punitive power *from the inside*. The extent to which prisons have been converted into counter-hegemonic spaces, the site of escape, fulfilment, education and resistance, is exceptional. At the forefront of this tradition is Harriet Jacobs. *Incidents* hinges upon a prison sequence that documents the bodily and psychological trauma of incarceration. However, Jacobs shows that even in prison she is not without resources. As Valerie Smith notes, the choice of the term 'loophole' for her retreat is apposite, since it denotes not only 'an avenue of escape', but also a gap in a fortress wall through which to fire at enemies.[111] From this vantage, Jacobs outwits her master by securing freedom for herself and her children. Self-incarceration also inverts the panoptic practices of slavery: the seen becomes unseen, not merely avoiding the disciplinary gaze but usurping optic power by monitoring her oppressor's movements and conversations.

A number of other slave narratives feature self-incarceration as a strategy for survival and escape. Both Henry Box Brown and Cato Beaufort secured passage to the free states by packing themselves in crates, whilst Robert the Hermit spent 14 years in a cave eluding his pursuers. In twentieth-century fiction, Baldwin's 'The Man Who Lived Underground' and Ellison's *Invisible Man* repeat this gesture of escaping into self-made prisons. In women's writing this conceit is articulated through a gothic suturing of tombs and wombs. The underground cell that holds Paul D in *Beloved* is both a coffin and the site of rebirth. The chain, the symbol of white punitive power that binds the convicts, becomes an umbilical cord, a lifeline that drags them up into the air as the flood waters break over the convict camp. In Jacobs' *Narrative*, the cell constricts but is also protective and productive. The loophole is a secure enclosure provided by her grandmother, and this retreat to a figurative womb robs slavery of its means of reproduction. Jacobs' loophole, like the garret occupied by her contemporary, Emily Dickinson, or the attic in Charlotte Perkins Gilman's 'The Yellow Wallpaper', is a conflicted site of confinement and creativity. The patriarchal prison, the (not-so-great) indoors to which many black and white women were confined, might be converted into spaces of maternal power through a recognition, in Dickinson's terms, that 'Captivity's consciousness, So's Liberty'.

African-American history repeatedly demonstrates that resistance is still possible when incarceration is enforced rather than self-imposed. Despite the aspirations of their guardians, neither the plantation nor the prison-industrial complex have functioned as total institutions. In fact, these punitive zones have often been the site of self-empowerment by their captives through political education and expression. The desire to silence African-Americans with the whip, the gun, the cell and the noose has been integral to the punishment practices of the dominant white culture. Slaves were kept in a state of enforced illiteracy, and strict penalties were imposed on those who assisted in their education; slaves were routinely flogged for talking back or out of turn; silence was sometimes coerced with the bit. Equiano reports that he was greeted upon his arrival at a Virginia plantation by the sight of 'a black woman slave ... cruelly loaded with various kinds of iron machines; she had one particularly on her head, which locked her mouth so fast that she could scarcely speak; and could not eat or drink'.[112] In *Beloved*, Paul D is similarly muzzled with 'neck jewellery' and Sethe's mother 'had the bit so many times she smiled. When she wasn't smiling she smiled' (pp.273, 203). Morrison recognises that the denial of literacy to slaves was mirrored by sadistic inscription on the slave's body. Sethe's back is written on as part of Schoolteacher's punitive pedagogics, and Sixo is given welts to drive home the lesson that 'definitions belonged to the definers – not the defined' (p.190). As Foucault remarks, feudal disciplinary practice demanded that semiotic sovereignty reside in the King. Only the King, or his representative, was entitled to right behaviour by writing on the body of the law-breaker. Slavery sustained this practice by leaving conspicuous signs of punitive violence on the bodies of African-Americans as testimony to transgression and its rewards.

The strict regulations governing communication in prison reflect the institutional legacy of the monastery, but also sustain the gagging of black voices. Communication amongst prisoners is permitted only at specified times and in specified spaces. Letters are censored and reading material closely monitored. At the same time, as on the plantation, education and expression have been possible. Malcolm X's act of copying out words from a dictionary whilst in prison itself copies Douglass' self-education in the *Narrative*. Literacy allowed Douglass to forge the pass that secured his liberty, and once Malcolm X discovers reading,

months passed without my even thinking about being imprisoned. In fact, up to then, I never had been so truly free in my life ... I don't think anybody ever got more out of going to prison than I did. In fact, prison enabled me to study far more intensively than

I would have if my life had gone differently and I had attended some college.[113]

Less sanguinely, Abu-Jamal notes that the prohibition on slave learning is being repeated in a prison-industrial complex where federal government is rolling back on education programmes whilst illiteracy rates amongst prisoners are soaring. *Live From Death Row* hints at the logic behind these developments when its author notes that he is denied access to a typewriter, since it is classified as a potentially dangerous weapon. Jean Genet confirmed this policy in his preface to *Soledad Brother*, a text which was confiscated as contraband throughout the Californian corrections system, and which illustrated that writing can be 'a weapon, a means of combat'.[114]

The letters written by Jackson during his seven years in solitary confinement, like those penned by Jacobs during her seven years of confinement, or Martin Luther King's 'Letter from Birmingham Jail', or Abu-Jamal's letters from death row, are inspired by the same refusal to be muzzled by white power. In both slave and prison narratives the act of writing itself becomes a potent means of resistance, a textual space in which to develop critiques of the dominant culture, which seeks to marginalise its author. White punitive power variously writes on black bodies, but African-Americans have always attempted to write back, to claim the right of self-authorship. In *Beloved* the defined offer their own definitions, reading the marks inscribed by Schoolteacher on Sethe's back as a 'choke-cherry tree', a 'pattern of roses and blood' and a 'wrought-iron maze'. The marks of the master can be at least partly erased; the master's tools used against him. Frederick Douglass pauses to inform his reader, in sexual symbols at least as extravagant as Morrison's, that the cracks in the soles of his feet are so wide he could place the pen with which he is composing his *Narrative* inside them.

Writing back against punishment has been central to a process of self-education. Slave and prison narratives often merge with the *bildungsroman* in their insistence that education, as Douglass wrote, might be 'the pathway from slavery to freedom' (p.85). The whip and the cell have always been deployed with pedagogical imperatives, but often the lesson that has been learnt is of resistance rather than rehabilitation. From Douglass' *Narrative* to X's *Autobiography*, *Soledad Brother* and *Soul on Ice*, imprisonment becomes an opportunity to unlearn the lessons taught by the dominant culture. Angela Davis recognised that prison life could encourage awareness

> of the specific oppressive structures of the penal system in their relation to the larger oppression of the social system ... Black revolutionaries do not drop from the moon ... We are being manufactured in droves in the ghetto streets, places like attica, san quentin, bedford hills, leavenworth, and sing sing. They are turning out thousands of us.[115]

Although the long history of the punishment of African-Americans problematises the periodisation of *Discipline and Punish*, it also verifies Foucault's maxim that there are no relations of power without relations of resistance. The record of oppression is scored by a communal chronicle of subversion and survival. The authors of this chronicle encourage their readers to see them not as exceptions whose situation necessitates empathy, but as representatives whose experiences require action. From death row Abu-Jamal reminds us that '[t]ools change with the times' (p.55). Although the plantation has given way to the SuperMax, the whip to the stun gun and the noose to the lethal injection, the prominence of punishment within the African-American experience remains alarmingly consistent. For African-Americans, from the middle passage to the new slave ship, social relations have always been underwritten by the pervasive threat of punitive violence. Only by recognising this long history and resisting its current practice can the binds that unite a divided nation be untied.

> It reminds me of two sets of handcuffs that have all four of us tied up together, holding all black and white flesh in a certain mould.[116]

5
The Whip, the Noose, the Cell and their Lover: Melville and Masochism

Gabriel Prosser, a 28-year-old slave, was one of the first and most infamous inmates at Virginia's state penitentiary in Richmond. Imprisoned in 1800 for plotting to organise a mass slave insurrection, Prosser and his co-conspirators were subjected to several weeks of intimidation and questioning, but managed to maintain a stoic silence throughout. After a prison visit to Prosser, James Monroe wrote to Thomas Jefferson that the slaves had 'exhibited a spirit, which, if it becomes general, must deluge the Southern country in blood ... They manifested a sense of their rights, and contempt of danger, and a thirst for revenge which portend the most unhappy consequences.'[1] Following their unsuccessful interrogation, Prosser and 34 of his followers were executed. Just over a decade later, in Louisiana in 1811, Charles Deslondes led a revolt that killed two white southerners and razed several plantations to the ground. Marching along the Mississippi river, their ranks swelled to over 500. Following a bloody battle with US troops, Deslondes and 15 of his closest supporters were publicly executed in New Orleans: 'their heads were placed on poles on roads leading from the city'.[2] An identical punishment was inflicted on 15 rebels in the wake of the slave revolt led by Nat Turner in 1831: the victims' heads were skewered and posted at a highway intersection in Jerusalem, Virginia, which was subsequently dubbed 'Blackhead signpost'.

In the decade before Monroe's prophecy of the Southern country deluged in blood was fully realised in civil war, Herman Melville wrote *Benito Cereno*, his tale of slave insurrection. It takes place in 1799, the year before Prosser's arrest, and although set at sea *Benito Cereno* includes resounding echoes of the land-locked uprisings in Virginia and Louisiana: thwarted rebellion, bloody vengeance, execution and, most loud of all, the silence:

Seeing all was over, [Babo] uttered no sound, and could not be forced to. His aspect seemed to say, since I cannot do deeds, I will not speak words ... Some months after, dragged to the gibbet at the tail of a mule, the black met his voiceless end. The body was burned to ashes; but for many days, the head, that hive of subtlety, fixed on a pole in the Plaza, met, unabashed, the gaze of the whites.[3]

This is one of the most striking images in the long history of Melville's intimacy with the art of punishment. Melville's family tree, like that of his friend, Nathaniel Hawthorne, included involvement with criminal justice: several of his relatives and ancestors were prisonkeepers, lawyers and judges. Melville's relation to punishment, however, represented a marked departure from the family tradition. He developed an acquaintance with naval discipline during his time on the South Seas, was imprisoned on Tahiti in 1842 for his involvement in a mutiny, and ironed on a French ship. When he retired as a sailor he continued this association with punishment in his writing. Prison episodes feature explicitly from the early romances, such as *Typee* and *Omoo*, to later works such *Pierre*; while the experience of incarceration is central to short stories such as 'Bartleby, the Scrivener' and 'The Two Towers', flogging features prominently in *White-Jacket* and *Redburn* and, following *Benito Cereno*, hanging figures in *Battle Pieces* and is the centrepiece of Melville's final work, *Billy Budd*. In his representation of punishment the occasional custom house officer (another trait shared with Hawthorne) seems to be compiling a counter-hegemonic inventory of the tools of discipline in nineteenth-century America: the whip, the rope and the cell. However, alongside the forceful moral and political critiques that Melville offers, one can also detect traces of an amatory attraction. Deviance can mask a desire for discipline, and in the elaborately foregrounded theatricality of Melville's fiction one can trace the outlines of an S&M masquerade. As with *The Scarlet Letter*, the crossings of discipline and desire within Melville's work have rarely been the subject of critical interrogation, except in forms that tend to abstract the punitive from contemporary historical developments. This chapter will aim to return Melville's representation of punishment to its cultural and historical contexts, with detailed attention to the entanglements of ethics, erotics and power in *White-Jacket*, *Benito Cereno*, 'Bartleby, the Scrivener' and *Billy Budd*.

WHITE-JACKET AND THE NECESSITY OF DISCIPLINE

What we Americans stand in need of is a daily whipping like a naughty boy.

Franci Lieber[4]

'[T]hough the subject of punishment in the Navy ... is every way a most unpleasant and grievous one to enlarge upon ... a feeling of duty compels me.'[5] Given the amount of time devoted to this distasteful topic in White-Jacket, Melville's sense of duty must have been admirably fervent. This semi-autobiographical account, of the 14 months he spent as a common seaman on the frigate United States, travels widely, but returns regularly to the subject of punishment. White-Jacket charts the full range of martial corrections, from 'holy-stoning' (being forced to wash the decks without shoes in freezing weather) to the yard-arm, from a gentle tap with a colt to a hundred lashes with a cat-o'-nine-tails. This last practice, known as 'flogging through the fleet', involves transporting the offender to several ships to secure the maximum number of spectators. Naval discipline, as well as being an extravagantly public affair, was also highly publicised. Each month the captain's clerk stood at the mainmast and recited the articles of war. White-Jacket recalls listening in terror as each transgression of authority appeared to be greeted with the mantra: 'Shall suffer death!' (p.296). Even more terrifying is the phrase 'Shall suffer death, or such punishment as a court martial shall adjudge':

> ... tell us, hangman, what punishment is this, horribly hinted at as being worse than death? ... is it to be imprisoned in a cell, with its walls papered from floor to ceiling with printed copies, in italics, of these Articles of War? (p.296)

The audience for these highly publicised punishments is convinced of the immanence of authority's judgement. White-Jacket and his fellows feel 'liable at any time to be run up at the yard-arm, with a necklace, made by no jeweller, round my neck!' (p.298). This anxiety is exacerbated by the extent of the disciplinary presence on-board. Whilst, in theory, only the captain can order punishment, in practice the process can be initiated by a number of figures in a punitive hierarchy. The seaman faces the threat of discipline from lieutenants, midshipmen, the master-at-arms who is a 'very Vidocq in vigilance', his assistants and informers, and the marines who are 'what turnkeys are to jails … their muskets are their keys' (pp.28, 377). Each level in this hierarchy disciplines the lower whilst themselves living with the constant threat of being disciplined from above: 'It is as if with one hand a schoolboy snapped his fingers at a dog, and at the same time received upon the other the discipline of the usher's ferule' (p.223). White-Jacket notes with bemused irony that, despite the severity of punishment and the prevalence of those who administer it, a typical man-of-war exists in a state of constant criminality. In anticipation of Foucault, Melville disregards ruling definitions of punishment as an instrument of crime prevention to highlight the use of discipline to manufacture certain forms of manageable criminality. The clamp-down on drinking, gambling, cards and other minor social ills both enhances the allure and covert organisation of these activities and channels potentially radical energies away from more overtly mutinous challenges to authority. White-Jacket recognises that punishment in the navy does not exist 'to convert Sin to Virtue, but to divide them, and protect Virtue and legalised Sin from unlegalised Vice' (p.250).

Although, in this respect, White-Jacket's understanding of the crime and punishment dialectic anticipates *Discipline and Punish*, the centrepiece to Melville's critique of naval discipline questions Foucault's genealogy. In place of a transition from 'classical' to 'modern' regimes, *White-Jacket* foregrounds the tenacity of torture. The labyrinth of locked rooms below deck on the *Neversink* is compared to 'the dungeons and cells of the Inquisition' (p.129). The surgeon's quarters seem to be the inner sanctum of these vaults, replete with a skeleton suspended from the ceiling, an array of 'glittering knives and saws' and a doctor 'tenderly feeling the edge of his knife' (pp.262, 259). However, alongside these tropes, White-Jacket also repeats the homology of ship and prison. The *Neversink* is described as 'a sort of state prison afloat', a 'sort of sea-Newgate' (pp.177–8). Both sailor and prisoner serve a sentence during which they must wake and sleep at specified times, are told what to wear (the sailor's uniform is 'aptly manufactured for him in a state prison ashore'), have an armed sentry monitoring their movements, face the difficulty of killing time, and are subject to summary punishment by their respective authorities (p.380). On the *Neversink* the first lieutenant is called Bridewell, and the master-of-arms' right-hand man served as a turnkey in the New York Tombs. Sailors, 'all under lock and key; all hopeless prisoners', have even less chance of escape than their land-locked counterparts, because 'the landless horizon hoops you in' (pp.175, 299). *White-Jacket* makes general analogies with prison, and also draws connections with the specific form of incarceration practised on Southern plantations. Life under the Articles of War is intolerable because it converts 'into slaves some of the citizens of a nation of free men' (p.145). The ship, with its isolation ('it is a state in itself'), constant surveillance, semi-feudal social organisation and draconian punishments, is refigured as plantation-prison (p.23). Lieutenants and midshipmen, like drivers, order sailors 'to and fro like a slave', whilst the captain is 'lord and master of the sun' (pp.23–4). This correspondence converges on slavery's key symbol. The critique of naval punishment in *White-Jacket*, offered by the ex-sailor who was forced to witness 163 floggings in just under a year on the *United States*, centres on the use of the whip. Michael Rogin explains how, in this respect, Melville's images intersect with a campaign during the 1840s to abolish flogging in the navy.

> Antislavery forces led the campaign against naval flogging; slave-state congressmen opposed them ... The whip, emblem of chattel slavery, symbolised shipboard authority for Melville. The 'sea-lords' were, like plantation owners in popular discourse, 'lords of the lash' ... Indeed, there is more whipping on an American ship, complains Redburn, than on a Southern plantation.[6]

White-Jacket, as a neoslave narrative, includes pivotal flogging scenes. In the first episode a group of sailors are punished for fighting; in the second the narrator himself narrowly misses being 'degraded at the gangway' (p.139). Melville uses the opportunity of the group flogging to explore different responses to the lash. One of the victims receives his dozen silently and then boasts about its ineffectuality, one curses authority throughout, and the third remains stoically silent. In anticipation of *Billy Budd*, the climax to this scene is the flogging of Peter, 'a handsome lad about nineteen years old ... a great favourite in his part of the ship' (p.137). Melville highlights how ceremonial precision is designed to detract from the essential barbarism of this ritual, and the sub-text of slavery surfaces in references to Peter's complexion: 'The day before his cheek had worn its usual red, but now no ghost was whiter ... As he was being secured to the gratings ... the shudderings and creepings of his dazzlingly white back were revealed' (p.139). White-Jacket's response when he is confronted by the whip, his hysterical fantasies of suicide and murder, similarly suggest cracks in racial and gender identity. Flogging forces the white male into subject positions normally associated with the African-American and the feminine. White-Jacket, however, is spared a ritual reminder that his naval father possesses the phallus by the intervention of his friend Jack Chase. Significantly, the captain at this point is reduced from a 'lord of the lash' to a 'slave to fate' (p.286). In a mirror image of the relation he enjoys to the crew, the captain's temporary diminution of authority symbolically places him in bondage to a higher authority. A sequence that is prefaced by the flogging of two black sailors thus concludes with a fleeting but significant slippage between master and servant. This transposition becomes increasingly conspicuous in Melville's subsequent writing.

White-Jacket chooses not to pursue this inversion, but his meticulous consideration of the tools of discipline, alongside images of medieval torture, prisons and plantations, compose a forceful aquarelle of the ship as a punitive apparatus: 'The whole body of this discipline is emphatically a system of cruel cogs and wheels, systematically grinding up in one common hopper all that might minister to the moral well-being of the crew' (p.378). In a foreshadowing of the carceral vision that emerges in his later works, Melville intimates that the cruel disciplinary machine on the *Neversink* may be a microcosm, an 'index to the true condition of the present civilization of the world' (p.297). The ship 'is but this old-fashioned world of ours afloat, full of all manner of characters – full of strange contradictions' (p.395). However, strange contradictions, which jeopardise this censure of a prison society, are also apparent throughout *White-Jacket*. The source of these contradictions is intimated early on by a phrase that is central to the text's engagement with punishment: 'the necessity of ... discipline' (p.7). *White-Jacket* has routinely been described as a critique of naval discipline, despite the fact that it often resembles an apology for it. Melville regrets some of its excesses, but still recognises the exigency of a tough disciplinary regime: 'Certainly the necessities of navies warrant a code for its government more stringent than the law that governs the land' (p.145). Significantly, during the scene in which White-Jacket is about to be flogged for not knowing his place on the ship, he blames his situation not on a surfeit of discipline but its desideratum: 'such was the state of discipline ... that very few of the seamen could tell where their proper stations were' (p.282). In a similar vein, White-Jacket notes that although the strict prohibition against lying on the deck at night 'caused much growling, it was far better for our health to be thus kept on our feet' (p.123). Not only is discipline necessary, it can be good for your health.

The reading of *White-Jacket* as a critique of naval punishment requires refinement. Melville expresses reservations about specific punishment practices, but at no point does he challenge the principle of discipline per se. *White-Jacket* aims for an alternative administration of discipline rather than its abolition. Doctorow's Daniel noted, with regard to improvements in penal process, that '[r]eform is complicity'.[7] Amelioration can be an effective tool for sustaining oppressive regimes through the diffusion of oppositional impulses. This tactic seems to be working well in *White-Jacket* since there are almost no instances of resistance against the powers that punish. Rebellion on the *Neversink* is limited to a refusal by the crew to shave off their beards. This insurgence is short-lived, and the narrative concludes with an injunction 'never [to] train our murderous guns inboard; let us not mutiny with bloody pikes in our hands' (p.404).

The strange contradictions produced by Melville's insistence on the necessity of succumbing to discipline are fused with his feelings towards those who administer and receive punishment. 'Were it not for these regulations a man-of-war's crew would be nothing but a mob, more ungovernable stripping the canvass in a gale than Lord George Gordon's tearing down the lofty house of Lord Mansfield' (p.7). Melville's mixed class ancestry can be unearthed beneath this analogy. The Melville-de Gansevoort's had aristocratic affiliations until Melville's father's bankruptcy and death entailed a rapid decline in social standing. Melville's movement along the class spectrum produces ambivalent responses towards both the common seamen, known as 'the people', and the 'sea-kings and sea-lords' (p.29). In amongst democratic expressions of sympathy for the masses there are flashes of anxiety about the mob which seem to justify a strict disciplinary regime. When this regime is removed, during shore leave, it results in an orgy of violence and self-destruction: 'Such are the lamentable effects of suddenly and completely releasing *the people* of a man-of-war from arbitrary discipline. It shows that, to such, "liberty", at first, must be administered in small and moderate quantities' (p.231). However, when a small and moderate quantity of liberty is permitted on the *Neversink*, during a period of prolonged cold weather, '*the people*' seem ill-equipped to cope: 'It was a Babel here, a Bedlam there, and a Pandemonium everywhere ... Gangs of men, in all sorts of outlandish habiliments, wild as those worn at some crazy carnival, rushed to and fro, seizing upon whomsoever they pleased' (p.104).

An earlier instance of this 'crazy carnival' occurs during a dramatic production for the crew's entertainment. The enjoyment is so intense that 'all discipline seemed gone forever', and White-Jacket concludes that 'this now is as it should be. It is good to shake off, now and then, this iron yoke around our necks' (p.98). The slave imagery here seems to reproach naval discipline unequivocally, but at exactly the moment when the frivolities reach their peak, with officers and crew mixing as equals, a tempest appears that 'terminated that day's theatricals' (p.97). The crew are so enthralled in the entertainment that they fail to respond quickly and the ship is imperilled: 'There is no knowing what would have ensued, had not the bass drum suddenly been heard, calling all hands to quarters, a summons not to be withstood' (p.97). The timing of this tempest seems a little fortuitous, as though nature itself were conspiring to insist on the necessity of discipline. The muted Calvinism in *White-Jacket*, hinted at by occasional references to the 'predestined necessities of things', offers ideological support to this edict (pp.251, 264). In this respect, *White-Jacket* might be compared to *The Scarlet Letter*, written by Melville's close friend in the same year. Roger Chillingworth propounds an identical Calvinist legitimation for discipline, when he insists that 'it has all been a dark necessity'.[8] (p.146). Both texts seem structured around an opposition between the dangers of freedom and the necessities of cruel discipline, between the crazy carnival and the law. Published in the same year as the Compromise designed to prevent the civil unrest provoked by slavery, Hawthorne's and Melville's works may be seen to express contemporary anxieties within the dominant culture, and justify an extension of punitive power.

Melville's insistence upon the necessity of discipline is driven partly by a fear of disorder amongst the people, but it is also partly attributable to a respect for their rulers, such as Captain Claret, who is 'the father of his crew' (p.92). A range of power relations in mid-nineteenth-century America – including those between captain and crew, slave and master, employer and worker, warden and prisoner – sought ideological sanction by association with the cult of domesticity. The self-image of the military, the plantation, the factory and the penitentiary was traced through an oedipal stencil. To resist any figure of authority was, therefore, to challenge the natural prerogative of the patriarch. Since it is the Father who implements the punishments to which White-Jacket objects, one would expect a hostile response to this figure. Melville, however, appears keen to offer excuses and commendations for the 'indulgent father of the crew' (p.280). Although the captain is envisaged with 'the Articles of War in one hand, and the cat-o'-nine tails in the other', the severity of this image clashes with the benevolence Claret displays elsewhere (p.304). In both minor and major issues of discipline the captain appears 'unusually lenient': against naval regulations he permits theatricals, checkers, and generous shore leave, and even forgives major breaches of discipline such as Jack Chase's desertion (p.308). When the father figure behaves less leniently, White-Jacket emphasises the loneliness and responsibility of positions of authority and insists that the system is more culpable than the individuals whose actions perpetuate it: 'It is not that the officers are so malevolent ... Some of these evils are unavoidably generated through the operation of the naval code' (p.379).

The suppressed admiration that White-Jacket feels towards the captain flowers fully into love in his relationship with Jack Chase. White-Jacket's immediate superior is worshipped not despite but because he is an authoritarian father figure: 'a little bit of a dictator ... a bit of a tyrant ... the sailors loved him all round' (p.35). Melville's homage to the strict father is part of the homoeroticism of *White-Jacket*. The narrative's most poignant moments involve the romance of male bonding: 'by night we became more romantically inclined', listening to the 'ever-noble Jack Chase, matchless and unmatchable Jack Chase' reciting from *The Luciads* (pp.402, 313). These expressions of homosocial desire are accompanied by conventional homophobic strictures against those 'sea-dandies' and 'rose-water sailors' who fail to match Jack Chase's masculine ideal. White-Jacket moves seamlessly from loving descriptions of his hero's physique, 'his muscles and tendons are all set true, trim, and taut', to barely coded outrage at 'evils, so direful that they will hardly bear even so much as an allusion ... The sins for which the cities of the plain were overthrown still linger in some of these wooden-walled Gomorrahs of the deep' (pp.35, 379). The strident moral tones employed to denounce degenerate pleasures repeat those used to castigate flogging. Both acts transgress 'the essential dignity of man ... in a word we denounce it as religiously, morally, and immutably *wrong*' (p.148). Such strident outbursts, however, appear somewhat compensatory for the strange contradictions that surface throughout *White-Jacket*. Homosexual desire is forbidden, but in the 'fragrant night' the narrator kisses 'that noble hand of my liege lord and captain of my top, my sea-tutor and sire' (p.400). Flogging is unequivocally wrong, but any man that disagrees ought to be 'scourged at the gangway till he recanted!' (p.148). This latter inconsistency might be read as a rhetorical simulation of emotion overtaking logic, but it is also indicative of the aporia within White-Jacket's critique of punishment. In places, strange contradictions even threaten to blossom into full-blown moral and erotic relativism:

> We perceived how that evil was but good disguised, and a knave a saint in his way; how that in other planets, perhaps, what we deem wrong, may there be deemed right ... it was only our mis-apprehension of these things that made us take them for woeful pains instead of the most agreeable pleasures. I have dreamed of a sphere, says Pinzella, where to break a man on the wheel is held the most exquisite of delights you can confer upon him. (pp.188–9)

As Tony Tanner suggests, the 'treatment of flogging in White-Jacket is not quite as uncomplicated a matter as might first appear'.[9] Rogin pursues these complications from the public to the private sphere: 'Flogging was not just a political issue for White-Jacket. The whip exercised over him hypnotic, aversive, personal fascination, as it did for some abolitionists.'[10] When White-Jacket is compelled to attend a flogging he insists fervently on a lack of agency: 'the strong arm that drags him in view of the scourge, and holds him there till it is over; forcing upon his loathing eye and soul the sufferings and groans' (p.135). Despite his desire to distance himself from the enthusiasm of some of his peers, those who are 'eager to obtain a good place on the booms, to overlook the scene', White-Jacket still confesses that the 'summons to witness punishment carries a thrill' (p.136). This sensation recalls White-Jacket's response whilst witnessing Jack Chase's chastisement of a young sailor: 'it made me shake all over' (p.16). Rogin argues that responses to the whip, at sea and on the plantation, awaken 'the erotic sadomasochism of a child being beaten ... the internalised meanings of flogging, the regression to childhood it might stimulate in wielders, victims, and observers alike'.[11] White-Jacket's explanation for the enthusiasm with which young midshipmen take up the whip similarly hinges on the concept of regression: 'It would almost seem that they themselves, having so recently escaped the posterior discipline of the nursery and the infant school, are impatient to recover from those smarting reminiscences by mincing the backs of full-grown American freemen' (p.222). Melville merely gestures towards those formative experiences that might produce deviant desires, and his cure for sadism and the attendant 'thrills' of voyeurism unintentionally recalls the 'posterior discipline of the nursery' in its blasé recourse to Christian masochism: 'turn the left cheek if the right be smitten' (p.325).

White-Jacket has been celebrated as the novel that brought about the abolition of flogging in the American navy. At the time of its publication, however, this practice was already on the verge of extinction. Tanner notes this fact and goes on to remark that, in comparison with contemporary anti-flogging tracts such as Dana's *Two Years Before the Mast*, there is remarkably little graphic depiction of this punishment in Melville's work. The narrator manages to elude the whipping-post, and in place of first-hand experience offers rather dry rhetorical denouncements. One might detect a strategy of evasion here, an effort to suppress the unstable erotic economies of punishment. *White-Jacket* may intend to oppose the whip, but there are also, as Rogin contends, 'signs of a forbidden attraction to it, suggesting that at the same time it punished disobedience and desire, it was as well a sign of love. The whip established a connection to patriarchal authority.'[12] *White-Jacket's* ethical critique of punishment is undercut by a forbidden attraction to the father who wields the whip. Oedipal identification confuses the lines between 'woeful pains' and 'agreeable pleasures', between defiance and eroticised submission. This dynamic is similarly apparent in Melville's subsequent engagement with the subject of discipline.

BENITO CERENO AND THE PERFORMANCE OF PUNISHMENT

Everything that acts is a cruelty.

The Theatre of Cruelty, Antonin Artaud[13]

In *White-Jacket*, Melville condemns 'general quarters', the practice of mock battle, suggesting that 'there is always a vast difference – if you sound them – between a reality and a sham' (p.71). It has been proposed, however, that the battle he wages in this work is itself somewhat counterfeit. Melville's assault on flogging in the navy was offered on the eve of its abolition and displays ambivalence towards the enemy and his weapons. Revealingly, when the *Neversink* is engaged in a real battle, the conflict is described with theatrical metaphors. White-Jacket notes that the 'wardrobe' of the officers is markedly different, and the ship seems like 'an extensive mansion preparing for a grand entertainment' (p.71). The narrator also comments on the irony of celebrating the 4th of July with a dramatic production on the *Neversink*, since 'if ever there was a continual theatre in the world, playing by night and day, and without intervals between the acts, a man-of-war is that theatre, and her planks are the *boards* indeed' (p.93). Punishment on the *Neversink* is represented as part of a continual theatre. In *Benito Cereno* this conceit is taken further.

Delano's first impressions upon boarding the *San Dominick* are that the 'ship seems unreal; these strange costumes, gestures and faces, [are] but a shadowy tableau just emerged from the deep'.[14] The American captain is oblivious to the fact that a slave revolt has taken place, and he is being presented with an elaborate *mise-en-scène* of normality. Behind the stage-management is the meticulous and inventive direction of Babo, the leader of the insurrection. Babo feeds lines to the deposed Spanish captain, he chooses his costume, invents dramatic confrontations and takes his protégé to one side intermittently to insist on a more realistic performance. Babo also directs the performances of other major players (Atufal) and the chorus (a group of oakum-pickers), he co-ordinates the use of props (padlocks, keys, shaving implements) and makes crucial set adjustments (such as tying canvas over a figurehead that has been decorated with a skeleton). Despite the efforts of the director, however, his one-man audience has his suspension of disbelief repeatedly disturbed. Delano questions the *vraisemblance* of his counterpart: 'would a gentleman, nay, any honest boor, act the part now acted by his host? The man was an impostor' (p.29). Watching Babo shaving his master, Delano is once again struck by a vague sense that they are acting out

> some juggling play before him ... But then, what could be the object of enacting this play of the barber before him? At last, regarding the notion as a whimsy, insensibly suggested, perhaps, by the theatrical aspect of Don Benito in his harlequin ensign, Captain Delano speedily banished it. (p.61)

Delano continues to will his suspension of disbelief even when members of the ensemble, specifically the captive sailors, try to steal the show with significant glances and improvised dialogue, intended to arouse his suspicions.

The action on the boards of the *San Dominick* is thus presented as an elaborate masquerade. Since *Benito Cereno* offers an allegory of slavery, it invites a reading of stagecraft within the plantation economy. Against the slaveocracy's self-imaging as an institution based on organic relationships, with reciprocal domestic bonds binding white father and black children, Melville presents the plantation as the scene of artifice and role-play. Delano's periodic doubts about the scene before him coincide with disruptions in the performance when figures act out of character. When he raises his voice 'the blacks paused, just where they were, each negro and negress suspended his or her posture, exactly as the word found them – for a few seconds continuing so' (p.50). Conversely, Delano's sense of normality is often restored by theatrical gesture, as for example when a slave ushers him into lunch with 'continual smiles and bows' in an exaggerated display of servility (p.56). *Benito Cereno* presents deference not as the innate character trait of a subservient race, but as a dramaturgical device to evade the master's suspicions and punishment. Drama in *Benito Cereno* is provided by Delano seeing and then not seeing through the charade, but the political imperative is to suggest a theatricality attendant upon all power relations, to which the American captain remains consistently blind. Epistemological elisions in *Benito Cereno* go beyond simple inversion. In place of the conventional opposition of 'sham' and 'reality', Melville offers a far less stable understanding based on the performative nature of both individual and institutional identities.

Melville's drama of racial conflict in *Benito Cereno* opens with some extravagant displays of colour:

> Everything was mute and calm; everything grey. The sea, though undulated into long roods of swells, seemed fixed, and was sleeked at the surface like waved lead that has cooled and set in the smelter's mould. The sky seemed a grey mantle. Flights of troubled grey fowl, kith and kin with flights of troubled grey vapours among which they were mixed, skimmed low and fitfully over the waters, as swallows over meadows before storms. Shadows present, foreshadowing deeper shadows to come.
>
> To Captain Delano's surprise, the stranger, viewed through the glass, showed no colours. (p.3)

The American captain's problems begin with a colour blindness which prevents him from envisaging any blur in the spectrum between black and white. In the slave narrative, fugitives relied on this form of conditioned myopia amongst their pursuers when attempting to pass as white. In *Benito Cereno*, Babo, passing as a slave, both underlines the performative nature of race identity and uncovers the ideological lenses through which white Americans, such as Delano, saw the world. Any unsettling of the natural colour bar was seen as evidence of demoniacal forces. In New York, in 1741, mass executions were arranged following an alleged conspiracy to revolt by black slaves in coalition with white servants and sympathisers. Thirty-one slaves and four white co-conspirators were executed and their bodies left hanging as a warning against future insurrections. In his account of *The New York Conspiracy*, Horsmanden notes that the bodies of two of the victims became a cause for public concern, and confirmed the consensus opinion that natural order had been challenged. A black slave (Caesar) and white servant (John Hughson) seemed to undergo an abject metamorphosis that pronounced gothic judgement on passing:

> [Hughson's] face, hands, neck and feet were of a deep shining black ... and the hair of Hughson's beard and neck ... was curling like the wool of a negro's beard and head; and the features of his face were of the symmetry of a negro beauty; the nose broad and flat, the nostrils open and extended, the mouth wide, lips full and thick, his body swelled to gigantic size ... [his body] dripped and distilled ... from the great fermentation and abundance of matter within him ... [it] burst and discharged pail fulls of blood and corruption. [Caesar's] face was at the same time somewhat bleached or turned whitish, insomuch that it occasioned a remark, that Hughson and he had changed colours.[15]

Melville's allegory of changing colours in *Benito Cereno* confirms the assessment offered in African-American writing, that punishment is integral to slavery and the policing of racial boundaries. Tools of discipline are the text's central symbols: the rope, the chain, the lock and key, the blade, the gun and the gallows. As in *White-Jacket*, the ship is a prison: Babo is the warden, the oakum-pickers and hatchet-polishers are his jailers. The bell sounds repeatedly, 'as of the tolling for execution in some jail-yard', and also signals a figurative jail-break when Benito dives overboard (p.9). Since the *San Dominick* is an allegorical representation of the plantation, part of the function of this imagery is to highlight contiguities between the lives of prisoners and slaves. Most importantly, in this context, there is Babo's ploy of having Atufal present himself to Benito: 'The black mounted the steps of the poop, and, like a brave prisoner, brought up to receive sentence, stood in unquailing muteness before Don Benito ... "Say but the one word *pardon*, and your chains will be off"' (p.25). The emphasis here, as in the contemporary penitentiary regime, is not simply on enduring but on accepting one's punishment with an act of contrition. The fact that this is being stage-managed might suggest that the prison, like the plantation, was home to carefully choreographed movements, scripted speech and role-playing. The penitentiary, with its system of indeterminate sentencing, put the onus on the inmate to perform the role of model prisoner, in the same way that slaves were encouraged to avoid discipline by assuming the mask of a willing servant. Although he recognises key aspects of modern punishment, Foucault's insistence on the disappearance of drama underplays the theatricality that persists at every stage in the punitive process, from sentencing and induction to release.

Babo's elaborate mime of the plantation-prison suggests another aspect of punishment practice in antebellum America. Tolerance is preached above board on the *San Dominick* whilst, below deck, deadly discipline is administered. The dominant punishment system in the antebellum North still contained strong traces of residual practices. And of course, below the Mason-Dixon line, the semi-feudal tortures associated with slavery continued as the dominant disciplinary mode. Melville mirrors this structural overlay of modes of punishment in the spatial organisation of his ships. Medieval tortures await below deck on both the *Neversink* and the *San Dominick*. Benito's cuddy echoes the torture chambers of the Inquisition, furnished with missals and muskets, crucifixes and cutlasses:

> There were also two long, sharp-ribbed settees of malacca *cane*, black with age and uncomfortable to look at as inquisitors' racks, with a large, misshapen armchair, which, furnished with a rude barber's crutch at the back, working with a screw, seemed some grotesque, middle-age engine of torment. (p.55)

Melville's intention here is less to emphasise Babo's cruelty than to underline an observation offered in *White-Jacket*: 'Depravity in the oppressed is no apology for the oppressor; but rather an additional stigma to him, as being, in a large degree, the effect, and not the cause and justification of oppression' (p.144). For daring to usurp the power to punish, Babo is dragged to the gibbet, hanged and then beheaded, but his eyes continue to meet 'unabashed, the gaze of the whites' as a mirror of their own violence (p.105). This denouement counter-points two acts of terror. The state fixing Babo's head on a pole repeats the renegade slave's own fixing of his master's skeleton to the prow of the ship. Accordingly, the distance collapses between 'savage' acts and the legal murder practised by a 'civilised' state: '[Babo] had determined to kill his master, Don Alexandro Aranda ... to keep the seamen in subjection, he wanted to prepare a warning of what road they should be made to take did they or any of them oppose him' (pp.89–90). It is no surprise that Babo proves adept in the semiotactics of punishment, since he was subjected to them systematically as a slave. The execution is committed publicly and followed by a number of crew and passengers being 'thrown alive into the sea' (p.92). Rather than random instances of barbarism, Babo is performing acts carefully calculated to produce compliance, acts which repeat the African-American experience of punishment, of cautionary executions and the middle passage's massive loss of 'cargo'.

At one point in the proceedings Delano fears that the *San Dominick* might be a 'slumbering volcano' that could 'suddenly let loose energies now hid' (p.29). Punishment in *Benito Cereno*, as on the *Neversink*, appears partly fuelled by libidinal 'energies'. The boards of the *San Dominick* seem, at times, to be staging an elaborate S&M masquerade. Babo's sadism impersonates the institutional sadism practised upon him. Abolitionist rhetoric asserted that slavery encouraged sexual deviancy, and even Delano recognises that 'slavery breeds ugly passions in man' (p.63). Thomas Jefferson argued that part of slavery's danger was that it unleashed 'the most boisterous ... the worst of passions', characterised by 'odious peculiarities ... the most unremitting despotism on the one part, and degrading submissions on the other'.[16] Jefferson's rather decorous synonyms, like Melville's euphemistic 'energies' and 'ugly passions', hint at the sexual dynamics of bondage. Abolitionists argued forthrightly that flogging was a

a source of sadistic pleasure for the masters. They imaged an erotic South, in which masters were stimulated by their power over slave bodies. Masters, on this understanding, whipped the forbidden source of pleasure which their power made available to them. To abolish slavery or shipboard flogging would free the victims from erotically charged, punitive, hierarchical relations.[17]

Erotically charged, punitive relations are everywhere evident on the *San Dominick*, although hierarchies seem obscure. Babo cuts Benito whilst shaving him, and then pretends to be the victim of revenge by using the razor on himself. Following this incident, Delano, who is adept at seeing the truth accidentally, describes the dispute between master and servant as but 'a sort of love-quarrel, after all' (p.63). An earlier act in this performance involves a disciplinary game, involving Benito and Atufal, of master and slave. During this play, in which the slave must appear before his master and beg his pardon, Babo pays close attention to casting, gesture and costume. Atufal, a 'gigantic black', confronts the slight Spanish captain wearing an 'iron collar about his neck, from which depended a chain, thrice wound round his body; the terminating links padlocked together at a broad band of iron, his girdle' (p.25). Atufal wears the costume of the victim, ready to be chastised in chains, whilst knowing that he cannot be hurt in this game. The real victim is dressed as the master: 'suspended by a slender silken cord, from Don Benito's neck hung a key' (p.27). Delano, as witness to this scene, provides unintentionally ironic commentary: 'So, Don Benito – padlock and key – significant symbols, truly' (p.27). Benito is tortured by the hollow mimicry of authority he is compelled to perform, involving the display of symbols signifying a punitive power he no longer possesses.

If bondage has encouraged the servant's sadism, it seems also to have promoted a masochistic streak in the master. The 'morbidly sensitive Spaniard' displays a predisposition towards suffering that is exacerbated by his relationship with Babo (p.30). First encountered by Delano as he stands 'passively by', with his 'small, yellow hands', the feminised Benito seems 'flayed alive', wracked by neurosis and nervous tension: 'like some hypochondriac abbot he moved slowly about, at times suddenly pausing, starting, or staring, biting his lip, biting his finger-nail, flushing, paling, twitching his beard, with other symptoms of an absent or moody mind' (p.28). According to Freud, 'feminine masochism' can be driven by a guilty recognition of one's erotic investment in the punishment of others. Following the revolt on the *San Dominick*, Benito is compelled to recognise his complicity in the sufferings he has produced, and he succumbs to a masochistic death-wish: a self-imposed confinement in a monastery becomes a death sentence, and he follows his leader to the grave.

Rogin suggests that this gloom-laden conclusion drives home the 'deepest subject of Melville's tale', namely, the 'inability of its characters to break free'.[18] *White-Jacket* was informed by an opposition between bondage (the American navy) and freedom (the American home). This opposition has disappeared in *Benito Cereno*, leaving only a sense of inevitable incarceration. In *Benito Cereno* there seems to be no alternative to the double binds of performance and punishment, no exit from the theatre of cruelty. Following the rebellion Babo is free, but only to mimic his master's sadism. Once the rebellion is put down Benito is free, but only to die in guilt-ridden melancholy. On the eve of the Civil War, many abolitionists believed that slave insurrection would lead to liberty. Conversely, Melville saw only a mirror image of slavery rising in its place. The stern-piece on the *San Dominick* displays a 'dark satyr in a mask, holding his foot on the prostrate neck of a writhing figure, likewise masked' (p.46). *Benito Cereno* suggests that the boot cannot be abolished, it can only change feet. Master and servant, director and actor, father and son: each seems unable to escape these roles. *Benito Cereno*, like *White-Jacket*, offers 'strange contradictions' in its presentation of punishment. Melville recognises that individual and institutional roles are a masquerade, but seems unable to imagine a way out of those parts scripted by the dominant culture.

'BARTLEBY' AND THE CARCERAL SOCIETY

… the silence within these vast walls … is that of death … We felt as if we traversed catacombs; there were a thousand living beings, and yet it was a desert solitude.

On the Penitentiary System in the United States,
Alexis de Tocqueville and Gustave de Beaumont[19]

It is itself the executioner's weapon; it is the world, the wall, that executes.

The Body in Pain, Elaine Scarry[20]

'Bartleby, the Scrivener, A Story of Wall-Street', offers a change of location from *White-Jacket* and *Benito Cereno*, but Melville's frame of reference for the representation of space remains the same. The lawyer's chambers, like the *Neversink* and the *San Dominick*, are depicted as a cell:

At one end they looked upon the white wall of the interior of a spacious sky-light shaft, penetrating the building from top to

bottom ... the view from the other end ... commanded an unob-
structed view of a lofty brick wall, black by age and everlasting
shade ... pushed up to within ten feet of my window panes.[21]

This image of a carceral city is apposite given that New York, from the
late eighteenth century, was a centre for prison growth and reform.
Thomas Eddy had been instrumental in establishing America's second
penitentiary, Newgate, in Greenwich Village in 1796, and the Auburn
penitentiary, built in 1817, became a paradigm for contemporary
prison design. The New York State prison, completed in 1799, was the
first large modern prison in America, and a flagship venture: 'the
state's first significant capital construction project and its leading
expenditure – more than roads or schools or any other activity'.[22]
Construction on this project took several years to complete, mainly
due to a distinctive architectural innovation: the walls were over 500
feet long on one side, 23 feet high in places, and included
watchtowers. As its sub-title suggests, walls are the dominant symbol
in 'Bartleby'. The pale scrivener seems caught in the glare from a
watchtower: 'Within three feet of the panes was a wall, and the light
came down from above, between two lofty buildings, as from a very
small opening in a dome' (p.118). Bartleby's cell also echoes the
design at Pennsylvania's Eastern Penitentiary, where the only source
of light was an eight-inch-diameter hole in the ceiling that could be
sealed if the prisoner broke rules. The architects of Eastern wanted the
exterior to 'exhibit as much as possible great strength, and convey to
the mind a cheerless blank indicative of the misery which awaits the
unhappy being who enters within its walls'.[23] Taking inspiration
from New York State, Eastern enclosed its cell blocks in walls that
were 30 feet high, twelve feet thick at the base, and enclosed
crenelated towers.

The lawyer's chambers in Melville's tale, like the cells designed for
solitary confinement at Eastern, are the space in which the 'mute,
solitary' Bartleby eats, dresses and sleeps, killing time by staring at a
'dead brick wall' (p.135). On one of the few occasions that Bartleby
leaves the chambers, his employer conducts the equivalent of a cell
search, discovering what seems like, in its Spartan simplicity, an
inventory of a prisoner's belongings:

... under his desk, I found a blanket; under the empty grate, a
blacking box and brush; on a chair, a tin basin, with soap and a

ragged towel; in a newspaper a few crumbs of ginger-nuts and a morsel of cheese. (p.129)

Read as a prison narrative, the key relationship in 'Bartleby', between lawyer and scrivener, becomes an allegory of the relationship between warden and inmate. This relationship begins with a misidentification: the warden mistakes Bartleby for a model prisoner – quiet, passive, pliable – an ideal addition to his '*safe*' institution. The prisoner, however, thwarts his keeper's 'natural expectancy of instant compliance' by refusing to obey simple commands (p.119). To discipline his subversive internee the warden tries, as was increasingly common practice in the new penitentiary regimes, to co-opt other prisoners to act as guards. The warden turns to his established cons, Turkey and Nippers, whose 'fits relieved each other like guards', and they enthusiastically offer to beat Bartleby into submission for resisting the regime into which they have been incorporated (p.116).

As a coded prison narrative 'Bartleby' offers an unexpected inversion of the power relationship between warden and prisoner. Bartleby obtains a key to the chambers, and when the lawyer comes to inspect his premises on a Sunday morning he is subjected to a lock-out. The cell can only perform its punitive function if a prisoner is held against his will, but Bartleby chooses to stay. This gives the prisoner a strange power, a 'wondrous ascendancy' over his keeper, so that the lawyer begins to feel like a prisoner in his own office. As Bartleby's resistance to discipline increases the lawyer is 'turned into a pillar of salt', and this reference to divine retribution signals the prisoner's theft of his keeper's disciplinary authority (p.140). It should be emphasised, however, that this inversion is not especially liberating for the prisoner. In *Benito Cereno* neither slave nor master were unfettered by temporarily exchanging roles. Similarly, Bartleby's subversion simply means that, to borrow a key phrase from *Pierre*, he becomes the 'jailer of himself'.[24] The prisoner's revolt is depicted as an essentially futile and sadomasochistic gesture, since, as Rogin suggests, 'Bartleby punishes the lawyer by punishing himself'.[25]

Melville underscores this futility by collapsing the distance between the lawyer's chambers and the New York Tombs where Bartleby is eventually taken to die.[26] In both locations he stands staring at walls of 'amazing thickness' which permit only a glimpse of sky above. The Turkey who had a key in the lawyer's office is replaced by a turnkey, and Nippers (a slang term for handcuffs) become literal upon arrival in the Tombs. In the prison yard a 'soft imprisoned turf grew under foot', a splash of colour in a carceral setting that mirrors the green screen which enclosed Bartleby in his previous monochrome cell (p.153). The lawyer insists that the prison, known colloquially as the Tombs, is referred to by its official title, the Halls of Justice. The scrivener replies with characteristically gnomic forcefulness: 'I know where I am' (p.151). Bartleby goes from deathly incarceration in the office, to the Tombs, to 'interment'. The cogency of Melville's critique stems from a spatial suturing that marks the distance between these locations as the law(yer)'s ideological mirage.

The critical cartography in 'Bartleby' extends beyond the contiguity of white-collar work on Wall Street and imprisonment in the Tombs. Barriers inside the lawyer's chambers (locked and folding doors, the screen) are repeated outside, thus transforming Wall Street into an ancient fortress city: 'Of a Sunday, Wall-Street is deserted as Petra' (p.129). Readings of the prison-city trope in 'Bartleby' have insisted that Melville's urban imagery does not decline into dystopian cliché. Michael Berthold, for example, argues that whilst Melville does see the prison as a central site of power in American society, he does not confirm the Foucauldian thesis of a totalisation of the carceral whole.[27] Referring to Weber's 'iron cage of rationalisation', as opposed to Foucault's 'carceral whole', Douglas Tallack similarly argues that 'Bartleby' resists the temptation to indulge in totalisation:

> [Melville] does not turn prison into a metaphor of modern existence, perhaps because he does not have an untrammelled ideal of freedom with which to oppose imprisonment ... Melville uses narrative to relate the prison, as inside, to the outside of the city in complex ways that rely as much on chance metonymical connections as on the metaphorical, all-inclusive, ones favoured by Romantic aesthetics.[28]

Examined in isolation, it is perhaps possible to argue that 'Bartleby' offers an experience of the city as carceral as opposed to a grand narrative of the carceral city. However, when seen alongside the prison-house fixation evident elsewhere in his writing, Melville seems far closer to the notion of a carceral whole than is suggested by 'chance metonymical connections'. The carceral city depicted in 'Bartleby' is not an abstract romantic formulation. Instead, this geo-graphical trope signifies a series of burgeoning material praxes, the regulation of social and economic relations in accordance with punitive models of control. Bartleby's cell, as previously noted, reflects key features of contemporary prison design. It also invokes the shaping influence of religion and the cult of domesticity, the eclipse of corporal punishments by an emphasis on the offender as a subject of knowledge within a panopticon, and critical equivalencies between the penitentiary, the madhouse and the factory.

As we have seen, the penitentiary was advocated not merely as a means of detaining criminals, but as nothing less than a sanctuary for spiritual education. Theodore Parker, in his 'Sermon on the Dangerous Classes', offered a mission statement that captured the reformer's conception of crime as disease: 'A jail ought to be a moral hospital where the offender is kept till he is cured.'[29] The discipline imposed in these moral hospitals mimicked practices established in the penitentiary's progenitor, the monastery: emphasis shifted from corporeal tortures to asceticism, solitary confinement to encourage meditation on one's sins, bread and water diets, and strict rules governing personal hygiene, contact, communication and sexual activity. Alexis de Tocqueville summarised the imperative behind the penitentiary system as follows:

> Formerly tyranny used the clumsy weapons of chains and hangmen. Despotism, to reach the soul, clumsily struck at the body, and the soul, escaping from such blows, rose gloriously above it; but in democratic republics ... tyranny ... leaves the body alone and goes straight for the soul.[30]

Throughout 'Bartleby' the narrator expresses sentiments that repeat the rhetorical legitimation of the penitentiary: 'I might give alms to his body; but his body did not pain him; it was his soul that suffered, and his soul I could not reach' (p.132). As Michael Clark suggests, the lawyer embarks on a 'quest for Bartleby's soul as a means of restoring discipline to his office'.[31]

The penitentiary, as well as seeking legitimation through appeals to religious discourse, also sought ideological sanction by modelling itself on the cult of domesticity. Moral hospitals were also homes in which society's wayward children could be brought back into the fold by the application of parental disciplines. The shift to modes of benevolent repression was accompanied by a restructuring of patriarchy, a transition from, in Rogin's terms, openly 'authoritarian' to more subtly 'manipulative' forms:

Both at home and in civil society, reformers proposed replacing physical force by a regularised, disciplined love. They urged parents not to scourge their children, but to substitute the mother's affection for the father's rod. Whipping was rejected not only because it was brutal but because it was ineffective. It coerced the child's body, but failed to reach the heart ... The discipline of love replaced the rod with two tangible weapons – physical isolation and food.[32]

The convergence between new methods of parental discipline being urged by liberal reformers on the one hand, and new methods of penal discipline on the other, are congruent with the lawyer's regime in 'Bartleby'. He aims consistently to adopt a paternalistic relation to his charges and to transform his chambers into a home. This aim is inspired by the notorious case of Colt and Adams, in which a murder could be blamed partly, the lawyer believes, on an office environment that was 'entirely unhallowed by humanising domestic associations' (p.141). With Bartleby facing the wall like an unruly child, and the lawyer trying to win him over with the discipline of love, their relationship bristles with oedipal enmity. When Bartleby initially rebels against paternal authority the lawyer is tempted to resort to the rod: 'I should have flown outright into a dreadful passion, scorned all further words, and thrust him ignominiously from my presence' (p.121). However, new modes of discipline in prison and the bourgeois home advocated restraint and reason rather than 'dreadful passion'. Accordingly, the lawyer begins to 'reason with [Bartleby]', to offer privileges, including 'taking wholesome exercise in the open air', to allow remission from work and offer to discuss his history and problems. The lawyer aspires, like the administrators of the new penal paradigm, to paternalistic management without physical coercion: 'There was no vulgar bullying, no bravado of any sort, no choleric hectoring, and striding to and fro across the apartment, jerking out vehement commands' (p.138).

Although it placed a premium upon souls and salvation, penitentiary science also relied heavily upon bureaucratic procedure. According to Foucault, the modern prison is a bureaucratic machine designed to produce 'knowledge of each inmate, of his behaviour, his deeper states of mind, his gradual improvement; the prisons must be conceived as places for the formulation of clinical knowledge about the convicts'.[33] The penitentiary aimed to convert its subjects into objects of technical knowledge. Paper prisons flourished to complement and extend the power inherent in the physical infra-structures of punishment. Upon arrival in a penitentiary, prisoners would be interviewed at length by the warden or chief guard. A file would be composed and then regularly updated, detailing not only criminal history, but family history, religious beliefs, behaviour patterns and general demeanour, which in turn produced larger systems of convict classification. Motivated by his conviction that knowledge is the key to redemption, the lawyer repeatedly interrogates Bartleby. The prisoner, however, stubbornly resists all lines of questioning:

> 'Will you tell me, Bartleby, where you were born?'
> 'I would prefer not to.'
> 'Will you tell me *any thing* about yourself?'
> 'I would prefer not to.'
> 'But what reasonable objection can you have to speak to me?'
> (pp.132–3)

Bartleby's rhetorical ploy anticipates that relied upon by communists who took the Fifth Amendment during the McCarthy witch trials, as well as the original catechisms at Salem. Michael Clark suggests that the lawyer views the scrivener 'the same way a Puritan magistrate would – as a sign hiding its true significance'.[34] Correspondences with the witch trials increase when Bartleby's words begin to infect the lawyer's office. Nippers and Turkey start repeating the term 'prefer', and had this 'unusual possession of the clerks' tongues' occurred one hundred and fifty years earlier in Salem, the narrator's conclusion would have been enough to get Bartleby arrested as a witch, if not convicted'.[35] The lawyer never specifically charges Bartleby with witchcraft, but he does rely on gothic metaphors to articulate his anxieties about the 'cadaverous' presence colonising his chambers: the copyist is a 'spectre', an 'incubus' and a 'ghost'.

In gothic narrative, suspicions of the supernatural result in increased levels of surveillance, and in 'Bartleby' the ghostly scrivener is subjected to the increasingly intense gaze of the lawyer. Developments in the technologies of surveillance were a key component in the contemporary drive to convert the prisoner into an object of knowledge. The panopticon was the architectural correlative of this drive. Prisoners in the penitentiary were subjected to constant monitoring, both within and in movements to and from their cells. At Auburn an 'inspection avenue' was introduced behind the workshops, separated only by a thin board containing numerous eye-holes. This passageway was continually patrolled by guards wearing moccasins. A committee reporting on the Auburn regime commended the authorities on this innovation:

> [N]o convict knows, at any time, but that the invisible eye of a keeper is fastened directly on him. Thus the apertures of the partition between the avenue and the shop are like so many eyes constantly fixed on the convicts; and the effect is, to make them feel, at all times, that any violation of the rules of the institution, whether under the eye of the shopkeeper or not, must be at the risk of incurring a severe penalty.[36]

Prominent prison reformer Reverend Louis Dwight commended Auburn 'as a model worthy of the world's imitation', and this advice seems to have been heeded by Bartleby's employer.[37] The lawyer positions his employees carefully behind ground-glass doors and screens around which he can glance, at any moment, without warning. Despite the deployment of all the tactics which the penitentiary system has to offer – the discipline of love, interrogation, panopticism – the file on Bartleby remains woefully incomplete:

> I believe that no materials exist for a full and satisfactory biography of this man ... Bartleby was one of those beings of whom nothing is ascertainable ... What my own astonished eyes saw of Bartleby, *that* is all I know of him. (p.109)

Conversely, the scrivener's response to the lawyer during his first prison visit suggests that, rather than just resisting his reduction to an object of knowledge, he is threatening to reverse reification: 'I know you ... and I want nothing to say to you' (p.151). In the penitentiary the prisoner is reduced to an anonymous number, but in 'Bartleby' it is the warden who is unnamed and *known*.

In subverting the conventions governing the relationship between warden and inmate, Bartleby also undermines reason, the philosophical lynchpin to new punishment practices: 'At present I would prefer not to be a little reasonable' (p.134). Penal codes during the colonial period had been characterised by irrational acts of violent vengeance. The new Republic prided itself that it could devise alternative, rational methods of benefit both to the criminal and society. In Bartleby, Melville offers an Imp of the Perverse, who challenges

Enlightenment assumptions concerning order and human perfectibility. Since reason fails to explain his behaviour the lawyer is forced to turn to unreason. The copyist's resistance to reformation is written off as madness, and he is defined as 'demented', 'deranged' and 'a little *luny*'. In *The Discovery of the Asylum*, David Rothman comments on the 'structural homogeneity of madhouse and prison-house', another contemporary institution keen to reify individuals as objects of technical knowledge.[38] Whilst reformers advertised the success of the penitentiary in curing social and spiritual ills, little publicity was given to the fact that Theodore Parker's moral hospitals were producing mental health problems in a large number of their patients. Prison inspections in New York penitentiaries routinely uncovered cases of self-destructive behaviour. This was especially prevalent amongst prisoners subjected to prolonged solitary confinement, some of whom were driven to eating their own faeces, chewing the skin of their hands, or smashing their heads continually into the walls of their cell. Bartleby's symptoms are not as demonstrative, but it is possible to read his acute agoraphobia, prolonged silence and listlessness as mental illness produced by incarceration.

At the same time that it was becoming difficult to distinguish between the prison and the madhouse, it was also proving harder to separate the penitentiary from the factory. Following Frankfurt School sociologists Rusche and Kirchheimer, a number of historians of punishment (including Melossi and Pavarini, Michael Ignatieff and Scott Christianson) have commented on the critical contiguities between these institutions.[39] In the late 1790s Samuel Slater, having introduced industrial innovations at his cotton mill in Pawtucket, was being celebrated as the 'creator of the American factory system'.[40] Inspired by Slater's success, Thomas Eddy, a key figure in penal reform in the early nineteenth century and the 'father of the New York State Prison', began the process of industrialising America's prisons. Eddy was keen to promote labour as the path to redemption, and encouraged the reconfiguration of the prison as an industrial centre. Following Eddy's example, governors across America established workshops and schedules that massively increased the productivity of prisons, converting some of the more successful, such as Auburn and Sing Sing, into profit-making institutions. Even when they failed to become self-financing, the prison-factories still trained prisoners in the requisite disciplines of industrial labour. Governor Elam Lynds converted Auburn into the model fortress-factory:

> Auburn carried asceticism and frugality – other hallmarks of factory
> organisation in the outside world – as far as possible, short of
> death. Its institutional regimen was made totally formal and
> impersonal, symbolic of the new industrial relationship ... Daily
> schedules and workplans became highly refined ... Clocks, bells,
> whistles and horns marked the time relentlessly.[41]

Following his success at Auburn, Lynds stood down to supervise the
construction of Sing Sing, whose location at Mount Pleasant was
chosen because of proximity to marble beds, silver and copper ore
deposits, and the Hudson river. During the 1830s Sing Sing boasted
a significant financial surplus. Horace Lane, a prison-labourer with
firsthand experience of this regime, reported the difficulty inmates
had in sleeping due to the noise of coffin construction taking place
at night. Prison governors intensified discipline to levels that their
industrial counterparts could only dream of: inmates could be
literally chained to their work-benches, as opposed to the figurative
shackles of wage-slavery.

The penitentiary system and industrialisation developed hand in
hand. Prisons became places of work at the same time that places of
work were being organised along increasingly penal lines. Melville
examines this integration in detail in another of the *Piazza Tales*,
'The Paradise of Bachelors and the Tartarus of Maids'. In the second
half of this tale a lawyer visits a Berkshire paper mill that seems indistinguishable from a women's prison. The segregation of the sexes
and the choice of rural locations were key features of both industrial
and penal organisation in Jacksonian America. In the 'Tartarus of
Maids' the narrator is unsettled by the eerie silence in which the
women work at their machines. As with the Lowell textile mill girls,
or at the ironically nicknamed Sing Sing, there were strict regulations
in the prison-factory controlling communication: 'singing, whistling,
scuffling, loud immoderate laughter, provoking witticisms or severe
sarcasm' were all punishable offences.[42]

In the nascent penitentiary system there were, as we have seen,
two main models, and each had distinctive ideas about the role of
labour in the reformation process. In the Auburn model prisoners
were forced to labour collectively in workshops, whilst the
Pennsylvania system kept prisoners in solitary, and only permitted
work in their cells as an occasional privilege. The lawyer's chambers
in 'Bartleby' seem to offer a composite of the congregate and
segregate systems. On one side of the folding doors Turkey, Nippers

and Ginger Nut work in tandem; on the other, cordoned-off behind his screen, the solitary Bartleby is inactive. Melville might be intimating that the integration of punishment and labour extends beyond the factory floor to the office and an industrialisation of the white-collar sector. Situated on Wall Street, the hub of urban-industrial capital, the lawyer's building 'hums with industry' (p.112). Initially the lawyer is willing to tolerate the idiosyncrasies of his new employee because of 'his incessant industry' (p.118). However, as Bartleby begins to disrupt schedules his employer considers various means of removing him:

> 'Would you like a clerkship in a dry-goods store?'
> 'There is too much confinement about that ... '
> 'Too much confinement,' I cried, 'why you keep yourself confined all the time!' (p.148)

The narrator fails to comprehend Bartleby's objection since it is based upon an experience of wage-slavery as incarceration, an experience produced by a system the lawyer sustains without having to endure.

The penitentiary system was a source of national pride in the fledgling republic, a testament to the Old World of their pioneering modernity. 'Bartleby' offers a dissenting vision of this system, showing the penitentiary not as a humanitarian advance but a refinement in strategies of social control. Reformers argued that in America even prisoners enjoyed certain inalienable rights. Melville suggested, alternatively, that even outside prisons individuals are subject to oppressive discipline. The penitentiary was a paradigmatic space since it was here that punishment practices becoming more pervasive throughout society – in the home, the factory, the office – were more clearly visible. Melville's account of Southern slavery, *Benito Cereno*, suggested that there was no escape from the prison house. Towards the close, Delano tries to cheer Benito by encouraging him to turn to nature. However, the conventional signifiers of liberty yearned for from the prison-house, 'yon bright sun ... and the blue sky', no longer offer an escape for the Spanish captain, for whom even the 'mild trades' seem to 'waft me to my tomb' (p.104). Don Benito turns his back on nature for a retreat into silence and a self-imposed sentence in a monastic cell on Mount Agonia. 'Bartleby' can be read as Melville's account of northern slavery and it reaches a similarly pessimistic conclusion. Towards the close the lawyer tries to cheer Bartleby by visiting him in the prison courtyard and encouraging him to turn to nature: 'Look, there is the sky, and here is the grass' (p.151). Bartleby's reply is even more succinct than Benito's: 'I know where I am' (p.151). He turns his back on nature to face the prison wall, retreats into silence, dies in the Tombs and thus joins the burgeoning ranks of suicides in the new penitentiary system.

In *White-Jacket* an ex-con called Shakings openly expresses a desire for discipline that is elsewhere covertly cherished: 'he almost wished he was back again in Sing Sing, where he was relieved from all anxieties about what he should eat and drink, and was supported ... He used to have such a snug little cell, all to himself' (p.177). The most disturbing feature of the encounter with the carceral society, North and South, in Melville's short fiction after *White-Jacket* is that his eponymous anti-heroes seem to share Shakings' prison wish. 'Bartleby' offers an incisive critique of the carceral society and at the same time confronts us with the enigma of a figure who seems to long for incarceration. It might be argued that Bartleby's masochism and death-drive have been conditioned by the carceral society and that he achieves a pyrrhic victory by becoming its perfect victim. Alternatively, it could be suggested that Bartleby fails to escape because there is nowhere to escape to, there is no outside to the prison house. Rather than reading the grass inside the Tombs as a sign of a redemptive natural realm beyond, Bartleby, seeing the 'soft, *imprisoned* turf', recognises a symbol of the extent to which nature itself is being incarcerated by urban-industrial capital. Nature becomes merely another anxious cryptogram for the carceral city.

Such readings can resolve the contradiction that exists in 'Bartleby' between the critique of and the desire for enclosure. However, in an extravagantly metafictional text such as this, these lines of interpretation also offer an uncomfortable parallel between reader and narrator. A sensible interpretation of masochism in 'Bartleby' sides the reader with the lawyer who is unwilling to accept the contradiction of a figure who seems both to love and loathe his punishment. The alternative to these reasoned readings that resolve textual contradictions and enable Bartleby to be known, is to recognise the prison wish as a positive value rather than a negative consequence. In this sense 'Bartleby' can be read as a narrative on enclosure that prefers not to offer closure. According to Reik, the 'characteristic of the masochistic tension-curve is the tendency to prolong the tension, while we meet with the opposite intention, of resolving the tension, in normal sexual life'.[43] Bartleby and 'Bartleby' exemplify the masochistic sensibility and its perverse negativity at odds with the dominant culture. The prolonged tensions produced by the code of enigma in 'Bartleby' repeat the messy entanglements uncovered in Melville's other works. On the one hand, we encounter ethical and political hostility towards punishment and on the other the seductive and 'nonsensical' attractions of subjugation and submission. These entanglements are central to Melville's final novel, *Billy Budd*, in which he completes his vision of the perfect victim.

BILLY BUDD AND THE PERFECTION OF PUNISHMENT

In *Billy Budd*, Melville returns to the sea and the subject of naval discipline. He insists at the outset that his subject is restricted to the 'inner life of one particular ship and the career of an individual sailor'.[44] However, in the context of this ex-sailor's own literary career, this 'inside narrative' marks the florescence of the problems with punishment germinating in his previous fiction. *Billy Budd* is set in 1797, following the rebellions at Spithead and Nore, during a period of increased anxiety about the prospect of mutiny in the British Navy. A young sailor, having been impressed aboard the warship *Bellipotent*, finds himself falsely accused by the master-at-arms of plotting mutiny. In a fit of rage Billy Budd lashes out and accidentally kills Claggart, his superior officer. The captain believes that the initial charge was without foundation but, in the drumhead court that follows, argues nonetheless that the immediate execution of the defendant is both inevitable and necessary. Budd receives his sentence and standing at the gallows his final words seem to suggest that he accepts his fate unequivocally: 'God bless Captain Vere!' (p.318).

H. Bruce Franklin has commented that in amongst a mass of critical responses, 'nobody seems to have noticed that ... [the] subject of capital punishment and its history' is at the heart of *Billy Budd*.[45] During the period that the novel was being drafted a national controversy was raging over capital punishment and this centred on New York, the city in which Melville lived and worked. Edmund Clarence Stedham, a prominent campaigner against the gallows, was Melville's patron at this time. The New York presses were the focal point for public debates concerning the ethics and mechanics of capital punishment. Many editorials were devoted to the 'Battle of the Currents' which climaxed with the execution of William Kemmler, just eight months before work on the manuscript of *Billy Budd* was halted by Melville's own death. In this context the response of the crew on the *Bellipotent* to Budd's last words is noteworthy: 'Without volition, as it were, as if indeed the ship's populace were but the vehicle of some vocal *current electric*, with one voice from alow and aloft came a *resonant* sympathetic echo: "God bless Captain Vere!"' (p.318, my italics). When the captain hears these words he seems gripped by a 'momentary paralysis induced by emotional shock, [he] stood erectly rigid as a musket in the ship-armourer's rack' (p.319). Franklin ignores the resonance between these lines and the chair, but proceeds to argue that *Billy Budd* must be read as Melville's contribution to the campaign against the death penalty:

> *Billy Budd* strips away the illusions of justice and deterrence to reveal the essence of capital punishment: human sacrifice, a ritual of power in which the state and the ruling class demonstrate, sanctify, and celebrate their ultimate power – the power of life and death – over the classes they rule.[46]

Franklin makes a case for reading *Billy Budd* as a critique of capital punishment, but only by collapsing the distance between Melville and his eponymous martyr-figure: 'To deal in double meanings and insinuations of any sort was quite foreign to his nature' (p.240). Whilst Billy Budd, apparently, is incapable of insinuation, *Billy Budd* is ceaselessly suggestive. When he gets close to elucidation, Melville declares that the affair on the *Bellipotent* is fuelled by passion:

> Passion, and passion in its profoundest, is not a thing demanding a palatial stage whereon to play its part. Down among the groundlings, among the beggars and rakers of garbage, profound passion is enacted. And the circumstances that provoke it, however trivial or mean, are no measure of its power. (p.269)

As in the passion plays observed on the *Neversink* and *San Dominick*, dramatic interest on the *Bellipotent* is provided by the performance of punishment and intimations about its cause: concerning the master-at-arms' motivation, the captain's designs and the victim's own experience of his death sentence. The irony of the subtitle, 'an inside narrative', is that we never get unmediated access to the protagonists. Melville does, however, leave hints that are too definite to be ignored.

On a ship at sea, 'every day among all ranks, almost every man comes into more or less of contact with almost every other man' (pp.263–4). From the opening homage to the 'Handsome Sailor' and the powerful charm that this figure exerts over his fellows, *Billy Budd* is laced with homoerotic periphrasis. The men on Billy's previous ship 'took to him like hornets to treacle ... they all love him' (p.233). When he arrives on the *Bellipotent*, Billy, nicknamed 'Beauty', is similarly worshipped amongst the crew and even provokes 'ambiguous smiles' and a 'peculiar favourable effect ... upon the more intelligent gentlemen of the quarterdeck' (p.261). The figure upon whom Billy seems to have the most 'peculiar' effect is Claggart, the master-at-arms. As in *White-Jacket*, *Billy Budd* awkwardly combines the homoerotic and the homophobic and this confusion centres upon the relationship between Claggart and Billy. Their first major encounter is loaded with Melville's typically irreverent sexual symbolism. Claggart is walking across the mess hall, 'official rattan in hand', when Billy spills a 'greasy liquid' across his path:

> He was about to ejaculate something hasty at the sailor, but checked himself, and pointing down to the streaming soup, playfully tapped him from behind with his rattan, saying in a low musical voice peculiar to him at times, 'Handsomely done, my lad! And handsome is as handsome did it, too!' (pp.261–2)

Billy fails to notice 'the involuntary smile, or rather grimace, that accompanied Claggart's equivocal words', nor the fact that he proceeds to attack a drummer-boy who crosses his path, 'impetuously giving him a sharp cut with the rattan' (p.262). The S&M frisson in this scene between the Master(-at-arms) and the Boy, with its slippage between pleasure and pain, release and restraint, dominate Melville's subsequent description of this relationship.

'[Billy] thought the master-of-arms acted in a manner rather queer at times' (p.258). This confusion is exacerbated when an older sailor explains that the master-at-arms has a 'sweet word' for Billy because 'he's down on you' (p.261). Billy seems unable to decipher the code he is offered, but the reader cannot afford to be coy. Interestingly, there is as much attention to Claggart's physicality in the text as to Budd's. Whereas, however, the Handsome Sailor's form produces pleasure, Claggart's causes concern. Along with his peculiar 'musical voice', the master-at-arms has noteworthy eyes and forehead, delicate hands, an 'ostentatious manner' and is 'not only neat but careful in his dress' (p.267). Despite his sartorial preferences, however, there are signs of the unwholesome in Claggart's complexion which

'seemed to hint of something defective or abnormal in the constitution and blood' (p.268). Melville hints at some 'romantic incident'
between Claggart and Billy that might resolve the 'enigma ... in the
case', but the main frame of reference for dealing with the 'abnormal'
master-at-arms is the gothic, the genre which revolves around trans-
gressive sexuality:

> And yet the cause necessarily to be assumed as the sole one
> assignable is in its very realism as much charged with that prime
> element of Radcliffian romance, the mysterious, as any that the
> ingenuity of the author of *The Mysteries of Udolpho* could devise.
> (p.263)

Claggart's feelings towards Billy are associated with infernal imagery:
'a subterranean fire, was eating its way deeper and deeper into him'
and upon any 'unforeseen encounter a red light would flash forth
from his eye like a spark from an anvil in a dusk smithy' (p.264). The
narrator seems at times to share Billy's confusion about Claggart,
insisting that this fiery feeling 'partakes nothing of the sordid or the
sensual', whilst recognising its source as Billy's 'significant personal
beauty' (p.265).

A comparable confusion is apparent in Melville's portrayal of the
captain. Like Claggart, whose passion assumes 'various secret forms
within him', Vere's feelings towards Billy are diverse and partially
concealed (p.269). The connection between Captain and crew on
the *Bellipotent*, as on the *Neversink*, assumes an oedipal aspect and it
is even hinted that the 'child-man' may be the Vere's literal rather
than simply figurative offspring. Not only is Vere 'old enough to
have been Billy's father', but his class identity, as 'the Honourable
Edward Fairfax Vere' makes him a prime candidate, since '[n]oble
descent was as evident in [Billy] as in a blood horse' (p.239). An
oedipal reverberation is simultaneously conspicuous in Vere's
decision to punish 'Baby Budd'. The captain explains the dilemma
facing the court in terms of a patriarchal collision, between Heavenly
Father and their earthly patron, the King. Although in the eyes of
God they will be condemning an innocent, their first allegiance must
be to King. Vere's alibi hinges on deference to the law of the father.
This allows the executioners to elude culpability, since the martial
code would be 'operating through us' (p.303). It may appear that
Melville gives Vere an intentionally feeble vindication to discredit his
position. However, it needs to be recalled that precisely the same

pretext was used to defend Captain Claret and his officers on the Neversink. In White-Jacket, Melville distinguished between the disciplinary system and those who administer it and in Billy Budd, Vere argues that for the 'law and the rigour of it, we are not responsible' (p.304). In White-Jacket, Melville also concedes that extreme circumstances may justify extreme measures, a position ventriloquised by Vere in defending Budd's execution: 'We proceed under the law of the Mutiny Act. In feature no child can resemble his father more than that Act resembles in spirit the thing from which it derives – War' (p.306).

Following the public call for Budd's punishment, a private scene takes place in which father and son, apparently, are reconciled to their respective fates. This is the moment in which they can share, according to Rogin, the 'masochistic bond of victims'.[47] In oedipal terms Billy is the perfect son, the one who castrates himself for his father by surrendering unconditionally to his law. At the same time, Vere is a victim insofar as he relinquishes power to be tortured by the same law that demands the sacrifice of his son. This relationship displays a hyperbolic oedipality and also combines the two dominant strands of contemporary punishment: the residual feudal tortures of public execution and the privatised discipline of love (forms of benevolent repression typically practised behind closed doors). Love is Vere's most potent weapon in preventing Billy from resisting the punishment he inflicts and its results are spectacular: the new ideal of self-punishment is perfected as Billy's asks God to bless his executioner.

Alternative readings of Vere's decision to punish his son might be proposed. If, as we have seen in Melville, acts of rebellion may be collateral calls for discipline, then acts of oppression might be reinterpreted as covert wishes for resistance. In this vein, Barbara Johnson's reading of Billy Budd suggests that all plots contain the possibility of subversion and authority can manufacture 'the scene of its own destruction'.[48] Vere argues that anything less than an execution might promote rebellion, since the crew will think their masters have lost their will to punish. This wilfully ignores the fact that the execution of an innocent man is at least as likely to provoke dissent. Read in this way the son's execution becomes a secondary expression of the father's desire to be rebelled against, a masochistic desire for the destruction of an unjust law as it is embodied in him. Vere realises at the outset that the law of the father requires the death of an 'angel' and may wish for the destruction of that system.

Accordingly, what Vere is punishing through his son is punishment itself. This could explain his mortification when the crew, his figurative children, mechanically repeat Billy's valediction: 'God bless Captain Vere!' Vere can thus be read both as the martinet who synthesises the residual and dominant modes of discipline and as the patriarch who longs for his law to be rebelled against.[49]

The confusions surrounding Claggart and Vere are repeated in the third corner of *Billy Budd*'s disciplinary triangle. When negotiations are taking place to secure Billy's services on the *Bellipotent*, his former captain explains his reluctance to let the Handsome Sailor go in relation to the pacifying effect he has upon his crew: like a 'Catholic priest striking peace in an Irish shindy' (p.233). The oxymoron at the centre of this analogy blurs the lines between violence and restraint and this inconsistency follows Billy onto the *Bellipotent*. Initially, a peaceful pliability is Billy's most conspicuous feature. He offers no resistance when impressed and the first image associated with him connects incarceration with a sense of the futility of resisting punishment: 'Billy made no demur. But, indeed, any demur would have been as idle as the protest of a goldfinch popped into a cage' (p.236). However, as it becomes clearer that Billy's 'uncomplaining acquiescence, [is] all but cheerful', the suspicion arises that violence has been internalised, directed against the self in a self-destructive masochism reminiscent of Bartleby's pathological passivity.

Melville, with predictable patriarchal logic, feminises his willing victim. Billy's features are compared to a 'rustic beauty', like the Hesperides of Greek mythology, a 'smooth face all but feminine in purity of natural complexion' (p.238). Unlike the abnormalities hinted at by Claggart's complexion, Billy's skin tone is likened to the lily and the rose and his voice to a nightingale: the 'clear melody of a singing bird on the point of launching from the twig' (p.240). During the trial, Vere significantly genders the clash in the case before them and insists on the necessity of punishing the feminine: 'Well, the heart here, sometimes the feminine in man ... must here be ruled out' (p.304). However, the apparently stable opposition offered in his rhetoric, between the father, law and punishment on the one side and mother, nature and sacrifice on the other is dextrously undercut by Melville's insinuations elsewhere. At times Billy seems to be the fair maiden, archetypal victim of ritual sacrifice, who is destined to be returned to the natural world with which he has been associated. When he is first accused he becomes tongue-tied and this gives 'an expression to the face like that of a condemned vestal priestess in the moment of being buried alive, and in the first struggle of suffocation' (p.291). Elsewhere, however, Billy seems more *femme fatale* than fair maiden. He is compared to the 'beautiful woman in one of Hawthorne's minor tales' ('The Birthmark') and there are also suggestions that, like Hester Prynne, he harbours those dangerous desires mythically associated with the dark lady. Claggart describes Billy as a 'cat's paw' (the attractive young sailors used to entice other men to volunteer) and a 'mantrap ... under the ruddy-tipped daisies' (p.267).

In *Benito Cereno* the role-play of domination and submission was destabilised and there are similar fractures in *Billy Budd*. This is not to say that Budd is another Babo, but Melville rarely allows innocence to appear entirely unbesmirched. On occasion Billy seems secretly aligned with the discipline that corrects him. Awaiting execution, shackled and lying in soiled white amongst coils of dirty black rope, Billy resembles 'a patch of discoloured snow in early April lingering at some upland cave's black mouth' (p.313). His reactions here, on the eve of execution, are puzzling: 'For now and then in the gyved one's trance a serene happy light ... would diffuse itself over his face, and then wane away only anew to return' (p.314). The religious imagery in *Billy Budd* encourages reading these moments of pleasure as the combined agony and ecstasy of Christian masochism. However, Budd seems less akin to a conventional Christian martyr and closer to the secular perversion of Bartleby's prison-wish.

If he is secretly desirous of the discipline he receives, Billy's 'accidental' actions – spilling the soup, killing Claggart – become more ambiguous. Vere assumes that there is no intention to kill when Budd lashes out at Claggart, but the defendant displays uncharacteristic composure on other occasions: 'in response came syllables not so much impeded in the utterance as might have been anticipated' (p.299). The Handsome Sailor's fists also have a history. On the *Rights of Man*, when provoked by an old sailor, Billy 'let fly his arm. I dare say he never meant to do quite as much as he did, but he gave the fellow a terrible drubbing. It took about half a minute, I should think' (p.234). Is this, or the later assault on Claggart, a proportionate or expected response from a figure elsewhere personified as innocence incarnate? The eponymous hero's name might be a cryptogram which crystallises psychosexual tensions: the 'bud' suggests nature and innocence, but the 'billy', as a tool of discipline, aligns him with the violence he provokes and performs. Whilst his name fuses love and an instrument of police violence, Claggart's nickname, 'Jemmy Legs', links him to a criminal tool. In *Billy Budd* the roles of victim and aggressor, law and disorder are strangely aligned. As Billy's fist delivers a death-blow to Claggart it could be read as a moment of masochistic consummation for the master-at-arms. Billy similarly seems to long for the discipline he receives and at his death phallic and punitive imagery combine: as he dies, falling 'like a heavy plank tilted from erectness', Melville puns on the S&M practice of erotic asphyxiation and the gallows' mythology of spontaneous ejaculation.

Claggart falls, Billy is hanged, Vere seems to go, figuratively, to the chair and on the *Bellipotent*, as on the *San Dominick*, it becomes difficult to dissociate submission and domination: 'innocence and guilt personified in Claggart and Budd in effect changed places' (p.307). Johnson summarises the fragile symmetries in this tale as follows: 'Billy is sweet, innocent, and harmless, yet he kills. Claggart is evil, perverted, and mendacious, yet he dies a victim. Vere is sagacious and responsible, yet he allows a man whom he feels to be blameless to hang.'[50] This deconstruction of binary logic is of course anticipated by Melville. In *Benito Cereno*, a tale about black and white opens with shades of grey. In *Billy Budd*, Melville returns to the palette to trace those liminal spaces of unfathomable hybridity between criminal and victim, masculine and feminine, good and evil, punishment and pleasure: 'Who in the rainbow can draw the line where the violet tint ends and the orange tint begins? Distinctly we see the difference of the colours, but where exactly does the one first blendingly enter into the other?' (p.295).

A precarious admixture is also apparent in the execution with which *Billy Budd* climaxes. Budd's sacrifice crosses the crucifixion with deviant desires. The rope, according to Rogin, 'is not simply a source of pain in Melville's fiction; it stimulates erotic associations as well'.[51] Billy's hanging is preceded by a kiss described as a 'consummation'. The 'emphasised silence' that follows recalls the articulate quiescence of Babo, Bartleby and the maids at Tartarus. The crew respond to this soundlessness with a 'strange human murmur' that seems to augur 'resistance around the scaffold'. However, this brief hint of defiance is dispelled by the whistles of the boatswain which signal the crew's somnambulist submission 'to the mechanism of discipline' (p.323). In *White-Jacket* Melville recalls an old sea saying: 'The gallows and the sea refuse nothing' (p.379). Contrary to Franklin's thesis, Melville's refusal of the gallows fails to get any louder than the murmur offered by the crew on the *Bellipotent*. In

White-Jacket, Melville had openly denounced the executions on the *Somers* (in which one of his cousins had been involved), but by *Billy Budd* the same event is passed over as '[h]istory, and here cited without comment' (p.286). Outrage at punishment drifts towards sacred and sexual whisperings and on into Melville's favoured silence.

In *White-Jacket* Melville had reproached Dibdin, a writer of patriotic sea-shanties, for his 'Mohammedan sensualism; a reckless acquiescence in fate, and an implicit, unquestioning, dog-like devotion to whoever may be lord and master' (p.386). However, traces of these selfsame traits surface repeatedly in Melville's own work. His moral condemnation of punishment is accompanied by a homoerotic fascination with the tools of discipline and a terminally ambivalent attitude towards the patriarchal authority that utilises them. White-Jacket had a secret attraction to the whip and the Father, Benito and Bartleby longed for their cells and Billy, completing the vision of punishment's perfect victim, submits to the patriarch with canine fidelity. Melville, like the old sailor with dirty hands in *Benito Cereno*, offers his reader narratives of punishment that are Gordian knots in which ethics and erotics, critique and fatalism are terminally entangled. His analysis of a carceral society makes connections between key institutions: the navy, the plantation, the factory, the office, the asylum, the penitentiary. At the same time, Melville's writing insists on there being no escape from the prison house and instead seeks compensation in deathly sadomasochistic play. Punishment practices are linked to specific socioeconomic systems, but discipline simultaneously seems scripted by transhistorical determinants as part of a timeless mythical drama of fathers and sons. Melville's critique recognises the performative aspects of punishment, but is paralysed by a sense of exitlessness from the theatre of cruelty. Wardens and prisoners, masters and servants, bosses and workers, captains and crew, each may temporarily assume the other's costume, but the masque of discipline grinds on. The effect is peculiar and powerful, located somewhere between subversion and hegemony, the violet and the orange: 'Distinctly we see the difference of the colours, but where exactly does the one first blendingly enter into the other?' (p.295).

6
Inside the American Prison Film

Go to a motion picture ... and let yourself go ... Before you know it, you are living the story ... All the romance, all the excitement you lack in your daily life are – in Pictures. They take you completely out of yourself into a wonderful new world ... Out of the cage of everyday existence! If only for an afternoon or an evening – escape.

Newspaper ad, cited in *Middletown: A Study in Contemporary American Culture*, Robert and Helen Lynd[1]

LAW/GENRE

The conjunction of sex and punitive cruelty which has been tracked from the Puritan colonies to the plantation and on into the conflicted fictions of Hawthorne and Melville, can be pursued further into contemporary US culture. In *Nightmare on Main Street*, Mark Edmundson suggests of the 1990s that the 'sadomasochistic psyche may be becoming the order of the day (somewhat as Christopher Lasch said that the narcissistic psyche was the order of the 1970s)'.[2] Throughout *Main Street* the signs of the times all lead back to S&M: from cult horror fiction by Stephen King and Anne Rice to film franchises that follow stalkers, slashers and serial killers, from music videos (Madonna's 'dominatrix' persona is singled out) to photography (Robert Mapplethorpe), from fashion (the vogue for leather and latex, boots and chains, body piercing and tattoos) to the media infatuation with tales of abuse, oc/cult murder and terrorism (in daytime talk shows and tabloid journalism). In self-fulfilling prophecy, *Nightmare on Main Street* develops a gothic vision of the metastasis of gothic culture in millennial America. For Edmundson, S&M is the *Ur*-narrative of this culture: 'For at the core of every Gothic plot is the S&M scenario: victim, victimiser, terrible place, torment.'[3] This scenario has spread far beyond the domain of the manifestly gothic: one could add various hardcore examples (internet bondage and snuff sites) and their softcore equivalents (various video game genres and the pantomime of WWF) to this pantheon of popular perversions.

Edmundson's list is expansive and yet there is a telling omission here. The interest in crime in *Nightmare on Main Street* ends at the televised courtroom, so that texts in popular culture that focus on the act of punishment itself are precluded. This is surprising given the applicability of Edmundson's précis of S&M culture to the prison narrative: victim, victimiser, terrible place, torment. The prison narrative has enjoyed something of a resurgence in the last 20 years, particularly in Hollywood. If S&M is an *Ur*-Gothic, then the prison film, with its recycled fantasies of victimhood and vengeance, might be read as the master (and servant) narrative of sadomasochistic desire. Edmundson's failure even to mention the genre is disappointing but not entirely unpredictable. The prison film has been criminally neglected by the academy. Whilst the genre has enjoyed success with audiences and mainstream critics, film studies has tended to ghettoise the prison film as a poor relation to the otherwise copiously covered and glamorous corpus of crime drama. Given the genre's lengthy rap sheet this is a puzzling lacuna. In the silent era, prison was a popular setting for short dramas (Barnsdale released *Prison Bars* in 1901) and comedies (Fred Evans starred in *Pimple's Prison* in 1914) as well as animations and public information films. Prison sequences were key to the formula in early gangster films (for example, the various versions of *Alias Jimmy Valentine* (1915, 1920, 1928)) and crime dramas (such as Paramount's *The Test of Honour* (1919)). In *Intolerance*, D. W. Griffith juxtaposed scenes of persecution through the ages that included the crucifixion, the siege and fall of Babylon and the slaughter of the Huguenots and chose an execution to epitomise contemporary sectarianism. Hollywood's inaugural death row drama focused on a young Irish worker who is wrongfully convicted and sentenced to the gallows. This might be read as an early example of the political ambivalence that often characterises the prison drama. The apparent proletarian sympathies of the storyline, with its backdrop of ruthless employers and oppressed workers, belie the film's own conditions of production: the Hollywood story itself began as an escape attempt, with Griffith following Cecil B. De Mille and the Nestor Company to the west coast haven of non-unionised labour.

As incarceration rates began to escalate in the early years of the Depression, a spate of successful prison dramas appeared, including *The Big House* (1930), *I am a Fugitive from a Chain Gang* (1932) and *20,000 Years in Sing Sing* (1932). Since these seminal contributions, thousands of formula films have been set inside although not all of them would qualify as prison films. Genre theory has established that most formulae are easier to recognise than define and this is testified to by the elusiveness of prison film. *Alias Jimmy Valentine*, *The Test of Honour* and *Intolerance* all include prison sequences, but are never identified as prison films. In *The Big House*, *I am a Fugitive from a Chain Gang* and *20,000 Years in Sing Sing*, a considerable portion of the action takes place on the outside and yet each is categorically classified as a prison film. Some visual representations of punishment focus on the crimes (including miscarriages of justice) that lead to prison, others are preoccupied with what happens once the walls have been left behind (escape, reintegration or, less frequently, alienation). In the classical prison drama, however, the before and after is entirely secondary to what takes place inside. The classical prison drama is invariably an all-male affair. Even when it enters a women's prison the genre routinely indulges in fantasies of rape and lesbianism tailored to a male voyeur. Although it is male-centred, the classical prison drama involves melodramatic excesses typically gendered female. The narrative hinges on a series of spectacular collisions between rebellious individuals and repressive institutions. In this respect, as in many others, the genre departs from those experiential realities of prison life which fail to lend themselves to the imperatives of commercial cinema. As Abu-Jamal suggests in *Live From Death Row*: 'The most profound horror of prisons lives in the day-to-day banal occurrences that turn days into months, and months into years, and years into decades.'[4]

Most Hollywood productions rarely go beyond a brief montage that simulates the monotony and routine of prison life, before hurriedly returning to a melodrama involving attempts to execute an escape or escape an execution. Although the classical prison film is either an escape or execution drama, it is complemented by a number of sub-genres and hybrids: the prison comedy (*Pardon Us* (1931), *Stir Crazy* (1980) and *Life* (2000)); the sports film (boxing in *Penitentiary* (1979) and *The Hurricane* (1999), football in *The Mean Machine* (1974)); the action film set in a prison (*The Rock* (1996) and *Half Past Dead* (2002)); the POW film (*Escape to Victory* (1981), which is also a sports film and *The Secret of Blood Island* (1965)); closely linked to the POW film is the overseas prison drama (*Midnight Express* (1978), which also belongs to the class of 'true life' prison dramas such as *Papillon* (1973) and *Escape from Alcatraz* (1979)); the legal drama (*Murder in the First* (1995)); prison/exploitation film (*Caged Heat II: Stripped of Freedom* (1994) and *Cellblock Sisters* (1995)); the prison horror film (*Prison* (1988)) and supernatural melodrama (*The Green Mile* (1999)). The last 20 years has also seen an upsurge in science fiction films that predict developments in correction with futuristic visions of high-tech facilities, prison cities and even prison planets (*Escape from New York* (1981), *Escape from LA* (1996), *Fortress I* and *II* (1993 and 2001)). On occasion, as in *Alien³* (1992) and *New Alcatraz* (2000), these dystopian prophecies cross-over with the prison horror film. The prison film, like the institution which is its star attraction, assumes multiple guises.

Despite this rhizomatic evolution, the scant scholarship that exists on prison film tends to justify its exclusion from more extensive research by focusing on what is repeated. The prison film follows individuals who break the law whilst scrupulously observing its own generic rule book. Consequently, the genre has been pilloried for a lack of rebellion, for a docile recycling of formulae that produces texts as bland and uniform as prison clothing. One might counter that this aesthetic crime is hardly unique to the prison film. In fact, constitutional recidivism dominates most commercial film-making and as Derrida has suggested, the very notion of genre is bound to concepts of rules and law:

> As soon as the word 'genre' is sounded, as soon as it is heard, as soon as one attempts to conceive it, a limit is drawn. And when a limit is established, norms and interdictions are not far behind: 'Do', 'Do not' says 'genre', the word 'genre', the figure, the voice, or the law of genre.[5]

The law of genre is always prominent in the genre of law. The prison film is a repeat offender on the counts of character, plot and *mise-en-scène*. Many of the essential 'do's' and 'don'ts' of the genre were established in the earliest prison films. In *Intolerance*, for example, the young worker is rescued from execution at the last moment by the arrival of his wife with a pardon from the governor. George W. Hill's *The Big House* (1930) introduces the major character types that are still conspicuous within the genre. Kent is the 'fresh fish' from a bourgeois background who is ill-equipped for prison life and must struggle to survive. In contrast, his cell mates are two seasoned cons: a wily and manipulative forger (John Morgan) and a bald, violent goon ('Machine Gun' Butch). Kent's entry into this alien culture involves formal and informal initiation ceremonies: the replacement of name by number and street clothes by uniform, the warden's speech, the goading by other inmates who are sceptical of the new boy's ability to survive. Subsequently Kent encounters, in the prison argot, a 'stool pigeon' and cruel 'screw' (the initiation is also lexical), he endures the horrors of the hole and mess hall and gets involved in a riot, a jail-break and a cockroach race.

For 70 years the prison film has largely failed to escape *The Big House*. Although the key thematic in the genre is the institutional repression of individuality, the typology of character in prison films does little to advance this critique. Since *The Big House*, both captives and overseers have conformed to a limited ethogram. The two main players are the 'prisoner-hero' and his nemesis the 'bad warden'. The prisoner-hero is typically an 'innocent inside', from a sheltered background, whose survival depends on adapting quickly to his harsh new environment. James Allen in *I am a Fugitive from a Chain Gang*, Jimmie Rainwood in *An Innocent Man* and Andy Dufresne in *The Shawshank Redemption* all follow in Kent's footsteps. The prisoner-hero will normally provide the spectator's point of view and be pivotal both to the *bildungsroman* narrative structure and moral design (which revolves around the unjust punishment of the innocent and the redemption of the guilty). The prisoner-hero's laudable credentials will often be underlined by association with the arts and the animal kingdom. Sometimes he or she will sketch or paint (Cindy Liggett in *The Last Dance*), or keep pets (Robert Stroud's aviary in *The Birdman of Alcatraz*), or, alternatively, they will be associated with minor characters, often on the edge and in need of emotional support, who rely on these pastimes (the Doc's painting in *Escape from Alcatraz* and Delacroix's mouse in *The Green Mile*). It is highly uncharacteristic for artistic materials and carefully nurtured birds, rodents and insects not to be destroyed or at least confiscated at some point in the proceedings. Aesthetics and wildlife are sledge-hammer symbols in the prison film which underline the essential humanity of the prisoners and the inhumanity of the system. On occasion, the artifacts (portraits of the villain) and menagerie (caged birds) will appear in the office of the bad warden to enforce this banal binary. Interior design in the warden's office is as predictable as the content of his inaugural address (in which he will insist on the impossibility of escaping his institution and his administration of a regime that is 'tough' but ultimately 'fair').

Waiting in the wings of the prison drama is a gallery of secondary figures who act largely as intermediaries between prisoner-hero and bad warden. Inmates may be persecuted by a bad guard (Percy in *The*

Green Mile) or befriended by a good guard (the rest of the staff in *The Green Mile*), but, inevitably, most of his acquaintances will be drawn from the prison population. As well as being assisted by various artists and zookeepers, the prisoner-hero will likely encounter at least one wily lifer, one black buddy and one kid. The seasoned con is keen to impart wisdom to the prisoner-hero on how to aspire to his own longevity (or, in less sanguine mode, to explain why longevity is unlikely). Although, in opposition to demographics within the US correctional system, the vast majority of prison films focus on Caucasian prisoners, a token African-American will sometimes appear to offer assistance to the hero (once again going against the historical grain so far as race relations are concerned). The black buddy usually appears as a stoic and muscular helper. John Coffey in *The Green Mile* is the most developed recent example of this undeveloped archetype and his history can be traced back to Sebastian, who helps James Allen to escape in *I am a Fugitive from the Chain Gang*. Although referred to as a 'big buck', Sebastian and subsequent black buddies typically conform to the Uncle Tom profile from antebellum mythology. The black buddy may sometimes be combined with other roles: for example, English in *Escape from Alcatraz* is both black buddy and wise lifer, Red in *The Shawshank Redemption* is black buddy, wise lifer and the fixer (a focal point for contraband in the prison community) and in *American History X*, the prisoner-anti-hero, a Nazi skinhead, is humanised by his encounters with one comical African-American he meets in the prison laundry room and one wise African-American on the outside (a history teacher). Whichever role, or combination of roles, they perform, however, the story of African-Americans inside is almost always subservient to a white master narrative.[6] As we will see in subsequent case studies, although it marginalises the African-American experience, the Hollywood prison film borrows from black cultural history to construct *white* slave narratives. Whilst there have been assaults on white masculinity from various quarters since the 1960s (second wave feminism, civil rights, gay rights), the prison narrative is an arena in which Caucasian males can be envisaged as downtrodden victims rather than oppressors.

The prisoner-hero receives fatherly advice from wise lifers and black buddies, but is sometimes permitted to perform a paternal role himself in relation to a new arrival: the kid. First Base in *Lock-up* and Tommy Williams in *The Shawshank Redemption* epitomise this figure: brash but ready to be moulded into manhood, they normally arrive at some mid-point in the film only to be sacrificed soon after to underline the wickedness of the warden. The prison authorities are not the only danger to the prisoner-hero and his surrogate family. The bad warden and his guards can be accompanied and sometimes displaced by the bad con: a gang leader who has usurped authority, a narc who rats on other inmates, or a Neanderthal who threatens sexual violence. The underdevelopment of character illustrated by this taxonomy is partly compensated for and partly attributable to the role played by setting. In a repetition of the decentring of subjectivity within prison, the built environment often plays a leading role in the prison drama. Before the spectator sees the prisoners' faces they will be confronted by low-angle shots of the prison's imposing façade. Then, bodies will be glimpsed in tiers of cells, through bars, crowded by bunks, basins and toilets. In a formal mirroring of its subjects' predicament, the camera in most prison films is fixed and largely restricted to tight, interior shots.

The institutional regime also seems to shape the narrative design in prison films. Certain setpieces appear with a routine inevitability of which any warden would be proud: the rude awakening by guards shouting and rattling their sticks against the bars; slopping-out and the shower; meal times in the mess hall (the menu of 'grease, fried dough, pig fat and sorghum' on offer in *I am a Fugitive from a Chain Gang* is representative of general levels of palatability); work on the chain gang, or in the factory, shop, kitchen, or library; lights out and a compulsory chiaroscuro shot of prisoner, in repose on bunk, illuminated by cross-hatched lighting filtered through the bars. This routine is then disrupted intermittently by the shake-down, the lock-down, or, often most painful of all, the visit. After establishing the quotidian schedule and key conflicts (institutional and internecine), most prison plots move with equal predictability towards escape (of which execution is one genus). Whilst the overwhelming reality of prison experience for inmates involves suspense, the interminable *waiting*, the prison film always provides closure by opening the prison doors, either literally (through release, pardon, or escape) or figuratively (death).

LAND OF THE FREE, OR S&M CULTURE?

Escape in the prison film is almost always viewed positively (ignoring problems such as institutionalisation, recidivism and forms of incarceration beyond the prison walls) and execution, at least superficially, as problematic. Hollywood liberalism has proffered images of wrongful execution from *20,000 Years in Sing Sing*, to *I Want to Live* and *The Last Dance*. Typically, the condemned either has not committed the crime for which they are sentenced, or they are no longer the same person who committed the crime due to rehabilitation. The apparent opposition to state murder in the execution film might casually be cited as evidence of a strong oppositional impulse within the genre. Although prison films are profoundly conservative in terms of form, the largely positive presentation of social deviants and the generally hostile perspective on state institutions seems more progressive. These oppositional impulses, however, are often ideological chimera. In fact, the prison, the institution that places most pressure on legends of the Land of the Free, has proved to be a cultural space in which myths of national identity can be reaffirmed.

This process begins with the de-criminalisation of the prisoner-hero, a *sine qua non* that can be achieved by a variety of means. The prisoner may be innocent and falsely imprisoned, or he may have committed a crime and subsequently reformed (although the authorities have failed to recognise this). Alternately, his wrong-doing might be marginalised within the narrative, or it might be justified by a variety of circumstances. If his punishment inside is severe enough (and it usually is) his criminal actions will be eclipsed by the greater crimes committed against him. Often, his criminality will be associated with the romance of outlaw culture and posited not as dangerous deviance so much as a healthy disregard for arbitrary regulations. The criminality of the prisoner is thus erased and he is elevated to folk hero status as victim, underdog, or pioneer spirit who embodies the rugged individualism and self-reliance of a frontier culture. Although the milieu of the prison film seems the obverse of frontier mythology it utilises the same mythical sign-posts and sometimes goes back further in its historical referencing. The prisoner can also be lionised by reference to Revolutionary and pre-Revolutionary mythology. The struggle between the warden and the prisoner can be mapped onto fables of the plucky American underdog standing up to his European oppressor (casting plays a crucial role here), breaking free from an oppressive old world order into the garden of a new world.

Despite its patina of progressive credentials, the American prison film generally fails to challenge conventional taxonomies of criminality or the legitimacy of the penal system. Although the presence of the prisoner-hero inside may be iniquitous, the justice of the institution per se tends not to be questioned. There may be bad prisons but it does not follow that all prisons are bad. This equation is enforced by the rogues gallery amassed behind the prisoner-hero. Whilst the individual prisoner might be innocent, or at least not guilty as charged, no such claims are advanced on behalf of the collective prison population and at least one irredeemably bad con is introduced to deflect from a more sweeping institutional indictment. When a prison *is* corrupt and oppressive, blame is attributed to the actions of an individual tyrant whose regime is coded as a political system inimical to the traditions of American democracy. The bad warden oversees a neo-Marxist, totalitarian order that insists on repressive conformity and rigid hierarchy. Conversely, the prisoner-hero, especially in his attempts to escape this grey world, will epitomise the virtues of capitalist romance: independence, initiative, mobility, risk-taking, work ethic and entrepreneurial spirit. The prison film thus never descends to the 'Tartarus of Maids'. The genre is incapable of representing prison as a specifically *capitalist* institution. Often the prison film will mirror the rhetoric of the marketplace by endorsing a crude social Darwinism. Although, on occasion, it permits visions of camaraderie amongst the prisoners alongside a survivalist ethos, instances of collective unity are typically fleeting and restricted to symbolic gestures. The prison population *en masse* may be allowed to triumph over guards on a sports field, or bang their canteens on the mess hall tables, but if they engage in full-blown rebellion their actions are portrayed as self-destructive anarchy. Inevitably, Hollywood's gaze is confined to loners, or small groups of risk-takers who manage to succeed against the odds where others fail. These smaller units in prison films will have a clearly defined leader and in their pretence of plurality (a middle class forger, an Italian-American hood, a Jew, an African-American) attempt to validate the myth of the melting-pot.

Beneath its veneer of dissent, then, the prison film provides a space in which the shibboleths of American mythology can be regenerated. Irrepressible individuals (representatives of American democracy) confront repressive institutions (the embodiment of communist regimes and the Old World order) and triumph by escaping to a brave new world of freedom in the garden. The ideological imperative of the prison film is to sustain myths about a freedom which always remains strategically nebulous in definition. As we saw in relation to Melville and slave literature, a massive cultural investment in the nineteenth century in the mythos of the Land of the Free functioned as a diversionary ruse, cloaking the curtailment of liberty not only in the penitentiary system, but in plantations, factories and the domestic sphere. In the late twentieth century, the prison film has perversely performed a similar role, as diversion and compensatory fantasy within an increasingly carceral society.

This is one of the social control functions performed by the prison film. Foucault's assertion that punishment, in the modern code, has becomes the least visible part of the penal process underestimates the role played by media representation. It might be contended that the prison film and other crime-based genres in popular culture are contiguous with those public spectacles of punishment which Foucault identifies as pivotal to the *ancien régime*. Cesare di Beccaria, one of the founding fathers of modern criminology, argued that crime prevention depends less on the severity of the punishment than on its certainty. The void left by the prohibition on public torture and execution has been filled in part by a meteoric expansion of visual narratives that aim to enforce a connection between certain crimes and certain punishments. Whilst individual films may oppose aspects of punishment – may suggest that a particular prison is barbaric, or that execution is uncivilised – the genre as a whole underlines the inevitability of correction for criminal deviance. At the same time, prison films collectively divert attention from the extremely low numbers of crimes that result in arrest, prosecution and punishment, sustain the illusion that prison is the solution to social deviance and preclude a broader structural understanding of the relationship between socioeconomic inequality and definitions of criminality.

It is thus possible to read the cinema of punishment as a dark panopticon that regulates the public gaze on law and order. The spectator enters an enclosed space to observe images of enclosed bodies, to witness the certainty of their punishment for acting out fantasies of deviance. The etymology of 'entertainment' (*entretenir* in Old French and *tenere* in Latin) suggests the carceral qualities of commercial cinema: film is a 'holding in', an ideological containment. It would be a mistake, however, to assume that the prison film operates as a total institution.[7] In the escape film the prisoners work hard to maintain a surface pretence of normality whilst secretly plotting and tunnelling. Similarly, throughout the prison genre, one can detect sub-textual burrowing just beneath the narrative surface. The prison film struggles continually and often unsuccessfully to contain its rogue elements. Institutional critique and valorisation can act as a cover for taboo fantasies. The prison film, like other narratives of punishment, lends itself to psychoanalytical interrogation and '[t]he door to the unconscious need not be picked; it is already slightly ajar, and ready to yield at the slightest pressure'.[8]

The central tension in most prison films, between the bad warden and the prisoner-hero, is redolent of oedipal allegory. The warden embodies the law of the father and the prisoner is infantilised in the Big House (sent to his room, told when to sleep, when to eat and when to clean himself). If the prisoner is the son and the warden signifies a cruel paternal and punitive imago, where is the mother in a genre that consistently marginalises women? Often the prisoner will have a wife, girlfriend, sister, or mother waiting for them on the outside. A brief and painful interview may take place during which the patriarch's power to separate mother and son will be symbolised by the guards, a table or perspex screen. In addition, the freedom denied to the prisoner is itself gendered: escape to mother nature and to a Liberty conventionally figured as female constitutes a triumph over the oedipal father.

Although the prison film may sometimes conform to the tidy symmetry of this pattern, more often its oedipal triangulation tends to be unruly. Not all prisoners go straight inside. Classical Freudianism proposes that the male subject experiences two oedipal dramas: one positive, resulting in the establishment of a socially-sanctioned gender identity, the second negative leading to the development of 'deviant' personalities. If the prison drama is a stage for the negative oedipal complex, driven by hostility towards the mother and desire for the father, then the Big House, rather than a paternal domain, could signify a maternal vessel. The prisoner-son experiences claustrophobic confinement in a concrete womb (the cell, the hole, the box), he is returned to uterine darkness and a pre-language of grunts and groans in a maternal space that provides no succour. Freud suggested that dreams of enclosed spaces, narrow passages and water were essentially fetal fantasies. The iconography of the prison film, with its emphasis on enclosure, tunnelling and escape through sewers to the outside world, collapses incarceration and invagination in a malevolent maternal body.

Antagonism towards the mother articulated in architectural tropes is complemented, in the narrative structure, by a desire for the father. The prison film, like other male-dominated commercial genres (the war epic, the action film, the sports drama) seeks to confirm hegemonic formulations of masculine subjectivity. The prison is posited as a testing-ground for masculinity, a space in which the hero's gender identity is put on trial because confinement produces symbolic feminisation. In a sense, all prisons are women's prisons, at least according to the gendered geographies of patriarchy. By making a prisoner subservient to a patriarch, by restricting him to a highly regulated existence indoors, by returning him to his body at the same time as denying corporeal control, the prisoner-hero is relocated in the feminine. The enforced passivity of prison life produces compensatory displays of hyperbolic masculinity and rituals of victimisation that aim to replicate the gender system outside.

In the absence of the heterosexual codes that structure narrative in other genres, male bonding in the prison film is offered as indemnity for bondage. Consequently, the borders between homosocial and homoerotic spectacle are traversed with as much frequency as the prison walls. The hole is a fecund symbol in the *mise-en-scène* of the prison film, connoting not only grave and womb, but also the rectum. To deflect from its homoerotic latency, the prison film resorts to routine homophobia. *Psycho* may boast the most famous shower scene in cinema history, but this is also a prerequisite in the prison genre and sometimes includes levels of sexual violence comparable to Hitchcock's seminal thriller.[9] Incidents of sexual violence inside are typically related to relations of domination and the conversion of a prisoner into a 'bitch.' Whilst such practices are well-documented, the genre appears incapable of recognising, except as comic interlude, the equally well-established fact of consensual sex and non-violent long-term relationships between inmates.

Clearly, the prison film resorts to queer-bashing because it has trouble staying straight. The virulence of the homophobia is inseparable from the intensity of the homosocial romance. This romance can be located in the relations between prisoners, but it can also surface in the ostensibly antagonistic struggles between the prisoner-hero and the bad warden. The prisoner, like the heroine in a straight romance, occupies a position of low social status, encounters a cruel superior, misreads his desires and displays an enmity that may cloak a deep attraction to the phallic father. In *The Ego and the Id*, Freud refers to the 'serviceable instinctual fusion' of cruelty and male sexuality: 'an element of aggressiveness – a desire to subjugate ... [it] seems to lie in the need for overcoming the resistance of the sexual object by means other than the process of wooing'.[10] The violence offered by the warden or bad guard might thus be read as a suitor's wooing in a boys' only romance. The negative oedipal complex that underpins this romance is linked by classical psychoanalysis to the over-development of the superego. According to Freud, a desire to be loved and punished for that love by the father is the root of the masochistic personality.

In 'Guilt without Sex', David Margolies examines the imbalance between prolonged frustration (repeated conflicts and confusions between the lovers) and the brevity of the closure (the happy ending) before classifying the pleasures of popular romance fiction as essentially masochistic.[11] A similar disparity is often evident in the prison narrative, which moves predictably from trials, torments and tortures, to a relatively evanescent moment of closure and release. According to Reik's definition of 'social masochism', end-pleasure is paramount: the punishment is only endured as a necessary prelude to the achievement of a guilt-free climax of orgasmic release.

> Finally Reik claims that the fantasies at the heart of masochism … always express the same desire … to be rewarded for good behaviour. Consequently, although they invariably dramatise the sufferings and defeats of the fantasising subject, that is 'only to make the final victory appear all the more glorious and triumphant.'[12]

However, if, as Silverman inquires, the objective is end-pleasure, 'why should he or she then delay the moment of gratification for as long as possible?'[13] The preoccupation with denouement in popular narrative forms and sadomasochistic play is founded on the assumption that only pleasure is pleasurable. This ignores the subject who seeks pain itself, for whom the climax of release is secondary and who thus 'seeks to prolong preparatory detail and ritual at the expense of climax or consummation'.[14] In its typical form the prison film is a lengthy spectacle of escalating tension, with rituals of suffering, defeat and degradation, leading to a final release. It is possible that the suffering with which the genre is preoccupied is not purely the price to be paid for this climax, but an implicit challenge to the binary coding of pain and pleasure.

Linda Williams' description of the *mise-en-scène* of sadomasochistic pornography might easily be a précis for many prison dramas:

Although the physical violence may be extreme, its effect hinges on careful timing, the suspense and anxiety of prolonged suffering, delayed consummations, surprise gestures of either cruelty or tenderness ... frequent role-playing, and inversions of hierarchies leading to confusion regarding who is really in power.[15]

Narrative structure in the prison film, as in the popular romance, is the socially acceptable face of masochism (with a hardcore skull still visible beneath the skin). But to whom does this face belong? The dominatrix, in a Freudian unmasking, is a disguise worn by a woman impersonating the oedipal father. However, a Deleuzean deconstruction of the S&M plot provides another turn of the screw in the prison drama. In *Coldness and Cruelty*, Deleuze proposes that the dominatrix is not a woman pretending to be the oedipal father, but a woman impersonating the pre-oedipal mother. The description Deleuze offers of this figure – a cold, severe, oral mother who 'swallows' her son – returns us to the gynophobic trope of prison as maternal body: 'A contract is established between the hero and the woman, whereby at a precise point in time and for a determinate period she is given every right over him.'[16] For the duration of this sentence the son is castrated and the mother invested with the phallus (the whip, the club, the gun, the chains, the bars of the cell). The ritual violence between these two is designed to negate the law, to destroy the patriarch as he is embodied in the submissive male partner: 'he is beaten ... what is beaten, humiliated and ridiculed in him is the image and likeness of the father'.[17] The masquerade of masochism seeks to subvert the law, since it is based on 'a pact between mother and son to write the father out of his dominant position within both masochism and culture, and to install the mother in his place'.[18]

Reading the prison film as sadomasochistic fantasy we are thus confronted by a disorderly triangulation of desire. The genre can express a positive oedipal complex, in which the prisoner-son battles with the warden-father to posses mother liberty. Alternatively, it might follow the path of the negative oedipal complex, in which the prisoner-son expresses hostility towards the Big House-maternal body and a covert attraction to the warden-father is played out in rituals of violence. According to the Deleuzean model, however, the role play may be even more convoluted: the Big House and the warden embody a powerful maternal figure who punishes the law of the father as it is embodied in the prisoner-son. This final line offers the most Gordian ravelling of images of bondage and also stakes the greatest claim for the genre's oppositional credentials. A Deleuzean perspective would encourage us to read this traditionally all-male genre as anti-oedipal, as a revolutionary return of repressed maternal power that banishes the father and commits an offence against patriarchy by investing the law in the mother.

The prison film is overcrowded with turbulent desires and these may not be confined to the screen. The genre offers the spectator oblique subject positions that traverse fantasies of mastery and submission, a sadomasochistic exchange in which s/he enjoys the privilege of a controlling gaze during scenes of torture, but is then locked into the point of view of the prisoner-hero subjected to the pain. In this respect, the prison film might be identified as a particularly purified form of the cinematic experience, at least as it has been analysed by psychoanalytical film theory. According to Mulvey's highly influential model of visual pleasure, patriarchal sadism is at the core of scopophilia and narrative structure: 'Sadism demands a story, depends on making something happen, forcing a change in another person, a battle of will and strength, victory/defeat.'[19] Conversely, several critiques of the Mulvey model, focusing on the passivity of spectatorship, have argued for the relevance of masochistic gratification to the suturing of onlooker and image. In 'Masochism and the Perverse Pleasures of the Cinema', Gaylyn Studlar insists that film encourages regression to pre-oedipal pleasures of fusion and submission where the tenebrous voyeur, like the child observing the primal scene, is more mastered than master.[20] If these psycho-analyses of film bear any relation to the cinematic experience, then post-*Star Wars* box office figures might suggest increasing currency in fantasies of sadistic mastery and masochistic submission. Whether or not this confirms Edmundson's thesis that millennial America constitutes an S&M culture, the specific genre of contemporary prison films is a productive site for anyone interested in the operations of power and fantasy, deviance and desire. The case studies that follow will interrogate individual prison films in relation to the taxonomy traced here: the reproduction of formula and its attempted subversion; the political instrumentality of prison film, especially in its departures from the recent history of a burgeoning prison-industrial complex; and the labyrinthine libidinal economies on display within the genre and its consumers.

THE ESCAPE FILM (1): *COOL HAND LUKE*

> In the end, the weapon returns, more concrete and cruel than it had been in the older writing ... The cross is unusual among weapons: its hurt of the body does not occur in one explosive moment of contact; it is not there and gone but against the body for a long time ... Jesus takes the place of the weapon.
>
> *The Body in Pain*, Elaine Scarry[21]

In the opening scene of *Cool Hand Luke* (1967), Paul Newman's character is caught vandalising parking meters with a pipe cutter. Luke makes no protest at his arrest and is similarly passive on arrival at a prison farm to serve a two-year sentence for 'maliciously destroying municipal property'. Gradually, however, he begins to perform defiant acts that win him a cult following amongst the convicts: he refuses to accept defeat despite being totally outmatched in a boxing contest; he wins a hand of poker (and his nickname) with an audacious bluff; he wins another bet by eating 50 eggs in one hour; and he makes repeated escape attempts. Aside from a short-lived period of docility after an especially severe beating, Luke remains refractory until his death at the hands of a prison marksman. In an epilogue delivered by Dragline, Luke's most ardent attendant, the martyr is seen to live on in chain gang folklore as a 'natural born world shaker'.

The closing images of *Cool Hand Luke* offer a God's-eye view of the chain gang toiling at a dusty intersection. In a gradual dissolve the cross-road is replaced by the cruciform tears in a photograph of Luke, at a bar, with his arms around two glamour models. This picture had earlier been torn up by one of Luke's followers when his idol confessed that it was a counterfeit costing him a 'week's wages'. The lacerated icon with which *Cool Hand Luke* closes may be a fake, but it seems to warrant the Christian symbolism associated with the film's martyr hero. On its initial appearance the photograph is described by Dragline as a 'vision of Paradise ... with two angels either side of my boy'. When it reappears at the close it now seems to signify crucifixion, with Luke flanked not by thieves but 'fallen ladies'. This tableau replays a 'God's-eye' shot following the egg-eating competition which showed Luke recumbent on a wooden table, head tilted, arms outstretched and lower legs crossed. The 50 eggs consumed at this festival correspond to the number of convicts held at the facility. Luke's subsequent accusation, that his followers are 'feeding off [him]', reverses the imagery of the egg festival and is prophetic, as, at his last supper before a final escape, each prisoner takes a spoonful of food from their leader's plate.

Although New Testament chronology is confused here, the imagery of Pentecost, crucifixion and sacrament is nonetheless conspicuous. Could road prison 36 be the site of a second coming? Luke's prison number, 37, might signpost a scriptural response: 'for with God, nothing is impossible' (Luke 1.37). Luke's nickname is confirmed by a bluff which proves that 'nothing can be a real cool hand'. This handful of nothing adds up to 36, the number of the road prison, thus reminding us of Luke's captivity. However, the sole picture card, a prominently displayed King of Hearts, hints at sovereignty and perhaps stigmata, through the conjunction of hands and blood red hearts. Following his execution, Luke's image appears alongside his devotees on the road and their faith in him assures he will live on in prison fable. At the same time, the fact that his apostles are left slaving in the wilderness, under the glare of cruel overseers, seems to confirm that Luke was no hard-boiled messiah.

In the epilogue, Dragline offers apocrypha to Luke's disciples about the execution.

Convicts: What'd he look like, Drag? Yeah, what'd he look like? He had his eyes opened or closed, Drag?

Dragline: He was smiling. That's right. You know, that, that Luke smile of his. He had it on his face right to the very end.

The montage that accompanies this epitaph underlines the significance of Luke's smile. It also recalls that this expression of pleasure is often linked to the experience of pain. Luke is happy when it hurts: he smiles at his arrest, when he's being beaten, when he's semi-conscious after consuming 50 eggs, when he's dying from a gunshot wound to the throat. Although his messianic credentials are doubtful, the pleasure he receives from pain aligns Luke with a distinguished history of saints who revelled in suffering. Generations of religious radicals and martyrs have embraced execution, torture and degradation as a chance to imitate the crucifixion, the primal scene of Christian masochism. The Christian masochist rejoices in pain since what is being punished, through them, is sin itself. Any agony can also be endured as an augury of ecstasy at the second coming and the Day of Judgement. Despite the Christian iconography littering Rosenberg's film, however, it is not certain that Luke's smile betokens a wholly spiritual joy. As in *The Scarlet Letter*, where Hawthorne hints strongly at the vicissitudes of the divine and the deviant, *Cool Hand Luke* imbricates the religious and the erotic through its foregrounding of Luke's masochism.

In 'The Economic Problem of Masochism' Freud suggested that 'in order to provoke punishment … the masochist must do what is inexpedient, must act against his own interests, must ruin the prospects which open out to him in the real world and must, perhaps, destroy his own real existence'.[22] Luke's actions follow precisely this trajectory: he begins by courting punishment from the police, then from other prisoners (the boxing match with Dragline) and after each escape he appears either to acquiesce in or even arrange for his recapture, encouraging increasingly severe beatings and ultimately his own demise. Luke never confesses to masochistic yearnings, but according to Freud, this complex remains 'as a rule hidden from the subject and has to be inferred from their behaviour … Even when punishment seems to derive from the external world, it is in fact the result of a skillful unconscious manipulation of "adverse incidents".'[23] For Freud, such behaviour is rooted in oedipal conflicts, has strong associations with homosexual desire and is ultimately under the sway of the death drive. Each of these signatures of the masochistic sensibility can also be detected in *Cool Hand Luke*.

During a thunderstorm Luke screams at the skies for a sign: 'You up there, Old Man? Love me, hate me, do anything. Just let me know you're there.' This forlorn attempt to open a dialogue represents one instance in a persistent 'failure to communicate' (the film's key phrase) that plagues father–son relations in the film. Luke never had the chance to know his biological 'Old Man' and his persistent challenging of the law might be read in relation to this paternal absence. When the Captain at the road prison asks why he wanted to cut the heads off parking meters, Luke answers that he was 'settling old scores'. The extent of the oedipal debt incurred by Luke is evidently severe: he gets into trouble with authority in the army, with Dragline, the alpha male amongst the inmates, with the Captain and the guards. The punishment which Luke receives seems less an unfortunate consequence of spirited individualism and more a longed for sign of recognition from the Old Man. With its enforced infantilisation of inmates, the prison is an ideal stage on which to act out this oedipal drama. On arrival Luke is familiarised with the 'house rules' concerning bed times, meal times, going to the toilet and the penalty for infraction, which is a night in 'the box', the darkest corner in the Big House. In her reading of Freud, Silverman describes the construction of the superego as a process dependent upon the introjection of the 'symbolic father' who signifies 'law, gaze, voice from above'.[24] At road prison 36, the state services superegos as well as transport infrastructure, attempting to develop Luke's respect for the law by subjecting him to a continual disciplinary gaze. As well as attempting to engage in dialogue with a heavenly 'voice from above', Luke is frequently positioned beneath authority figures during conversation (below porches and in ditches).

The suturing of Heavenly Fathers and earthly authority figures in *Cool Hand Luke* resonates with Freud's comment in *The Ego and the Id* that the superego 'contains the germ from which all religions have evolved'.[25] Freud went on to insist that the superego is always 'a substitute for a longing for the father'.[26] In this context, masochism is read as a reactivation of the negative oedipus complex: desire for the father and identification with the mother. Masochistic fantasies 'place the subject in a characteristically feminine situation; they signify, that is, being castrated, or copulated with, or giving birth to a baby'.[27] During the egg-eating competition, Luke's stomach swells impressively, leading one of the inmates to tap his belly and claim 'it's just about ready to pop'. The eggs connote fertility and this scene also echoes a common misconception amongst young children, reported by Freud, associating pregnancy with eating a special food and babies being born from the belly. According to Silverman, the masochist 'prefers the masquerade of womanliness to the parade of virility'.[28] In preparation for the competition, the mammoth Dragline assumes the role of Luke's trainer and massages the star attraction's far slighter frame, focusing on his stomach, whilst semi-naked inmates dance suggestively for each other in the background. Such moments, alongside Drag's nicknames for Luke – 'my darling', 'my baby' – might highlight the cipher in his own name.

During one of Luke's escape attempts, a guard is given heterosexual erotic fiction as a diversionary ruse. The guard reads a highlighted passage aloud but, as the temperature rises, his voice trails off into suggestive silences. The queer quiescence of *Cool Hand Luke* similarly relies on diversionary tactics. Classical Hollywood narratives often seek to deflect attention from gay sub-texts by introducing material that foregrounds heterosexual desire. In *Cool Hand Luke* this distraction is achieved by a car washing scene in which a country girl teases the chain gang. Although she is introduced to signpost how straight these criminals are, Dragline's naming of the anonymous girl, as 'Lucille', echoes the film's forbidden subject of desire. *Luc*ille functions as an intermediary between Luke and his lovers. At the climax of a subsequent set piece, in which Luke foxes the guards by encouraging the men to work feverishly whilst laying a new road, Dragline calls him a 'wild, beautiful thing' and as their idol reclines, surrounded by admirers, a broom handle rears up suggestively between his legs.

When they are not being symbolically satiated, forbidden erotic attractions can also be displaced into violence in classical Hollywood narrative. Following the car wash scene in *Cool Hand Luke*, the men initially cheer and then are disgusted by their pleasure, as Luke is beaten in a boxing match by Dragline for daring to question the sexual innocence of Lucille. When Luke wins the respect of the inmates he turns to the guards to satisfy his masochistic longing. The punishments he receives – the chaining of his legs and beatings with clubs and canes – recall Freud's remarks concerning masochistic fantasies of being 'copulated with' and 'castrated'. One of the punishments devised by the guards requires Luke to dig and refill holes repeatedly whilst apologising for the mess he is making. The climax to this ritual humiliation is attained when the Captain beats Luke with his cane, after which the victim abases himself by hugging his master's boots and begging for mercy. Throughout this pivotal scene Luke is watched closely both by guards and prisoners:

> in no case of masochism can the fact be overlooked that the suffering, discomfort, humiliation and disgrace are being shown and so to speak put on display ... one feels induced to assume a constant connection between masochism and exhibitionism.[29]

Luke's exhibitionism is projected onto Lucille, his female double and can also be inferred from all of the scenes in which he is punished. He is surrounded by the inmates during the boxing match and the egg-eating competition. In the opening scene Luke smiles as the police arrive to witness his offence and he is illuminated by the patrol vehicle headlights. This proves to be a curtain-raiser for the crowning glory of his death scene, as he beams, once again before the spotlights of a mass audience of law officials, before being gunned down.

During Luke's ritual humiliation by the Captain, one of his followers in the captive inmate audience offers his support by singing 'ain't no grave gonna hold my body down'. As a cadaverous Luke rises from the grave resurrection imagery is crossed with signs from the genre most associated with erotic deviance: the Gothic. The blood-spattered Luke's challenge to his disciples to 'stop feeding off me' carries connotations of vampirism and recalls Nietzsche's denouncement of the sacrament as cannibalism. The crucifix imagery at the close might thus be read as a promise of sanctuary for Luke, safe from his rapacious cult following. Psychoanalytical readings of vampire fiction and film have often been torn between different chapters in the family romance: the vampire has been unmasked as both oedipal father and pre-oedipal mother. As in vampire fiction and like its eponymous subject, the oedipal narrative in *Cool Hand Luke* is disjunctive and disorderly. At times Luke's rebellion appears to represent a coded expression of love for the father. The appearance of his mother, however, threatens to challenge this reading.

When Luke's mother arrives for a prison visit it is also a death bed scene. Terminally ill and lying in the back of a pick-up truck, Arletta delivers a message to her son: 'You ain't alone. Everywhere you go, I'm with you.' Arletta also confesses in relation to Luke that 'sometimes you just have a feeling for a child' and in the absence of his father, the son's bond with his mother is similarly intense. Once the mother enters the oedipal triangle, Luke's punishment assumes the guise of patriarchal vengeance for incestuous desires. When Arletta dies, the Captain puts Luke in the box. This punishment is designed to stop the son from 'getting rabbit in his blood' and attending his mother's funeral, but symbolically it diminishes the distance between them. The following three days in a vertical coffin are the catalyst to Luke's subsequent escape attempts, but it is not clear where, or to whom, he is running. The fugitive's insurgency guarantees attention from the father, but also promises, through death, a reunion with the mother. Luke's death scene suggests that whilst his sedition is initially motivated by a desire to communicate with patriarchal authority, it is subsequently driven by a need to return to pre-oedipal bonds.

After a third failed escape attempt, Luke goads his captors by repeating the Captain's maxim: 'what we have here is a failure to communicate'. Significantly, he is shot in the throat for mimicking his master's voice and this wound initiates a return to a pre-lingual (and ultimately pre-conscious) condition. The agent of phallic vengeance is Boss Godfrey, a figure whose name and resolute silence position him as the film's archetypal patriarch. In response to Luke's death, Dragline attacks Godfrey and the Boss's reflector sunglasses are smashed by the car carrying Luke's body. The breaking of the mirrored shades signifies not an oedipal blinding of the 'man with no eyes', however, so much as a regression to the imaginary. Lying near death in the back of a car, Luke's position replicates his mother's at their last meeting. Automobiles have been associated with the female body on two prior occasions: Arletta's death bed in the back of a pick-up truck (which seemed an extension of her ailing frame) and Lucille's car-washing exhibition. Luke is introduced whilst attacking parking meters and is last seen in the back of a police car. The Captain says confidently, 'he's ours', but Luke's smile, as the car pulls off and smashes Godfrey's glasses, suggests an escape to a pre-oedipal state beyond the father's law. The hearse is both tomb and womb. The Captain's decision to take Luke to the prison infirmary, rather than the local hospital nearby, is a death sentence, but Luke, smiling as his death drive is literalised, is on his way to achieving the coolest hand of all.

According to Freud, the superego, the primary agency in masochism, can 'promote a pure culture of death'.[30] Is Luke's death drive simply suicidal, or might it be read, in Deleuzean terms, as part of a subversive 'pact between mother and son'? Can such a drive be reconciled with Dragline's epitaph for Luke as a 'natural born world shaker' and with critical assessments that insist on what Reik termed the 'revolutionary fervour' of masochism? Luke might conform to Chasseguet-Smirgel's definition of the pervert, 'trying to free himself from the paternal universe and the constraints of the law. He wants to create a new kind of reality and to dethrone God the Father.'[31] In this context, the death drive might be read not as self-destruction so much as an assault on dominant forms of male subjectivity, especially as those forms are valorised in the figure of the hero. According to Silverman, the perversity of the masochist seethes with counter-hegemonic impulses. The masochist's

(barely) repressed desire runs directly counter to any reconcilia-tion of father and son, attesting irrefutably to the violence of the familial and cultural contract ... His sexuality, moreover, must be seen to be entirely under the sway of the death drive, devoid of any possible productivity or use value ... although he seems to subordinate himself to the law of the father, that is only because he knows how to transform punishment into pleasure, and severity into bliss ... [he] deploys the diversionary tactics of demonstration, suspense, and impersonation against the phallic 'truth' or 'right', substituting perversion for the *père-vision* of exemplary male subjectivity.[32]

Luke's intransigence uncovers the violence underpinning the Captain's rhetoric of rehabilitation and his impersonation of a model prisoner obscures the *père-vision* of the 'm[e]n with no eyes'. Like Bartleby, Melville's prototypical masochist, Luke's necromania might radiate a perverse negativity inimical to the dominant culture, eventually using his own body as an instrument with which to punish the law of the father.

Although utopian readings of masochism rarely specify the means by which it might translate into public political action, there are moments in *Cool Hand Luke* that hint at how perversion might be transported from the bedroom to the barricades. The scene in which Luke encourages the prisoners to shovel sand onto a newly-tarred country road at a frenzied pace, for example, allows them to share the ecstasy of masochism and achieve a temporary triumph over their baffled keepers. If Luke's perversion does offer the potential for public transgression, however, this scene needs to be weighed against the film's closing shots, in which the prisoners are working the road at a measured pace, contenting themselves with nostalgia for their dead leader rather than engaging in any 'world shaking' over their own. The docile acquiescence of his followers to authority suggests Luke's martyrdom achieved, at best, a pyrrhic victory over his oppressor. Luke's charisma seems to suggest revolutionary longing, but his death and the failure of his followers to rebel, betokens scepticism concerning the possibilities of translating utopian impulses into political action. *Cool Hand Luke* must thus be read as a political allegory, especially given its historical position in the hey-day of 1960s radicalism. As Ryan and Kellner argue in *Camera Politica*, the year that Rosenberg's film was released, 1967, was a

turning point year in Hollywood film. The period between 1966 and 1968 is a watershed of the sixties, a time when the economy was expanding, liberals in government were seeking to reform society, blacks were in revolt against oppression, drug use and sexual experimentation were changing traditional social values, and protest movements against the Vietnam War were gaining national attention for the New Left.[33]

Within this climate New Hollywood films, such as *The Graduate*, *Bonnie and Clyde*, *Midnight Cowboy* and *Easy Rider*, offered representations of

> the 'Establishment' as a set of outdated conservative values, of the police as an enemy rather than a friend, of the patriarchal family as an instrument for the oppression of women ... of sexuality as a rich terrain of possibility rather than an evil to be repressed.[34]

Cool Hand Luke echoes the sentiments of the New Hollywood, but ultimately seems to renounce them. Instead of optimism for the possibilities of radical change, Rosenberg offers a sombre scepticism. The rebel's triumphs are largely symbolic – a pair of broken glasses – his followers remain oppressed, repressed and unable to escape the house of the father except through death.

Ryan and Kellner's assessment of the New Hollywood relies on an orthodox opposition of 1960s radicalism and 1980s conservative counter-revolution. Surveying the same territory in *Vineland*, Thomas Pynchon challenges the dualism underlying this history with Brock Bond, a fascist bully boy whose 'genius lay in his recognition that all of this [1960s] rebellion was not an affront to authority so much as unacknowledged desire for it ... Children longing for discipline.'[35] *Cool Hand Luke* confirms this revisionist history of 'children longing for discipline'. It shows as much contempt for the mob who live vicariously through their rebel leaders as for the authorities. Radicalism is devalorised through association with deviant, infantile fantasy and self-destruction. The opening image of the film is a signifier of state authority – a 'STOP' sign on a parking meter – and Luke is last seen in a car beneath a traffic light changing from green to red. The thrust of the film seems to be a mournful confirmation of the necessity for obeying such signs. As the cruciform tears in the image of Luke are transposed over the crossroads at which the chain gang labour, Rosenberg's double cross of the spirit of 1960s radicalism is unwittingly visualised.

THE EXECUTION FILM (1): *THE GREEN MILE*

> In sentimentality there is repressed or unconscious hate, and this repression is unhealthy. Sooner or later the hate turns up.
>
> *Deprivation and Delinquency*, D. W. Winnicott[36]

Cool Hand Luke expresses romantic sympathy for the rebel, but ultimately associates this figure with immaturity and self-destructive violence. Stuart Rosenberg's reservations about radical defiance and a concomitant sympathy for the establishment were confirmed by his subsequent prison drama *Brubaker* (1980).[37] Whilst *Cool Hand Luke*, in the hey-day of the counter-culture, was preoccupied with a rebellious prisoner, *Brubaker*, which appeared on the eve of Reagan's election, follows the career of a reformist warden. In a prison-based spin on *The Prince and the Pauper* legend, Henry Brubaker arrives at his new prison disguised as an inmate and witnesses at first hand the corruption of the officials. Subsequently unveiled as the warden, Brubaker battles and eventually triumphs over the prison hierarchy and the local business community who have been benefiting from convict labour. *Brubaker*, by positioning itself between the oppressors and the oppressed, offered a liberal fantasy solution to problems within the prison industry, a remedy whose potency was about to be spectacularly disproved by history. The Reagan administration was instrumental in a profitable expansion of the prison industry as well as the rolling back of prisoner support, education and welfare programmes.

The African-American community, inevitably, bore the brunt of these developments and this makes the images in *Brubaker* of a white governor sensitive to the needs of his black prisoners seem especially unconvincing. The prison in *Brubaker* includes a significant African-American presence, perhaps in part as compensation for colour blindness in *Cool Hand Luke*, which had been located in the unlikely setting of a Southern correctional facility devoid of black prisoners. This omission is fortuitous, since the presence of black prisoners would have jeopardised the film's racial sub-text. *Cool Hand Luke* is a seminal example of the white slave narrative that figures conspicuously in Hollywood prison films. The long history of institutional symbiosis between slavery and the prison system extends to textual representations and the prison film borrows much of its narrative structure and iconography from the slave narrative. As we have seen, prison farms and chain gangs were the institutional replacements for plantations in the Southern penal economy. The road prison in *Cool Hand Luke* is divided into the Big House, residence of the Captain and the crowded quarters of his charges, sent out to work from dawn to dusk and supervised by guards called 'boss'. Luke's strategies of resistance on this prison-plantation recall those practised in the slave narrative. In a manner reminiscent of the trickster figure, Luke outwits his captors by performing as an 'eye-servant' whilst planning escape. As a fugitive, Luke is chased by dogs, he teams up with African-American children to lose his leg-irons and is seen running on a railroad (a literalisation of the figurative escape route taken by slaves). The analogies between Luke and Christ also reproduces a key generic signature of the slave narrative.

The palimpsest of the slave narrative beneath the prison story in *Cool Hand Luke* has particular significance against the backdrop of what Ryan and Kellner term the 'revolt against oppression' involving African-Americans in 1967.[38] Luke specialises, like the civil rights movement, in the tactics of passive resistance: he invites arrest by destroying state property, he allows the burly white Southerner, Dragline, to beat him until his audience are disgusted by the spectacle and ultimately he instigates his own assassination and martyrdom. Luke, the King of Hearts, is shot in the throat for passively resisting his white masters. The following year, Martin Luther King, primary spokesperson for black civil rights and passive resistance, was gunned down by a white assassin. In the same year, in the science fiction film *Planet of the Apes*, astronaut George Taylor is shot in the throat resulting in a 'failure to communicate' with his simian captors. As in *Cool Hand Luke*, against a backdrop of increasingly vocal African-American activism, *Planet of the Apes* offers a white slave narrative in which white men, women and children are herded into cages by whip-wielding apes. The representation of the apes resurrects antebellum racist propaganda about African-Americans as animal-human hybrids eager to subjugate their evolutionary superiors. At the same time, the division of the ape community into militant gorillas in black leather and more 'civilised' chimpanzees and orangutans maps neatly onto the division in contemporary African-American protest between, on the one hand, the Nation of Islam and the Black Panthers and on the other the civil rights movement.

The appearance of white slave narratives like *Cool Hand Luke* and *Planet of the Apes*, in the hey-day of African-American protest, allowed the dominant culture to experience the ethical privileges of the margin without risking any of its dangers. As various challenges to the authority of white masculinity were made in the late 1960s and subsequently, the prison narrative has served as an arena in which white male subjectivity can position itself as downtrodden victim rather than beneficiary of 'the system'. Frank Darabont's highly successful prison drama, *The Green Mile* (1999), represents a recent continuation of this signifying practice and also mirrors the ideological formulae at work in *Cool Hand Luke*, *Brubaker* and *Planet of the Apes*. Like *Cool Hand Luke*, *The Green Mile* features heavy-handed messianic imagery. Like *Brubaker*, *The Green Mile* offers an untypical focus on a benevolent white guard and his compassion for black prisoners, positioning its Caucasian hero as fellow victim alongside his African-American brother and proffering faith in the possibility of humanising the system from within. Like *Planet of the Apes*, *The Green Mile* has an urgent but displaced relation to the material conditions of race war in contemporary America and this relation will be the focal point of the following analysis.

During the three set-piece executions in *The Green Mile* there are repeated shots, compulsory to the *mise-en-scène* of the death house, of a quartz clock on the wall. This clock, however, like the death row inmate, is out of time. Darabont's film is set in 1935, but the quartz clock, invented by Morrison in 1927, was not even adopted in laboratories until the 1940s. The misplaced clock is suggestive of the confused timing in *The Green Mile*. The Depression setting disguises the film's attempt to supply symbolic resolutions to contemporary conflicts within the prison industry. In 1973 there were 134 prisoners on death row in the US and no executions. By the time of *The Green Mile*'s release, in 1999, there were 3,540 prisoners awaiting death and 98 executions. Almost 45 per cent of the death row population at this time were black and there were also disproportionately high numbers of Hispanic, Native American and Asian-American inmates. The racial and ethnic composition of death row in *The Green Mile* pays homage to these statistics and conforms to the melting-pot formula of prison narratives. The African-American is juxtaposed with one Native American, one Cajun and one clichéd specimen of poor white trash. To underline its liberal credentials all of the enmity is channelled away from the racial minorities and towards the redneck, Billy Wharton. This redirection is repeated with the prison authorities as the rogue deviant, Percy, exists primarily to underline the essential decency of the other guards. A systemic critique of capital punishment is thus foreclosed by facile moral antithesis: the ranks of philanthropic guards and dignified prisoners are disrupted by lone, puerile sadists. Cultural anxiety about crime and punishment is directed away from institutional systems towards individuals, or rather, platitudinous stereotypes of the 'bad seed'. The socioeconomic conditions that promote deviance are erased by Billy the Kid's cartooned criminality and when Percy tortures the prisoners, institutional violence is hidden behind individual sadism.

The Green Mile works hard to obscure the origins and nature of punitive violence. In the process, far from offering an indictment of capital punishment, it valorises the executioner's profession. Darabont reverses prison narrative formula by focalising through the guards and insisting on their fundamental decency. Paul Edgecombe, in the best tradition of liberal penologists, compares death row to the 'intensive care ward of a hospital'. *The Green Mile* suggests that individual compassion humanises even this most inhumane of environments. The measured protocols observed by Edgecombe and his men are seen to confer dignity on the condemned. Alternatively, one might argue that the tactics of disciplinary intimacy serve primarily to pacify the victims and cloak the barbarism of state slaughter. Violence, the essential ingredient in execution, is either hidden or displaced in *The Green Mile*. Before the first of three trips to the chair, Paul organises a rehearsal which does less to suggest the perverse theatricality of ritual butchery than to encourage sympathy for those who carry it out. As the first condemned man is dispatched with clinical precision, Darabont also encourages respect for the executioner's professionalism. This scene works in counterpoint with the second execution which is intentionally botched by the bad guard. When Percy neglects to apply water to Eduard Delacroix's head, a bad connection results that prolongs the electrocution and eventually results in a public burning. The pro-death penalty sympathies of the film are evident in Darabont's attributing of this grisly spectacle to Percy's sexual deviancy and an implicit sanctioning of the normally well regulated machinery of death. The problem posed by *The Green Mile* is not execution, but botched execution.

The film's most potent anti-death penalty imagery is undercut and this process is continued in the climactic execution of John Coffey. The preoccupation with Coffey's spiritual angst and Edgecombe's empathy confuses execution with euthanasia. Rather than offering an unequivocal anti-death penalty statement, *The Green Mile* translates state slaughter into mercy killing. The staging of Coffey's execution minimises violence and hints at ascension. There is only a brief glance at the chair before a sequence, accompanied by mawkish music, of slow-motion reaction shots of the guards who are silhouetted by a golden nimbus of exploding light bulbs (Edison's ghost doubly haunts this *mise-en-scène*). The extent to which *The Green Mile* condones the death penalty is underscored by its sentimental aestheticisation of murder and by the behaviour of John Coffey who is figured as both condemned man and executioner.

Before welcoming his own death, Coffey inflicts summary justice on disruptive elements within the Death House and explains: 'I punished the bad men, I punished them both.' A disease extracted from the governor's wife is injected into Percy who then shoots Billy the Kid. Thus, the good wife is saved, the child rapist and murderer is gunned down and the bad guard ends up traumatised in an asylum. *The Green Mile* replaces the state machinery of death with the *deus ex machina* of right-wing retribution fantasies. Perversely, the African-American body, which has historically been the subject of white violence, is transformed in this fable into a powerful instrument of punitive vengeance. Coffey directs the shooting of Wharton and sends Percy to an asylum before insisting on his own execution. In the coda that follows Coffey's execution, punitive power again changes hands as Edgecombe, the white guard, is seen to be enduring a life sentence, in an old people's home, passed down by the black prisoner.

The Green Mile offers symbolic resolution of the contemporary punitive oppression of African-Americans partly by obscuring the nature and origins of disciplinary power and partly through historical insouciance, epitomised by the misplaced quartz clock, in its depiction of punishment practices in the Depression era. John Coffey's mere presence on death row is an historical anachronism since, in Louisiana in 1935, even an accusation that white children had been sexually assaulted and murdered would certainly have resulted in summary lynching. Alternatively, *The Green Mile* focuses on sympathetic responses from white prison officials who listen to Billie Holliday on white radio stations and arrange nocturnal visits by convicted black felons to the bedrooms of white Southern women. This was the era of the infamous Scottsboro case, when nine young black men, falsely accused of gang-raping two white women, suffered legal lynching and were sentenced to death in Alabama. Louisiana State Penitentiary was popularly referred to as 'bloody Angola' at this time, due to its predominantly black population and its reputation as one of the most brutal prison regimes in America. In *The Green Mile*, although one of the guards is nicknamed 'Brutal', there is remarkably little violence. Flogging, water torture and extended solitary confinement were deployed routinely in penal institutions, but in *The Green Mile* the 'punishment room' has fallen into disuse and is serving as a storage space for furniture. During the Depression the living conditions in most American prisons were obscene: dilapidated infrastructure, filth, diseases and plagues of insects and vermin were not uncommon. Louisiana had a particularly appalling record in this respect and even its own State Board of Health decried the prison system as a 'relic of barbarism'.[39] Conversely, the gleaming floors of the 'Green Mile' are disturbed only by the antics of a single circus mouse.

The appearance of 'Mr Jingles' epitomises the flight from the historical conditions of punishment towards a Disneyfication of death row. *The Green Mile* is set in the nascent period of Disney's evolution (on the eve of *Snow White and the Seven Dwarves*), but Darabont replicates the polished Pavlovianism perfected by Disney's late twentieth century 'Imagineers'. Genre, narrative structure and character in *The Green Mile* are traced through the Disney-Touchstone template. This process begins with the decision to translate social problems (capital punishment and racial discrimination) into maudlin melodrama and transcend material conflicts by gesturing towards spiritualism. The main players in this sentimental spectacle conform precisely to the moral Manicheism that typifies Disney style and also underpins the contemporary legitimation of capital punishment. Any ethical nuances surrounding the professional executioner are dispelled by the casting of Tom Hanks, the dominant culture's embodiment of wholesome American normality. Michael Clark Duncan's performance as the child-like black giant similarly telegraphs his innocence from the outset and Coffey's supernatural powers are confirmed early on by the Spielbergean 'god-light' that accompanies his miracle work. This cartooning of character extends to the secondary roles, with a gallery of good prison officials and their families opposed to the bad prisoner (Billy the Kid) and the bad guard who conveniently eliminate each other (not before, in Dickensian fashion, Percy Wetmore has been humiliated by wetting himself). Eduard Delacroix is soothed on his way to the chair by the reassuring fantasy of 'Mouseville', a theme park retirement home for Mr Jingles. On the eve of his execution John Coffey is similarly heartened by a screening of *Top Hat*, a seminal example of those musical opiates eagerly consumed by Depression-ravaged America. 'Mouseville' and *Top Hat* might be read as self-reflexive motifs for *The Green Mile*'s own historical evasions and sentimental reassurances, its audacious attempt to deflect from conflicts within the *fin-de-siècle* prison-industrial complex.

Historical regression in *The Green Mile* goes further than the 1930s. Whilst *Brubaker* offered reassuring visions of the benevolent paternalism of white guards caring for black prisoners that dimly echoed the legitimising discourses of slavery, *The Green Mile* offers an unashamedly nostalgic recreation of antebellum ideology and iconography. *The Green Mile* is not too far from *Uncle Tom's Cabin*. Whilst Stowe's classic abolitionist text constituted the seminal response of sentimental white liberalism to slavery, Darabont's film represents a similar response from that same cohort to the new slave ship. Stowe's novel was inspired by a vision of a meek slave being mercilessly flogged to death and aimed to motivate white sympathy for black suffering. Darabont's film similarly relies on empathy for the plight of an African-American martyr as opposed to any critical understanding of the systems that produce racial oppression. John Coffey, like Uncle Tom, has an impressive physical presence, but at the same time is feminised through a focus on his child-like innocence, innate spirituality and passivity. *The Green Mile* resurrects the romantic racism of abolitionist propaganda. African-Americans are gentle, spiritual, capable of intense emotion and empathy but devoid of intellect: 'To tell you the truth Boss, I don't know much of anything, I never have.' Coffey's infantilisation and consequent dependence on the guiding hand of benevolent white patriarchs is highlighted upon his arrival at death row when he spells his name like a child and inquires timidly whether the lights are switched off at night: 'I's afraid of the dark.' When Coffey's defence lawyer, whose son has been scarred by the family dog, offers an analogy between 'negroes' and untrustworthy pets, Paul Edgecombe appears unconvinced, but the film's portrayal of John Coffey does little to challenge this equation. One of the guards, in reference to his faith-healing ingestion of a disease, even encourages Coffey to 'cough it up, boy'. Romantic racism reaches its climax in *Uncle Tom's Cabin* and *The Green Mile* with the climactic apotheoses and Passion of their respective martyr heroes. Uncle Tom embraces his death whilst refusing to flog his fellow slaves and John Coffey goes to the chair willingly after his summary execution of a fellow prisoner. Despite this difference, which crystallises Stowe and Darabont's respective positions on capital punishment, both figures achieve transcendence through execution which catalyses ethical self-consciousness in those around them. In both death scenes the black Christ (John Coffey) is ready to die for the sins of the white world, ready to forgive and redeem his persecutors. Uncle Tom prays for his white master even as he is being flogged to death and John Coffey blesses his executioners on the way to the chair: 'You're a good man Boss Brutal, Boss Edgecombe.'

In an echo of Uncle Tom's worship of white America, John Coffey declares, watching the 'I'm in Heaven' set piece from *Top Hat*: 'Why, they're angels.' Although both Stowe and Darabont are keen to desexualise the black Christ, it is, as we have seen, always difficult to segregate the spiritual from the sexual in narratives of punishment. John Coffey's faith-healing abilities involve a laying-on of hands and lips followed by the inhalation and exhalation of disease. Rather than a purely spiritual potency, this inspiration may be a coded artic-ulation of sexual energy. The black Christ appears in a dyad with the buck, associated since antebellum mythology with virile hypermas-culinity. In *Uncle Tom's Cabin*, Stowe repeated the abolitionist tactic of inverting racist stereotyping: the black rapist was replaced by an asexual, infantile figure playing innocently in the garden with Little Eva and kneeling respectfully by her death bed. In *The Green Mile*, John Coffey embraces the dead white girls and later kneels respect-fully by the bedside of the warden's dying wife. The ensuing oral exchange between the burly black man and the vulnerable white lady shakes the house to its foundations. Subsequently, John Coffey discharges this disease into the effeminate Percy by clenching the guard against the bars of his cell and forcing their mouths together. This is the third of three exchanges that occur through the bars of the cells on death row. In the first, the good prisoner (John Coffey) cures the good guard (Paul Edgecombe) of a urinary infection through a laying-on of hands. In the second the bad prisoner (Billy the Kid) sexually assaults the bad guard (Percy) by grabbing his genitals and kissing him. The third instance involves the good prisoner grabbing the bad guard and causing him to shoot the bad prisoner through the bars of his cell. The symmetry of these set pieces is accompanied by a desire to cordon off erotic connotations: whilst the second episode is unequivocally sexual, the first and third are presented as white magic performed by the black man. The structural contiguity of these scenes however, alongside the bedroom scene at the warden's house, make the lines between the spiritual, the sentimental and the sexual as pervious as the cells on the Green Mile. The choice of a urinary infection for the good guard may be coincidental, but it also anticipates Billy the Kid's sadistic assault on Percy. John Coffey explains to Paul, 'I got to give you a bit of myself' to achieve the cure. Later, after his fervent contact with a dying woman in the warden's bedroom, John 'give[s] … a bit' of the Southern Lady back to Percy. Following his own intimate encounter with Coffey's faith-healing techniques, Paul Edgecombe experiences ecstatic relief and promptly goes home to sleep with his wife. The emphasis on the longevity of their unseen conjugal reunion ('four times in one night') might be interpreted as compensatory for the conspicuous genital contact between black prisoner and white guard. When Percy (pronounced 'Pussy' in the Southern dialect) receives 'a bit' of the warden's wife and then empties his gun into Billy the Kid's cell it sustains the film's motifs of fluidity and orality. From the moment he arrives on death row, Billy the Kid is seen spitting out saliva, chocolate, feathers and expletives. Wharton grabs Percy's dick and causes him to wet himself and is later punished by being hosed down in his cell. Harriet Beecher Stowe believed strongly in the redemptive power of tears and offered her sentimental fiction as a form of baptism. The lachrymal aspirations of *The Green Mile*, however, are interfered with by a robust sexual symbolism. The sentimental tears in Darabont's Disneyfied death row melodrama are polluted by other fluids.

THE ESCAPE FILM (2):
THE SHAWSHANK REDEMPTION AND *ESCAPE FROM ALCATRAZ*

In Darabont's previous prison film, the narrator insists that 'prison is no fairy-tale world'. At times, *The Shawshank Redemption* does manage to avoid the Disneyfication of punishment evident in *The Green Mile*. Andy Dufresne, the vice-president of a Portland bank, arrives at Shawshank Penitentiary in 1947 for the murder of his wife and her lover. On arrival he is greeted by a gauntlet of jeering prisoners, callous guards and an austere warden. After his first night, during which a new inmate commits suicide, Andy continues to be intimidated by prisoners and staff and is subjected to assaults by a gang of rapists. The prison milieu in *The Shawshank Redemption* immediately appears less accommodating than in *The Green Mile*. Whilst the latter film threatens to lapse into an apology for the executioner's profession, the former offers elements of credible critique. *The Shawshank Redemption* highlights the futility of the parole ritual and the exploitation of prisoners as slave labour. Whilst the genre typically offers freedom as the grail, *The Shawshank Redemption* confronts the difficulties of adjusting to life *without* bars. An institutionalised yardbird finds it impossible to adapt to the outside and hangs himself: 'These walls are kind of funny. First you hate 'em, then you get used to 'em. Enough time passes, gets so you depend on them.'

In comparison with *The Green Mile*, the critique of punishment in *The Shawshank Redemption* is relatively trenchant and there is also a greater level of ambiguity in the depiction of the central crime. Whilst John Coffey's innocence is telegraphed from the outset, Andy Dufresne's denial of guilt initially seems to enhance suspicion. It would be a mistake, however, to emphasise the differences between Darabont's prison films at the expense of recognising their fundamental similarities. The distance between prison and a 'fairy-tale world' diminishes as *The Shawshank Redemption* unfolds. Andy Dufresne emerges as unbesmirched as John Coffey, cloaked in what a fellow inmate describes as an 'invisible coat' of goodness that is instinctively recognised by everyone he meets. When Paul Edgecombe presents John Coffey with home-made cornbread as a reward for his faith-healing, the prisoner insists that his peers on death row share this sacrament. After Andy Dufresne offers assistance to the prison guards, albeit in the more secular form of tax dodges, he is even more generous with his reward and the fact that he refuses the bounty of beer gratefully received by his fellows underlines his essential virtue. Subsequently, Andy works tirelessly on the guards' tax returns to secure privileges for the inmates, he writes thousands of letters to secure funds to stock the prison library and he helps young inmates to achieve educational qualifications. It is possible that Andy performs as a model prisoner to distract from his ongoing escape attempt, but his 'invisible coat' is still evident beneath this disguise.

Andy's canonisation eclipses the film's hostility towards the prison system and is accompanied by trite Hollywood maxims: 'Hope is a good thing, maybe the best of things, and no good thing ever dies.' The initial emphasis on the material conditions of prison life is gradually displaced by a more abstract focus on redemption, as Andy teaches the prisoners the importance of hope and thus returns the humanity which the system has stolen from them. Simultaneously, Andy manages to gain the respect of the guards, to fight for prisoner rights, to improve educational facilities and vocational training. These achievements are integral to the film's transition from institutional critique to valorisation of rehabilitative penal styles. As Andy's prestige within the prison increases he assumes the role of the good warden and engages in a power struggle with his nemesis, the institution's official custodian, Samuel Norton. Whilst Andy works tirelessly on behalf of the prisoners and reminds them of their humanity, the bad warden subjects his charges to excessive discipline and exploitative labour and insists on notions of sin. In the customary inaugural speech, Norton's affiliation with the *ancien régime* is underscored by his profession of faith in only two things, 'discipline and the Bible'.

Andy strives to create a progressive apparatus within this semi-feudal system, one founded on the possibility of redemption and legitimised by reference to the arts. Throughout his sentence at Shawshank, Andy is associated with texts and aesthetics. The figure of the artist-banker, a hybrid of particular appeal in Hollywood, uses his financial know-how to boost the fiscal balances of the guards and warden, but still finds time to accrue cultural capital of his own by reading, quoting Frost and Dumas, listening to classical music, sculpting, and playing chess. When he takes over the tax returns of guards and the prison accounts he is compared to Rembrandt – the commitment to rehabilitative penal styles is matched in intensity by a homage to white collar crime. Alongside his creative accountancy, Andy spends several years writing letters to request increases in funds to stock the prison library and this eventually results in the arrival of an avalanche of texts. The arts programme that Andy introduces at Shawshank suggests that despite the *disembourgeoisiement* symbolised by his prison overalls, his invisible coat has a freshly starched white collar. Class distinctions are evident in the opposition between Shawshank's two wardens: one is a Philistine who only reads the Bible, attends dinner parties and never gets his hands dirty; the other is an aesthete with a work ethic, who labours all night and day, pausing only to savour the arts. When a benefactor donates classical records to the Shawshank library, the good warden plays opera over the prison speakers, 'setting the prisoners free', which the film's bourgeois sentimentalism equates with subjection to a liberal arts education.

When Andy gives Red directions to a black box buried in a field, he describes a nearby wall as 'something out of a Robert Frost poem', thus indirectly indexing the film's hidden epigraph: 'Something there is that doesn't love a wall.'[40] The treasure that Red finds near this wall is under a small thicket of trees, perhaps the *shaw* at the end of Andy's *shank* (in prison argot a makeshift dagger or cutting implement). However, the *shank* in printing parlance, the body of the text between foot and shoulder, might be more apposite here. From the outset Red has difficulty reading Andy. He is described as a 'closed book ... A hard man to know'. One of the first things that Andy asks Red to acquire for him, as the prison fixer, is Rita

Hayworth. The female object of exchange that initiates the bonding between Andy and Red is requested in person and not as a reproduction. Andy's request for the real thing as opposed to her image, a poster for his cell, recalls his description as a 'Rembrandt' and the fakery with which the Dutch master is associated. Andy forges flawless tax returns, his escape is founded on a perfect imitation of the model prisoner and his request for Rita Hayworth in his cell is duplicitous since the image is designed to cover the reality of a hole in his cell wall. The succession of pin-ups that decorate Andy's cell – Hayworth is followed by Monroe and Raquel Welch – are thus doubly counterfeit: images of screen stars, rather than the women themselves and a screen covering Andy's escape route. When the warden tears down the poster in Andy's empty cell, the ruse is revealed and Andy's sexual gaze at female icons is de-eroticised into a lust for liberty. According to a psychoanalytical reading, however, the sexual dynamics here are not so easily eluded. The choice of sexual icons on the cell wall, behind which Andy's furtive nocturnal burrowing takes place, conforms to the gendering of liberty which characterises oedipal sub-texts in the prison genre. Andy escapes from the Big House of the father *through* the body of his fantasy women. His passage is decorated with birth imagery: squeezing through a narrow hole, struggling in a tunnel, emerging in waters, semi-naked and coated in waste to be born again on the outside. Andy escapes through a sewer, a 'river of shit' and then leads the authorities to the 'river of dirty money' that flows back to the warden. This might be read as oedipal vengeance for the symbolic toilet training he endured in the Big House (shining the warden's shoes, as well as laundering his shirts and his filthy lucre). Following his escape from the father's sphere of rules, language and writing, we never hear from Andy again: he is seen but silent. The escape is narrated by Red and the postcard that the fugitive sends to his friend is blank. Andy's flight to freedom is depicted as a passage from the symbolic to the semiotic (tunnelling behind pin-up posters, the 'two Italian ladies' singing a duet from *The Marriage of Figaro* and finally the ocean).

The silent reunion of Andy and Red by the Pacific at the close of *The Shawshank Redemption* anticipates the racial coding of *The Green Mile*. Both films develop utopian visions of interracial bonding that transcends bondage as compensations for social tensions inside and outside the contemporary US prison system. In *The Green Mile* homosocial union is accompanied by a homophobic demonisation of the sadistic Percy. This dynamic of desire and denial is similarly apparent in *The Shawshank Redemption*. The male love story that evolves between Andy and Red climaxes with a *mise-en-scène* borrowed straight from romance narrative: after painful separation the two are reunited, in the film's closing aerial shots, on a sun-soaked tropical beach and the camera pulls away to a decorous distance. The denial of any homosexual content to this relationship is effected earlier through the negative portrayal of a gang of male rapists known as the 'Sisters'. Despite his buddy's disclaimer, that the Sisters are 'not homosexual, they'd have to be human first', it seems clear that, as in *The Green Mile*, homosexual impulses in the film's central relationship are disowned by a demonisation of the queer other. At the same time, the fairy-tale ending of *The Shawshank Redemption* borders on camp parody of classical Hollywood closure. Racial conflict is resolved by the closing image of de-eroticised bonding between black and white soul mates and problems associated with punishment are rectified by the defeat of the *ancien régime* (embodied in the bad warden) and the enshrining of a progressive code.

Red claims that he has no faith in 'rehabilitation', it is 'a politician's word … a bullshit word', but Andy seems to embody the rehabilitative ethic and is part-buddy and part-parole officer to Red on his release. The choice of location for this promotion of the rehabilitative ethic is both pertinent and ironic. *The Shawshank Redemption* was shot at Ohio State Reformatory, designed in the late nineteenth century as a model institution geared to the rehabilitation of young offenders. In effect, Andy, especially in his tutoring of the new kid, Tommy Williams, rekindles the philosophy behind the original construction of the reformatory. At the same time, prison folklore at Ohio includes tales of a prisoner digging a tunnel through rocks with a spoon stolen from the mess hall and an escape through storm drains into the sewer system. One inmate even recalls an escape by two close friends through the sewers, one of whom was recaptured and then received an anonymous postcard from the Bahamas.

However, Ohio State was presumably not selected for its historical allegiance to a liberal penal style, or resonances with prison folklore, but for an impressively gothic architecture associated with the *ancien régime* of punishment. The design, drafted by the Cleveland architect Levi T. Scofield, was inspired by sketches of medieval German castles. Ohio State Reformatory was a monumental and hugely ambitious structure, that took over 20 years to build. Although the cornerstone was laid in 1886 the first prisoners did not arrive until a decade later and were promptly put to work on constructing the sewer system and a 25-foot-high stone wall surrounding the 15-acre complex. The arrival of the first prisoners was treated as a major event by people of nearby Mansfield. Prisoners were escorted through the town, treated to cigars by the crowds that gathered and photographed for the front pages of local and regional newspapers. Ohio was heralded as a flagship institution, but complaints of overcrowding began not long after its opening and these increased during the Depression. In 1978 the Counsel for Human Dignity filed a lawsuit on behalf of the 2,200 prisoners housed at Ohio, claiming that their constitutional rights were being violated by the brutalising and inhumane conditions. A US corrections evaluation team subsequently submitted a report recommending that Ohio be closed. When this advice was followed, in the late 1980s, the prison became, as it had been at its opening in 1896, the site of spectacle. In 1989 it was used as the location for the prison sequences in *Tango and Cash* (as it had previously been utilised in *Harry and Walter Go to New York* (1975), and this was followed by *The Shawshank Redemption* (1994) and *Air Force One* (1997)). Since its closure the gothic ambience of towers, cellblocks and dungeons has also been exploited by the music industry, including the performer Marilyn Manson, for photoshoots and videos. Partly in response to its growth as an icon in popular culture, Ohio Department of Rehabilitation and Correction now offers theme tours: visitors can take an online virtual tour, or a 'movie tour' which focuses on sites used in *The Shawshank Redemption*, or a 'haunted prison experience', which exploits local legends of a ghost.

Ohio is just one of a number of US prisons currently capitalising on local history. Since the 1980s, Eastern State Penitentiary, West Virginia Penitentiary, Anamosa State Penitentiary, 'Radisson Hotel', Old Idaho Penitentiary, Old Montana prison complex and Wyoming Frontier prison have all acquired museum status. The prototype for converting dilapidated prisons into touristscapes and one of the key icons in the history of American punishment is Alcatraz. Its name derives from *Isla de los Alcatraces* (Island of the Pelicans), following the Spanish settlement of the Bay Region in 1776. Its nickname, the Rock, is well chosen, since topographically the island is a drowned mountain, with only a thin skin of dirt that supports very little flora and fauna. Following a period of Mexican ownership that began in 1822, Alcatraz was declared property of the US government in 1846. The first major developments on the island, inspired by the economic boom of the Gold Rush, were a lighthouse (the first on the west coast) and a fortification established in 1854. This was followed by the establishment of a military stronghold in 1859 that included a prison. The carceral potential of the island was recognised early on by the US Army, who housed prisoners at Alcatraz during the Civil War and the Spanish–American war. The War Department built a state of the art military prison on the island in 1911, but over the next 20 years it fell into disuse due to high operating costs.

In 1933, however, the Department of Justice assumed control of the island with the intention of using it as the site of a 'Super Prison' designed to hold the most serious offenders and those who proved unmanageable in other institutions. Every prison has an interior disciplinary space, a prison *within* the prison and Alcatraz was designed essentially as 'the Hole' for the US corrections system itself. The Justice Department opened its flagship penitentiary in 1934 and partly because of its colourful clientele (Al Capone, 'Machine Gun' Kelly, 'Doc' Barker et al.) and partly due its role as a disciplinary threat to prisoners in other institutions, Alcatraz quickly cultivated a reputation as the most brutal prison regime in America. Prison folklore included tales of torture, beatings and murder: of prisoners by guards, guards by prisoners, prisoners by prisoners. The legends may have been apocryphal, but some of the cruelest components of prison life at Alcatraz had less to do with personnel than location. Alcatraz is adjacent to San Francisco and prisoners reported that, on New Year's Eve, they could hear the tinkling of champagne glasses and women's laughter carried across the bay by sea breezes.

Isolation was the key to the mythos of the island and its potency as a punitive symbol. Alcatraz was marketed assiduously as an escape-proof facility. There were, however, 14 documented escape attempts involving 34 prisoners: 23 inmates were recaptured, six were shot and killed, but there are five unaccounted for which the authorities insisted must have drowned in the Bay. The official explanation for the closure of Alcatraz in 1963 emphasised economics. By the early 1960s the infrastructure on the island was in need of major renovation and the costs of housing prison guards and their families on site and shipping supplies on a daily basis made the facility far more expensive than its mainland counterparts. The alternative explanation, one favoured by prisoners, centred on the missing prisoners and especially Frank Morris, who disappeared, along with John and Clarence Anglin in 1962. Following the Morris–Anglin escape, the prison lost much of its mystique and became simply another federal penitentiary. The mantle of America's most fearful prison passed to Marion (known as Son of Alcatraz) and then Pelican Bay (Son of Marion).

Following closure the island was abandoned until, in 1969, it was occupied for 19 months by Native American protestors who issued 'The Alcatraz Proclamation to the Great White Father and His People'. This symbolic reverse colonisation recalled both the earliest visitors to the island (the Miwok and Ohlone peoples who inhabited the Bay region before Spanish settlement) and the incarceration of Hopi Indians on the island by the US Army in 1895. Once the protesters departed a private company entertained plans to build an amusement park on the island. These plans were partially realised by the acquisition of National Park status in 1972. When public tours were introduced in the following year, Alcatraz proved to be one of the most popular destinations for sightseers in San Francisco. Foucault suggests that punishment becomes increasingly invisible in modern punitive regimes, but San Francisco tourist guides point out that alongside the Golden Gate Bridge, the Rock is the Bay's most conspicuous landmark. Punishment is big business in the United States and especially in California where the entertainment subsidiary of this growth industry is most apparent. From its inception as a modernist monument synonymous with suffering and alienation, Alcatraz has evolved into a postmodern playground offering a simulated prison experience.

The pecuniary and iconic value of the Rock has been restored by 30 years of tourism and an ever expanding number of books and films.[41] Only a few years after the facility was opened, Hollywood recognised the entertainment potential of *Alcatraz Island* (1937), and this has remained a popular destination for film-makers and audiences ever since.[42] Possibly the most famous addition to this sub-genre, *Birdman of Alcatraz*, appeared on the eve of the prison's closure in 1962 and fictionalised the life of Robert Stroud (who actually conducted his famous bird studies not on the 'island of the pelicans', as the film suggests, but whilst serving time in Leavenworth). The legend of Alcatraz has subsequently featured in *Point Blank* (1967), *Escape from Alcatraz* (1979), *Terror on Alcatraz* (1986), *Murder in the First* (1995), *The Rock* (1996), *New Alcatraz* (2000) and *Half Past Dead* (2002). Within this prison film sub-genre Don Siegel's *Escape from Alcatraz* constitutes a particularly pure example of the formula associated with the escape film.[43] Unlike *The Shawshank Redemption*, which disguises its generic credentials by positioning the spectator with the guards and prisoners who are unaware of Andy's tunnelling,

Escape from Alcatraz signals its subject from the outset. The opening set piece spotlights the tools of discipline with lengthy holds on handcuffs and leg irons, cells and bars, guards, guns and watch towers. Alcatraz is established as a fortress consisting of concentric circles of confinement: first the Bay waters, then the rugged island, then the high prison walls, then barred corridors divided by electronically-controlled doors leading to the cell with the threat, for the recalcitrant prisoner, of the journey continuing on and down into 'D Block'. The attention given to entering Alcatraz, in a film with *Escape* in the title, is clearly intended to signal the difficult return journey that lies ahead for the prisoner-hero.

Whilst in many escape films, such as *The Shawshank Redemption*, the material setting serves essentially as a backdrop to pseudo-spiritual odysseys of self-discovery, *Escape from Alcatraz* remains remarkably confined to its physical milieu. Andy Dufresne's excavations are witnessed fleetingly, in retrospect, in a montage that climaxes with rebirth on the outside and is followed by arrival at a picture postcard Pacific. Conversely, *Escape from Alcatraz* focuses intensely on the sheer physical exertion involved in chipping away at a cell wall, night after night and then fails to reward the spectator with a guarantee of liberty for the fugitives last seen struggling in the biting waters of the Bay. Frank Morris' endurance is the cornerstone of the film's masculine masquerade. The casting of Clint Eastwood, an icon as imposing as the Rock itself in late twentieth-century popular culture, is integral to the film's construction of male subjectivity.

Eastwood's star persona in the 1960s and '70s is often taken as synonymous with an upsurge of reactionary fantasies in popular culture provoked by the rise of second wave feminism. In Eastwood's spaghetti westerns (*The Good, the Bad and the Ugly* (1967), *A Fistful of Dollars* (1967), *The Outlaw Josey Wales* (1976)), war movies (*Kelly's Heroes* (1970)) and urban crime dramas (the *Dirty Harry* trilogy also directed by Siegel), male identity is founded on violent gunplay and reduced to such cartooned simplicity that it borders ambivalently on camp subversion. In *Escape from Alcatraz*, however, Eastwood's performance seems to diverge from the hyperbolic he-man and his queer shadow. In place of a magnum .45, Frank Morris uses a pair of nail scissors to tunnel through his cell wall, he is involved in very few violent confrontations and relies on ingenuity far more than aggressive display. At the same time, the film's preferred definition of the male subject repeats key characteristics from previous Eastwood roles that suggest, in terms of sexual politics, partial redefinition as opposed to abnegation of hegemonic codes. In terms of masculine role models, *Escape from Alcatraz* is organised in a triangular structure: Frank Morris is positioned opposite the warden and the 'Wolf', the film's negative embodiments of male subjectivity. The warden is established at the outset as the sort of desk-bound bureaucrat that Dirty Harry routinely came into conflict with.[44] His conservative suit and emphasis on paperwork suggest a modern prison manager, but beneath this façade his penal style is clearly uncontaminated by progressive thinking: 'no good conduct programmes, no inmate counsel ... We don't make good citizens here, but we make good prisoners.' The 1960s and early '70s saw an increase in liberal programmes of penal reform based on the rehabilitative ethic and Rosenberg's *Brubaker* might be read as a flagship film for this movement. *Escape from Alcatraz* appeared in the same year as *Brubaker*, on the eve of Reagan's first term in office and its depiction of the warden seems more prophetic of contemporary shifts occurring in penal philosophy.

Whilst the warden dons a suit to disguise the fundamental barbarism of his regime, Clint is seen naked or in prison issue denim that might recall the grungy functionality of the 'Man with No Name'. Frank Morris, like Eastwood's other screen roles, is laconic and undemonstrative and these qualities are juxtaposed with the wordiness and posturing of the warden. Male vanity is not only suspect in *Escape from Alcatraz*, but the key to the warden's downfall. As the warden listens to his own inaugural speech to the prisoner, Morris is busy stealing some nail clippers from the desk with the intention of putting them to more manly purpose. The opposition between the neatly manicured bureaucrat and the industrious manual labourer suggests both the Auburn paradigm and the tendency towards a romanticisation of manual toil in popular culture during a period which has witnessed extensive bleaching of American blue-collars. Unlike *The Shawshank Redemption*, which attempts to bridge class differences in the figure of Andy Dufresne (accountant by day, but a miner on his night shift), *Escape from Alcatraz* maintains an unequivocal class polarity between the feminised bureaucrat and the butch proletarian, the worlds of administration and muscular action.[45]

Although their class narratives diverge, the oedipal sub-texts in *Escape from Alcatraz* and *The Shawshank Redemption* intersect. The son's possession of the phallus (rock hammer, nail clippers) is the key to escape from the Big House and to ascendancy over the father (who takes his own life, or loses his authority and is summoned to face his own patriarchal superiors in Washington). *Escape from Alcatraz* does not develop a homosocial romance as conspicuously as *The Shawshank Redemption*, but it does include its own strain of homophobic demonisation. The practically bestial Wolf, like the Sisters, is inserted to equate homosexuality with sadistic savagery and to confirm the hero as hetero. Frank Morris has spent much of his life behind bars in single sex communities, arrives at Alcatraz on the doorstep of the gay capital of America, befriends a character called Butts, complains that his spoon 'looks like it's been stuck up someone's arse' and spends his nights slipping in and out of narrow passages. In this context, the shower scene with the Wolf aims to contain the latent homoeroticism that habitually slips through the bars of the prison narrative.

The banal opposition of good hetero and evil homo prisoner in *Escape from Alcatraz* is representative of the film's fundamental moral design. Siegel reduces the social and ethical dramas of punishment to a cartoon. The breadth of brushstroke here is illustrated by a cut from a Second World War film on the prison television, displaying Nazi tanks and swastikas, to a medium shot of the warden patrolling the mess hall. The unequivocal villainy of the warden is mirrored by the emphatic decency of the prisoners. According to the warden, Alcatraz is where they 'put all the rotten eggs in one basket', but with the exception of the Wolf, the inmates appear uniformly virtuous. *Escape from Alcatraz* illustrates the stratagems by which Hollywood prison films enable audience identification with the criminal class. Frank Morris is sent to Alcatraz not because he robbed banks, but because he 'broke the rules' in other prisons, which conveniently translates the opposition between criminal and law into rebellious individual against faceless bureaucracy. The offences committed by Morris' fellow inmates are occluded by the conventional repertoire of references to aesthetics, small animals and family. The prisoners at Alcatraz quote Twain, paint, take care of mice and are seen with daughters, wives, sisters and mothers during tearful prison visits.

The only prisoner in Alcatraz who confesses to murder is English, the ageing African-American librarian who explains that he was acting in self-defence in the face of racist provocation. *Escape from Alcatraz* fails to explore the prison experiences of African-Americans in any detail but instead offers reassuring images of interracial union: black and white hands holding through the bars, black and white musicians in the prison band, or engaging in sports and friendly banter in the yard. In some of these shots a sullen mass of undifferentiated black faces can be seen sitting on a wall in the yard, but they fail to do anything other than sit on that wall and their story is unheard. In fact, their story is stolen. The analogy between the prison system and a slave ship is hinted at in the film, but only in relation to the white prisoner-hero. When Frank Morris arrives on the island, in leg irons, his first experience is of a strip search and medical and these humiliating rituals contain visual echoes of the slave warehouse and auction block. The first communication Morris has with another prisoner involves an African-American inmate telling him to 'button up your collar, *boy*'. This injunction reinforces the status of Frank Morris' story as a white neoslave narrative. During a period in which black prisoners have come to outnumber whites in US prisons, *Escape from Alcatraz*, like *Cool Hand Luke*, *The Green Mile* and *The Shawshank Redemption*, marginalises and expropriates the African-American experience to serve the visual pleasures of the dominant white culture.

THE EXECUTION FILM (2):
DEAD MAN WALKING AND *THE LAST DANCE*

The first [execution] turned me quite hot and thirsty, and made me shake so that I could hardly hold the opera-glass.

Letters, Lord Byron[46]

And then the Windows failed – and then
I could not see to see –

'I heard a Fly buzz – when I died', Emily Dickinson[47]

Alcatraz has been at the forefront of rekindling the nineteenth-century vogue for recreational prison tours. Following Siegel's film in 1979, the island played host to an annual televised 'escape from Alcatraz' triathlon, and in 1987 it was the stage for a David Copperfield 'escapology spectacular'. The prison island has become a key icon for the incorporation of punishment into entertainment in the US. One probable trajectory for this merger is suggested by a landmark legal case that took place in 1991 in California. In *KQED v. Daniel B. Vasquez*, a public television station based in San Francisco sued the warden of San Quentin for the right to televise an execution.

Wendy Lesser has argued that this case constituted a logical extension of the burgeoning elision between media, legal and penal cultures.[48] An incestuous hyperreality was evident throughout the ten-week trial, as local and national media promoted a case concerning media spectacle into media spectacle. KQED's legal team asserted that their request was supported by the First Amendment and merely a continuation of the principle established in *Richmond Newspapers Inc. v. Commonwealth of Virginia*, the case which had sanctioned the presence of press cameras in courtrooms. In 1980, the year in which a Hollywood president arrived in the White House, Chief Justice Burger ruled that the media was equipped to satisfy the

> fundamental, natural yearning to see justice done – or even the urge for retribution. The crucial prophylactic aspects of the administration of justice cannot function in the dark; no community catharsis can occur if justice is done in a corner [or] in any covert manner.[49]

The ruling in *Richmond Newspapers* paved the way for 'Court TV', docu-soaps such as NBC's *Crime and Punishment*, *Judge Judy* and its imitators and these have been accompanied by a massive upsurge in legal dramas (series such as *LA Law*, *Family Law*, *The Practice* and numerous adaptations of John Grisham novels). The commercial success of this genre may testify to a 'natural yearning', but as these shows dissolve distinctions between the dramatic and the documentary by capitalising on the inherent theatricality of the trial, it also confirms the increasingly simulacral nature of US justice.

The commercial successes in the 1990s of cult prison drama *Oz* (which includes numerous formal and informal executions) and the Hollywood death row drama (*Dead Man Walking*, *The Green Mile*, *The Monster's Ball*, *The Life of David Gale*) might hint that the prophylactic aspects of judicial process are due to extend beyond the courtroom to the dead centre of US Justice. The cameras are zooming in on death row. In late 2002, in Texas, legal wrangling began to ensure the right to televise jury deliberations in death penalty cases. The proponents of this initiative argued that this is the last remaining phase of judicial proceedings to be kept hidden from the public. This argument repeats the rhetoric from *KQED v. Daniel B. Vasquez*, where the prosecution proposed that *Richmond Newspapers* had established the right of the media to utilise all the 'tools of the trade' in their coverage of a public event and that the people had the right to witness an act committed in their name. The defence strategy in *Vasquez* was to side-step these rights by focusing on strictly functional concerns and in particular the potential security threat posed by the presence of cameras. It was contended that the televising of an execution might incite a riot (by prisoners or death penalty protesters), could jeopardise the anonymity of guards and witnesses, or that those present might be more immediately imperilled should heavy equipment crash into the glass walls of the gas chamber. Although they remained a persistent sub-text throughout this legal drama, ethical questions concerning the potential impact of televised executions on the viewing public were rarely referred to directly. However, the prosecution observed that most people already had access to images of execution and murder, both in documentary (coverage of crime, wars and assassinations) and fictionalised form (specific reference was made to an episode of *LA Law* which centred on an execution). The judge, evidently unconvinced by these claims, ruled against the plaintiff. Although the glass walls of San Quentin's gas chamber were not threatened by KQED's cameras, the media provided extensive and graphic coverage of the subsequent execution of Robert Alton Harris, the largely silent African-American prisoner at the physical centre of the trial: 'There was a panel discussion afterward about whether he jerked or twitched, whether he lowered his head or moved it to the right, whether his left finger moved. It got to be very gruesome in terms of the detail they kept going over and over and over.'[50]

The tidy symmetry of Foucault's genealogy of punishment, with its opposition of a performative, feudal justice visited on the body and an invisible discipline aimed at the mind, is repeatedly disrupted by the tenacity of spectacle in American culture. The media audience for the execution of Robert Alton Harris, or the numbers who followed reports of the administering of a lethal injection to Timothy McVeigh, far exceeded the 10,000 spectators who attended, in 1936, the last public hanging in the US. When Gary Gilmore was executed by a firing squad in 1977, various commentators deplored the 'media circus', the 'super bowl of violence' surrounding the execution that inaugurated a new era of state culling. Gilmore's execution was followed exhaustively in visual and print media and was subsequently adapted in fiction and film. In *The Executioner's Song*, Norman Mailer devoted over one hundred pages to the scene of Gilmore's execution. Mailer's strategy of gothic overkill here extended a position he had previously outlined in *The Presidential Papers*:

I would like to see a law passed which would abolish capital punishment except for those states which insisted on keeping it. Such states would then be allowed to kill criminals provided that the killing is not impersonal but personal and a public spectacle: to wit that the executioner be more or less the same size and weight as the criminal (the law here could specify the limits) and that they fight to the death using no weapons, or weapons not capable of killing at a distance ... The benefit of this law is that it might return us to moral responsibility. The killer would carry the other man's death in his psyche. The audience, in turn, would experience a sense of tragedy, since the executioners, highly trained for this, would almost always win ... In the flabby American spirit there is a buried sadist ... Since nothing is worse for a country than repressed sadism, this method of execution would offer ventilation for the more cancerous emotions of the American public.[51]

Mailer manages to evade the ethical ironies of contributing to a spectacle by decrying it, but underplays the extent to which modern executions, like that of Gilmore, were already spectator sports. The cancerous emotions of repressed sadism are both fulfilled and fuelled by ceaseless necrotic display in news coverage and cinematic simulation. As the number of executions in the US has grown, along with public support for capital punishment and impatience with delays in its implementation, liberal factions in Hollywood have responded by returning to the sub-genre of death row dramas. What follows will be a close reading of two examples that appeared in the mid 1990s: *Dead Man Walking* and *The Last Dance*.

Robbins' and Beresford's films appeared within a few months of each other and bore so many similarities that *The Last Dance* was derisively dubbed *Dead Woman Walking*. Robbins' script was based loosely upon Sister Helen Prejean's account of her experiences amongst Louisiana death row inmates. Set in the buckle of the Bible Belt, *Dead Man Walking* documents the last weeks in the life of Matthew Poncelet, awaiting execution for the rape and murder of a teenage couple. Sister Prejean is appointed as spiritual counsellor for his final days and after failing to assist in the overturning of the death sentence she concentrates on persuading Poncelet to accept responsibility for his actions. Poncelet, who seems initially content to conform to a caricature of Southern white trash, is duly persuaded and achieves redemption on the way to lethal injection. *The Last Dance* follows the relationship between Cindy Liggett, a death row murderess and Rick Hayes, a young lawyer assigned to her clemency case. Hayes' crusade to rescue his client is ultimately unsuccessful and *The Last Dance* climaxes with Liggett's death by lethal injection.

The similarities between *Dead Man Walking* and *The Last Dance* are multiple. Both films share a setting in the late twentieth century South and revolve around an odd couple. Although the gender of the condemned partner in each pairing is different, class and genealogical oppositions remain constant: the working class criminal from a 'broken' family is juxtaposed with the stable family units of middle class victims and saviours. Poncelet and Liggett both participated in double murders that shattered the sanctuaries of bourgeois privacy (dragging a teenage couple from their car and shooting a married couple in their bedroom). The scene of their respective crimes is reconstructed in piecemeal fashion, through black-and-white flashbacks and it is revealed that both condemned figures were under the sway of a partner – a father figure and a lover – who subsequently escaped the death penalty due to more proficient legal defence. The centrepiece of *Dead Man Walking* and *The Last Dance* is the bond that evolves between the death row inmate and their new partners. The consummation of these relationships is the intimacy shared on the eve of execution and the anguish in the death chamber. In both films the last exchange of looks is spliced with shots of bureaucratic procedure and the technology of death. Since execution films, as a sub-genre of the prison drama, tend to follow the narrative curve of the *bildungsroman*, these death scenes embody the final lesson in the education of the protagonists. Once the criminal has accepted responsibility for their actions they achieve redemption and their moral and spiritual metamorphosis is underscored with crucifixion imagery.

Despite, or rather because of their extensive similarities, *Dead Man Walking* and *The Last Dance* enjoyed very different receptions. Whilst Robbins' film saw considerable commercial and critical success, garnering numerous awards, Beresford's effort was dismissed as an inferior copy. This mainstream critical judgement ignored the extent to which both films complied compulsorily to established conventions. Needless to say, commercial imperatives underlined this adherence to formula, but in the case of the execution film, spectators might also be witnessing the cinematic equivalent of repetition compulsion. Execution is the state's response to murder. Almost all twentieth-century executions in the US have been of convicted murderers, or, as in the Rosenberg case, of individuals allegedly responsible by default for mass murder. Whilst murder involves a breakdown in structure, the rituals of the state and the formulae of the culture industry aspire to the mastery of traumatic disorder through repetition.

Although one might assume that the death row drama opposes capital punishment it often eases (or, in *The Green Mile*, strides) towards a representation of execution as a vital act associated with salvation and transcendence. The adumbrated critique in most death row dramas is typically compromised by pseudo-religious iconography and mystifying sentimentalism. In the crowd gathered outside the penitentiary in *Dead Man Walking* placards are visible bearing the biblical injunction: 'Thou shalt not kill.' The ambiguity surrounding the addressee (it could be directed towards the murderer or the state) makes this an emblematic sign for the political incoherence of the Hollywood execution film. The case against capital punishment tends to be undermined by the generic imperatives of romantic and sentimental melodrama. Additionally, the structural interrogation of punishment is displaced by a liberal ethics that isolates morality from questions of power. The political capital of execution as a vote-winner and the legal inequities associated with who does and does not get sent to death row appear largely as background to the drama. The class identity of the condemned may confirm historical reality, but the possibility that socioeconomic inequality is a major determinant of crime is given very little weight. Instead, *Dead Man Walking* and *The Last Dance* move towards white collar fantasies of class reconciliation through ethical exchange: the bourgeois learns about blue collar suffering whilst the condemned learns to recite middle class moral maxims concerning responsibility. This *embourgeoisement* is depicted as part of the condemned prisoner's progress towards humanity and the possibility of alternative class affiliation is precluded by the virtual disappearance of other death row inmates from both films.

The exclusion of other prisoners serves the function of relocating the execution film from the predominantly same-sex environment of prison to Hollywood's preferred heterosexual terrain. In *Dead Man Walking*, Sister Prejean performs an orthodox female role as the redeemer of a sinful man, curbing masculine excesses with moral and spiritual sensitivity. Although the system takes his body she saves his soul. Sister Prejean follows in the footsteps of early female Quakers and reformers such as Eliza Farnham who were at the forefront of the development of the rehabilitative ethic with its emphasis on spiritual instruction. Whilst *Dead Man Walking* resurrects traditional formulae concerning the containment of male lawlessness by True Womanhood, *The Last Dance* feeds off the obverse of this mythology and discursive figurations of Depraved Womanhood. In her drab prison uniform and with her dogged insistence on accepting punishment 'on my own terms', Cindy Liggett is a contemporary Hester Prynne who articulates the feminine as anarchic and uncontrollable. In this respect, Liggett's character offers confirmation of and for recent developments in the punishment of women in the US and the attendant neo-Puritan resurgence in the demonisation of the deviant woman. Women currently represent around 16 per cent of the total number of US citizens under correctional supervision, but the numbers of women and young female offenders inside increased by 500 per cent between 1980 and 2000.[52]

The female lawbreaker is less easily tolerated than her male equivalent, who can be accommodated by reference to mythical notions of American individualism and frontier spirit. Anne Morey has explored how women's prison films tend to present the Big House as 'an agent to return women to domesticity'.[53] In *Caged* (1950), *Women's Prison* (1955), *Girls in Prison* (1956) and *House of Women* (1962), women are unable to effect this transformation for themselves and their redemption is dependent upon the intervention of a sympathetic male character: warden, doctor or chaplain. In *The Last Dance* the disciplinary domestication of the female deviant hinges upon the involvement of Rick Hayes, Cindy's lawyer. Cindy tries initially to assert autonomy, but her character curve follows a predictable path from criminal subject to love object and eventually an Angel in the Big House. Cindy was the passive partner in the original crime, and in prison she still plays a secondary role to her male lawyer.

The political dynamics of capital punishment are typically obscured in the execution film by gender mythology and narratives of class conversion and also by a preoccupation with *seeing* the scene of the crime. Inevitably, narratives of punishment are interwoven with crime stories and the manner in which the latter is represented impacts crucially upon responses to the former. When a death row drama returns to the scene of the crime it can confirm hegemonic formulations that ring-fence crime and punishment. This simplistic binary implicitly sanctions the punishment by conflating the criminal with the crime, thus excluding the structural determinants of social deviance and the criminality of state violence. In *Dead Man*

Walking and *The Last Dance* the crime scene is revealed accretively: Poncelet's crime is constructed through a series of flashbacks focalised through Sister Prejean's imagination; Liggett's crime is initially glimpsed in photographs from police reports and then in progressively longer and more authoritative flashbacks. Each film is obsessed with solving the mystery of *what* happened and largely ignores more complex questions concerning causality. In the process they sanction the legal fiction that the crime scene can be known definitively and therefore punished unproblematically. The cross-cutting between Poncelet's homicide and execution might underscore his final words: 'I just wanna say I think killin' is wrong, no matter who does it, whether it's me or y'all or your government.' Equally, however, the splicing of shots of the bullets entering the victim's bodies and the administering of the lethal injection could emphasise the essential contingency of these acts. In *The Last Dance*, the use of slow-motion during both homicide and execution similarly secures the nexus of crime and punishment.

In place of exploring the socioeconomic determinants of crime, the Hollywood execution film pedals homilies on individual responsibility. The epiphany in *Dead Man Walking* occurs when Poncelet accepts Prejean's injunction to 'take responsibility' for his actions. Although her lawyer wants to blame external factors (class background, upbringing and drug addiction), Cindy Liggett seems similarly determined to embrace culpability. In both films redemption is achieved through the heroic acceptance of agency and guilt. Hostility towards the death penalty is thus diffused as the criminal fulfils their obligation within the modern disciplinary system of accepting the ethical burden of punitive power. The ensuing moment of redemption seems to imply that executions are less intolerable when the criminal accepts masochistic martyrdom. One of the functions of punishment is to maintain the subject positions of 'criminal' and 'victim'. The execution film may traverse these categories through the exercise of sympathy, but the moral binary remains intact. Perversely, however, it is the act of accepting their criminality that allows the condemned to aspire to saintly victimhood.

The trajectory of the typical execution film thus heads away from the historical towards perfunctory spiritual melodrama. Following his confession, Poncelet is strapped onto a cruciform structure in the death chamber and in the final scene of *The Last Dance*, Rick Hayes follows Cindy's final sketches of the Taj Mahal to Agra. It may be possible, however, to resist this path. Cindy Liggett's drawings of the tomb could express a coded death wish rather than a western tourist's synonym for spirituality; the embrace of execution might betoken a longing for an end to the torture of twelve years on death row as opposed to an acceptance of the state's judgement. Similarly, in *Dead Man Walking*, Poncelet's confession might be read less as spiritual epiphany and more as *mauvaise foi*. At the scene of the crime and in court, in front of the media and amongst other inmates, Poncelet works hard at maintaining the masculine masquerade. This performance is evident in his gestures and grooming (the handling of a cigarette, the goatee and pompadour), his recitation of macho clichés about 'showing people' and 'taking things like a man', and an attempted flirtation with Prejean. During the crime he follows the lead of his older partner and in prison he parrots the polemic of the Aryan Brotherhood. It is possible that the Poncelet we see in the death chamber is part of another performance, directed from the wings this time by Prejean. In 1935 five actors from the Curran Theatre in San Francisco, presumably keen to acquire insider knowledge for death scenes, applied successfully for permission to attend an execution at San Quentin. The climax to *Angels with Dirty Faces*, released a few years later in 1938, as Cagney's character performs the role of the coward on the way to the chair, might hint at reciprocal exchanges between the boards and the state-sponsored theatre of cruelty. In *The Executioner's Song*, Mailer applauds Gilmore's ability to deliver 'the kind of acting that makes you forget you are in a theatre', and Poncelet might be engaged in a comparable performance.[54]

The popularity of the death row drama is attributable as much to a desire to witness this finale as to Justice Burger's 'fundamental, natural yearning to see justice done'. The spectator, like the audience for Benjamin's Storyteller, is drawn in part by the 'hope of warming his shivering life with a death he reads about'.[55] The optics of the Hollywood obituary can be problematic. The execution film entangles the unseen and the unseeable, the obscene and the obscure. The desire to witness the administration of justice, as Hollywood restages the *mise-en-scène* of state slaughter, can be accompanied by less innocent forms of death wishfulness. In *Discipline and Punish*, Foucault decries the assumption that the replacement of dramatic spectacle by bureaucratic procedure constitutes progress, since 'justice no longer takes public responsibility for the violence that is bound up with its practice'.[56] At the public execution, people 'were summoned as spectators ... Not only must people know, they must see with their own eyes.'[57] Simultaneously, at the 'scene of terror ... the role of the people was an ambiguous one'.[58] What drew the crowds to the gallows spectacle? The wish to witness retribution? Voyeurism and blood lust? The opportunity to protest and practise carnivalesque 'disturbances around the scaffold'?[59] *Angels with Dirty Faces* was screened in 1938, just two years after the last public execution in the US. The execution film might be read in part as a surrogate for the lost gallows spectacle. It promises, like its predecessor, a convoluted admixture of voyeurism and vengeance, a curiosity about the exotic and the potential for resistance.

Undoubtedly part of the appeal of the execution film is the promise of assuming a taboo ocular power, to see behind the scenes, to be an eye witness to the death of the 'I'. This promissory enticement is inevitably frustrated, however, since, as Elizabeth Bronfen has argued, 'every representation of death necessarily represses what it purports to reveal ... *Every representation of death is a misrepresentation.*'[60] The execution film seems to offer insights into our own death, but these are illusory. The experience must be vicarious in the same way that Freud noted the unavoidable third person perspective adopted in dreams about dying. In *Dead Man Walking* and *The Last Dance* we see very little. The intrusion into that most private of moments, one's death, permits a doubled voyeurism, but we see what others are seeing because the subject itself is profoundly invisible. The camera eye, like the infamous spiral out of Marion Crane's eye in *Psycho*, circles round a subject it cannot enter.[61]

The self-incarcerated American poet Emily Dickinson wrote, utilising gallows imagery, that with death a 'Plank in reason' breaks and we are 'Finished Knowing – then –'.[62] Confronted by this appalling blankness, both *Dead Man Walking* and *The Last Dance* predictably offer codas that focus on the survivor. The absence of death is twofold since it involves both erasure and a terrifying void. As Kenneth Burke remarks: 'the imaging of death necessarily involves images not directly belonging to it ... [Death] lies beyond the realm of such images as the living body knows'.[63] This problematic is intimated by the title of Robbins' film: how can a dead man walk? The condemned prisoner becomes a revenant, an uncanny figure forging a chiasmus between death and representation. In accordance with patriarchal logic, this liminal figure, the living dead, is also associated with the feminine. The supremely symbolic act of execution, an exercise in law and power, entails a move towards the semiotic, into spaces before and after language. As Hélène Cixous has argued, death and the feminine have often been connected by patriarchy as consummate embodiments of the other, the unknown. The 'social death' inflicted on women has been accompanied by a mythological feminisation of death. Elizabeth Bronfen has explored this equation in *Over Her Dead Body*:

> Death, as the limit of cultural representation, has been associated with that other enigma, the multiply coded feminine body ... Like the decaying body, the feminine is unstable, liminal, disturbing. Both mourning rituals and representations of death may seek strategies to stabilise the body, which entails removing it from the feminine and transforming it into a monument, an enduring stone.[64]

In the final scenes of *The Last Dance*, Rick Hayes is left observing the Taj Mahal, the subject of Cindy Liggett's final sketches prior to execution. The equation between death and the feminine is self-evident in *The Last Dance*, which fuses the execution drama with a conventional romance plot (man as saviour, woman as victim), but it is also apparent in *Dead Man Walking* in signs that problematise the gender identification of the film's title. In his final hours, Poncelet's aggressive posturing is replaced by passive resignation and loud bragging is silenced by whisperings, crying, choking. Poncelet has his leg shaved and then, in the death chamber, is confined and penetrated by syringes. The cross-cutting that combines crime and punishment – between rape and lethal injection – symbolically associates Poncelet with the body of his female victim as both are pinned down and invaded by foreign fluids.

Poncelet's death is coded as sexual assault, but perhaps the most immediate frame of reference for execution is torture. As Scarry has argued, the imposition of bodily hurt aims to erase the contents of consciousness in simulation of death: 'The two are the most intense forms of negation ... physical pain always mimes death and the infliction of physical pain is always a mock execution.'[65] Given the increase in the average duration of death row confinement, the practice of capital punishment in contemporary US justice converges even more closely with the practice of 'mock execution' favoured by dictatorships in the Philippines and Latin America. In 'Reflections on the Guillotine', Camus proposed that a man is undone by waiting for capital punishment well before he dies. Two deaths are inflicted on him, the first being worse than the second … Compared to such torture, the penalty of retaliation seems like a civilised law … . For there to be equivalence, the death penalty would have to punish a criminal who had warned his victim of the date at which he would inflict a horrible death on him and who, from that moment onward, had confined him at his mercy for months. Such a monster is not encountered in private life.[66]

The time of death is difficult to fix in relation to capital punishment and not simply because of the long history of botched execution. The process of dying is initiated automatically when someone is subjected to acute reminders of mortality: 'Whenever death can be designated as "soon" the dying has already begun.'[67] As well as taking the prisoner's life, the state-as-executioner, like the torturer, aims to take his or her death by translating this most intimate of experiences into a sign of the system's omnipotence. The tortured body of the condemned is a site of contestation, one which the state hopes to inscribe with its own insignia, to underscore its power, to translate it into a sign of 'Justice' and the 'Law', to pervert 'the enlarged map of human suffering into an emblem of the regime's strength'.[68] The emphasis on confession in *Dead Man Walking* and *The Last Dance*, on accepting responsibility for one's crimes, projects a fraudulent sense of ownership, since the execution is precisely concerned with assuming control of both the criminal's body and their identity at the time of death.

In *Discipline and Punish*, Foucault remarks on how torture is initiated by the sight of the weapon. In confirmation of this, Scarry refers to the repeated testimony of torture victims who were forced 'to stare at the weapon with which they were about to be hurt'.[69] A similar compulsion, both for the condemned and the spectator, is evident in *Dead Man Walking* and *The Last Dance*, which in their voyeuristic preoccupation with the technology of death do for lethal injection what *The Green Mile* accomplishes for the electric chair. Scarry has argued that one consequence of the inexpressibility of pain is a compensatory digression towards the sign of the weapon and the wound. In the case of execution, however, the strategy of the state is to eliminate all traces of torture behind the façade of 'scientific', bureaucratic procedure. Modern execution aims to minimise the marks of vengeance on the body of the victim. The electric chair was initially heralded as a humane alternative to

hanging, a technological advance beyond the prolonged asphyxia-
tions and grisly decapitations common on the gallows. However,
ever since the inaugural botched execution of William Kemmler, the
chair has been the site of grotesque affliction. In the case of *Glass v.
Louisiana*, a witness was cited as remarking that the 'force of the
electric current is so powerful that the prisoner's eyeballs sometimes
pop out on his cheeks'.[70] Alternative forms of capital punishment
have found it equally difficult to eliminate the legacy of the *ancien
régime*. In 1992, in the Arizona gas chamber, a condemned man
suffered convulsions for six minutes in front of an increasingly
appalled audience. The gas chamber is also haunted by the Holocaust,
the *Ur*-text of anti-textuality which perhaps also explains its
expulsion from the execution film sub-genre.[71]

Currently the state's preferred mode of execution is the lethal
injection, which aims to confuse murder with medical procedure.
This confusion is apparent in execution scenes which encourage
sympathy by linking the condemned to the terminally ill, who
inhabit a similar uncanny location between life and death. In *The
Last Dance*, in contrast to the murder scene with its graphic images
of a hand swinging the lethal weapon, the execution is administered
by machine in a bloodless, antiseptic operation. The screams and
struggle at the murder scene are replaced by the sight of Liggett
drifting into eternal sleep, her body devoid of the marks of state
violence. Ultimately, Beresford responds to the 'banality of evil', to
borrow Hannah Arendt's chilling description of the Nazi bureaucrati-
sation of genocide, with the aesthetic crime of banality. *The Last
Dance*, like *The Green Mile*, offers a dangerously sentimental
translation of execution into maudlin melodrama. The mobilisation
of sympathy intends to bypass political intelligence. The spectator
is made to *feel* bad about this subject but not encouraged to *understand*
its causes and possible solutions. The formula of romantic tragedy
takes over and the look of the lover obscures the gaze of the social
critic. Closure is achieved, precisely when it ought to be resisted, with
the favoured ploy of classical Hollywood narrative: the replacement
of the bad couple who represent social deviance (Liggett and her
original partner) by the good couple who embody social responsibility and self-sacrifice (the reformed Liggett and her new legal partner).

By centring on the emotional hurt of the lovers, *The Last Dance*
reinforces the state strategy of eliminating the signs of bodily pain
from capital punishment.[72] As well as ignoring the long history of
botched lethal injections, Beresford's images suppress the fact that the

lethal injection, rather than allowing a painless death, deploys drugs to prevent the condemned from screaming.[73] This fact is recognised in *Dead Man Walking*, when Poncelet's lawyer explains to Prejean that whilst the first shot of drugs is designed to immobilise the victim, those that follow result in the collapsing of the lungs and biological 'Armageddon' for the internal organs. For all its technological trappings, lethal injection is ultimately aligned with the gallows as a mode of execution by asphyxiation. The withdrawal of capital punishment from the public stage to private performances (which often commence with the raising of a curtain to reveal the death chamber) reaches a new level of interiority here. Death by lethal injection represents the state's aspiration to the total eclipse of bodily pain. Pain wages war on words, reducing the subject to a prelanguage of moans and screams, but with lethal injection even the pre-language that silences words is silenced. The prolonged close shot of Poncelet's face, transformed by chemicals into its own death mask, makes this silence scream. In her mapping of the 'invisible' geographies of pain, Scarry comments on the image of the scream in western culture:

> [it appears frequently] in the visual arts, which for the most part avoid depictions of auditory experience. The very failure to convey the sound makes these representations arresting and accurate; the open mouth with no sound reaching anyone in the sketches, paintings, or film stills of Grünewald, Stanzione, Munch, Bacon, Bergman, or Eisenstein, a human being so utterly consumed in the act of making a sound that cannot be heard, coincides with the way in which pain engulfs the one in pain but remains unseen by anyone else.[74]

As *Dead Man Walking* progresses towards execution the barriers between Prejean and Poncelet gradually dissolve. This development is literalised by Robbins in the *mise-en-scène*: the early interviews take place through thick wire mesh, grilles, bars and perspex screens which blur focus or reflect sunlight. However, whilst the narrative climax points affirmatively towards emotional and spiritual convergence between Prejean and Poncelet, the final image in the death scene forcibly reimposes a barrier and reminds us of the immeasurable distance between the living and the living dead.

In *Discipline and Punish*, Foucault refers to the scaffold as a place where one could decipher crime and innocence, the past and the future, the here below and the eternal. [The hanging] was a moment of truth that all the spectators questioned: each word, each cry, the duration of the agony, the resisting body, the life that clung desperately to it, all this constituted a sign.[75]

The final shot of Poncelet involves no words, no cries, no visible agony by the resisting body, but this is itself a potential source of resistance. Whilst various voices aspire to the status of master discourse in *Dead Man Walking* – the nun, the grieving family, the law – authority should reside with this mute image, since, as Benjamin argued, '[e]verything about history that, from the very beginning, has been untimely, sorrowful, unsuccessful, is expressed in a face – or rather in a death's head'.[76] In 'The Storyteller', Benjamin went on to argue for a fundamental conjunction between the moment of death and the transmission of truth:

> It is, however, characteristic that not only a man's knowledge or wisdom, but above all his real life – and this is the stuff that stories are made of – first assumes transmissible form at the moment of his death. Just as a sequence of images is set in motion inside a man as his life comes to an end – unfolding the views of himself under which he has encountered himself without being aware of it – suddenly in his expressions and looks the unforgettable emerges and imparts to everything that concerned him that authority which even the poorest wretch in dying possesses for the living around him. This authority is at the very source of the story.[77]

Observing the shot of the 'death's head' in *Dead Man Walking*, we might, after Benjamin, detect the 'crystal of the total event in the analysis of the small, individual moment'.[78] Poncelet's face informs us that we cannot see inside. This moment thus becomes an irresistible metaphor for the prison film genre itself.

> The camera is getting smaller and smaller, ever readier to capture the fleeting and secret moments whose images paralyse the associative mechanisms in the beholder ... Is it not the task of the photographer – descendant of the augurs and haruspices – to reveal guilt and to point out the guilty in his pictures?[79]

Whilst *The Last Dance* imprisons the spectator with the look of the lover, the final execution image in *Dead Man Walking* aspires to Benjamin's definition of the responsibility of the photographer. Poncelet's skeletal stare returns the spectator's guilty gaze; his immobility reflects our own political passivity and encourages us to recognise, as Daniel does in Doctorow's execution novel, the extent to which 'innocence is complicity'.[80] The dead man walking has no mouth but he must scream. For these screams to go unanswered would mean that the 'dead will be killed again'.[81] There are currently 2,700 prisoners awaiting execution in death rows across the US.

PRISON FILMS AND POSTMODERNISM:
DOWN BY LAW, NATURAL BORN KILLERS AND *OZ*

In the conclusion to the prison plot in *Intolerance*, a young worker is rescued from execution at the last moment by the arrival of his wife with a pardon from the governor. When, 80 years on, Robert Altman needed a fake finale in *The Player* to underline his satire of Hollywood formula, he recycled the recycling of Griffith's execution story. In a studio screening room, a select audience are watching *Habeas Corpus* (the film within the film) and offer rapturous applause at the 'new' ending (the old one 'tested poorly'): the district attorney (a partially-attired Bruce Willis) rescues his innocent lover (Julia Roberts) from the gas chamber just as the pellets drop, taking out the plexiglas with a machine gun. *The Player* mocks postmodern platitudes concerning the blurred lines between real and reel in Tinsel Town, but the career of its eponymous hero confirms this confusion. The Player, Griffin Mills, a studio executive who rewrites the original script of *Habeas Corpus*, is played by Tim Robbins, who subsequently made his own spectacular prison-break in *The Shawshank Redemption* before rewriting Sister Helen Prejean's *Dead Man Walking* as a well-received death row drama. The postmodern phase of prison film, as with other commercial genres, has seen a spiralling self-referentiality. When the guard in *The Green Mile* repeats the phrase 'dead man walking' it seems far more convincing as intertextual homage than prison lingo.

A number of *auteurs*, alongside Altman, have offered sequences in their work that break out of *The Big House* by playfully subverting the prison genre formula. In *Raising Arizona*, for example, the Coen brothers present prison purely as an MTV montage accompanied by a Cajun rendition of Beethoven's *Ode to Joy*. (The Coens went on to similarly excessive hybridity by splicing prison escape film, road movie, musical and classical legend in *O Brother Where Art Thou?*) *Raising Arizona* offers an affectionate pastiche of the genre's replications by having a repeat offender caught in a cycle of repetitions. In the opening scenes, the hero, Hi, is arrested three times and dispatched on each occasion to the same prison. Here Hi is greeted by the same Neanderthal con mopping a floor and the same wise black prisoner offering fake folk wisdom before facing the same parole board repeating the same questions about his recidivism. Nicholas Cage, who plays Hi, returned to prison in *Face/Off* (1997) as FBI agent Sean Archer. In this John Woo action film, the detective hero is falsely imprisoned after going undercover to impersonate his criminal nemesis, Castor Troy, in an operation that involves the two swapping faces. In the same year, in David Lynch's *The Lost Highway*, Fred Madison, a jazz saxophonist on death row for the murder of his wife, mysteriously mutates into Pete Dayton, a garage mechanic. Although they appear to offer very different profiles of prison – Woo's is comic book, Lynch's surrealist *noir* – both *Face/Off* and *The Lost Highway* essentially are farces that decentre subjectivity through excessive genre play and deliver a postmodern pastiche of notions of prisoner identity crisis. In this section we will examine, in more detail, two disparate examples of postmodern prison sequences in films by Jim Jarmusch and Oliver Stone.

Down by Law (1986) pretends to play along with the prison film rulebook. In separate incidents, a pimp and an unemployed disc jockey are framed and end up acrimoniously sharing a cramped cell in the Orleans Parish Prison. This odd couple, Jack and Zach, becomes an even quirkier trio following the arrival of a new cellmate, Roberto, an Italian tourist afflicted by exasperating optimism. Although initially fractious, the threesome begin to bond and manage to escape into the bayous where Roberto improbably discovers his one true love waiting for him at 'Luigi's Tintop', an Italian restaurant in the middle of the Louisiana backwaters. Jack and Zach, who began as jaded hipsters and mortal enemies have, by the close of the film, been revitalised and developed a grudging mutual respect. Jarmusch manages some revitalisation of his own, energising this conventional plot through a delinquent and self-reflexive *mise-en-scène*. *Down by Law* energises the tired clichés of prison narratives in part by focusing on what Abu-Jamal terms the most profound horror of incarceration: the listlessness, the inactivity and all those banal occurrences traditionally excluded from the genre. The pace is set by an opening tracking shot that pans slowly past a row of cells before arriving at a medium shot of Zach, resting against the bars. This is followed by a series of lengthy holds on Zach lying on his bunk, sitting on his bunk and leaning against the wall. Several minutes pass before what would be conventionally termed a significant 'event': the arrival of Zach's cellmate, Jack. However, the promise of this incident is initially thwarted as interaction between the two is minimal, consisting largely of monosyllabic bickering and strained silence, accompanied by further lengthy holds on images of enforced indolence. Jump cuts between scenes underline the monotony by allowing no indication of how much time has passed. Our only indication as to precise chronology is the series of scratch marks that Zach makes on the cell wall. This time-keeping provokes a complaint from Jack that crystallises Jarmusch's interest in *un*doing time: 'Don't you know you're making time go slow?'

Down by Law deliberately underplays the drama in the scenes leading up to Zach and Jack's arrests. There is no substantial explanation for the frame-ups that lead to their imprisonment and no courtroom drama building to a climactic sentencing. Once they are imprisoned for doing next to nothing Zach and Jack do next to nothing in a 30-minute sequence during which the camera never leaves the confines of the cell. There is no bad warden to deliver an inaugural address, no bad guards and after the opening tracking shots we never see any other prisoners. At one point, the most animated in the sequence, we do *hear* the other inmates as, in mockery of the conventional prison riot and clichés concerning alienation, the entire cellblock joins Roberto in conjugating the children's verse: 'I scream, you scream, we ALL scream for ice cream.' This disturbance is quickly quelled by the guards and in the only other animated incident, a fight between Zach and Jack, we leave the confrontation shortly after it begins with a jump cut to another bunk shot where the combatants' bumps and scrapes are prominently displayed. A more substantial elision takes place in relation to the escape which is typically the highpoint of sensation in a prison drama. Roberto broaches the subject of escape, the prisoners are then seen leaving the cell for the first time for exercise in the yard and this is followed, after 30 minutes of close shots, by an unrevealing long shot as they scramble through a sewer. Jarmusch escapes from escape-film cliché by omitting the planning, the preparation and suspenseful execution. In fact, there is no need to supply these because the prisoners, like the spectators, are already fully familiar with the formula:

Roberto: Today, in the yard, I make a discovery, very interesting. And I think a film I have seen it in. Very good. An American film. Lots of action. It was a prison film. When a ... how do you say in English? When a ... when the man go out the prison and make away?
Jack: Escape.
Roberto: What?
Jack: Escape.
Roberto: Escape. Yes, escape.

As they make their way into the forest the fugitive's flight is accompanied by a cacophony of bells, sirens and barking dogs and Roberto underscores the familiarity by remarking: 'We have escaped. Like in the American movies.'

Roberto continually consults a self-assembled phrase book of American idioms and recycles colloquial cliché from his arrival in the cell – 'not enough room to swing a cat' – to his farewell to Jack and Zach – 'wish you were here'. Jarmusch performs a similar operation with cinematic customs to foreground the prison film's 'fourth wall' (the screen). During one of their squabbles, Zach responds to Jack's decision to 'blank' him with the following: '*You* don't exist. This floor doesn't exist. This prison isn't here. These bunks aren't here. The bars aren't here. None of this is really here. None of this is really here at all.' Subsequently, Roberto draws a fake window frame on the wall that is not really there and inquires innocently:

Roberto: Excuse me. Do you say in English 'I look at the window' or do you say in English 'I look out the window'?
Jack: Well in this case Bob, I'm afraid you gotta say 'I look at the window.'

Roberto's love of American movies leads to the jailbreak and his fairytale meeting with Nicolette: 'Now I have found my love at last. She has asked me if I will stay here with her for ever and ever. Like in a children's book.' Roberto's cinephilia leads to conventional Hollywood closure for the happy couple and his passion for American poetry signposts Jack and Zach's denouement. Roberto quotes Walt

Whitman (poet of the Open Road) and Robert Frost ('The Road Less Travelled') in Italian. The final image in *Down by Law* is of Jack and Zach going their separate ways at a fork in the road, which is also a crossroads between East and West, Europe and America, elite and popular aesthetics. In *Down by Law* it is the foreigner, the innocent abroad, who enables Americans to recover their national myths of travel, innocence and wonder. Whilst Roberto quotes English idioms and recites American verse in Italian, Jarmusch, taking the road less travelled, quotes from the idiom of European cinema in the native tongue of American formula film. Elements of *noir*, the prison and escape film and the road movie are crossed with literary allusion, a quixotic open-endedness and privileging of image over narrative associated with poetic cinema.

Roberto claims to be inspired by American cinema but hints at standardisation by failing to name any specific films. The identity of the prison film – 'with lots of action' – that inspires Roberto's escape attempt remains a mystery, but it certainly could not be *Natural Born Killers*. The basic narrative structure of Stone's controversial work is identical to *Down by Law* (crime, punishment, escape) and both are hybrid prison-road movies, but here the similarities end. In contrast to the minimalist and monochrome *Down by Law*, *Natural Born Killers* is kinetic and kaleidoscopic: over 3,000 shots in under two hours (an average shot length of two and a half seconds) which splice a variety of film stocks (colour and black and white, Super 8 and 35mm) and styles (music video, newsreel, sitcom, natural history documentary and cartoon). Both films include references to Whitman, but Stone is preoccupied with Charles (the mass murderer who shot passers-by from a clock tower on the University of Texas campus) rather than the good grey poet. Whilst Jarmusch exercises restraint and draws from European cinematic tradition, Stone aims for carnivalesque excess and borrows from MTV and tabloid sensationalism. The antithesis between the *mise-en-scène* of each film is best captured during the escape sequences. Whilst the breakout disappears from *Down by Law*, Stone offers a 20-minute spectacular of carnage inspired by the New Mexico uprising.

Despite these differences, however, both films are engaged in their own flight from the prisonhouse of formula film-making. Whilst Jarmusch seeks to slip outside through subterfuge, Stone opts for smashing through the walls with a sledgehammer. *Natural Born Killers* follows the career of Mickey and Mallory Knox on their 'Route 666' killing spree. Following their capture, the golden boy and girl of tabloid culture are pursued into prison by a slavering media. Mickey's pronouncement, live from death row, that he is a 'natural born killer' sparks a prison riot during which the couple escape, execute their interviewer and are last seen, a few years down the line, back on the road in a Winnebago with their children. Ultimately, *Natural Born Killers* is less interested in the killers and their destiny than the culture they personify. Mickey and Mallory's actions are vigilante vengeance visited on a necrophile nation; their bloodlust appears almost wholesome alongside the grotesque pageant of journalists, fans and law enforcement officials who pursue them. At the same time, however, the killers' road trip seems less a mirror held up to a degraded Thanatocracy than a rear view image of the implosion of the social into simulacra. All of the outlaws' travels are in media hyperreality and intertextual allusions far exceed images of violence. Mickey and Mallory are not a modern Bonnie and Clyde so much as a postmodern *Bonnie and Clyde* (with a detour through Terence Malik's *Badlands*). The killings are re-enacted for primetime television shows, the FBI arrange for the arrest to be videotaped (in a scene which reenacts the videotape footage of Rodney King's punishment beating) and the cameras subsequently follow them into prison for an interview. The name of the institution in which they are held, Batongaville, might seem to suggest the fusion of law and police violence, but the instruments here really belong to the cheerleaders. The screening of Wayne Gale's 'exclusive' live interview and the subsequent prison riot on Superbowl Sunday accents the rivalry between sports and crime and punishment dramas as national pastime. During this spectacular, Mickey and Mallory manage to escape Batongaville, but, as the authors of 'Mad Love, Mobile Homes and Dysfunctional Dicks' suggest, Stone is primarily concerned with the 'possibility of escaping what Guy Debord calls "the society of the spectacle"'.[82] Leong's conclusion, however, that 'the media is ultimately rejected at the end of the film in favour of privacy, tourism and the mobile home', ignores the extent to which space in *Natural Born Killers* is always already mediated.[83] Whilst Jarmusch is hopeful of escape, Stone seems to offer no outside. Batongaville is simply a microcosm for the carceral hole of hyperreality.

Although *Natural Born Killers*, like *Down by Law*, concludes on the open road, the tour spirals inwards in nihilistic self-erasure. The Knox family are accompanied, at the close, by images from a gallery of media folk devils – including O. J. Simpson, the Menendez brothers and Lorena Bobbitt – which signposts *exitlessness* from the precession of simulacra. Leong proposes that the fugitives do manage to escape and their getaway is consummated by the execution of Wayne Gale, the anchorman on *American Maniacs* who epitomises the moral void of media culture. Stone claimed that the Wayne Gale interview of Mickey was inspired by Geraldo Rivera's interview of Charles Manson and his show is a composite of tabloid television coverage of crime and punishment in *Hard Copy*, *Current Affairs* and *America's Most Wanted*. However, the extent to which Gale's execution signifies an escape is instantly undercut by the death sentence Mickey delivers: 'Killing you and what you represent is a statement. I'm not 100 per cent sure exactly what it's saying ... ' The increasing impregnability of a carceral hyperreality is perhaps intimated here by the presence of Robert Downey Jr. As research for the role of Gale, Downey shadowed the host of *Current Affairs*, Steve Dunleavy, but this role subsequently became a rehearsal for the Brat Packer's own performances on *Celebrity Justice*. Since starring as the celebrity who becomes a criminal in *Natural Born Killers*, Downey has been the subject of continual media coverage as a celebrity criminal, with several arrests and prison time for drink- and drug-related offences and probation violations. Downey's subsequent rehabilitation was signalled by a starring role as a lawyer in *Ally McBeal* until an arrest in 2001 led to him being fired from the show. A similar annulation is evident in the casting of Gale's executioner, Mickey Knox. Woody Harrelson's father, Charles Voyde Harrelson, is a convicted murderer who was picked up for questioning near the 'grassy knoll' following the assassination of President Kennedy. The circle here is completed by *JFK* (1991), in which Stone framed the Kennedy assassination as the inaugural killing that spawned a culture of violence whose self-parodic paradigm is *Natural Born Killers*.

In 'Way Cooler Than Manson', David Courtwright pinpoints the accidental manslaughter of an Indian shaman living alone in the desert as 'the act on which the film turns ... the one mortal sin that sends Mickey and Mallory to Batongaville hell'.[84] Mallory screams: 'Bad, bad, bad, bad, bad. You killed life!' Their victims prior to this act have been complicit in the necrophile fantasies of a degenerate culture, but the shaman 'lived outside the media-polluted world'.[85] One could question, however, whether the shaman is any more convincing than the process footage of the desert behind Mickey and Mallory's studio-bound car. Stone's shaman is played by Russell Means, the Oglala/Lakota Sioux actor, who rose to national prominence as the first national director of AIM (the American Indian

Movement which caused a media stir in 1972 during a standoff with the US government at Wounded Knee). Means' militancy, however, was not responsible for his casting in *Natural Born Killers*. Stone chose the actor following his role as Chinachgook in *The Last of the Mohicans* and Means went on to provide the voice of Powhatan in Disney's *Pocahontas* (1994). *Natural Born Killers* opposes media simulation not with a shaman but a media simulation of the 'noble savage' who has escaped the global village.

When Mickey is asked to explain his homicidal tendencies he recites a pop stereotype of Indian culture: 'The wolf don't know why he's a wolf.' The motif of predatory animals and insects (snake, hawk, scorpion, praying mantis) seems to hint at an explanatory context for the killer's violence. There is, however, nothing natural in *Natural Born Killers*. The Indian in the desert belongs to the western and new-age fadism and the wildlife images are lifted from natural history documentaries. Social Darwinism is discredited as an explanation for the killer's violence and scientific ('rogue genes') and religious exegesis ('demoniac possession' by elemental evil) seems largely throwaway. Ultimately, all causality is cartooned and traced back to Mickey (Mouse's) origins in media myth. When Mickey refers to 'some awful, secret thang' in his past and Mallory's abuse by her father is presented as a sitcom, complete with canned laughter, Stone foregrounds the extent to which the 'abuse excuse' has become a hackneyed cliché of talk show culture.

Incest may be another throwaway alibi for violence in *Natural Born Killers*, but it is also the essence of its vision of in-breeding between social reality and the media. Stone has claimed that his intention was to capture 'that mean season, from '92 to '94, when there was one bloody tabloid scandal after another … Bobbitt, Menendez, Harding, King, Buttafuoco'.[86] The intention of copying media representations of crime and punishment has not saved *Natural Born Killers* from accusations of causing copycat crimes. Of the twelve killings to date allegedly linked to the film perhaps the most infamous is that of William Savage. In 1995, Ben Darras and Sarah Edmondson confessed to taking LSD, watching Stone's film six times and then driving off to kill Savage in the small Mississippi town of Hernando. The infamy of this case has been guaranteed by the involvement of another celebrity and friend of the deceased. John Grisham, the ex-lawyer whose courtroom fictions have been translated into Hollywood blockbusters, has lent his high-profile support to a lawsuit against Stone charging him with 'product liability' in relation to *Natural Born Killers*.

In what seems like a homage to *Natural Born Killers*, an episode of *Oz*, the cult prison drama, focused on a star reporter arriving at a maximum security facility to make a *vérité* exposé, getting too close to his subject and being punished with a brutal beating. *Oz* transports the ultra-violence and self-referentiality of Stone's film to its logical home in soap opera. Although it has been regularly praised and denounced for its documentary realism, *Oz* in fact represents the pinnacle of postmodern self-reflexivity in contemporary prison drama. Each episode is framed by one of the prisoners, a wheelchair bound Augustus Hill, delivering a streetwise sermon on the weekly installment from inside a glass cage – a Brechtian device that foregrounds the other glass-screened box containing the inmates. The prison warden, his aides and charges invariably appear on television within the show each week due to *Oz*'s notoriety. The prisoners are also repeatedly seen watching television and are particularly fond of a children's show, or rather its female presenter. When the network axes *Miss Sally's Schoolyard*, the inmates launch a letter writing campaign to complain and it is difficult not to hear an echo of the career of *Oz*'s creator here. (Tom Fontana developed his prison drama with HBO after NBC axed his crime drama *Homicide: Life on the Streets*.)

During the six seasons since its premiere in 1997, the Oswald Maximum Security Prison has proven to be a Pandora's Box of prison film cliché. Each episode is overcrowded with melodramatic excesses: murders and executions, fighting and time in the hole, lock-downs and shake-downs, riots and escape attempts, bonding and tearful prison visits. The roster in *Oz* is a roll call of prison film archetypes. Tobias Beecher is prominent, amongst a gallery of 'innocents inside', as a lawyer who killed a child whilst drink-driving and makes a rapid transition from brutalised victim to hardened con. Beecher's main adversary, one of a pack of bad cons, is Vern Schillinger, head of the Aryan Brotherhood. Schillinger rapes Beecher, forces him to cross-dress as his 'bitch' and then experiences the agony of being unable to protect his own drug-addict son when he is arrives at Oz. Ryan O'Reilly plays an Irish American schemer, gleefully playing factions off against each other but, like Mickey Knox, haunted by some 'dark, secret thang' from his childhood. The factions that O'Reilly manipulates include the Wiseguys (who have been transferred from the prison sequence in Scorcese's *Goodfellas*), gangbangers (relocated from New Jack gangsta cinema) and a Brotherhood of Black Muslims led by Kareem Said (a principled imam and clone of Brother Malcolm in Spike Lee's biopic). Oz also boasts an artist-prisoner whose credentials are underlined by his name: Poet. The authorities in the Emerald City, beneath some PC-inspired casting choices, are similarly familiar: a tough black warden, a sensitive Asian-American priest and a nun with a tragic past (played by *West Side Story* star Rita Moreno) who is also the prison psychiatrist.

Beneath its glossy recycling of prison film formula, *Oz* also conforms to the genre's basic profile: S&M masquerade coated with a patina of political content. The focal point of the drama, the 'Emerald City', is an experimental wing within Oz designed by McManus, a white liberal who adheres to the rehabilitative ethic. This unit replaces bars with perspex screens and is officially dedicated to non-violent 'problem resolution', safety, educational programmes and counselling that offers the inmates an opportunity to reform. Em City, however, proves to be an ironic misnomer. The good warden-wizard is an imposter and the ideal of transformation a progressive fairy-tale. Despite the rehabilitative aspirations of prison management, the inmates degenerate into an endless cycle of violence, drug wars, turf wars and full-scale riots. The perspex screens in Oz mirror social disunity on the outside as different classes, ethnic groups (Latinos, African-, Asian-, Italian- and Irish-American), political and religious factions (White Supremacists and Black Muslim Separatists) and various gangs (including bikers and the Russian Mafia) scrap for power and limited territory. Meanwhile, the well-intentioned prison authorities struggle ineffectually to contend with corrupt guards and politicians. *Oz* discredits liberal solutions to these problems, suggesting in fact that they exacerbate the situation. At the same time, by failing to offer any radical alternatives the series risks implicitly sanctioning the conservative fatalism that has fuelled the expansion of a conflict-ridden prison-industrial complex.

Unable to offer solutions, *Oz* resorts to the aestheticisation of penal crisis. Each episode automatically includes at least one lavishly depicted scene of ultra-violence: a beating or eye-gouging, a lynching or burning, a poisoning (being fed ground glass or injected with HIV), a crucifixion or a (refreshingly simple) shooting.[87] Inmates appear unable to shower without being 'shanked' or 'shiv'd'. When, on rare occasions, the prisoners fail to murder each other the state obliges. *Oz* has seen the capital punishment of men and women by gas and the gallows, lethal injection and firing squad and even a request by a prisoner for stoning as his preferred means of execution. Sexual assaults are even more frequent than executions but, needless to say, all of the violence in *Oz* is sexual. As it heads towards its fiftieth episode *Oz* comes increasingly to resemble a De Sadean treasury. The end of each season usually provides a climactic orgy of violent destruction (a riot, explosion, or fire, sometimes simultaneously). However, the climax always fails to deliver closure since the soap opera format permits the perpetual deferment of end-pleasure. Suffering is never the prelude to release but only the progenitor to further tortures. Plots and sub-plots are terminated (typically with murder), but only to be instantly replaced with new plots of sensational affliction, sacrifice and degradation. The serial format, with its interminable delays and digressions, comes close to a paradigmatic S&M simulation. The frustration may be enhanced since this simulation is trapped in the postmodern prisonhouse. The success of *Oz* is founded on its graphic depiction of sexuality and violence. But, for the voyeur, the orgy is doubly vicarious, since the postmodern prison spectacle can never offer images of violence, only images of images.

SCIENCE FICTION PRISON FILMS: *ALIEN³* AND *THE TRUMAN SHOW*

In a science-fiction slant on the drug testing on prisoners, a sub-plot in several episodes of *Oz* entertained the possibility of inmates choosing chemically-produced accelerated decrepitude instead of serving time. Prisoners were given the option of taking a drug that rapidly enhanced the aging process, thus fulfilling the requirements of their sentence and saving the state considerable expenditure. Needless to say, this experiment did not end well. Routinely fatalistic and even dystopian predictions for the future of punishment are evident throughout contemporary science fiction. The expansion of the prison-industrial complex in the post-Vietnam era has been greeted by apocalyptic visions of mega-complexes, entire cities and even planets devoted exclusively to mass incarceration. When the first of the *Alien* films was released, in 1979, the US prison and jail population was around 300,000. By the time of *Alien³* (1992), just over a decade later, the number of inmates in custody had risen by over 400 per cent to 1.3 million.[88] David Fincher's contribution to the *Alien* franchise is set on Fiorina (Fury) 161, an inhospitable prison planet whose designation might hint at the scale of the corrections industry in the twenty-third century. The majority of the 5,000 inmates at this 'Maximum Security Work Correctional Facility' has been relocated due to industrial redevelopment leaving only a custodial contingent. This group consists of 25 violent offenders – primarily murderers and rapists – who have formed a religious cult, taken vows of celibacy and chosen to remain on Fury as a 'good place to wait for the End'.

Despite the science fiction milieu, the inmates in *Alien³* all belong to the tradition of the classical prison film. Following her crash landing on Fury, Ripley performs the conventional role of the prisoner-heroine: although innocent of any crime, her head is shaved, her clothing replaced with prison issue and she is confined with a pack of bad cons. Ripley's first encounter is with Clemens, a doctor found guilty of accidental homicide whilst intoxicated (and who thus belongs to the ranks of intemperate bourgeois felons, from Kent Marlowe in *The Big House* to Tobias Beecher in *Oz*). Following an inevitable shower scene, the 'fresh fish' goes on to meet a warden who loves to deliver speeches, an inmate who takes care of a dog and a prisoner on the edge who is even more dangerously unstable than his peers. The head con, Dillon, proves to be both black buddy who offers assistance and wise lifer who delivers sage contemplations to the prisoner-heroine: 'Why, the innocent punished?'

Whilst the inmates of the future are drawn from the 'Gen Pop' of the prison film, the facility that holds them calls on alternative models from the history of punishment. Given the vast distances that the convicts have been transported to barren territory, Fury 161 sustains the legacy of the penal colony. At the same time, the religious fervour displayed by the prisoners elides colonial subjects with pilgrims. In an early draft of Vincent Ward's script the setting was to have been a gothic monastery occupied by a colony of Luddite monks. The design of the prison complex in *Alien³* is a palimpsest beneath which a crumbling cathedral is still visible, inhabited by a sealed community of celibate, bald inmates, who wear monastic robes and light candles in labyrinthine corridors. The overlaying of prison and monastery recalls the institutional origins of the penitentiary in Philadelphia and also indexes the subcultures of contemporary US prisons. Clemens describes the laity as 'some apocalyptic, millenarian, Christian cult', but they are also linked with Islamic fundamentalism (through their African-American Imam), the Black Panthers (a clenched fist salute at a funeral) and gang culture (the tattoos, violence and endless expletives). Ripley is initially shunned by this sect as 'intolerable' temptation and challenged by Dillon on the subject of her faith. However, she subsequently transcends the figure of Eve in an industrial garden and becomes a saviour by sacrificing herself to deliver the world (before her *Resurrection* (1997) in the franchise's next instalment).

Fiorina 161 is several centuries not to mention star systems away from Eastern penitentiary, but, like its progenitor, still promises salvation. The prison-monastery, however, is in the process of being upgraded to prison-factory. The convict coiffure which underlines spiritual aspirations also reveals a barcode imprinted on the back of the head. Fury 161 is under the control of the Company which has been using prison labour to run a lead works. The foundry, which becomes a site of salvation at the close, recalls the Auburn model as much as the Philadelphia design and motions towards the contemporary privatisation of the prison landscape. The introduction of the Private Sector Prison Industry Enhancement Certification Program was a watershed in this development.[89] The 'PIE' programme was passed by Congress in the same year that *Alien* appeared and the film franchise, with its twinning of the extraterrestrial predator and a ravening Company, has grown alongside the prevalence of private capital in US prisons. In 1985, public support for the programme was enhanced by the intervention of Chief Justice Burger, who delivered speeches and articles on the subject of 'Prison Industries: Turning Warehouses into Factories with Fences'. Prison factories have traditionally manufactured products for state and federal authorities such as licence plates, street signs and clothing for hospitals and public schools. The PIE legislation, however, has effectively paved the way for a return of the convict lease system. The total value of goods manufactured in prison topped $1 billion for the first time in the year of *Alien³*'s release. Given that prison growth since the early 1990s has averaged almost 10 per cent per annum and that the cost of housing an inmate for one year is around $70,000, 'there is every reason to believe that productive prison labor programs will gain even greater importance'.[90]

Whether it is seen as a prophetic prison-factory, a monastic cell or a penal colony, the key feature of Fury 161 is the spectacular absence of improvement in correctional conditions. The technological advances that have facilitated interplanetary travel and the manufacture of androids do not appear to have reached the prison industry. Fury 161 is a dilapidated, unsanitary, low-tech dungeon. Scientific advances at the 'Core', however, are singalled at the outset by the classification of the inmate population as 'Double Y Chromosome'. XYY syndrome is a chromosomal abnormality that produces 'Super-Males' who are typically over six feet tall and produce high levels of testosterone. Some of the earliest studies of the XYY genotype were conducted in prison and proposed that it was linked to low IQs and a genetic predisposition towards aggressive behaviour and homosexuality. The 'XYY boys' in Fiorina are generally belligerent, one is nicknamed '85' (his IQ score) and most have taken vows of celibacy 'that include women'. Despite their sexual abstinence, however, the prisoners are still unprotected and fall one by one to an adversary initially identified as an 'unwelcome virus'. The *mise-en-scène* in *Alien³*, like an animated prison tattoo, is splattered with images of blood, skulls and syringes. Fincher's film clearly belongs alongside Carpenter's *The Thing* and Cronenberg's *The Fly* as science fiction AIDS allegory. The screenplay writer Vincent Ward, in his previous film, *The Navigator*, followed an attempt to escape the Black Death which involved tunnelling from a village in medieval England and arriving in twentieth-century New Zealand. In *Alien³*, a new 'Black Death' stalks a men's prison. The unstoppable, 'unwelcome virus' is configured as the gay plague which was seen by the moral majority, like its medieval predecessor, as divine punishment. Since the mid 1980s it has been feared and in some quarters hoped that retribution would be particularly severe in US prisons. Given the prevalence of unprotected sex and needle-sharing, some early studies predicted that prison time could become a de facto death sentence. At the time of *Alien³*'s release, some estimates of HIV infection among prisoners were as high as 18 per cent. In a 1991 essay, Nancy Neveloff Dubler and Victor W. Side argued that 'the figures on HIV infection suggest that prisons are about to become hospital conduits and nursing homes if planning and funding are adequate, or charnel houses if they are not'.[91] Simultaneously, the media was eagerly latching on to prison fables about inmates with HIV using their saliva, blood and semen as dangerous weapons. In *Alien³*, apocalyptic prophecies and demonology converge in the figure of a slavering creature which has deadly acid for blood and proceeds to wipe out all but one of the staff and inmates in Fury 161.

'No rubbers, no women, no guns, no shit.' Dillon's précis of prison life equates lack of contraception with vulnerability to the new Black Death. Since its official policy is that sexual relations in prisons constitute a prosecutable offence, the US corrections industry refuses to provide inmates with contraception, but, at the same time, these activities are covertly sanctioned in the interest of prisoner pacification. The absence of any authorities to protect the inmates in Fury 161 mirrors the experiences of many victims of sexual assault inside: in prison, no one wants to hear you scream. Consequently, the convicts in *Alien³* are forced to improvise weaponry and go on the offensive. Their assailant is a science fiction hybrid of folk devils: plague carrier, bad con, black rapist. The attacks are coded as sexual violence and represent a spectacular return of the repressed for the alien's celibate victims. An archetypal rapist, the creature stalks its victims, waits until they are isolated and then sadistically savours their terror.[92] The dirty passages in which most of the assaults occur might connote anal rape and on one occasion the alien is seen thrusting its pelvis into a prone victim. Typically, however, the focal point of sexual violence is the head, violently penetrated by a shaft which appears from the creature's salivating jaws in a consummation that signifies oral rape or even necrophile skull fuck.

Studies of sexual violence in modern US prisons state that the majority of rapes (70–85%) involve black aggressors and white victims. In this context, the bestial, jet-black alien can be read as a science fiction reincarnation of the Bad Nigger exacting phallic revenge on white culture. The alien's white victims cower in terror before this figure, but the film's other black super-male, Dillon, offers considerable resistance during his assault. In an earlier scene, Dillon beat a gang of white prisoners with a lead pipe to prevent their attempted rape of Ripley. This may appear as another instance of the black buddy aiding the white prisoner-heroine. Dillon, however, introduced himself to Ripley as a 'murderer and rapist of women', described her as 'intolerable … temptation' and may actually be more concerned with 're-educating the brothers'. The nature of this lesson requires close attention to the customs and argot of prison sexualities. The majority of sexual assaults inside involve 'new jacks' who are being claimed as the property of an older con or gang. The victim is often 'turned out' even before he arrives at prison, in a jail cell and it is not uncommon for drugs to be used to pacify the victim. In *Alien³*, before Ripley arrives on the prison planet, she has already been subjected to oral rape, whilst in a drug-induced stasis in her hypersleep pod. On arrival at Fiorina, the alien creature selects a large dog as its primary host and subsequently assumes canine characteristics. The sexual aggressor in prison vernacular is often known as a 'wolf', and his victim is known by a series of terms all associated with Ripley: 'bitch', 'sister' and 'queen'. Following the initial proprietorial rape, the wolf will offer protection to his bitch from other potential attackers. This observance might explain why the alien-wolf refuses to harm Ripley whilst eliminating the other inmates. The violence in *Alien³* can thus be read as an allegory of gang war for the possession of a queen. The alien-wolf disposes of Clemens soon after he sleeps with Ripley, before moving on to the convicts who attempted to rape her and then finally confronts Dillon, the rival alpha male.

A final suitor, the Company, arrives too late to save the queen-bitch. Before her final dive into the foundry, Ripley has twice attempted suicide: firstly, by confronting the alien-wolf and then by encouraging Dillon to perform euthanasia. The large numbers of prison suicides are often victims of abuse and the violent actions of inmates can sometimes mask a covert death wish. When she tracks the alien-wolf to 'the basement … where he's always been', Ripley is motivated both by a death drive and the perverse bonding that can characterise relations between abuser and victim. In the basement, the 'sister' identifies herself as 'one of the family' and this highlights parallels between sexual violence in the Big House and incest. The prison and the home are closed systems where the victim is forced to live in close proximity to their abuser. Both institutions enforce silence and secrecy. Offenders typically escape punishment whilst victims blame themselves. The futuristic Big House in *Alien³* is also a home and it hides a secret pregnancy. Fiorina's nickname, Fury, recalls the mythical snake-haired winged goddesses who mercilessly punished wrong-doing within the family. The Furies are twinned in classical legend with the Eumenides, three fertility goddesses and Fiorina 161, like the settings of the other *Alien* films, is heavy with reproductive imagery. In this respect, Ripley's role is Janus-faced for she is both queen mother and reginicide. This duality is a function of the protean nature of Ripley's gender identity. The gender system in prison is designed to reproduce patriarchal oppositions in a same-sex society. Inmates are encouraged to perform scripted identities as either super-males or queens. Ripley epitomises the gender-bending latent within this unstable polarity by traversing both roles. An androgynous woman in an all-male prison (genre) threatens to transgress conventional sexual coding.

At the close, Ripley's self-sacrifice plunges her gender identity into further contradictions. A prisoner in her own maternal body, she chooses to take her life and simultaneously execute the queen inside. Maternal subjectivity, however, is instantly reinscribed as the alien emerges from Ripley's stomach and is cradled in gothic parody of breast-feeding. Ripley's escape from confinement is realised perversely at the moment of (post-natal) confinement. This break-out is witnessed by Bishop, the figurative father and Company Man who had arrived with a cage to capture the birth of a valuable commodity, but is himself caught screaming behind a chain link fence. The oedipal dynamics of this moment seem to repeat those of the classical prison drama: the prisoner triumphs over the father and possesses the mother. However, the phallic appearance of the alien queen that Ripley embraces problematises the symbolism of this anti-Electral drama. *Alien³* seeks to extricate itself from gender trouble by having the 'intolerable' Ripley take her own life. The religious symbolism associated with this act, however, sustains the sexual indeterminacy: Ripley is aligned with the fate of gender-bending religious warriors such as Joan of Arc and the 'feminised' Christ, pierced and bleeding on the cross. The prisoner-heroine fails to escape the Big House of the future and *Alien³* articulates anxious impulses about flight from the prisonhouse of gender.

The Company is prevented from rescuing the alien creature by the vast distances it has to travel to get to Fury 161. The prison-factory, as with other industrial functions within the global restructuring of late capitalism, is banished to the margins and rendered increasingly invisible. Conversely, in Peter Weir's *The Truman Show*, we shift sights from the prison-factory to a postindustrial panopticon in which punishment is obscenely and incessantly visible. Truman Burbank, adopted at birth by a media corporation, has become the unwitting star of the most successful show in television history. His entire life has been on air, his every movement and even his sleep is scrutinised by 5,000 hidden cameras that beam his image around the globe to hordes of adoring fans. *The Truman Show* raises questions about voyeurism and exhibitionism in contemporary media culture, especially as technological advances corrode the boundaries between public and private spheres: the lives of star icons are 'invaded' by zoom lenses whilst a new generation of internet celebrities broadcast their daily existence live on-line. The reading offered here, however, will focus on *The Truman Show* as the contemporary culmination of the American prison film and its implications for current developments in disciplinary technology.

'The Truman Show', as both mass entertainment and prison, represents the ultimate glass house. Initially, Truman is a model inmate in a model town serving a life sentence that is devoid of the violent excesses typically endured by the innocent prisoner-hero. However, as he begins to develop consciousness of his captivity this 'soft' time recalls Scarry's critique of torture:

> the prisoner is forced to attend to the most intimate and interior facts of his body (pain, hunger, nausea, sexuality, excretion) at a time when there is no benign privacy, and there is no benign public, for there is no human contact, but instead only an ugly inverting of the two.[93]

This recognition signals the transformation of 'The Truman Show' into an escape film. Following several failed attempts at flight to Fiji, Truman adopts a strategy familiar from numerous prison films such as *Escape from Alcatraz* and *The Shawshank Redemption*: he pretends to play along with the rules whilst secretly tunnelling, manufactures a model to fool his watchers and then sneaks out at night, leaving the prison island behind for a picture postcard seascape.

During one of his initial unsuccessful escape attempts, Truman receives commiseration from an African-American bus driver. The sympathetic black buddy is just one of a familiar cast of prison film caricatures that the prisoner-hero encounters, including a stool pigeon who pretends to be his closest ally and a warden who monitors his every move. Truman is provided on the show with a fake father, but his relationship to the 'televisionary' Christof is the locus of oedipal tensions and an archetypal embodiment of the collision between prisoner-son and warden-father. During a rare unscripted moment, Truman meets Lauren/Sylvia, who attempts to reveal his incarceration by the 'Big Guy'. This intimate interlude is broken up by Christof, in a manner that echoes the denouement of many prison visit scenes, when Lauren is dragged away by her on-screen father. She leaves behind a cardigan, to which Truman clings like a comforter, and a challenge: 'Get out of here. Come and find me.' The prisoner-hero's rebellion against a punitive father is aligned with the recovery of a feminised freedom and mother nature. Following a path well-travelled since Forster's 'The Machine Stops', Truman decides to break out of a utopian, machine-controlled world into the natural world where he can recover an 'original' mother-figure.

In *Cool Hand Luke*, the first of our case studies, a similar pattern of oedipal rebellion was evident which was accompanied by laboured Christian iconography. Religious imagery in *The Truman Show*, however, makes Rosenberg's film appear understated. In this scheme,

Christof is a false media messiah, less Christ than Christo (Javacheff), the Bulgarian performance artist famous for large-scale cover-ups. Lauren is both a pre-oedipal and a Holy Mother. The beads she wears are emblems of the rosary and the crystal blue ocean with which she is associated are Mary's colour. Lauren is also seen interceding for Truman in prayer at the hour of his death whilst he is sailing through storms towards her on a boat called the *Santa Maria*. During the storm, Truman is figuratively baptised and saved by tying himself to the wooden vessel in a cruciform pose. Following these trials, Truman walks on water, climbs a staircase towards heaven and then, unlike the unanswered Cool Hand Luke, finally gets to talk to the 'Old Man'. At the end, religious imagery in *The Truman Show* reverts to Genesis. The 'Creator', who has made the sun and moon from a control booth in the heavens, summons storms to punish the unbeliever, whilst Truman is figured as an Adamic rebel choosing to leave the Garden having tasted the forbidden fruit of knowledge first offered by the unruly Lauren.

Truman's flight from a technologically simulated prison-garden is a mainstay of science fiction and belongs alongside 'The Machine Stops', Robert Heinlein's 'They', Frederick Pohl's 'The Tunnel Under the World', Arthur C. Clarke's *The City and the Stars* and William F. Nolan's *Logan's Run*. *The Truman Show*'s originality lies in splicing this premise together with the sub-genre of surveillance cinema. Weir's ostentatious foregrounding of framing and spectatorship belongs to a canon of metacinematic works that are either videocentric (*Rear Window, Peeping Tom, The Thousand Eyes of Dr Mabuse, The Secret Cinema*), or audiocentric (*The Anderson Tapes, The Conversation, Blow Out*). More recent additions to this sub-genre have responded to advances in private security systems (*Sliver* and *Panic Room*) and surveillance technology which integrates satellites and information databases (*Enemy of the State* and episodes of television series such as *The X-Files* and *24*). In the late 1990s in the US, the Lexi-Nexis corporation sparked a furore by marketing its online P-Trak Person Locator: a software package which offered to provide a profile on any individual that included present and past addresses, social security number and credit history. The controversy surrounding this service centred on privacy rights and the threat of stalking, but the corporation defended itself by insisting that it was merely collating materials that were already quite readily available. In information economies, subjects are already shadowed by a statistical avatar, an informational double composed of employment, medical and criminal records, shopping and leisure habits, telephone and internet activities. It has been estimated that, during a trip to the mall, an individual's image will be captured on approximately 200 separate security cameras. The 'entire life caught on an intricate network of cameras' in 'The Truman Show' constitutes a projection of conditions within the surveillance state where each subject is twinned with their virtual doppelgänger.

The Truman Show revolves around elaborate doublings and patterns of repetition. Truman offers an insurance policy called the 'doppelgänger special' to twins and his fake family history includes mention of his father being a twin. Rather than signalling his 'Everyman' status, the eponymous hero's name is an ironic misnomer signalling his own evil twins and the genealogy of the prison that holds him. *Truman* can be tracked back to Harry Truman (the founding father of the surveillance state who created the CIA in 1947) and *Burbank* to the 'Entertainment Capital of the World' (north of Los Angeles and the headquarters of numerous media corporations). Truman Burbank is the franchise name for a profitable merger between agencies of surveillance and entertainment and yet he is, at least initially, oblivious to his situation. 'The Truman Show' is thus founded on the principle of *inverted* panopticism, with the many watching the one who must not know he is the subject of incessant scrutiny. Although it transposes the optical dynamics of Bentham's model, this system is still structured by the imperatives of control. One of the co-stars boasts of the show that: 'It's all true, it's all real. Nothing you see on this show is fake. It's merely *controlled*.' Truman's actions are continually manipulated and 'any unpredictable behavior must be reported' immediately. Gradually, however, he develops suspicions about the extent of his freedom. Truman's paranoia could be diagnosed less as individual pathology and more as the psychological correlative of material conditions within a surveillance state.

The Truman Show progresses beyond an allegorical critique of advances in surveillance technology to locating carceral conditions with late capitalism. Seahaven might be read as a paradigmatic site for the interlocking of panoptic modes of regulation with the scripting of consumer subjectivities. The Pleasure Dome is a microcosm of key locations within commodity capitalism: the suburb, the mall and the theme park. The historical setting of the show, in an endless 1950s, traces the construction of this gilded cage to the post-war emergence of new spaces of consumption and leisure, media culture and suburbanisation. The seacoast town that holds

Truman seems like a succession of Norman Rockwell vignettes played out against backdrops lifted from the photography of Joel Meyerowitz. Each day, after acting out pop culture fantasies of escape before the bathroom mirror, Truman steps out of a picture-perfect suburban home, greets his cheery neighbours (a black family, a white family, a black and white Dalmatian), before driving downtown to his white collar role in an insurance company. The first major disruption to this routine involves a spotlight crashing to the street in front of his house whilst he is leaving for work one morning. In *The Theatre and its Double*, Artaud reminds his reader of the lesson that Truman must learn: 'We are not free. And the sky can still fall on our heads.'[94] Truman's discovery of his imprisonment hinges on moments of Artaudian cruelty in which illusion and reality, theatre and its double, are unexpectedly inverted: the intrusion of non-actors onto the stage, an actress improvising an unscripted scene, a glimpse 'back-stage' behind a set simulating an elevator. In each of these instances Truman, like the audience to Artaud's theatre of cruelty, is 'shocked bodily into an awareness of the undomesticated or the uncanny. It is as if, suddenly, in the midst of reassuringly familiar forms, a space opens up, lit by a strange light.'[95]

The mounting paranoia in a small-town 1950s setting twins *The Truman Show* with *Invasion of the Body Snatchers*. As in Siegel's seminal science fiction allegory of Cold War America, the protagonist begins to suspect that the surfaces of his social world are counterfeit and the everyday becomes increasingly charged with surreal menace. Truman's suspicions are aroused by doublings and the uncanny seriality of his suburban existence. Close observation reveals suburban rituals being repeated with the precision of a prison timetable. The same acts are performed by the same people in the same manner *ad infinitum*: 'They just go round and round.' The unveiling of Truman's environment as an assembly line hints at the extent to which late capitalism is the historical era in which the superstructure itself has been subject to industrialisation. This is confirmed by Truman's inability to escape from advertising. Since 'The Truman Show' is broadcast continuously without commercial interruption it generates revenue through persistent product placement and celebrity endorsement. The intrusion of product placement into his home and workplace testifies to the implosion of the imperatives of advertising within private and public spaces. On 'The Truman Show' there is no substantial distinction between entertainment and capitalism's official art form since both are geared towards the promotion of individual products, 'lifestyles' and values. In Seahaven, the channels of Truman's desire are shaped by the nostalgia mode of American popular culture and advertising. His acute aquaphobia highlights the contingency of consumer culture on the programming of bodily fears and wants. The prominence of advertising in Truman's home testifies to the structural integration of suburbia and spaces of shopping. The biosphere that contains Truman's hometown mimics the architecture of increasingly gargantuan and hermetically-sealed shopping complexes. Seahaven, like a super-mall, boasts a vast number of themed zones and storefronts in ersatz idyllic settings behind which operates a network of surveillance cameras and security guards.[96] Truman's situation, as the subject of some 5,000 cameras strategically positioned around the fake city, may seem hyperbolic, but is in fact closely comparable to the supervision of subjects within most malls and inner city shopping precincts.

The paradigm for a sealed utopian community, under constant surveillance and covert control geared towards maximising consumption, is the theme park. Seahaven is set in Tampa Bay, Florida and seems modelled on the Main Street section of its near neighbour Disneyworld. The theme park might be read as an *Ur*-landscape for the trajectory of consumer capitalism. The smooth functioning of themed enclosures is dependent on maintaining the 'innocence' of the visitor and Truman is similarly shielded from the artifice, labour and meticulous manipulation taking place behind the scenes. In *The Truman Show*, the future of social control predicted in *The Book of Daniel* has come to pass. Daniel's wry comment on the 'real achievement' of Disneyland could equally apply to Seahaven:

> ... the handling of crowds ... Plain-clothes security personnel appear in any large gathering with walkie-talkies. The problems of mass ingress and egress seem to have been solved here to a degree that would light admiration in the eyes of an SS transport officer.[97]

Doctorow's narrator captures the regressive impulses, both political and psychological, within these developments by noting the intrauterine design of Disneyland: 'This famous amusement park is shaped like a womb.'[98] 'The Truman Show' began with glimpses of the star's foetal existence and in a sense he has never left the womb:

Seahaven is a sanctuary surrounded by water in which Truman is continually provided for and protected. When he decides to break out of this high-tech womb it is figured, as is common in prison film iconography, as a rebirth. Truman embarks on a perilous voyage across water and then steps through an aperture into the outside world.

Truman's decision to reverse uterine flight is motivated by his consciousness that beneath the patina of pre-oedipal perfection, Seahaven belongs to the symbolic sphere of authority and rules. The landscape of power is well hidden, but its topography can be uncovered by transgression. The instant that an unauthorised presence appears in Seahaven, it is swiftly ushered away by plain-clothes security teams. Once Truman begins his rebellion he is met by a counterforce. Initially this appears in a benevolent guise, such as a policeman interested only in public safety. However, as Truman's insurgency escalates the full security apparatus is unveiled. Following his escape, the moon becomes a spotlight, sirens wail and the friendly neighbourhood Dalmatian (perhaps in homage to Disney) is transformed into a rabid tracker dog. This conversion hints at the disciplinary apparatus underlying the butterscotch façade of theme parks, malls and leafy suburban vistas. As Truman runs from the hometown mob there is a clear allusion to Siegel's *Invasion of the Body Snatchers*, but also, perhaps, a haunting sense of contemporary US suburban paranoia: the proliferation of private patrols, neighbourhood watches, curfews, guard dogs, security lighting, sensors, alarms, fencing, CCTV, guns and an assortment of personal defence devices. Surveillance technology originally pioneered in corrections for the monitoring of parolees is now being aggressively marketed at middle class parents to 'keep track' of their children. Following highly publicised child abduction cases, electronic tagging has been deemed only partially reliable and trials are currently taking place that involve the implantation of tracking devices beneath the skin of suburban children.

As Truman seeks to escape the suburban theme park prison, Christof insists that 'Seahaven is the way the world should be'. *The Truman Show* allows few glimpses of the world outside Seahaven and aside from a token Japanese family the 'world' predictably appears to signify America. The televisionary's declaration, however, seems to detract from the extent to which this world already *is* Seahaven. To paraphrase Baudrillard's aphoristic assault on Disneyland, perhaps Seahaven exists to disguise the fact that the rest of America is Seahaven. Such a recognition is partly undermined by the dynamics of identification in *The Truman Show*. Far from being a representative figure, Truman is cast as exceptional. Camera rhetoric invites the spectator to share the ocular power of the show's creators and audience. In the process, potential affinities with Truman's position as the object of a disciplinary gaze in landscapes of power are erased. *The Truman Show*'s conclusion enables it to escape from the implications of its allegorical critique of a carceral society by repeating the classic prison film cliché that freedom lies just beyond the prison walls. Weir's film maintains a fake opposition between the fake prison world of Seahaven and liberty on the outside. As the star steps jauntily out of his gilded cage with a cheery wave and corny dialogue, *The Truman Show* is given a happy ending from a 1950s sitcom, a denouement that suggests an underlying consonance with the reactionary nostalgia renounced elsewhere. Christof's judgement is discredited by his prisoner's successful escape, but maybe, this time, the warden should get the last line: 'Truman prefers his cell ... You're afraid, that's why you can't leave.'

7

Image Burn: A *Minority Report* on the Future of US Punishment

I have also known omnipotence, opprobrium, imprisonment. Look: the index finger on my right hand is missing. Look: through the rip in my cape you can see a vermilion tattoo on my stomach … I come from a dizzy land where the lottery is the basis of reality.

'The Lottery in Babylon', Jorge Luís Borges[1]

'Is it now?'
   Minority Report

The Truman Show was loosely based on *Time Out of Joint* and is thus one of several contemporary science-fiction films, including *Blade Runner*, *Total Recall*, *Screamers*, *Impostor* and *The Matrix*, to have been inspired by the fiction of Philip K. Dick. When Dick, like Truman, had his life turned into a film (in both *The Gospel According to Philip K. Dick* (2001) and *The Nervous Breakdown of Philip K. Dick* (1996)), the centrepiece was a disturbing perception, once again like Truman, that there was a world beyond the one he could see:

I remember [the world] in detail. I do not know who else does. Perhaps all of you were always here. But I was not. In March 1974 I began to remember consciously, rather than unconsciously, that black iron prison police state world.[2]

Following what he referred to as his '2.3.74' experience, Dick was convinced that he had crossed over from a parallel universe in which the Second World War had been won by the Axis powers. As well as pre-empting the 1990s vogue for 'alternative history', this might be read as a mantic vision of the massive expansion of the US prison-industrial complex in the post-Vietnam era. Dick's troubling dreams, like the visions that plague Doctorow's Daniel at Disneyland, situated 'somewhere between Buchenwald and Belsen', map the future of American fascism.

One of the most recent additions to the expanding canon of Dick films, Spielberg's *Minority Report* (2002), offers slick shots of law enforcement in black leather storming into civilian homes. These images, however, appear to be offered as progressive developments in the future of US policing. The year is 2054 AD and in the District of Columbia, John Anderton heads the 'Department of Pre-Crime' which has been responsible for reducing major felonies by 99.8% in a six-year period. Anderton's mentor and the mastermind behind the Pre-Crime project is Burgess (played by Max von Sydow, in carbon copy of the role he performed in *Judge Dredd* (1995), another computer-generated cartoon of the future of crime and punishment). Whilst *Judge Dredd* offered a neo-fascist fantasy of justice inflicted by leather-clad law-makers on the streets, *Minority Report* goes one step further to envisage the administering of justice even before the crime has been committed. In place of high rates of homicide, low rates of detection, lengthy investigation and prolonged legal wrangling, the Pre-Crime department delivers near instantaneous detective work, due process and discipline. The success of this programme, in the former murder capital of America, has resulted in a rather redundant referendum on whether Pre-Crime should be adopted nation-wide. The key figures in this experiment are a triumvirate of genetically-altered mutants who possess the power to foresee violent crimes. The 'Pre-Cogs' are kept in a flotation tank, their visions are translated to digital video and used by the Pre-Crime team to arrest perpetrators prior to the commission of the crime. Anderton examines the Pre-Cogs' 'data stream' on a holographic computer interface for evidence. This is witnessed by two judges on video link-up who then offer judicial sanction for the troops to descend on the criminal-to-be and instantly impose a life-sentence. Whilst Anderton motions gracefully with cybergloved hands, moving digital information across a 3-D screen, his gestures are accompanied by Schubert's 'Unfinished Symphony'. This soundtrack completes the aestheticisation of mid twentieth-century police work and also includes distant echoes of the Nazi liquidation of the ghetto, to the accompaniment of J. S. Bach, in Spielberg's *Schindler's List*.[3] The computer technology that permits the integration of police, judicial and criminal proceedings, much favoured by totalitarian regimes, includes an anachronistic low-tech component reminiscent of Borges' 'The Babylon Lottery'. Once the vision is received, the names of the murderer and their potential victim are inscribed on coloured balls (red signifies unpremeditated crimes of passion) which roll down plastic tubes like lottery numbers. This disparity in crime-fighting technology is repeated in the penal system. Those convicted of Pre-Crime are permanently suspended in cryogenic containers. The comments of the sentry at the containment facility suggest a high-tech perfection of the Quakers' segregationist model: 'Look how peaceful they seem. But inside: busy, busy, busy.' At the same time, however, Anderton's encounter with a former felon establishes that the traditional prison system remains intact alongside these futuristic advances: 'Confinement was a real eye-opener ... For true enlightenment there's nothing like taking a shower whilst this large fellow with an attitude you can't knock down with a hammer whispers in your ear "oh Nancy, oh Nancy".'

The initial setpiece in *Minority Report* is also an 'eye-opener' in which the spectator watches Anderton scrutinising the video evidence of an imminent murder seen from multiple perspectives by the Pre-Cogs. In this vision of the future, based on the concept of foresight, the eye is a critical subject. Spielberg compiles a catalogue of eye images (including glasses, blindings and 'third eyes'), 'eye-lines' ('the eyes of the nation are on us' and 'in the land of the blind, the one-eyed man is King') and self-reflexive optical allusions (to *Un Chien Andalou*, *Psycho*, *A Clockwork Orange* and *Blade Runner*). The founder of pre-crime technology is Dr Iris Hineman and her symbolic daughter, Agatha, repeats a challenge to Anderton throughout the film: 'Can you see?' When Anderton, somewhat inevitably, goes on the run from his Pre-Crime peers, he undergoes eye transplant surgery to evade the panopticon police state. Justice in the future is anything but blind, as citizens are continually subjected to retinal scans. Biometric technology automatically identifies individuals as they enter buildings or use public transport, and the poor are routinely subjected to optical interrogation by robotic 'spiders' in their homes. Eye-scanners were initially designed for use in maximum security prisons and military facilities, but *Minority Report* predicts they could become a conspicuous feature on the urban landscape. When the film was in pre-production, in 1999, Spielberg brought together a think tank to 'imagineer' a US city in the mid twenty-first century. The team included authors, academics and assorted experts on media, architecture, biomedicine, computing, transport, the environment and fashion. One of their key predictions concerned the imminent integration of scanning technology with targeted advertising. In Washington, 2054, retinal scanning in shopping centres is as commonplace as contemporary CCTV and every surface is the potential site of consumer spectacle. The same technology that allows the futuristic state to monitor an individual's daily movements permits retailers to track all spending. Consequently, consumers are continually bombarded by custom-made commercials: digital images are wrapped around buildings and floating billboards, the interiors and exteriors of cars become mobile adverts, cereal packets are activated at breakfast time with cartoon animations, and jingles and virtual shop assistants welcome customers to every store with queries about prior purchases.

Instead of indulging in fanciful speculation, the city of the future constructed in *Minority Report* is thus firmly founded on current technology which includes retinal scanning (now deployed at a number of international airports), holographic billboards (prominent in some major city centres) and personalised commercials (an increasingly integral component of internet shopping). However, despite recognising that the all-seeing eye of the state and consumer capitalism share the same tools, tactics and databases, Spielberg's film refuses to acknowledge any connection between the hard and soft faces of social control. The application of scanning to shoppers hints visually at the consumer's status as the key product in commodity culture, but this is not identified as a correlative of the objectification and false consciousness endured by the Pre-Cogs. In place of a politicised awareness of affinities between the situation of the Pre-Cogs and the channelling of consumer consciousness, Spielberg develops the doubling of Agatha and Anderton. The two are twins who share symbolic parents (Burgess and Iris) and foetal imprisonment: the drugged Agatha is trapped in womb-like stasis replaying video memories of the loss of her murdered mother who was drowned; Anderton is shown immersed in an ice bath, is underwater at a swimming pool when he loses his son and subsequently develops an addiction to drugs and replaying his memories on holographic home movie. Agatha is rescued by her twin and their break-out from the Pre-Cogs' uterine enclosure is accompanied by a symbolic breaking of waters that repeats the familiar prison film motif which equates the cell with the maternal body. More specifically, the water motif in *Minority Report* has both baptismal and lachrymal connotations. The hard edges of political critique are dissolved repeatedly by Spielberg's sentimental preoccupation with spiritual redemption and tears. Any alarm concerning the emergence of an Orwellian police state is washed away by a mawkish insistence on the humanity of the Pre-Cogs. The potentially false imprisonment of the hundreds accused of 'pre-crime' is entirely secondary to the situation of the child-like Agatha.[4] When the invasive colonisation of public and private space by consumer capital is confronted by Spielberg it is utilised, as in *The Truman Show*, for comical as opposed to critical effect. When Anderton is tracked by an advert for a 'getaway' holiday whilst on the run, or Agatha predicts the behaviour of shoppers in a mall with uncanny accuracy, such incidents are offered as amusement rather than political questioning. The mysterious 'third man', who oversees the crime scene where Anderton shoots a suspect, is humourously revealed as an advertising image for designer sunglasses. Although this iconic figure cannot be scanned, the spectator of *Minority Report* is repeatedly the target of product placement by companies ranging from The Gap and Guinness, to Lexus, Nokia and Reebok.[5]

The mystery plot in *Minority Report* hinges on tampering with visual evidence and the film is itself guilty of erasing its own visual testimony to cabals between overt and covert modes of social discipline. *Minority Report* could also be charged with suppressing evidence of links between crime and poverty. The city of the future is sharply divided into areas of middle class affluence (luxurious high-rises, malls and a gleaming business district) and the 'Sprawl' (consisting of filthy alleyways and impoverished federal housing). Spielberg's lack of concern for those who occupy the latter is illustrated during a chase scene in a mall during which a beggar scrambling for coins appears only as an opportunity for slapstick humour. Despite the gross inequalities that characterise this city of the future major crime, which of course does not include poverty, has been eradicated. In place of a socioeconomic framework, the understanding of crime and punishment in *Minority Report* is underpinned by a pseudo-religious determinism. The Pre-Cogs are worshipped as saints and kept in a space known as the 'Temple'. The pre-crime detectives, conscious of their role in shaping destiny, claim that they are 'more like clergy than cops ... the power's always been with the priests'. The criminals caught by these priests of pre-crime are immobilised with headsets nicknamed 'halos' and sent for life to a subterranean punishment chamber, known as 'hell', presided over by a sentry called Gideon. *Minority Report* begins, like *The Scarlet Letter*, with an act of adultery and its unification of religion and law suggests how far we have failed to come since our initial investigation of the Puritan penal code. The concept of pre-crime is little more than a science-fiction updating of predestination. The musical accompaniment to Anderton's investigation of the Pre-Cogs' visions, Schubert's 'Unfinished Symphony', alongside the insistence that you can change your future, appears to endorse the principle of human agency. This concept seems to exist, however, only in the sense that Jonathan Edwards outlined in *Freedom of the Will*, which is to say that the elect are free to perform good deeds whilst the preterite can choose the path of wickedness. Agatha's justification is signalled by a halo of Spielbergean 'god-light' and Anderton displays the perseverance of the saints, enduring even banishment to hell, before his inevitable ascension. Beneath the palimpsest of foreordination according to classical Hollywood narrative, one can still detect the scripting of Calvinist fatalism.

The religious underpinning to *Minority Report* precludes a wholesale renunciation of the principle of punishment for pre-crimes. The mystery plot hinges on the revelation that some of those banished to hell may not have gone on to commit the crimes for which they were punished. The three Pre-Cogs occasionally disagree on destiny but the 'minority report' has been suppressed to maintain the appearance of infallibility. In fact, the very first case, involving the drowning of Agatha's mother by Burgess, the patriarch of pre-crime, is revealed as a cover-up. The key clue in the case of Ann Lively, the dead lady in the lake, is the direction of the waves (they go one way in the visions of Dashiell (Hammett) and Arthur (Conan Doyle), but the other in the minority report of Agatha (Christie)). The waves go both ways in *Minority Report* itself, as the film is profoundly inconsistent with regard to the ethics and efficacy of pre-crime. Following the disclosure of Burgess' crime and cover-up, the Department of Pre-Crime is disbanded, the gates of hell are opened and over 1,000 ex-cons are released back onto the streets of Washington. Given that we have only seen two dubious cases and Agatha, the most gifted of the pre-cogs has never been wrong, this clemency appears somewhat equivocal. The denouement grants amnesty but not absolution. Crucially, although Spielberg displays reservations about glitches in the methodology of the pre-crime experiment, the principle of a crime-free police state is not itself renounced.

Minority Report evinces liberal qualms about miscarriages of justice, but is still seduced by the paradigm of fascist penality. One of the commercials that appears in the film is an infovert for 'pre-crime' that parades the people who would have been the victims of murder and rape and ends with a chorus of children claiming: 'Pre-crime: it works.' This advert might be read as a parody of law and order sloganeering and recalls the infamous Wille Horton campaign used to discredit Dukakis, but its resonance in the post-9.11 political climate might not be wholly ironic. *Minority Report*, as well as feeding off a range of millennial *bêtes noires* (drug-addicted mothers and genetic experimentation, paedophiles and child abduction), was uncannily pre-cognitive in relation to contemporary developments in US penal culture. The so-called 'war on terrorism' has been used to legitimate massive encroachments into civil liberties and widespread 'pre-emptive arrests'. The Bush administration claimed the right of 'anticipatory self-defence' and John Ashford insisted that due process had become an unaffordable luxury. Undisclosed numbers of individuals, not found guilty in civilian courts, have been sentenced to indefinite detention, often in military facilities, based on the suspicion that they might plan or assist in future acts of terrorism. Largely, the liberal media has shown as much interest in the situation of these permanent detainees as *Minority Report* does for the prisoners held for life in cryogenic freezers without actually committing any crime. The most substantial debates that have occurred in relation to the situation of detainees has not addressed the legal or moral issue of their incarceration, but the legitimacy of torture as an interrogation technique for terrorists.

As the concept of 'thoughtcrime' is codified in US criminal justice, the framework for punishing those deemed to possess a predisposition to criminal activities is consolidated. Of course, as we have seen in relation to religious radicals, political militants, racial minorities and others deemed a threat to social order, the practice of pre-emptive punishment is hardly a recent addition to the American scene. Potential transgressions have been systematically fabricated to justify the punitive practices of the justified. Today's folk devil, the terrorist, like the drug dealer and bad nigger, the atom spy and the apostate, the witch and the sexual deviant, the radical and the unruly worker, is associated by the dominant order with apocalyptic excesses to legitimate the cruelty of its own disciplinary apparatus. A history of punishment as a political tool in the US underscores the extent to which criminals exist because the law needs them. When George Bush refers to the US offensive against terrorism as a 'war of Good against Evil', his Manichean metaphors can be traced back through the rhetoric of the 'war on drugs', Cold War and race war in the ante- and postbellum South, to the Puritan crusade against the wonders of the invisible world.

The chiaroscuro of the Puritan imagination, alongside its preoccupation with supernatural forces, demons, sexuality, punishment and sin, is the forebear of a gothic tradition which has always been prominent in American cultural history. It was precisely this quality that Melville detected in Hawthorne's work:

> a touch of Puritanic gloom ... this great power of blackness in [Hawthorne] derives its force from its appeals to that Calvinistic sense of Innate Depravity and Original Sin ... You may be bewitched by his sunlight – but there is the blackness of darkness beyond.[6]

This description has often been seen as an equally valid précis of Melville's own aesthetic. Despite the oppositional urges in his fiction, Melville, like Hawthorne, ultimately succumbs to a conservative fatalism that is fixated on the tragic inevitability of punishment. As the walls close in on Wall Street and the revenant figures of Babo, Bartleby and Budd call silently from the grave, Melville's carceral vision also mirrors Poe's desperate preoccupation with premature burial and the undead. Each of the narratives of punishment which have been studied here might be read as a vibrant strand in the long history of gloomy American gothic. From Hawthorne and Melville to the literature of slavery and neoslave narratives, from the spiritual iconography of the Cold War to the sadomasochistic spectacles of the American prison film, punishment narratives operate as the uncanny of the American Dream.

In his 1995 adaptation of *The Scarlet Letter*, Roland Joffé ends not with 'Puritanic gloom' but bewitching sunlight. Hester Prynne triumphs over her Puritan oppressors and tosses away the sign that symbolises her punishment. The film's closing image is a close-up on the letter, trampled into the earth by the wheels of the carriage taking Hester, Dimmesdale and Pearl towards new beginnings. The closure here constitutes a feeble form of (dirty) protest by the liberal imagination against the politico-cultural hegemony of the new conservatism, but it is purely compensatory. Needless to say, Hawthorne's original ending was far less sanguine. The closing image in *The Scarlet Letter* returns us to the beginning. A narrative about a letter penalty is framed by the first letter and concludes with the image of a scarlet 'A', burning brightly on Hester's black tombstone:

> It bore a device, a herald's wording of which may serve for a motto and brief description of our now concluded legend; so sombre is

it, and relieved only by one ever-glowing point of light gloomier than the shadow: –

'ON A FIELD, SABLE, THE LETTER A, GULES'[7]

Following Hawthorne and Hester back to where we began, with the polysemic sign of punishment, the scarlet 'A' on its sable backdrop has acquired new 'deep meaning'. The black and the red signifies the history of punitive oppression endured by America's racial and political outsiders – the black speaks to the gothic tinge within that long history; whilst the red embodies the cruelty, the bloodshed, branding and burning. The cyclical structure of *The Scarlet Letter* might finally betoken the interminable cycles of profit and loss in the political and libidinal economies of cruel and usual punishment.

Notes

1. THE BIRTH OF A PRISON NATION

1. Nathaniel Hawthorne, *The Scarlet Letter* (Bedford, St Martin's Press: New York, 1991) p.41. All subsequent references are to this edition.
2. Ogden Nash, *The Face is Familiar: The Selected Verse of Ogden Nash* (Little, Brown and Company: Boston, 1940), p.209.
3. Ralph Waldo Emerson, 'English Traits' in *Essays and Lectures* (Viking Press: New York, 1983), p.849.
4. Cited in Scott Christianson, *With Liberty for Some: 500 Years of Imprisonment in America* (Northeastern University Press: Boston, 1998) p.46.
5. Ibid., p.7.
6. Ibid., p.51.
7. Alexis de Tocqueville, *Democracy in America* (A. A. Knopf: New York, 1945), p.94.
8. Thomas Paine, 'An answer to a friend regarding *The Age of Reason*', May 12, 1797, in *Collected Writings* (Viking: New York, 1995), p.712.
9. Cited in Scott Christianson, *With Liberty for Some*, p.88.
10. Ibid.
11. Alexis de Tocqueville and Gustave de Beaumont, *On the Penitentiary System in the United States and Its Application in France. With an appendix on penal colonies and also statistical notes*, Francis Lieber trans. (Carey, Lea and Blanchard: Philadelphia, 1833), p.201.
12. Ibid., p.211.
13. David Rothman, *The Discovery of the Asylum: Social Order and Disorder in the New Republic* (Little, Brown and Company: Boston, 1971), p.83.
14. See Daniel Burton-Rose, Dan Pens, Paul Wright (eds), *The Celling of America: An Inside Look at the US Prison Industry* (Common Courage Press: Portland, Maine, 1998).
15. Fyodor Dostoyevsky, *Memoirs from the House of the Dead* (Oxford University Press: London, 1956), p.12.
16. Sigmund Freud, 'The Economic Problem of Masochism', in *The Complete Psychological Works of Sigmund Freud Vol. XIX* (Hogarth: London), p.162.
17. Ibid.
18. Sigmund Freud, 'A Child is Being Beaten', in *The Complete Psychological Works of Sigmund Freud Vol. XII* (Hogarth: London), p.185.
19. Kaja Silverman, *Male Subjectivity at the Margins* (Routledge: New York, 1992), p.190.
20. Ibid.
21. Ibid., p.191.
22. Ibid., p.211.
23. Ibid.

24. Gilles Deleuze, *Masochism: Coldness and Cruelty* (Zone Books: New York, 1991), p.58.
25. Ibid.
26. Kaja Silverman, *Male Subjectivity at the Margins*, p.186.
27. Georg Rusche and Otto Kirchheimer, *Punishment and Social Structure* (Columbia University Press: New York, 1939), p.18.
28. Ibid. p.23.
29. Norman Mailer, introduction to Jack Henry Abbott, *In the Belly of the Beast: Letters from Prison* (Vintage Books: New York, 1991), p.xii.
30. Scott Christianson, *With Liberty for Some*, p.xiv.

2. *THE SCARLET LETTER* AND THE
LONG FOREVER OF PURITAN PUNISHMENT

1. Nathaniel Hawthorne, *The Scarlet Letter* (Bedford, St. Martin's Press: New York, 1991), p.92. All subsequent references are to this edition.
2. Since this inaugural slaughter, approximately 15,000 people have been executed in North America.
3. Cited in Scott Christianson, *With Liberty for Some: 500 Years of Imprisonment in America* (Northeastern University Press: Boston, 1998), p.7.
4. Karen Kupperman, 'Apathy and Death in Early Jamestown', *Journal of American History*, 66 (June 1979), pp.24–40.
5. It should also be noted that the Puritan penal code was founded in part on a long history that included the vagaries of English common law and Levitical exegesis.
6. William Bradford, *Of Plymouth Plantation, 1620–1647* (Knopf: New York, 1970), p.3.
7. Michael Wigglesworth, *The Day of Doom: Or a Poetical Description of the Great and Last Judgement, with a Short Discourse about Eternity* (Thomas Fleet: Boston, 1751), Nos. 37, 139.
8. Cited in Kai Erikson, *Wayward Puritans: A Study in the Sociology of Deviance* (John Wiley & Sons: New York, 1966), p.186.
9. Ibid., p.188.
10. Ibid.
11. Lawrence Friedman, *Crime and Punishment in American History* (BasicBooks: New York, 1993), p.32.
12. Jonathan Edwards, *Sinners in the Hands of an Angry God, A Sermon, Preached at Enfield, July 8th, 1741, at a Time of Great Awakenings, and Attended with Remarkable Impressions on Many of the Hearers* (Riggs and Stevens: New York, 1815), pp.15–16.
13. Michael Wigglesworth, *The Day of Doom*, p.20.
14. John Winthrop, *A Model of Christian Charity*, in Paul Lauter et al. (eds), *The Heath Anthology of American Literature*, 4th edition (Houghton Mifflin: Boston, 2002), p.232.
15. Cited in Robert Martin, 'Hester Prynne, C'est Moi', in Joseph Allen Boone and Michael Cadden (eds), *Engendering Men: The Question of Male Feminist Criticism* (Routledge: London, 1990), p.110.

16. William Bradford, *Of Plymouth Plantation, 1620–1647*, p.228.
17. Michael Wigglesworth, *Day of Doom*, p.63.
18. Kai Erikson, *Wayward Puritans*, pp.168–9.
19. John Winthrop, *A Model of Christian Charity*, p.228.
20. Kathy Acker, *Blood and Guts in High School, Part Two* (Grove Press: New York, 1989), pp.66, 69.
21. Cited in Bruce Daniels, 'Did the Puritans Have Fun? Leisure, Recreation and the Concept of Pleasure in Early New England', *Journal of American Studies*, 25.1 (1991), p.17.
22. Kai Erikson, *Wayward Puritans*, p.157.
23. See Carol F. Karlsen, *The Devil in the Shape of a Woman: Witchcraft in Colonial New England* (Norton: New York, 1997).
24. Cited in Elizabeth Reis, *Damned Women: Sinners and Witches in Puritan New England* (Cornell University Press: Ithaca, 1997), p.114.
25. Cited in Roger Thompson, 'Attitudes Towards Homosexuality in the Seventeenth-Century New England Colonies', *Journal of American Studies*, 23.1 (1989), p.30.
26. Cited in Bruce Daniels, 'Did the Puritans Have Fun?' p.8.
27. Friedrich Nietzsche, *On The Genealogy of Morals: A Polemic by way of Clarification and Supplement to my Last Book 'Beyond Good and Evil'*, Douglas Smith trans. (Oxford Paperbacks: Oxford, 1998), pp.42–3.
28. Michael Wigglesworth, *Meat Out of the Eater, or Meditations Concerning the Necessity, End, and Usefulness of Afflictions unto God's Children* (T. Green: Connecticut, 1770), p.61.
29. Elisabeth Bronfen, *Over Her Dead Body: Death, Femininity and the Aesthetic* (Routledge: New York, 1992), p.218.
30. Cited in Elizabeth Reis, *Damned Women: Sinners and Witches in Puritan New England*, p.116.
31. Roger Thompson, 'Attitudes Towards Homosexuality in the Seventeenth-Century New England Colonies', p.34.
32. Ibid., p.31. It should be noted that execution for 'sodomitical uncleaness' was practically non-existent in seventeenth-century New England. Several cases were brought to court and William Plaine of Guildford was hanged for 'corrupting youths', but colonial court records actually contain more cases of bestiality. Between 1641 and 1673, there were five executions involving charges of unnatural relations with animals. Notoriously, in the case of Thomas Granger in 1642 in Plymouth, this involved the mass butchery of a mare, a cow, two goats, five sheep, two calves and a turkey. Investigative procedure included placing the suspect in close proximity with his 'partners' to see if they behaved in an 'aroused' fashion. It was also technically possible for animals themselves to be sentenced to death for promiscuous conduct.
33. René Girard, *Deceit, Desire and the Novel: Self and Other in Literary Structure*, Yvonne Frecerro trans. (Johns Hopkins University Press: Baltimore, 1976), p.21.
34. Nathaniel Hawthorne, 'Mrs. Hutchinson', in *Tales and Sketches* (Viking Press: New York, 1982), p.21.
35. Ibid.
36. For the record, Judge Hathorne ordered a Quaker woman to be stripped to the waist and severely flogged.

37. Cited in Scott Christianson, *With Liberty for Some*, p.19.
38. Cesare Beccaria's seminal *On Crimes and Punishments* (1764) and John Howard's *The State of Prisons in England and Wales* (1777) are noteworthy in this respect.
39. Alexis de Tocqueville and Gustave de Beaumont, *On the Penitentiary System in the United States and Its Application in France, with an appendix on penal colonies and also statistical notes*, Francis Lieber, trans. (Carey, Lea and Blanchard: Philadelphia, 1833), p.175.
40. Charles Dickens, *American Notes, for General Circulation* (New York: 1972), p.155.
41. Michel Foucault, *Discipline and Punish: The Birth of the Prison* (Vintage: New York, 1995), p.189.
42. John Winthrop, 'City on a Hill', in Lauter et al. (eds), *The Heath Anthology of American Literature*, 4th edition, p.233.
43. Kai Erikson, *Wayward Puritans*, pp.169–70.
44. Cited in Michael Rogin, *Subversive Genealogy: The Politics and Art of Melville* (University of Wisconsin Press: Madison, 1983), p.267.
45. This was also a *de facto* policy of birth control amongst 'undesirables'. Such a policy was officially adopted after 1870, when the nascent eugenics movement encouraged legislation prohibiting criminals, with their inferior 'germ plasm', from reproducing.
46. Charles Dickens, *American Notes*, pp.146–7.
47. See, for example, Larry Reynolds' '*The Scarlet Letter* and Revolutions Abroad', *American Literature*, 57.1, (1985), pp.44–67, and Jonathan Arac, 'The Politics of *The Scarlet Letter*', in Sacvan Bercovitch and Myra Jehlen (eds), *Ideology and Classic American Literature* (Cambridge University Press: London, 1986), pp.247–65.
48. Larry Reynolds, '*The Scarlet Letter* and Revolutions Abroad', p.51.
49. Cited in Kai Erikson, *Wayward Puritans*, pp.117–18.
50. Angelina Grimké, 'Appeal to the Christian Women of the South', in Lauter et al. (eds), *The Heath Anthology of American Literature*, 4th edition, p.853.
51. Nathaniel Hawthorne, 'Mrs. Hutchinson', p.18.
52. Cited in Kai Erikson, *Wayward Puritans*, p.105.
53. Nathaniel Hawthorne, 'Mrs. Hutchinson', p.18.
54. Cited in Richard Brodhead, 'Sparing the Rod: Discipline and Antebellum Fiction', *Representations*, 21, 1998, Winter, p.73.
55. Ibid., p.70.
56. Cited in Bruce Daniels, 'Did the Puritans Have Fun?' pp.19–20.
57. American Anti-Slavery Society, 'The Declaration of Sentiments', in Lauter et al. (eds), *The Heath Anthology of American Literature*, 4th edition, p.902.
58. Cited in Kai Erikson, *Wayward Puritans*, p.202.
59. Ibid., p.201.
60. Ibid., p.202.
61. Mark Colvin, *Penitentiaries, Reformatories and Chain Gangs: Social Theory and the History of Punishment in Nineteenth-Century America* (Macmillan: London, 1997), p.107.
62. Cited in Scott Christianson, *With Liberty for Some*, p.178.

63. Scott Christianson, *With Liberty for Some*, p.19.
64. For example, a bumper sticker sold at the 1995 National Federation of Republican Women Convention declared the following: 'THE MIRACLE OF AIDS TURNS FRUITS INTO VEGETABLES.'
65. Cited in Gary Wamser, 'The Scarlet Contract: Puritan Resurgence, the Unwed Mother and Her Child', in Bruce Rockwood (ed.), *Law and Literature Perspectives* (Peter Lang: New York, 1996), p.385.
66. Ibid. p.380.

3. READING THE ROSENBERGS:
THE PUBLIC BURNING AND *THE BOOK OF DANIEL*

1. Robert Coover, *The Public Burning* (Grove Press: Berkeley, 1997), p.211. All subsequent references are to this edition.
2. Cited in Stanley Goldberg, 'The Secret about Secrets', in Marjorie Garber and Rebecca Walkowitz (eds), *Secret Agents: The Rosenberg Case, McCarthyism and Fifties America* (Routledge: New York, 1995), p.45.
3. Ibid., p.46.
4. Cited in Robert Coover, *The Public Burning*, p.250.
5. Ibid., p.466.
6. See Paul Maltby, *Dissident Postmodernists: Barthelme, Coover, Pynchon* (University of Pennsylvania Press: Philadelphia, 1991). Studies by LeClair and Ramage are singled out for failing to contain a single reference to the Cold War. See Thomas LeClair, 'Robert Coover, *The Public Burning* and the Art of Excess', *Critique: Studies in Contemporary Fiction*, 23.3, 1982, pp.5–28 and John Ramage, 'Myth and Monomyth in Coover's *The Public Burning*', *Critique: Studies in Contemporary Fiction*, 23.3, 1982, pp.52–68.
7. Paul Maltby, *Dissident Postmodernists*, p.101.
8. Michel Foucault, *Discipline and Punish: The Birth of the Prison* (Vintage: New York, 1995), p.199. All subsequent references are to this edition.
9. Richard Godden, 'So That the Dead Shall Not Be Killed Again: Mailer, Doctorow and the Poetics of a Persecuting Society', in Michael Klein (ed.), *An American Half-Century: Post-War Culture and Politics* (Pluto: London, 1991), pp.30–58.
10. Cited in Michael Paul Rogin, *'Ronald Reagan', The Movie and Other Exercises in Political Demonology* (University of California Press: Berkeley, 1987), p.239.
11. Bruce Robbins, 'Helplessness and Heartlessness: Irving Howe, James Bond and the Rosenbergs', in Marjorie Garber and Rebecca Walkowitz (eds), *Secret Agents*, p.144.
12. E. L. Doctorow, *The Book of Daniel* (Picador: London, 1972), pp. 134–5. All subsequent references are to this edition.
13. Joyce Nelson, 'TV, the Bomb, and the Body: Other Cold War Secrets', in Garber and Walkowitz (eds), *Secret Agents*, p.38.
14. Robert Proctor, 'Censorship of American Uranium Mine Epidemiology in the 1950s', in Garber and Walkowitz (eds), *Secret Agents*, p.60.

15. Friedrich Nietzsche, *The Genealogy of Morals: A Polemic by way of Clarification and Supplement to my Last Book 'Beyond Good and Evil'*, Douglas Smith, trans. (Oxford Paperbacks: Oxford, 1998), pp.47–8.

16. Mikhail Bakhtin, from *Rabelais and his World*, in Pam Morris (ed.) *The Bakhtin Reader. Selected Writings of Bakhtin, Medvedev and Voloshinov* (Edward Arnold: London, 1994), p.204.

17. Sylvia Plath, *The Bell Jar* (Faber: London, 1992), p.3.

18. Sylvia Plath, *The Unabridged Journals of Sylvia Plath* (Anchor: New York, 2000), pp.81–2.

19. Cited in Blanche Weisen Cook, 'The Rosenbergs and the Crimes of the Century', in Garber and Walkowitz (eds), *Secret Agents*, p.25.

20. Mikhail Bakhtin, from *Rabelais and his World*, in Pam Morris (ed.) *The Bakhtin Reader*, p.217. All subsequent references are to this edition.

21. Andrew Ross, 'The Work of the State', in Garber and Walkowitz (eds), *Secret Agents*, p.297.

22. Alice Jardine, 'Flash Back, Flash Forward: The Fifties, The Nineties, and The Transformed Politics of Remote Control', in Garber and Walkowitz (eds), *Secret Agents*, p.150.

23. Richard Godden, 'So That the Dead Shall Not Be Killed Again: Mailer, Doctorow and the Poetics of a Persecuting Society', in Michael Klein (ed.), *An American Half-Century*, p.42.

24. Ibid., p.45.

25. Joyce Nelson, 'TV, the Bomb, and the Body: Other Cold War Secrets', in Garber and Walkowitz (eds), *Secret Agents*, p.33.

26. Karl Klare, 'Arbitrary convictions? The Rosenberg Case, the Death Penalty, and Democratic Culture', in Garber and Walkowitz (eds), *Secret Agents*, p.277.

4. PUNISHMENT, RESISTANCE AND
THE AFRICAN-AMERICAN EXPERIENCE

1. Toni Morrison, *Beloved* (Picador: London, 1987), p.181. All subsequent references are to this edition.

2. John Edgar Wideman, 'Introduction', in S. E. Anderson and Tony Medina (eds), *In Defence of Mumia* (Writers & Readers: New York, 1996), p.127.

3. George Jackson, *Soledad Brother. The Prison Letters of George Jackson* (Penguin: Harmondsworth, 1970), p.127.

4. Ibid., p.204.

5. Elaine Scarry, *The Body in Pain. The Making and Unmaking of the World* (Oxford University Press: New York, 1985) p.109.

6. Angela Davis, *Women, Race and Class* (Women's Press: London, 1981) p.177.

7. Olaudah Equiano, *The Interesting Narrative of the Life of Olaudah Equiano, or Gustavus Vassa, The African* (Penguin: Harmondsworth, 1995, first published in 1789), pp.55, 58.

8. See Kali Tal, *Worlds of Hurt: Reading the Literatures of Trauma* (Cambridge University Press: New York, 1996).

9. Olaudah Equiano, *The Interesting Narrative*, p.58.
10. Scott Christianson, *With Liberty for Some: 500 Years of Imprisonment in America* (Northeastern University Press: Boston, 1998), p.29.
11. Olaudah Equiano, *The Interesting Narrative*, p.55.
12. Peter Parish, *Slavery: History and Historians* (Harper and Row: New York, 1989), p.8.
13. Peter Kolchin, *American Slavery, 1619–1877* (Hill and Wang: New York, 1993), p.52.
14. James Walvin, *Questioning Slavery* (Routledge: London, 1996), p.58.
15. Cited in Edward Ayers, *Vengeance and Justice: Crime and Punishment in the 19th Century American South* (Oxford University Press: New York, 1984), p.133.
16. Elaine Scarry, *The Body in Pain*, p.58.
17. Cited in John Blassingame, *The Slave Community: Plantation Life in the Antebellum South* (Oxford University Press: Oxford, 1979), p.236.
18. Frederick Douglass, *Narrative of the Life of Frederick Douglass, an American Slave and Incidents in the Life of a Slave Girl* (Modern Library: New York, 2000), p.35. All subsequent references are to this edition.
19. Scott Christianson, *With Liberty for Some*, p.54. In *The Peculiar Institution*, Kenneth Stampp argued that the plantation 'strongly suggested a prison with cruel wardens'. In *Slavery*, Stanley Elkins drew a controversial equation between the plantation and the concentration camp. In a similar mould, David Brion Davis proposed that 'throughout history enslavement has been used as a form of punishment, while some penal systems have acquired many of the characteristics of chattel slavery'. See, 'The Crime of Reform', *New York Review of Books*, No.27, June 26, 1980, p.14.
20. Harriet Jacobs, *Incidents in the Life of a Slave Girl* (Harvard University Press: Cambridge, 1987), p.52. All subsequent references are to this edition.
21. Octavia V. Rogers Albert, *The House of Bondage, or Charlotte Brooks and Other Slaves* (Oxford University Press: New York, 1988), p.1.
22. Mary Titus, 'This Poisonous System: Social Ills, Bodily Ills and *Incidents in the Life of a Slave Girl*', in Deborah M. Garfield and Rafia Zafar (eds), *Harriet Jacobs and Incidents in the Life of a Slave Girl: New Critical Essays* (Cambridge University Press: New York, 1996), p.202.
23. Deborah M. Garfield, 'Earwitness: Female Abolitionism, Sexuality and *Incidents in the Life of a Slave Girl*', in Garfield and Zafar (eds), *Harriet Jacobs and Incidents in the Life of a Slave Girl: New Critical Essays*, p.87.
24. Sandra Gunning, 'Reading and Redemption in *Incidents in the Life of a Slave Girl*', in Garfield and Zafar (eds), *Harriet Jacobs and Incidents in the Life of a Slave Girl: New Critical Essays*, p.140.
25. Ibid.
26. Olaudah Equiano, *The Interesting Narrative*, p.63.
27. Frederick Douglass cited in Edward Ayers, *Vengeance and Justice*, p.135.
28. Lawrence Friedman, *Crime and Punishment in American History* (BasicBooks: New York, 1993), p.86.
29. Frederick Douglass, *My Bondage and My Freedom* (Miller, Orton and Mulligan: New York, 1855), p.273.

30. Cited in John Blassingame, *The Slave Community*, p.83.
31. Ibid., p.85.
32. Cited in Edward Ayers, *Vengeance and Justice*, p.44.
33. Ibid., p.102.
34. Cited in Deborah M. Garfield, 'Earwitness: Female Abolitionism, Sexuality and *Incidents in the Life of a Slave Girl*', in Garfield and Zafar (eds), *Harriet Jacobs and Incidents in the Life of a Slave Girl: New Critical Essays*, p.106.
35. Jenny Franchot, 'The Punishment of Esther: Frederick Douglass and the Construction of the Feminine', in Eric J. Sundquist (ed.), *Frederick Douglass: New Literary and Historical Essays* (Cambridge University Press: Cambridge, 1990), p.141.
36. Ibid.
37. Robert William Fogel and Stanley L. Engerman, *Time on the Cross: The Economics of American Negro Slavery* (Norton: London, 1989), p.145.
38. Ibid.
39. John Blassingame, *The Slave Community*, p.261.
40. Octavia V. Rogers Albert, *The House of Bondage, or Charlotte Brooks and Other Slaves*, p.25.
41. Cited in H. Bruce Franklin (ed.), *Prison Writing in 20th-century America* (Penguin: Harmondsworth, 1998), p.4. My italics.
42. Ibid., pp.24–5.
43. Ibid.
44. Ibid., p.7.
45. Cited in Edward Ayers, *Vengeance and Justice*, p.178.
46. H. Bruce Franklin (ed.), *Prison Writing in 20th-century America*, p.5.
47. David M. Oshinsky, *'Worse than Slavery': Parchman Farm and the Ordeal of Jim Crow Justice* (Free Press: New York 1996), p.59
48. Cited in Edward Ayers, *Vengeance and Justice*, p.193.
49. Ibid.
50. See David M. Oshinsky, *'Worse than Slavery': Parchman Farm and the Ordeal of Jim Crow Justice* and Mark Colvin, *Penitentiaries, Reformatories and Chain Gangs: Social Theory and the History of Punishment in Nineteenth-Century America* (Macmillan: London, 1997), especially Chapter 9, 'From Slavery to Reconstruction: Penitentiaries and Chain Gangs', pp.201–26.
51. Mark Colvin, *Penitentiaries, Reformatories and Chain Gangs*, p.248.
52. Ibid.
53. Ibid., pp.252–3.
54. Cited in Abdul JanMohamed, 'Rehistoricising Wright: The Psychopolitical Function of Death in *Uncle Tom's Children*', in Harold Bloom (ed.), *Richard Wright* (Chelsea House: New York, 1988), p.198.
55. Mark Colvin, *Penitentiaries, Reformatories and Chain Gangs*, p.251.
56. Ida B. Wells-Barnet, *On Lynchings: Southern Horrors, A Red Record, Mob Rule in New Orleans* (Arno Press: New York, 1969), p.26.
57. Cited in Eric J. Sundquist (ed.), *Frederick Douglass: New Literary and Historical Essays*, p.238.
58. Frederick Douglass, 'Why is the Negro Lynched?' (African Islamic Publications: New York, 1988), p.23.
59. Cited in Edward Ayers, *Vengeance and Justice*, p.240.

60. Angela Davis, *Women, Race and Class*, pp.175, 183.
61. Cited in Peter Linebaugh, 'Qui Vive? The Farce of the Death Penalty', in S. E. Anderson and Tony Medina (eds), *In Defence of Mumia*, p.166.
62. Ibid.
63. Richard Wright, *Native Son* (Perennial: New York, 2001), p.331. All subsequent references are to this edition.
64. Richard Wright, *Black Boy: A Record of Childhood and Youth* (Harper: New York, 1945), p.16.
65. Richard Wright, *Uncle Tom's Children* (Harper and Row: New York, 1965) p.31.
66. Ibid., p.49.
67. Ibid., pp.45–7.
68. Roger Rosenblatt, 'Bigger's Infernal Assumption', in Harold Bloom (ed.), *Richard Wright's Native Son* (Chelsea: New York, 1988), p.24.
69. Cited in John Blassingame, *The Slave Community*, pp.235–6.
70. Mike Davis, *City of Quartz: Excavating the Future in Los Angeles* (Vintage: London, 1992), p.253.
71. John Edgar Wideman, 'Introduction', in S. E. Anderson and Tony Medina (eds), *In Defence of Mumia*, p.127.
72. Etheridge Knight, 'The Warden Said to Me the Other Day', in H. Bruce Franklin (ed.), *Prison Writing in 20th-century America*, p.231.
73. Eldridge Cleaver, *Soul on Ice* (Jonathan Cape: London, 1969), p.59.
74. Ibid., p.4.
75. Ibid., pp.157–8.
76. Ibid., p.14.
77. Ibid., p.13.
78. George Jackson, *Soledad Brother*, p.27.
79. Ibid., p.43.
80. Cited in Edward Ayers, *Vengeance and Justice*, p.61.
81. George Jackson, *Soledad Brother*, p.130.
82. Ibid.
83. Angela Davis, *Women, Race and Class*, p.38.
84. Ibid., p.148.
85. See Assata Shakur, *Assata: An Autobiography* (Lawrence Hill: New York, 1988).
86. Angela Davis, *Women, Race and Class*, p.11.
87. Nancy Reagan, cited in Mike Davis, *City of Quartz*, p.267.
88. Ibid., p.288.
89. Mumia Abu-Jamal, *Live From Death Row* (Avon: New York, 1995), p.8. All subsequent references are to this edition.
90. Robert Gooding-Williams, 'Introduction', in Robert Gooding-Williams (ed.), *Reading Rodney King, Reading Urban Uprising* (Routledge: London, 1993), p.2.
91. Ibid., p.5.
92. Toni Morrison, *Playing in the Dark: Whiteness and the Literary Imagination* (Harvard University Press: Cambridge, Mass., 1992).
93. Cited in Robert Gooding-Williams (ed.), *Reading Rodney King, Reading Urban Uprising*, p.112.

94. Judith Butler, 'Endangered/Endangering: Schematic Racism and White Paranoia', in Robert Gooding-Williams (ed.), *Reading Rodney King, Reading Urban Uprising*, p.19.
95. Elaine Scarry, *The Body in Pain*, p.59.
96. Robert Gooding-Williams, 'Look, a Negro!' in Robert Gooding-Williams (ed.), *Reading Rodney King, Reading Urban Uprising*, p.168.
97. Mike Davis, *City of Quartz*, p.224.
98. Ibid., p.254.
99. Staci Rodriguez, in S. E. Anderson and Tony Medina (eds), *In Defence of Mumia*, p.87.
100. Mike Davis, *City of Quartz*, p.256.
101. Eldridge Cleaver, *Soul on Ice*, pp.129–30.
102. George Jackson, *Soledad Brother*, p.126.
103. James Walvin, *Questioning Slavery*, p.117.
104. Cited in ibid. p.121.
105. John Blassingame, *The Slave Community*, p.209.
106. Cited in Eugene Genovese, *Roll Jordan Roll: The World the Slaves Made* (Vintage: New York, 1976), p.299.
107. Cited in John Blassingame, *The Slave Community*, p.123.
108. Ibid., p.139.
109. Delivering her inaugural lecture at UCLA, Davis focused on Frederick Douglass' significance as a figure who taught that 'the first condition of freedom is an open act of resistance – physical resistance, violent resistance'. See Angela Davis, *Women, Race and Class*, p.197.
110. See Bruce Jackson (ed.), *Wake Up Dead Man: Hard Labor and Southern Blues* (University of Georgia Press: Atlanta, 1999).
111. Valerie Smith, 'The Loophole of Retreat', in Garfield and Zafar (eds), *Harriet Jacobs and Incidents in the Life of a Slave Girl: New Critical Essays*, p.174.
112. Olaudah Equiano, *The Interesting Narrative of the Life of Olaudah Equiano*, pp.62–3.
113. Malcolm X, *The Autobiography of Malcolm X* (Penguin: London, 1968), pp.267, 275.
114. George Jackson, *Soledad Brother*, p.18.
115. Angela Davis, *Women, Race and Class*, pp.33, 209.
116. Eldridge Cleaver, *Soul on Ice*, pp.162–3.

5. THE WHIP, THE NOOSE, THE CELL AND THEIR LOVER: MELVILLE AND MASOCHISM

1. Cited in Scott Christianson, *With Liberty for Some: 500 Years of Imprisonment in America* (Northeastern University Press: Boston, 1998), pp.107–8.
2. John Blassingame, *The Slave Community: Plantation Life in the Antebellum South* (Oxford University Press: Oxford, 1979), p.217.
3. Herman Melville, *Benito Cereno*, in *Shorter Novels of Herman Melville* (Liveright: New York, 1942), p.105. All subsequent references are to this edition.

4. Cited in Michael Paul Rogin, *Subversive Genealogy: The Politics and Art of Herman Melville* (University of California Press: Berkeley, 1985), p.265.
5. Herman Melville, *White-Jacket, or the World in a Man-of-War* (Oxford World's Classics: Oxford, 1990), p.372. All subsequent references are to this edition.
6. Michael Paul Rogin, *Subversive Genealogy*, pp.90–1.
7. E. L. Doctorow, *The Book of Daniel* (Picador: London, 1972), p.233.
8. Nathaniel Hawthorne, *The Scarlet Letter* (Bedford, St Martin's Press: New York, 1991), p.146.
9. Tony Tanner, 'Introduction' to *White-Jacket, or the World in a Man-of-War* (Oxford World's Classics: Oxford, 1990), p.xvi.
10. Michael Paul Rogin, *Subversive Genealogy*, p.85.
11. Ibid., p.93.
12. Ibid., p.189.
13. Antonin Artaud, 'Theatre and Cruelty', in *Collected Works*, Vol.4, Victor Corti, trans. (Calder and Boyars: London, 1968), p.64.
14. Herman Melville, *Benito Cereno*, in *Shorter Novels of Herman Melville* (Liveright: New York, 1942), p.112. All subsequent references are to this edition.
15. Cited in Lawrence Friedman, *Crime and Punishment in American History* (BasicBooks: New York, 1993), p.47.
16. Cited in Michael Paul Rogin, *Subversive Genealogy*, p.92.
17. Ibid.
18. Ibid., p.213.
19. Alexis de Tocqueville and Gustave de Beaumont, *On the Penitentiary System in the United States and Its Application in France. with an appendix on penal colonies and also statistical notes* Francis Lieber, trans. (Carey, Lea and Blanchard: Philadelphia, 1833), p.175.
20. Elaine Scarry, *The Body in Pain: The Making and Unmaking of the World* (Oxford University Press: New York, 1985), p.45.
21. Herman Melville, 'Bartleby the Scrivener, A Story of Wall Street', in *Shorter Novels of Herman Melville* (Liveright: New York, 1942), p.111. All subsequent references are to this edition.
22. Scott Christianson, *With Liberty for Some*, p.96.
23. Cited in ibid., p.132.
24. Herman Melville, *Pierre, or the Ambiguities* (Northwestern University Press: Evanston, 1971), p.381.
25. Michael Paul Rogin, *Subversive Genealogy*, p.66.
26. Coincidentally, this was also where Greenglass and Gold, the state's key witnesses in the Rosenberg trial, were held.
27. Michael Berthold, 'The Prison World of Melville's *Pierre* and "Bartleby"', *ESQ: A Journal of the American Renaissance*, 1987, 33.4, p.246.
28. Douglas Tallack, *The Nineteenth-Century American Short Story: Language, Form and Ideology* (Routledge: London, 1993), p.166.
29. Cited in Michael Paul Rogin, *Subversive Genealogy*, p.241.
30. Alexis de Tocqueville, *Democracy in America* (A. A. Knopf: New York, 1945), p.108.

31. Michael Clark, 'Witches and Wall Street: Possession is Nine-tenths of the Law', *Texas Studies in Literature and Language*, 1983, Spring, 25.1, p.63.
32. Michael Paul Rogin, *Subversive Genealogy*, pp.187–8.
33. Michel Foucault, *Discipline and Punish: The Birth of the Prison* (Vintage: New York, 1977), p.82.
34. Michael Clark, 'Witches and Wall Street: Possession is Nine-tenths of the Law', p.140.
35. Ibid., p.141.
36. Cited in Scott Christianson, *With Liberty for Some*, p.116.
37. Ibid., p.117.
38. David Rothman, *The Discovery of the Asylum: Social Order and Disorder in the New Republic* (Little, Brown and Company: Boston, 1971), p.48.
39. See Georg Rusche and Otto Kirchheimer, *Punishment and Social Structure* (Columbia University Press: New York, 1939); Dario Melossi and Massimo Pavarini, *The Prison and the Factory* (Barnes and Noble: Totowa, New Jersey, 1981); Michael Ignatieff, *A Just Measure of Pain: The Penitentiary in the Industrial Revolution, 1750–1850* (Pantheon: New York, 1978); and Scott Christianson, *With Liberty for Some: 500 Years of Imprisonment in America* (Northeastern University Press: Boston, 1998).
40. Scott Christianson, *With Liberty for Some*, p.98.
41. Ibid., p.115.
42. Ibid.
43. Theodore Reik, *Masochism in Sex and Society*, cited in Kaja Silverman, *Male Subjectivity at the Margins* (Routledge: New York, 1992), p.193.
44. Herman Melville, *Billy Budd, Sailor* in *Shorter Novels of Herman Melville* (Liveright: New York, 1942), p.302. All subsequent references are to this edition.
45. H. Bruce Franklin, '*Billy Budd* and Capital Punishment: A Tale of Three Centuries', *American Literature: A Journal of Literary History, Criticism and Bibliography*, 1997, June, 69.2, p.337.
46. Ibid., p.352.
47. Michael Paul Rogin, *Subversive Genealogy*, p.309.
48. Barbara Johnson, 'Melville's Fist: The Execution of Billy Budd', in Myra Jehlen (ed.), *Herman Melville: A Collection of Critical Essays* (Prentice Hall: New Jersey, 1994), p.242.
49. The doctor on the *Bellipotent* introduces a third possibility, one that repeats the conjunction of punishment and madness introduced in 'Bartleby': 'Was Captain Vere suddenly affected in his mind? He recalled the unwonted agitation of Captain Vere and his excited exclamations, so at variance with his normal manner. Was he unhinged?' (p.343).
50. Barbara Johnson, 'Melville's Fist: The Execution of Billy Budd', p.247.
51. Michael Paul Rogin, *Subversive Genealogy*, p.92.

6. INSIDE THE AMERICAN PRISON FILM

1. Cited in Robert and Helen Lynd, *Middletown: A Study in Contemporary American Culture* (Harcourt, Brace: New York, 1929), p.265.

2. Mark Edmundson, *Nightmare on Main Street: Angels, Sadomasochism and the Culture of the Gothic* (Harvard University Press: Cambridge, Mass., 1997), p.132.

3. Ibid., p.133.

4. Mumia Abu-Jamal, *Live From Death Row* (Avon: New York, 1995), p.53.

5. Jacques Derrida, 'The Law of Genre', *Glyph*, 7 (1980), p.203.

6. Exceptions to this trend include the *Penitentiary* trilogy, *Stranger Inside* and the prison sequences involving Denzel Washington in *Malcolm X* and *The Hurricane*. Other racial minorities are even less well represented. Edward James Olmos' *American Me* and Taylor Hackford's *Blood In, Blood Out*, with their focus on the Chicano prison experience, are notable anomalies in this respect.

7. A vibrant tradition of documentaries by independent film-makers offers one highly effective way out of mainstream representations of prison. Notable examples include the following: *Lockdown USA*, produced by the Deep Dish Network; *Framing the Panthers in Black and White*, by Chris Bratton and Annie Goldson, a work which explores the infamous FBI COINTELPRO group; Lisa Rudman's work includes *Geronimo Pratt*, *Resistance Conspiracy* and *Have You Seen La Nueva Mujer Revolucionaria Puertoriquena?* The 'Women in the Director's Chair' group produced *Mistreating Prisoners: Health Care Behind Bars*. Kari Mokko's *The New Gulag* offers an inside look at the SuperMax facilities that have been repeatedly denounced by Amnesty and other international organisations. Felicia Sullivan's *Life Beside Bars* looks at the building of a prison near a housing estate in Boston. *Prison Labor, Prison Blues*, by the California Working Group, concentrates on the increasing prevalence of private capital and exploitation of inmate labour in US corrections.

8. Kaja Silverman, *Male Subjectivity at the Margins* (Routledge: New York, 1992), p.210. The classical Freudian imagination might itself be read in relation to carceral tropes: the unruly id is monitored by the super-ego and yet continually manages to slip past the psychic guards. According to the reading offered here, the return of the repressed is a figurative jailbreak that rules the prison genre.

9. Following a prison shower assault in *American History X*, for example, Derek Vinyard requires over 30 stitches around his anus.

10. Sigmund Freud, *Three Essays on Sexuality*, in *The Complete Psychological Works of Sigmund Freud Vol. VII* (Hogarth: London), p.162.

11. David Margolies, 'Mills and Boon: Guilt without Sex', *Red Letters: A Journal of Cultural Politics* 1982–3 Winter, 14, pp.5–13.

12. Kaja Silverman, *Male Subjectivity at the Margins*, p.196.

13. Ibid., p.199.

14. Ibid.

15. Linda Williams, *Hard Core: Power, Pleasure and the 'Frenzy of the Visible'* (University of California Press: Berkeley, 1989), p.212.

16. Gilles Deleuze, *Masochism: Coldness and Cruelty* (Zone Books: New York, 1991), p.58.

17. Ibid.

18. Ibid., p.62.

19. Laura Mulvey, 'Visual Pleasure and Narrative Cinema', in Bill Nichols (ed.), *Movies and Methods, Volume II* (University of California Press: Berkeley, 1985), p.311.

20. Gaylyn Studlar, 'Masochism and the Perverse Pleasures of the Cinema', in Bill Nichols (ed.), *Movies and Methods, Volume II*, pp.602–21.

21. Elaine Scarry, *The Body in Pain: The Making and Unmaking of the World* (Oxford University Press: New York, 1985), pp.213–14.

22. Sigmund Freud, 'The Economic Problem of Masochism', in *The Complete Psychological Works of Sigmund Freud Vol. XIX* (Hogarth: London), p.170.

23. Ibid.

24. Kaja Silverman, *Male Subjectivity at the Margins*, p.194.

25. Sigmund Freud, *The Ego and the Id*, in *The Complete Psychological Works of Sigmund Freud Vol. XX* (Hogarth: London), p.274.

26. Ibid., p.281.

27. Sigmund Freud, 'The Economic Problem of Masochism', p.175.

28. Kaja Silverman, *Male Subjectivity at the Margins*, p.213.

29. Theodore Reik, *Masochism in Sex and Society*, cited in Kaja Silverman, *Male Subjectivity at the Margins*, p.197.

30. Sigmund Freud, 'The Economic Problem of Masochism', p.180.

31. Cited in Kaja Silverman, *Male Subjectivity at the Margins*, p.187.

32. Ibid., pp.210, 213.

33. Michael Ryan and Douglas Kellner, *Camera Politica: The Politics and Ideology of Contemporary American Film* (Indiana University Press: Bloomington, 1988), p.4.

34. Ibid., p.18.

35. Thomas Pynchon, *Vineland* (Secker and Warburg: London, 1990), p.237.

36. D. W. Winnicott, *Deprivation and Delinquency* (Tavistock: London, 1984), p.114.

37. *Brubaker* was inspired by the career of Thomas Mott Osborne, an industrialist who was invited to chair a commission on prison reform during the Progressive Era. Osborne took the unusual move, as background research, of posing as an inmate to spend a week at Auburn penitentiary. His experiences after this short stay resulted in a report that recommended the immediate closure of Auburn and Sing Sing, alongside sweeping reforms throughout the penal system. Osborne was subsequently appointed as warden at Sing Sing, where he abolished the notorious regulations on silence and introduced prisoner self-government schemes.

38. Michael Ryan and Douglas Kellner, *Camera Politica*, p.108.

39. Cited in Lawrence Friedman, *Crime and Punishment in American History* (BasicBooks: New York, 1993), p.298.

40. A line from Robert Frost's, 'Mending Wall', in *Collected Poems of Robert Frost* (Garden City: New York, 1936), p.87.

41. The literary sub-genre includes historical surveys (Marilyn Tower's *Alcatraz Prison in American History*); biographies of famous inmates (Jolene Babyak's *Birdman: The Many Faces of Robert Stroud*); prisoner autobiographies (Alvin Karpis' *On the Rock: Twenty-Five Years in Alcatraz*, Jim Quillen's *Alcatraz From Inside: The Hard Years, 1942–1952*, and Leon 'Whitey' Thompson's *Rock Hard: The Autobiography of a Former Alcatraz*

Inmate); biographies and autobiographies by prison staff (George Gregory's *Alcatraz Screw: My Years As a Guard in America's Most Notorious Prison* and Milton Daniel's *Alcatraz Island: Memoirs of a Rock Doc*); collections of photographs and paintings (John Mercer's *Island of the Pelicans*, Ron Levine's *Prisoners of Age: the Alcatraz Exhibition*); poetry (Henry Floyd Brown's *Real Prison*); novels (Tara Ison's *A Child out of Alcatraz*); and novelisations based on escape attempts (Don Denevi's *Riddle of the Rock: The Only Successful Escape from Alcatraz*).

42. The first 20 years of screening the Rock saw *King of Alcatraz* (1938), *Those High Grey Walls* (1939), *The House Across the Bay* (1940), *Passport to Alcatraz* (1940), *Seven Miles from Alcatraz* (1942), *Road to Alcatraz* (1945), *Train to Alcatraz* (1948) and *Experiment Alcatraz* (1950).

43. As is often the case in the genre, it is difficult to shake the suspicion of parody, given Siegel's remorseless regurgitation of prison film cliché, from the lightning strike that coincides with the guard's 'welcome to Alcatraz', to the closing image of a wild flower symbolising freedom. Characterisation is similarly hackneyed. The supporting cast are cardboard cut-outs, and even Eastwood's character, Frank Morris, struggles to be more lively than his model papier-mâché head. *Escape from Alcatraz* pretends to charge prison with an assault on individuality, but its uninspired reproduction of generic platitudes simply repeats the offence.

44. Ironically, the warden is played by Patrick McGoohan who is most famous for his role in cult TV series *The Prisoner*.

45. *Escape from Alcatraz* is unable, unsurprisingly, to articulate these oppositions in relation to capitalist class relations. Siegel relies instead on banal generalisations concerning the 'individual' and the 'system'. An amorphous version of the 'system' permits the valorisation of the individual, who displays the capitalist virtues of a positive work ethic and entrepreneurial ingenuity whilst ignoring the structural integration of capitalism and the prison system.

46. Lord Byron letter quoted in Leonard Michaels, *I Would Have Saved Them if I Could* (Farrar, Straus and Giroux: New York, 1982), p.133.

47. Emily Dickinson, 'I heard a Fly buzz – when I died', in *The Complete Poems of Emily Dickinson* (Little Brown & Co: 1976), p.412.

48. See Wendy Lesser, *Pictures at an Execution* (Harvard University Press: Cambridge, Mass., 1993).

49. Cited in ibid., p.32.

50. Cited in ibid., p.249.

51. Norman Mailer, *The Presidential Papers* (Berkeley Pub.: Berkeley, 1964), p.11.

52. The 'war on drugs', so central to the needs of the Justice Juggernaut and a conservative social agenda, has been the motive force behind these changes. Between 1991 and 1997 the number of women incarcerated for drug-related offences doubled. African-American and Latina women, like their male counterparts, have been the main targets here, and are around seven times more likely to go to prison than white women. There are now more women on death row than at any time in US history, and one-third of them are African-American. *The Last Dance*

works to confirm right-wing phobias concerning increases in female criminality, but obscures vital statistics. Women account for around 10 per cent of homicides in the US, but offenders are far less likely than men to have criminal records, are far more likely to have acted alone, and their victim is far more likely to be a spouse or intimate relation. *Last Dance* inverts each of these trends.

53. Anne Morey, '"The Judge Called Me an Accessory": Women's Prison Films, 1950–1962', *Journal of Popular Film and Television*, 1995, 23.2, p.80.

54. Norman Mailer, *The Executioner's Song* (Little, Brown and Company: Boston, 1979), p.658.

55. Walter Benjamin, 'The Storyteller', in *Illuminations*, Harry Zohn trans. (Harcourt, Brace and World: New York, 1968), p.154.

56. Michel Foucault, *Discipline and Punish: The Birth of the Prison* (Vintage: New York, 1995), p.150.

57. Ibid., p.58.

58. Ibid.

59. Ibid., p.60.

60. Elizabeth Bronfen, *Over Her Dead Body: Death, Femininity and the Aesthetic* (Routledge: New York, 1992), pp.19–20.

61. The closest cinematic approximation to the act of seeing death requires a POV shot as used by the Coen brothers in the closing scene of *Blood Simple*. As a character lies dying on a bathroom floor, looking up at the plumbing under a sink, the screen unexpectedly cuts to black. A similar effect is used in *The Monster's Ball*, where an execution scene concludes with a black-out synchronised with the placement of the hood on the head of a condemned man.

62. Emily Dickinson, 'I heard a funeral in my brain', in *The Complete Poems of Emily Dickinson* (Little Brown and Company: Boston, 1976), p.380.

63. Kenneth Burke, 'Thanatopsis for Critics: A Brief Thesaurus of Deaths and Dying', *Essays in Criticism* 2.4 (1952), p.369.

64. Elizabeth Bronfen, *Over Her Dead Body*, p.13.

65. Elaine Scarry, *The Body in Pain*, p.31.

66. Albert Camus, 'Reflections on the Guillotine', in *Resistance, Rebellion and Death*, Justin O'Brien trans. (Vintage: London, 1995), p.181.

67. Elaine Scarry, *The Body in Pain*, p.31.

68. Ibid., p.56. In the idiom of state slaughter, the executioner represents the law, the execution represents justice, the audience represents the public and the condemned figure comes to represent the power of the system he opposed.

69. Ibid., p.27.

70. Cited in Wendy Lesser, *Pictures at an Execution*, p.54.

71. One notable exception here is the appearance of the gas chamber in the parodic denouement to Altman's *The Player*. Surely, if this genre wished to deliver its most effective statement against the death penalty, it would evoke the Final Solution more frequently?

72. The focus on romance behind bars also denies the historical realities of abuse. Most US women prisoners are guarded by men. Around 50 per

cent of them claim to have been the victims of physical and/or sexual abuse, and 27 per cent state that they have been raped.

73. In the past 20 years, there have been almost 20 separate instances of 'technical difficulties' in executions by lethal injection. Many of these cases involve problems with the insertion of IVs in prisoners who are drug users and in poor physical condition. Delays of up to 50 minutes have been documented, during which the condemned has often had to offer assistance. IVs have also been dislodged whilst the chemicals were being injected. In Texas, in 1998, Joseph Cannon had to inform the execution team of this error during his execution. The curtains were drawn for 15 minutes whilst the problem was rectified. In the execution of Emmitt Foster, in Missouri in 1995, the injections appeared not to be working. The coroner noted that the condemned man had been strapped so tightly to the gurney that it was prohibiting the flow of the chemicals. Death by lethal injection, depicted as an orderly and rapid affair in the films under consideration, is often accompanied by seizures, spasms, severe facial contortions, and choking fits, and can last up to 80 minutes from the point that the drugs are first administered.

74. Elaine Scarry, *The Body in Pain*, p.52.

75. Michel Foucault, *Discipline and Punish*, p.44.

76. Walter Benjamin, *The Origin of German Tragic Drama*, John Osborne trans. (Verso: London, 1977), p.166.

77. Walter Benjamin, 'The Storyteller', in *Illuminations*, p.152.

78. Walter Benjamin, 'N (Re. The Theory of Knowledge, Theory of Progress)', cited in Gary Smith (ed.), *Benjamin: Philosophy, Aesthetics, History* (Chicago UP: Chicago, 1989), p.48.

79. Walter Benjamin, 'A Small History of Photography', in *One-Way Street, and Other Writings*, Edmund Jephcott and Kingley Shorter trans. (New Left: London, 1979), p.256.

80. E. L. Doctorow, *The Book of Daniel* (Picador: London, 1972), p.264.

81. Walter Benjamin, 'Theses on the Philosophy of History', in *Illuminations*, p.222.

82. Ina Leong, Mike Sell and Kelly Thomas, 'Mad Love, Mobile Homes and Dysfunctional Dicks: On the Road with Bonnie and Clyde', in Steven Cohan and Ina Rae Hark (eds), *The Road Movie Book* (Routledge: London, 1997), p.83.

83. Ibid.

84. David T. Courtwright, 'Way Cooler Than Manson', in Robert Brent Toplin (ed.), *Oliver Stone's USA: Film, History and Controversy* (University Press of Kansas: Lawrence, 2000), p.200.

85. Ibid.

86. Oliver Stone, cited in David T. Courtwright, 'Way Cooler Than Manson', p.191.

87. *Oz* has offered more deaths at one institution than normally occur in the entire US penal system each year. Official statistics state that there are between 70 and 100 murders per annum inside American prisons.

88. Coincidentally, the same year also saw the first in a trilogy of *Prison Planet* films.

89. The PIE initiative enables companies to acquire prison labour with minimal incidents of absenteeism and turnover, and to pay the minimum wage without health benefits. Meanwhile, inmates are expected to pay tax and contribute towards their keep. This opportunity has been grasped by industrial and postindustrial concerns: convict labour is being used to build and maintain prisons, to manufacture furniture and office supplies and computer components for IBM and US Technologies. Since the mid 1990s Microsoft has been using prison labour from Washington's Twin Rivers Corrections Center, near its Seattle headquarters, to package its products. In 1995 the Corrections Corporation of America controlled about 50 per cent of the market on prison labour. Its stock rose by 360.5 per cent in that year, making it the fourth-best performer on the New York Stock Exchange.

90. William Stone, 'Rehabilitation Revisited', in Jocelyn M. Pollock (ed.), *Prisons: Today and Tomorrow* (Aspen: Gaithersburg, 1997), p.126.

91. Nancy Neveloff Dubler and Victor W. Side, 'Aids and the Prison System', in Dorothy Nelkin, David P. Willis and Scott V. Parris (eds), *A Disease of Society: Cultural and Institutional Responses to Aids* (Cambridge University Press: New York, 1991), p.82.

92. An identical formula is used in the low budget *Alien³* clone, *New Alcatraz*, where a 100-foot boa constrictor pursues its victims through a high-tech prison complex built beneath the Antarctic tundra.

93. Elaine Scarry, *The Body in Pain*, p.54.

94. Antonin Artaud, *The Theatre and its Double*, Mary Caroline Richards trans. (Grove Press: New York, 1958), p.12.

95. Susie J. Tharu, *The Sense of Performance: Post-Artaud Theatre* (Prometheus Books: New York, 1983), p.57.

96. The metastasis of fantasy environments also extends into informational landscapes. The internet is a hyperspace of themed sites beneath which users' movements and communications can be secretly monitored and manipulated.

97. E. L. Doctorow, *The Book of Daniel*, p.296.

98. Ibid., p.292.

7. IMAGE BURN: A *MINORITY REPORT*
ON THE FUTURE OF US PUNISHMENT

1. Jorge Luís Borges, *Labyrinths: Selected Stories and Other Writings* (New Directions: New York, 1964), p.30.

2. Cited in Lawrence Sutin, *Divine Invasions: A Life of Philip K. Dick* (Citadel Press: New York, 1991), p.192.

3. Coincidentally, 'Jesu, Joy of Man's Desiring' is being performed by the sentry at the containment facility where pre-criminals are held indefinitely. This chain of musical connections can be taken further. Whilst the detainees at the concentration camp in *Schindler's List* are forced to run naked as Billie Holliday sings 'God Bless the Child' on a gramophone, Lady is piped over the sound system in the futuristic Gap store in *Minority Report* as Anderton chooses an outfit for Agatha. His

selection of striped trousers for the emaciated and shorn figure of the Pre-Cog seems to complete her visual replication as a camp survivor.

4. A less sanguine conclusion, involving the discovery that the entire film consisted of the visions of Anderton confined in the 'hell', was apparently dropped by Spielberg during production.

5. Tom Cruise's production company recruited the 3 Ring Circus agency to design a series of commercials for use in *Minority Report* which, given the innovative media involved, also function as adverts for capitalism's official art-form itself. Lexus purportedly donated $5 million to the film and a $62,000 convertible to its director to include one of their concept cars. Nokia handed over $2 million to ensure the use of their handsets. Coincidentally, Nokia was a major sponsor of *The Matrix*, another fashionably dystopian and profoundly inconsistent science-fiction fantasy which utilised state of the art technology to advance a neo-Luddite philosophy.

6. Herman Melville, 'Hawthorne and his Mosses', in Paul Lauter et al. (eds), *The Heath Anthology of American Literature*, Vol. 1, second edition (D. C. Heath: Lexington, MA, 1994), p.2617.

7. Nathaniel Hawthorne, *The Scarlet Letter* (Bedford, St.Martin's Press: New York, 1991), p.214.

Bibliography

Abu-Jamal, Mumia *Live From Death Row* (Avon: New York, 1995)

Acker, Kathy *Blood and Guts in High School* (Grove Press: New York, 1989)

Albert, Octavia *The House of Bondage, or Charlotte Brooks and Other Slaves* (Oxford University Press: New York, 1988)

Anderson, S. E. and Medina, Tony (eds) *In Defence of Mumia* (Writers & Readers: New York, 1996)

Arac, Jonathan 'The Politics of *The Scarlet Letter*', in Sacvan Bercovitch and Myra Jehlen (eds), *Ideology and Classic American Literature* (Cambridge University Press: London, 1986), pp.247–65.

Artaud, Antonin 'Theatre and Cruelty', in *Collected Works*, Vol.4, Victor Corti trans. (Calder and Boyars: London, 1968)

—— *The Theatre and its Double*, Mary Caroline Richards trans. (Grove Press: New York, 1958)

Ayers, Edward *Vengeance and Justice: Crime and Punishment in the 19th Century American South* (Oxford University Press: New York, 1984)

Benjamin, Walter *The Origin of German Tragic Drama*, John Osborne trans. (Verso: London, 1977)

—— 'A Small History of Photography', in *One-Way Street, and Other Writings*, Edmund Jephcott and Kingley Shorter trans. (New Left: London, 1979)

—— 'Theses on the Philosophy of History', in *Illuminations*

—— 'The Storyteller', in *Illuminations*, Harry Zohn trans. (Harcourt, Brace and World: New York, 1968)

Berthold, Michael 'The Prison World of Melville's *Pierre* and "Bartleby"', *ESQ: A Journal of the American Renaissance*, 1987, 33.4, pp.227–52

Blassingame, John *The Slave Community: Plantation Life in the Antebellum South* (Oxford University Press: Oxford, 1979)

Bloom, Harold (ed.), *Richard Wright* (Chelsea House: New York, 1988)

—— *Richard Wright's Native Son* (Chelsea: New York, 1988)

Borges, Jorge Luís *Labyrinths: Selected Stories and Other Writings* (New Directions: New York, 1964)

Bradford, William *Of Plymouth Plantation 1620–1647* (Knopf: New York, 1970)

Brodhead, Richard 'Sparing the Rod: Discipline and Antebellum Fiction', *Representations*, 21, 1998, Winter

Bronfen, Elizabeth *Over Her Dead Body: Death, Femininity and the Aesthetic* (Routledge: New York, 1992)

Burke, Kenneth 'Thanatopsis for Critics: A Brief Thesaurus of Deaths and Dying', *Essays in Criticism* 2.4 (1952)

Burton-Rose, Daniel, Pens, Dan and Wright, Paul (eds), *The Celling of America: An Inside Look at the US Prison Industry* (Common Courage Press: Portland, Maine, 1998)

Camus, Albert 'Reflections on the Guillotine', in *Resistance, Rebellion and Death*, Justin O'Brien trans. (Vintage: London, 1995)

Christianson, Scott *With Liberty for Some: 500 Years of Imprisonment in America* (Northeastern University Press: Boston, 1998)

Clark, Michael 'Witches and Wall Street: Possession is Nine-tenths of the Law', *Texas Studies in Literature and Language* 1983, Spring 25.1, p.63

Cleaver, Eldridge *Soul on Ice* (Jonathan Cape: London, 1969)

Colvin, Mark *Penitentiaries, Reformatories and Chain Gangs: Social Theory and the History of Punishment in Nineteenth-Century America* (Macmillan: London, 1997)

Coover, Robert *The Public Burning* (Grove Press: Berkeley, 1997)

Courtwright, David T. 'Way Cooler Than Manson', in Robert Brent Toplin (ed.), *Oliver Stone's USA: Film, History and Controversy* (University Press of Kansas: Lawrence, 2000)

Daniels, Bruce 'Did the Puritans Have Fun? Leisure, Recreation and the Concept of Pleasure in Early New England', *Journal of American Studies*, 25.1 (1991)

Davis, Angela *Women, Race and Class*, (Women's Press: London, 1981)

Davis, Mike *City of Quartz: Excavating the Future in Los Angeles* (Vintage: London, 1992)

Deleuze, Gilles *Masochism: Coldness and Cruelty* (Zone Books: New York, 1991)

Derrida, Jacques 'The Law of Genre', *Glyph*, 7 (1980)

Dickens, Charles *American Notes, for General Circulation* (Penguin: New York, 1972)

Doctorow, E. L. *The Book of Daniel* (Picador: London, 1972)

Dostoyevsky, Fyodor *Memoirs from the House of the Dead* (Oxford University Press: London, 1956)

Douglass, Frederick *Narrative of the Life of Frederick Douglass, An American Slave, and Incidents in the Life of a Slave Girl* (Modern Library: New York, 2000)

——— 'Why is the Negro Lynched?' (African Islamic Publications: New York, 1988)

Dubler, Nancy Neveloff and Side, Victor W. 'Aids and the Prison System', in Dorothy Nelkin, David P. Willis and Scott V. Parris (eds), *A Disease of Society: Cultural and Institutional Responses to Aids* (Cambridge University Press: New York, 1991)

Edmundson, Mark *Nightmare on Main Street: Angels, Sadomasochism and the Culture of the Gothic* (Harvard University Press: Cambridge, Mass., 1997)

Edwards, Jonathan *Sinners in the Hands of an Angry God, a Sermon, Preached at Enfield, July 8th, 1741, at a Time of Great Awakenings, and Attended with Remarkable Impressions on Many of the Hearers* (Riggs and Stevens: New York, 1815)

Emerson, Ralph Waldo 'English Traits' in *Essays and Lectures* (Viking Press: New York, 1991)

Erikson, Kai *Wayward Puritans: A Study in the Sociology of Deviance* (John Wiley & Sons, New York, 1966)

Equiano, Olaudah *The Interesting Narrative of The Life of Olaudah Equiano, or Gustavus Vassa, The African* (Penguin: Harmondsworth, 1995)

Foucault, Michel *Discipline and Punish: The Birth of the Prison* (Vintage: New York, 1995)

Fogel, Robert William and Engerman, Stanley L. *Time on the Cross: The Economics of American Negro Slavery* (Norton: London, 1989)

Franchot, Jenny 'The Punishment of Esther: Frederick Douglass and the Construction of the Feminine', in Eric J. Sundquist (ed.), *Frederick Douglass: New Literary and Historical Essays* (Cambridge University Press: Cambridge, 1990)

Franklin, H. Bruce (ed.), *Prison Writing in 20th-century America* (Penguin: Harmondsworth, 1998)

—— '*Billy Budd* and Capital Punishment: A Tale of Three Centuries', *American Literature: A Journal of Literary History, Criticism and Bibliography*, 1997 June, 69.2

Freud, Sigmund *Three Essays on the Theory of Sexuality*, in *The Complete Psychological Works of Sigmund Freud Vol. XII* (Hogarth: London)

—— 'A Child is Being Beaten', in *The Complete Psychological Works of Sigmund Freud Vol. XVII* (Hogarth: London)

—— 'The Economic Problem of Masochism', in *The Complete Psychological Works of Sigmund Freud Vol. XIX* (Hogarth: London)

—— *The Ego and the Id*, in *The Complete Psychological Works of Sigmund Freud Vol. XIX* (Hogarth: London)

Friedman, Lawrence *Crime and Punishment in American History* (BasicBooks: New York, 1993)

Garber, Marjorie and Walkowitz, Rebecca (eds), *Secret Agents: The Rosenberg Case, McCarthyism and Fifties America* (Routledge: New York, 1995)

Garfield, Deborah M. and Zafar, Rafia (eds) *Harriet Jacobs and Incidents in the Life of a Slave Girl: New Critical Essays* (Cambridge University Press: New York, 1996)

Genovese, Eugene *Roll Jordan Roll: The World the Slaves Made* (Vintage: New York, 1976)

Girard, René *Deceit, Desire and the Novel: Self and Other in Literary Structure*, Yvonne Frecerro trans. (Johns Hopkins University Press: Baltimore, 1976)

Godden, Richard 'So that the Dead Shall Not Be Killed Again: Mailer, Doctorow and the Poetics of a Persecuting Society', in Michael Klein (ed.), *An American Half-Century: Post-War Culture and Politics* (Pluto: London, 1991)

Gooding-Williams, Robert (ed.), *Reading Rodney King, Reading Urban Uprising* (Routledge: London, 1993)

Hawthorne, Nathaniel 'Mrs. Hutchinson', in *Tales and Sketches* (Viking Press: New York, 1982)

—— *The Scarlet Letter* (Bedford, St Martin's Press: New York, 1991)

Ignatieff, Michael *A Just Measure of Pain: The Penitentiary in the Industrial Revolution, 1750–1850* (Pantheon: New York, 1978)

Jackson, Bruce (ed.), *Wake Up Dead Man: Hard Labour and Southern Blues* (University of Georgia Press: Atlanta, 1999)

Jackson, George *Soledad Brother: The Prison Letters of George Jackson* (Penguin: Harmondsworth, 1970)

Jacobs, Harriet *Incidents in the Life of a Slave Girl* (Harvard University Press: Cambridge, 1987)

Johnson, Barbara 'Melville's Fist: The Execution of Billy Budd', in Myra Jehlen (ed.), *Herman Melville: A Collection of Critical Essays* (Prentice Hall: New Jersey, 1994)

Karlsen, Carol F. *The Devil in the Shape of a Woman: Witchcraft in Colonial New England* (Norton: New York, 1997)

Kolchin, Peter *American Slavery, 1619–1877* (Hill and Wang: New York, 1993)

Kupperman, Karen 'Apathy and Death in Early Jamestown', *Journal of American History*, 66 (June 1979), pp.24–40

LeClair, Thomas 'Robert Coover, *The Public Burning* and the Art of Excess', *Critique: Studies in Contemporary Fiction*, 23.3, 1982, pp.5–28

Leong, Ina, Sell, Mike, and Thomas, Kelly 'Mad Love, Mobile Homes and Dysfunctional Dicks: On the Road with Bonnie and Clyde', in Steven Cohan and Ina Rae Hark (eds), *The Road Movie Book* (Routledge: London, 1997)

Lesser, Wendy *Pictures at an Execution* (Harvard University Press: Cambridge, 1993)

Mailer, Norman *The Presidential Papers* (Berkeley Pub.: Berkeley, 1964)

—— *The Executioner's Song* (Little, Brown and Company: Boston, 1979)

—— Introduction to Jack Henry Abbott, *In the Belly of the Beast: Letters from Prison* (Vintage Books: New York, 1991)

Maltby, Paul *Dissident Postmodernists: Barthelme, Coover, Pynchon* (University of Pennsylvania Press: Philadelphia, 1991)

Margolies, David 'Mills and Boon: Guilt without Sex', *Red Letters: A Journal of Cultural Politics* 1982–3 Winter, 14, pp.5–13

Martin, Robert 'Hester Prynne, C'est Moi', in Joseph Allen Boone and Michael Cadden (eds), *Engendering Men: The Question of Male Feminist Criticism* (Routledge: London, 1990)

Melossi, Dario and Pavarini, Massimo *The Prison and the Factory* (Barnes and Noble: Totowa, New Jersey, 1981)

Melville, Herman *Shorter Novels of Herman Melville* (Liveright: New York, 1942)

—— *White-Jacket, Or the World in a Man-of-War* (Oxford World's Classics: Oxford, 1990)

—— *Pierre, or the Ambiguities* (Northwestern University Press: Evanston, 1971)

Michaels, Leonard *I Would Have Saved Them if I Could* (Farrar, Straus and Giroux: New York, 1982)

Morey, Anne '"The Judge Called Me an Accessory": Women's Prison Films, 1950–1962', *Journal of Popular Film and Television*, 1995, 23.2

Morris, Pam (ed.) *The Bakhtin Reader: Selected Writings of Bakhtin, Medvedev and Voloshinov* (Edward Arnold: London, 1994)

Morrison, Toni *Beloved* (Picador: London, 1987)

—— *Playing in the Dark: Whiteness and the Literary Imagination* (Harvard University Press: Cambridge, Mass., 1992)

Mulvey, Laura 'Visual Pleasure and Narrative Cinema', in Bill Nichols (ed.), *Movies and Methods, Volume II* (University of California Press: Berkeley, 1985)

Nietzsche, Friedrich *On The Genealogy of Morals: A Polemic by Way of Clarification and Supplement to My Last Book 'Beyond Good and Evil'*, Douglas Smith trans. (Oxford Paperbacks: Oxford, 1998)

Oshinsky, David M. *'Worse than Slavery': Parchman Farm and the Ordeal of Jim Crow Justice* (Free Press: New York, 1996)

Paine, Thomas *Collected Writings* (Viking: New York, 1995)

Parish, Peter *Slavery: History and Historians* (Harper and Row: New York, 1989)

Plath, Sylvia *The Bell Jar* (Faber: London, 1987)

—— *The Unabridged Journals of Sylvia Plath* (Anchor: New York, 2000)

Pollock, Jocelyn M. (ed.), *Prisons: Today and Tomorrow* (Aspen: Gaithersburg, 1997)

Rafter, Nicole Hahn *Shots in the Mirror: Crime Films and Society* (Oxford University Press: New York, 2000)

Ramage, John 'Myth and Monomyth in Coover's *The Public Burning*', *Critique: Studies in Contemporary Fiction*, 23.3, 1982, pp.52–68

Reis, Elizabeth *Damned Women: Sinners and Witches in Puritan New England* (Cornell University Press: Ithaca, 1997)

Reynolds, Larry '*The Scarlet Letter* and Revolutions Abroad', *American Literature*, 57.1, 1985, pp.44–67

Rogin, Michael Paul *Subversive Genealogy: The Politics and Art of Melville* (University of Wisconsin Press: Madison, 1983)

—— '*Ronald Reagan', The Movie and Other Exercises in Political Demonology* (University of California Press: Berkeley, 1987)

Rothman, David *The Discovery of the Asylum: Social Order and Disorder in the New Republic* (Little, Brown and Company: Boston, 1971)

Rusche, Georg and Kirchheimer, Otto *Punishment and Social Structure* (Columbia University Press: New York, 1939)

Ryan, Michael and Kellner, Douglas *Camera Politica: The Politics and Ideology of Contemporary American Film* (Indiana University Press: Bloomington, 1988)

Scarry, Elaine *The Body in Pain: The Making and Unmaking of the World* (Oxford University Press: New York, 1985)

Shakur, Assata *Assata: An Autobiography* (Lawrence Hill: New York, 1988)

Silverman, Kaja *Male Subjectivity at the Margins* (Routledge: New York, 1992)

Smith, Gary (ed.) *Benjamin: Philosophy, Aesthetics, History* (Chicago UP: Chicago, 1989)

Studlar, Gaylyn 'Masochism and the Perverse Pleasures of the Cinema', in Bill Nichols (ed.), *Movies and Methods, Volume II* (University of California Press: Berkeley, 1985)

Sundquist, Eric J. (ed.), *Frederick Douglass: New Literary and Historical Essays* (Cambridge University Press: Cambridge, 1990)

Sutin, Lawrence *Divine Invasions: A Life of Philip K. Dick* (Citadel Press: New York, 1991),

Tal, Kali *Worlds of Hurt: Reading the Literatures of Trauma* (Cambridge University Press: New York, 1996)

Tallack, Douglas *The Nineteenth-Century American Short Story: Language, Form and Ideology* (Routledge: London, 1993)

Tanner, Tony 'Introduction' to *White-Jacket, Or The World in a Man-of-War* (Oxford World's Classics: Oxford, 1990)

Tharu, Susie J. *The Sense of Performance: Post-Artaud Theatre* (Prometheus Books: New York, 1983)

Thompson, Roger 'Attitudes Towards Homosexuality in the Seventeenth-Century New England Colonies', *Journal of American Studies*, 23.1 (1989)

Tocqueville, Alexis de *Democracy in America* (A. A. Knopf: New York, 1945)

Tocqueville, Alexis de and Gustave de Beaumont *On the Penitentiary System in the United States and Its Application in France, with an appendix on penal colonies and also statistical notes* Francis Lieber, trans. (Carey, Lea and Blanchard: Philadelphia, 1833)

Walvin, James *Questioning Slavery* (Routledge: London, 1996)

Wamser, Gary 'The Scarlet Contract: Puritan Resurgence, the Unwed Mother and her Child', in Bruce Rockwood (ed.), *Law and Literature Perspectives* (Peter Lang: New York, 1996)

Wells-Barnet, Ida B. *On Lynchings: Southern Horrors, A Red Record, Mob Rule in New Orleans* (Arno Press: New York, 1969)

Wigglesworth, Michael *Meat Out of the Eater, or Meditations Concerning the Necessity, End, and Usefulness of Afflictions unto God's Children* (T. Green: Connecticut, 1770)

—— *The Day of Doom: or a poetical description of the great and last judgement, with a short discourse about eternity* (Thomas Fleet: Boston, 1751)

Williams, Linda *Hard Core: Power, Pleasure and the 'Frenzy of the Visible'* (University of California Press: Berkeley, 1989)

Winnicott, D. W. *Deprivation and Delinquency* (Tavistock: London, 1984)

Winthrop, John *A Model of Christian Charity*, in Paul Lauter et al. (eds) *The Heath Anthology of American Literature, 4th edition* (Houghton Mifflin: Boston, 2002)

Wright, Richard *Black Boy: A Record of Childhood and Youth* (Harper: New York, 1945)

—— *Uncle Tom's Children* (Harper and Row: New York, 1965)

—— *Native Son* (Perennial: New York, 2001)

Index